FRONTIERS OF AEROSPACE LAW

To my sister, Suranganee,
for her many acts of kindness

Frontiers of Aerospace Law

RUWANTISSA I.R. ABEYRATNE

ASHGATE

Published by
Ashgate Publishing Limited
Gower House
Croft Road
Aldershot
Hants GU11 3HR
England

Ashgate Publishing Company
131 Main Street
Burlington, VT 05401-5600 USA

Ashgate website: http://www.ashgate.com

British Library Cataloguing in Publication Data
Abeyratne, R. I. R. (Ruwantissa Indranath Ramya), 1951–
Frontiers of aerospace law
1. Aeronautics – Law and legislation 2. Space law
I. Title
341.4'6

Library of Congress Control Number: 2001099673

ISBN 0 7546 1949 4

Typeset by Manton Typesetters, Louth, Lincolnshire, UK.
Printed and bound in Great Britain by Antony Rowe Ltd, Chippenham, Wiltshire.

Contents

Foreword

It gives me great pleasure to write a foreword to the latest work of Dr Ruwantissa Abeyratne, a scholar who continues to make a significant contribution to the literature on aerospace law through his incisive vision of future developments in that field.

My pleasant introduction to Dr Abeyratne, a senior member of the international civil service, was during one of my visits to Montreal in the early 1990s which I made in my capacity as visiting professor to McGill University. Dr Abeyratne had, by then, already published numerous articles on various subjects, in addition to several books, and was well on his way towards making a name for himself as a respected and learned scholar in international law and aerospace law.

Dr Abeyratne distinguishes his writings by documenting them meticulously and building sustained analyses from available facts. He has made excellent use of his distinguished service as an aviation lawyer and economist at the International Civil Aviation Organization by addressing current and topical issues in their true perspective and practical application. Dr Abeyratne's writings are therefore most esoteric, covering a wide spectrum of practical issues, and they bear ample testimony to his exposure, knowledge and experience in the field of aerospace law and economics.

The present volume, *Frontiers of Aerospace Law*, deals with a wide range of developments in space law. However, being an expert in air law, Dr Abeyratne has also made quite a number of pertinent observations relevant to aviation issues. His current work primarily reviews the links between air law and space law in the broadest sense of the word and contains a critical survey of the philosophical aspects of aerospace law, their interpretation through international law, and the principal tents of space law.

There is also an extensive commentary on the frontiers of both air law and space law, with particular reference to the status of the aeroplane. The book also contains the author's analyses of the role of states as providers of space technology in the field of navigation and the new Global Navigation Satellites System, bringing to bear once again his expert knowledge of air law. His exposé on the legal aspects of human conduct concerning extraterrestrial intelligence is the first of its kind and blazes a trail for more deliberation on the subject.

A separate chapter touches on emergent issues with regard to new activities in outer space, three of which are currently of great importance: trade secrets in the outer space exploration industry, trademarks in outer space industry, and cyber terrorism in outer space. The author proceeds to offer a number of conclusions on matters of outer space, while going on to air law issues in a separate chapter. Comments and issues which show the wide experience and profound knowledge of the author and the originality of his ideas in air law are reflected in a masterful dealing with such subjects as the funding of an international financial facility for aviation safety, the smuggling of illegal migrants by air and the economy class and aerotoxic syndromes. He arrives at sound conclusions, with a penetrating analysis of these topical and contentious issues, in the chapters to follow.

Dr Abeyratne makes a most apposite remark in the Preface to his book, where he states that the recommendations contained therein are geared to look future reality in the face and find legal solutions. This he accomplishes with his usual competence and authority, while emphasizing, quite rightly, that there is no single coherent dispute settlement mechanism in space law, which is badly needed at present and will be needed even more in future.

This book fills a great lacuna in the legal literature pertaining to current and future issues in aerospace law which have thus far not been given sufficient attention. It also emphasizes the growing links between air and space activities and attempts to find solutions to problems of great actuality and impact. This is a fascinating, original book and an asset to existing literature.

Professor I.H.Ph. Diederiks-Verschoor
Leiden University

Preface

This book introduces issues of aerospace law which are likely to flow into the new millennium as challenges that have to be addressed. These issues are corollaries to the fundamental and overriding trend in this area of the law which is seeing a gradual merger between two hitherto isolated regimes of human conduct pertaining to air and space law separately. The use of information technology is arguably the foremost compelling force responsible for the unity of aviation and space activities of man. It is therefore inevitable that information technology, computer law and the laws pertaining to state and individual responsibility are inextricably intertwined in a net of legal issues which will emerge in the new millennium.

The issues addressed in this book range from space law issues such as legal liabilities pertaining to extraterrestrial intelligence, environmental pollution in outer space and the conduct of persons in outer space, to cyber crimes affecting outer space activities, to air law issues such as aircraft noise, to economic trends of airports and air navigation services, funding for aviation safety projects, and emergent aeromedical issues and privacy of airline pilots. The recommendations contained in this book are geared to look future reality in the face and find legal solutions. In the realm of public international law, remedial measures are almost non-existent in the field of aerospace law, except for a solid foundation given to the Council of the International Civil Aviation Organization to hear disputes between states on matters pertaining to civil aviation, a facility which until now has scarcely been used in the organization's 55-year history.

It is also worthy of note that, except for a few provisions in the various space law conventions, there is no single coherent dispute settlement mechanism at space law. The increasingly rapid proliferation of space activities in the coming years and their diversity leave no room for doubt that new laws will have to be put into place and new mechanisms to combat problems will have to be carefully thought out. It is hoped that this book will be a precursor to such thinking.

Ruwantissa Abeyratne
Montreal, January 2001

Table of Cases

Chapter 1

Space Law Concepts

1 INTRODUCTION

Whether it be in the discipline of air law or in space law, the fundamental postulates of any system of human conduct are broadly based on democracy. As the aerospace industry moves into the new millennium, a whole new attitude may be required to cope with the unimaginably rapid progress the industry will make in the first 25 years of the millennium. However, despite this metamorphosis, it is doubtful that mankind will veer from the democratic umbrella which has so effectively sheltered modern legal structures. Aerospace law is no exception.

The basis of modern democracy is Hobbes' *Leviathan*, which begins with the premise that the supreme power, whether it be a man, woman or assembly, is called the sovereign. Hobbes (1588–1679), recognized initially that the powers of the sovereign are unlimited, untrammelled and unchallenged. The sovereign has the right of censorship over all expression of opinion, on the basis that the main interest of the sovereign is the preservation of internal peace. Therefore a true sovereign will not use the power of censorship to suppress the truth, because a doctrine which is at variance with peace cannot be true. Hobbes emphasized that the laws of property should be entirely the purview of the sovereign, for in absolute nature, and in its pristine purity, there is no property, as property is created by government.

Hobbes believed that, even if a sovereign were to be despotic, the worst despotism was better than anarchy. The interests of governments become singularly identifiable with the interests of the subjects. Above all, rebellion is wrong: not only because it usually fails, but also, if it succeeds, it sets a bad example. The most noble of the great philosophers, Spinoza (1632–77), derived his political philosophy from Hobbes, but differed from Hobbes on the subject of freedom of opinion, which should not, in Spinoza's view, be subject to governmental control. But Hobbes and Spinoza held the common view that any kind of rebellion against a sovereign was bad.

The influence of the early philosophers on the modern philosophers becomes apparent with the thrust of Aristotle's *Politics*, which fundamentally held that a government is good when it aims at the good of the whole community, and bad when it cares only for itself. Aristotle was emphatic when he made the distinction between oligarchy and democracy by using the economic status of the governing party as the only criterion for the distinction: oligarchy is when the rich govern without consideration for the poor; and democracy is when the sovereign gives power to the hands of the poor and needy in initial disregard for the interests of the rich. Aristotle argued that monarchy was better than aristocracy and aristocracy was better than polity. The greatest political sin, according to Aristotle, was the corruption of the best in a political society. He placed tyranny as the worst form of government next to oligarchy, and placed democracy over both categories. Aristotle concluded that, among actual governments, democracies were the most liked and beneficial.

The Utilitarian school, of which Jeremy Bentham was a protagonist, recognized democracy as being composed of four essential and basic elements: subsistence, abundance, security and equality. According to Bentham, a good democracy had to ensure these elements for its community. He observed: 'wars and storms are best to be read of, but peace and calms are better to endure'. The two fundamental postulates which he attributed to good government were equality and security, which to Bentham added the cornerstone of a balanced sovereign.

The above philosophical beliefs bring one to the inexorable conclusion that democracy is government for all – in equality and unity. The inevitable question which follows is: can a community which, in its constitutional essence, favour a few require the majority to be content with the second best? Plato and Aristotle answered in the affirmative, purely to support intellectual independence, which was essentially a flawed perception of the era they belonged to, if one were to take their positions literally. If, however, one were to interpret the position of these two philosophers as giving the few in power the discretion to decide for the betterment of the entire community with the ultimate aim of ensuring its safety and security, it follows that democracy should focus on a lean executive charged with this task. This interpretation is wholly consistent with religious philosophy and democratic ethics which incontrovertibly hold that the most valuable assets of human life are power and property and that a political system which is unjust in these respects is unacceptable.

Immanuel Kant (1724–1804) who wrote, in his *Perpetual Peace* in 1795, recommending a federation of free states, bound together by a covenant eschewing war, was more emphatic about prohibiting war than considering the virtues of the political clustering of states. He viewed war as a problem which only an international government could quell. The group of states, according to Kant, should be republican in civil constitution, with a distinct separation of powers between the executive and the legislature. Kant attacked democracy on the ground that a democracy gave overt and unjust powers to the executive which were invidious to a state. Of course, his theory against democracy, favouring a community of states under one international government, fell into disfavour in his own country in 1933 and has not gained official acceptance since.

John Locke (1632–1704), a moderatist philosopher, deviated from dogma, while essentially retaining his faith in the goodness of positive morality. This led to his abiding faith in religous tolerance and parliamentary democracy as the two necessary elements of basic governance. Locke is believed to be the father of empiricism, which was founded on the premise that all knowledge is based on experience. There is evidence in philosophical history that Locke applied the theory of empiricism to parliamentary democracy, ascribing to democracy a certain imperative which brings to bear a compulsive element. Accordingly, democracy, although reflecting the overall will of the people, would succeed only if practised with empirical dependence upon past experience. Political decision making, according to the empirical democracy doctrine, should therefore not be destitute of past experience, whatever the overall will of the community may be.

The wisdom of Locke's empirical democracy is perceived in its application to democracy in the modern context, which is also consistent with the Aristotelian view, that the highest virtue is for the governing few, who could, if the interests of the community dictate, subject conservative and theoretical ethics to political necessity and prudence. Although Aristotle required a president or prime minister to be magnanimous in this regard, the modern interpretation and context of good government does not necessarily require a leader to be magnanimous, but to be different from the average citizen; and to have certain merits connected with his or her status.

The essence of modern practical democracy is to curb unnecessary power of the central government and not to buttress the authority of the state to the point of corruption and self-service. The end result is personal freedom and a society which precedes the state. Also there is a compelling need in a functional democracy for a loyal opposition which does not portend a real threat to national security. This does not, however, mean that democracy should make the executive impotent. On the contrary, a strong and lean executive, as Aristotelian philosophy recommends, is an essential tool of a workable democracy.

The above principles, enunciated by the founding fathers of democracy, eminently accord with the vision that development through democracy is an effective tool of political economics for the next millennium.

Current theory of democracy and development

Present-day lawyers would define democracy as the form of government in which the sovereign power resides in and is exercised by the whole body of citizens directly or indirectly through a system of representation. Put more simply, the above definition means that democracy is a system where ordinary citizens have a meaningful and compelling role in the affairs of the state, including the formulation of policy and the development and implementation of legislation. A typical democracy as enunciated by the Western philosophers whose views have already been discussed would separate the state and its instrumentalities from the Church or other religious body. It would be composed of three separate and intrinsic powers, the legislature, the executive and the judiciary. This separation of powers in a democracy facilitates the sustenance of fundamental human rights of the individual by giving legal protection to a citizen through an independent judiciary. In a social democracy, the protection of the social and economic rights of a person could be very strongly entrenched as an essential principle of the philosophy of government.

Development, in the modern sense, is not merely concerned with material well-being and economic affluence, but covers in a broad sense all forms of human progress and a better quality of life. In this sense, the development brought about by an honest democracy would be measured, not merely by the increased per capita income of the citizens, but also by their political and economic freedom and their equal enjoyment of the fruits of growth. The trend towards development through democracy, attained mostly through the indigenous efforts of a nation, commenced in 1968 with the 27th meeting of the United Nations International Conference on Human Rights which adopted the Proclamation of Iran. This trend was followed assiduously by the world community for 20 years and strengthened in 1986 through the United Nations by the United Nations General Assembly Declaration on the Right to Development. More recently, the United Nations Declaration of Human Rights of 1993 endorsed the twin elements of democracy and development and emphasized that development includes economic, social and cultural as well as fundamental political rights.

Economic progress and development are not necessarily always synonymous, and it is a fact that there is no empirical evidence to suggest that democracy is a precondition to economic growth. However, it is logical to assume that democracy, which supports stability and sustains fair distribution of goods and services, would be a good basis and launching pad for economic progress.

Both democracy and development denote a continuous change which is brought about over a sustained period of time through indigenous efforts. Sustainable development, achieved through democracy, must in essence be rooted in local conditions and emerge from real forces within a society. This does not exclude assistance from outside sources provided such sources are properly channelled when applied internally and are granted on the basis that the assistance would foster good governance.

One of the main thrusts of development in a democratic society is the encouragement of fair and equal competition in trade through the fundamental economic right of free trading. Today's commercial competition has transcended the past era, where dominant markets protected their established market shares. Most mega commercial activity was then the purview of governmental control under instrumentalities of state which were mostly cumbersome bureaucracies at best. Perhaps the best analogy is the biggest commercial market – the United States – which had, until recently, extensively regulated larger commercial activities pertaining to energy, transport and telecommunications.

Happily, over the past decade, commercial enterprises have broken the shackles of rigid regulation to form strategic alliances among themselves. These alliances have been formed in the realization that the performance of a company can be affected by two factors: the average performance of all competitors in the industry, and whether the company concerned is a superior or inferior performer in the industry. Michael Porter, in his book *Competition*, encapsulates these two factors in the single premise that any business achieves superior profitability in its industry by attaining either higher prices or lower costs than rivals. Curiously, in most industries, it is the latter – lower costs – which has been the cornerstone of strategic alliances. A progressive democracy will not only foster internal competition in trade but will also encourage international competition among nations, in order that the citizens of that country will have access to equality and fair distribution of goods, and private enterprise within the state will be given a free hand at competition, without interference from the state.

2 LINKS BETWEEN SPACE LAW AND AIR LAW

The philosophy of space law

The legal and philosophical bases of space law are the antithesis of those applicable to air law in that space law is grounded on the principle that outer space is the common heritage of mankind and that no state or individual can therefore claim *rights in rem* to any portion of outer space. Air law, on the other hand, is firmly entrenched in the principle of sovereignty of states, so that a state may lay claims to rights over the airspace above its territory.[1] This essentially means that, while the implementation of air law is heavily influenced by municipal law, space law is solely grounded on legal principles binding on the community of nations. Principles of public international law therefore play an exclusive part in the application of space law principles.

In terms of jurisprudence, space law represents the Idealist school which supports community interest over national interest, while air law represents the Realist school which advocates that national interests are pre-eminent considerations for all purposes. The Idealist school believes that individual interests should best be served by collective intercourse and is best illustrated by the view of Lauterpacht: 'a community may be said to be the body of a number of individuals more or less bound together through such common interests as to create a manifold intercourse between single individuals'.[2] Legal principles relating to the international community necessarily emanate collectively from that community as a body of rules which require the consent of the community. An examination of the philosophy of space law therefore essentially requires an examination of the nature of public international law itself. This chapter will discuss the philosophical basis of the common heritage principle of space law, through an evaluation of public international law and its relevance.

Basic principles

Space law is one of the most recent additions to international jurisprudence. That it pertains to one of the most highly technology-intensive activities is an incontrovertible fact and was made evident with the successful launch of the space shuttle 'Columbia' on 12 April 1981, when the world entered a new age of space exploitation, leaving behind the period of space exploration which seemingly started in 1957 with the launch of the Russian 'Sputnik'. Understandably, the world was elated in 1981 with the phenomenon of the space shuttle to the extent that a space technologist at NASA declared: 'I am convinced that by 1990 people will be going on the shuttle routinely – as an aircraft.'[3] Of course, it has not happened quite that way yet. One must concede, however, that the expert's prophecy was at least partially correct, in that by 1990 we were actively involved with the concept of the aerospace plane, of which the space shuttle was a precursor.

The emergent philosophical problem posed by space law, in its offer to mankind of a new dimension of transport law and property law, was succinctly summarized by Professor Böckstiegel in 1983:

> [Space law] is the newest main field of international law ... and it depends more than most other fields on probable and fast technical progress ...[4] It is obvious that the application of space technology will lead to the growing commercialization of space activities, since such service – at least in the long run – can only be maintained and expanded, if it is self-financing.[5]

The blending of high technology with a new forensic code of conduct on hitherto uncharted territory has brought to bear the need for the community of nations to formulate a sustainable legal theory that would ensure non-exploitation of space resources by individuals or states, at the same time incorporating the element of responsibility and liability for individual and state conduct in outer space.

As mentioned earlier, the basic principle of space law is the 'common interest' (or common heritage) principle which emerged as a result of the first specific resolution on space law of the United Nations General Assembly in 1958.[6] The 'common interest' principle has since been incorporated in subsequent multilateral treaties, particularly the Outer Space Treaty of 1967,[7] article I(1) of which provides:

> the exploration and use of outer space, including the moon and other celestial bodies, shall be carried out for the benefit and in the interest of all countries, irrespective of their degree of economic or scientific development, and shall be the province of all mankind.

This provision, which binds signatory states, is seemingly a departure from the traditional 'national interest' approach of international air law and has represented a moral obligation to some,[8] while to others the provision has represented a *jus cogens* or mandatory legal principle.[9]

The International Court of Justice (ICJ), in the *North Sea Continental Shelf Case*,[10] held that legal principles that are incorporated in treaties, such as the 'common interest' principle, become customary international law by virtue of article 38 of the 1969 Vienna Convention on the Law of Treaties.[11] Article 38 recognizes that a rule set forth in a treaty would become binding upon a third state as a customary rule of international law if it is generally recognized by the states concerned as such. Article I(1) of the Outer Space Treaty, which declares that the use of space technology is achieved under the 'common interest' principle for the common good of humanity, therefore becomes a principle of customary international law, or *jus cogens*. Obligations arising from *jus cogens* are considered applicable *erga omnes*, which would mean that states using space technology owe a duty of care to the world at large in the provision of such technology. The ICJ, in the *Barcelona Traction Case*, held:

> an essential distinction should be drawn between the obligations of a State towards the international community as a whole, and those arising *vis à vis* another State in the field of diplomatic protection. By their very nature, the former are the concerns of all States. In view of the importance of the rights involved, all States can be held to have a legal interest in their protection; they are obligations *erga omnes*.[12]

The International Law Commission has observed of the ICJ decision: 'in the Court's view, there are in fact a number, albeit limited, of international obligations which, by reason of their importance to the international community as a whole, are – unlike others – obligations in respect of which all States have legal interest'.[13] The views of the ICJ and the International Law Commission, which has supported the approach taken by the ICJ, give rise to two possible conclusions relating to *jus cogens* and its resultant obligations *erga omnes*:

a obligations *erga omnes* affect all states and thus cannot be made inapplicable to a state or group of states by an exclusive clause in a treaty or other document reflecting legal obligations without the consent of the international community as a whole;

b obligations *erga omnes* pre-empt other obligations which may be incompatible with them.

Some examples of obligations *erga omnes* cited by the ICJ are prohibition of acts of aggression, genocide, slavery and discrimination.[14] It is indeed worthy of note that all these obligations are derivatives of norms which are *jus cogens* at international law.

Article VI of the Outer Space Treaty provides in part that state parties to the treaty shall bear international responsibility for national activities in outer space, whether such activities are carried out by governmental agencies or by non-governmental agencies. This provision clearly introduces the notion of strict liability *erga omnes* to the application of the *jus cogens* principle relating to outer space activities of states and could be considered applicable in instances where states hold out to the international community as providers of technology achieved and used by them in outer space, which is used for purposes of air navigation. Article VI further requires that the activities of non-governmental entities in outer space shall require authorization and continuing supervision by the appropriate state party to the treaty, thus ensuring that the state whose nationality the entity bears would be vicariously answerable for the activities of that organization, thereby imputing liability to the state concerned.

Article VII makes a state party internationally liable to another state party for damage caused by a space object launched by that state. The Registration Convention of 1974,[15] in article II(1), requires a launching state of a space object that is launched into earth orbit, or beyond, to register such space object by means of an entry in an appropriate registry which it shall maintain and inform the Secretary General of the United Nations of the establishment of such a registry. This provision ensures that the international community is kept aware of which state is responsible for which space object and enables the United Nations to observe outer space activities of states. Article VI of the Convention makes it an obligation of all state parties, including those that possess space monitoring and tracking facilities, to render assistance in identifying a space object which causes damage to other space objects or persons. Justice Manfred Lachs analyses these provisions of the Registration Convention to mean that the state of registry and the location of the space object would govern jurisdictional issues arising out of the legal status of space objects.[16] On the issue of joint launching of space objects, Justice Lachs observes:

> No difficulties arise whenever a State launches its own object from its own territory; the same applies to objects owned or launched by non-governmental agencies registered in that State. However, in cases of joint launching, agreement between the parties is required as to which of them is to be deemed the 'State of Registry'. A similar agreement is also necessary when a launching is carried out by an international organization.[17]

The above provision ensures the identification of parties responsible for specific activities in outer space and thereby makes it easier to impose liability for environmental damage caused.

The Outer Space Treaty,[18] while expostulating the fundamental principle in its article 1 that the exploration and use of outer space, including the moon and other celestial bodies, shall be carried out for the benefit and in the interests of all countries, explicitly imposes in article VII international liability and responsibility on each state party to the treaty for damage caused to another state party or to its populace (whether national or juridical) by the launch or procurement of launch of an object into outer space. In its preceding provisions, the treaty imposes international responsibility on states parties for national activities conducted in outer space. The treaty also requires its states parties to be guided by the principle of cooperation and mutual assistance in the conduct of all their activities in outer space.[19] This overall principle is further elucidated in the same provision:

> States Parties to the Treaty shall pursue studies of outer space, including the moon and other celestial bodies, and conduct exploration of them so as to avoid harmful contamination and also adverse changes in the environment of the Earth resulting from the introduction of extra-terrestrial matter.[20]

The Moon Agreement[21] of 1979 provides that, in the exploration and use of the moon, states parties shall take measures *inter alia* to avoid harmfully affecting the environment of the Earth through the introduction of extra-terrestrial matter or otherwise.[22] The Liability Convention[23] contains a provision which lays down the legal remedy in instances of damage caused by space objects. Article II provides: 'A launching State shall be absolutely liable to pay compensation for damage caused by its space objects on the surface of the Earth or to aircraft in flight',[24] thereby imposing a regime of absolute liability on the state that launches space objects such as satellites, which provide technology and communication that is used for air navigational purposes. Although, admittedly, both the Outer Space Treaty and the Liability Convention do not explicitly provide for damage caused by technology and communication provided by space objects, culpability arising from the 'common interest' principle and liability provisions of the two conventions can be imputed to states under these conventions.

Gorove states that, in the field of international space law, two clearly connected terms have been used: liability and responsibility.[25] Although 'responsibility' has not been cohesively interpreted in any legal treaty relating to outer space, 'liability' occurs in the Liability Convention and is sufficiently clear therein. This, however, does not mean that state responsibility is not relevant to the obligations of states law as, in international relations, the invasion of a right or other legal interest of one subject of the law by another inevitably creates legal responsibility. Professor Brownlie observes:

> today, one can regard responsibility as a general principle of international law, a concomitant of substantive rules and of the supposition that acts and omissions may be categorized as illegal by reference to the rules establishing rights and duties. Shortly, the law of responsibility is concerned with the incidence and consequence of illegal acts, and particularly the payment of compensation for loss caused.[26]

International responsibility relates both to breaches of treaty provisions and to other breaches of legal duty. In the *Spanish Zone of Morocco Claims* case, Justice Huber observed: 'responsibility is the necessary corollary of a right. All rights of an international character involve international responsibility. If the obligation in question is not met, responsibility entails the duty to make reparation'.[27] There is also explicit recognition that principles of international law apply to space law. The

General Assembly of the United Nations in 1961 adopted the view that international law, including the Charter of the United Nations, applies to outer space and celestial bodies.[28] It is also now recognized as a principle of international law that the breach of a duty involves an obligation to make reparation appropriately and adequately. This reparation is regarded as the indispensable complement of a failure to apply a convention and is applied as an inarticulate premise that need not be stated in the breached convention itself.[29] The ICJ affirmed this principle in 1949, in the *Corfu Channel Case*,[30] by holding that Albania was obliged under international law to pay compensation to the United Kingdom for not warning that Albania had laid mines in Albanian waters which caused explosions, damaging ships belonging to the United Kingdom. Since the treaty law provisions of liability and the general principles of international law as discussed complement each other in endorsing the liability of states to compensate for damage caused by space objects, there is no contention as to whether, in the use of nuclear power sources in outer space, damage caused by the space objects or use thereof would not go uncompensated. The rationale for the award of compensation is explicitly included in article XII of the Liability Convention, which requires that the person aggrieved or injured should be restored (by the award of compensation to him) to the condition in which he would have been if the damage had not occurred. Furthermore, under the principles of international law, moral damages based on pain, suffering and humiliation, as well as on other considerations, are considered recoverable.[31]

As discussed, both treaty law and general principles of international law on the subject of space law make the two elements of liability and responsibility a means to an end: that of awarding compensation to an aggrieved state or other subject under the law. Therefore, in view of the many legal issues that may arise, the primary purpose of a regulatory body which sets standards on state liability in issues concerning the use of space technology would be to consider carefully the subtleties of responsibility and liability and explore their consequences on states and others involved as they apply to the overall concept of the status of a state as a user of space technology which may cause harm or injury to the latter.

3 IMPLEMENTATION OF SPACE LAW THROUGH INTERNATIONAL LAW

The genesis of international law may well lie in the seminal European Charter – the Peace of Westphalia – which was signed in 1648. This document recognized unrestrained sovereignty of states and effectively consolidated the concept of world unity through sovereign states. The next significant step was the Concert of Europe, a haphazard system of consultation between the great countries of Europe, which was established by the Settlement of Vienna in 1815 and followed by the Congress of Aix-la-Chapelle in 1818. The Concert emerged as a corollary to the Napoleonic wars and provided a forum which maintained and balanced power between the

European nations for a century. One of the salient features of the Concert was that, although the treaty admitted of consultation and conference on the devolution of power among states, its findings or decisions had no obligatory effect on the Great Powers. This perceived inadequacy of the Concert resulted in its impotence and inability to impose adherence by states of its findings or decisions and is often attributed to states having a free hand in doing as they pleased to each other in World War I.

As history would demonstrate time and time again, the aftermath of a major disaster brings fresh thinking for reformation and revival. After World War I, states adopted the Paris Settlement of 1919, partially as atonement for the bankruptcy and inability of the Concert to ensure uniformity in international accord and also to introduce new ideas and rules of conduct for the international community. The Paris Settlement, which retained for the most part the spirit of the Peace of Westphalia, set the tone for the establishment of the League of Nations which further strengthened the bonds of unity between states, based on the wartime collaboration between associated and allied powers. The League of Nations adopted the principle that undertakings of international law would actively determine conduct among governments, without abdicating *jus ad bellum*, or the right of war. This in turn resulted in failure, as was seen in 1939, when, without reference to the League of Nations, Britain and France hastened to come to Poland's assistance when it was attacked by Germany.

At this stage in history, international law was considered as simply law binding upon states in their relations with each other. The Provisional International Court of Justice (the predecessor to the International Court of Justice) decided in the famous *Lotus* case of 1927:

> International law governs relations between independent States. The rules of law binding upon States therefore emanate from their own free will as expressed in conventions or by usages generally accepted as expressing principles of law and established in order to regulate the relations between those co-existing independent communities or with a view to the achievement of common aims. Restrictions upon the independence of States cannot therefore be presumed.[32]

The aftermath of World War II saw the advent of the United Nations and the United Nations Charter, the latter of which proclaims that the United Nations is based on the sovereign equality of all members. The Charter also provides that less powerful nations recognize the pre-eminence of the Great Powers as guardians of international peace and security.[33] With the exception of this predominant innovation of post-World War II accord, the rest of the Charter seems complacently to accord with the basic framework of international law which existed under the Peace of Westphalia. Judicial recognition of the United Nations as a subject of international law was given by the International Court of Justice (ICJ) in 1949, in the *Reparation for Injuries Case*,[34] where the ICJ pronounced the end of the old orthodoxy that states are the only subjects of international law, and advised that the United Nations, though not a state, had the capacity to bring certain kinds of claims directly against a state under the rubric of international law.

The many contributions of the United Nations to the development of international law have been both significant and sustained, ever since the United Nations General Assembly convened its first session in 1946. The General Assembly has been prolific in adopting numerous resolutions, declarations and conventions through diplomatic conferences. Guided by article 13 of the United Nations Charter which places an obligation on the General Assembly to initiate studies and make recommendations for encouraging the progressive development of international law and its codification,[35] the Assembly, in November 1947, established the International Law Commission whose members were entrusted with the formulation of principles of international law. One of the first tasks of the Commission was to write a Draft Code of Offences against Peace and Security of Mankind, which the Commission completed in 1954. The Draft Code provided that any act of aggression, including the employment by the authorities of a state of armed forces against another state for any purpose other than national or collective self-defence or in pursuance of a decision or recommendation of a competent organ of the United Nations, was an offence against the peace and security of mankind. The code also stipulated that any threat by the authorities of a state to resort to an act of aggression against another state was a similar offence.[36]

The sense of international responsibility that the United Nations ascribed to itself had reached a heady stage at this point, where the role of international law in international human conduct was perceived to be primary and above the authority of states. In its Report to the General Assembly, the International Law Commission recommended a draft provision which required: 'Every State has the duty to conduct its relations with other States in accordance with international law and with the principle that the sovereignty of each State is subject to the supremacy of international law.'[37] This principle, which forms a cornerstone of international conduct by states, provides the basis for strengthening international comity and regulating the conduct of states both internally – within their territories – and externally, towards other states. States are effectively precluded by this principle of pursuing their own interests untrammelled and with disregard to principles established by international law.

Development of international law through treaties

Treaties, conventions, agreements, protocols, exchanges of notes and other synonyms all mean one and the same thing at international law – that they are international transactions of a legal character. Treaties are concluded between states in written form and governed by international law, whether embodied in a single instrument or in two or more related instruments and whatever its particular designation.[38]

Each treaty has four constituent elements: the capacity of the parties thereto to conclude agreement of the provisions of the treaty under international law; the intention of the parties to apply principles of international law when concluding agreement under a treaty; *consensus ad idem* or a meeting of the minds of the parties;[39] and the parties must have the intention to create legal obligations among themselves. These four elements form a composite regulatory process whereby a treaty becomes strong enough at international law to enable parties to settle their differences within the parameters of the treaty, make inroads into customary international law if necessary, and transform an unorganized international community into one which may be organized under a uniform set of rules. Treaties are based on three fundamental principles of international law: good faith, consent and international responsibility.[40] Since international customary law does not prescribe any particular form for consensual agreements and requirements that would make them binding, the parties to a treaty could agree upon the form of treaty they intend entering into and make it binding among them accordingly. Legal bonds are established between nations because they wish to create them and, as is seen in the Preamble to the Outer Space Treaty, a statement to this effect is reflected in the treaty itself.[41] The main feature of a multilateral international agreement is that absolute rights that may have existed within states before the entry into force of such treaty would be transformed into relative rights in the course of a balancing process in which considerations of good faith and reasonableness play a prominent part. However, treaty provisions must be so written and construed as best to conform to accepted principles of international customary law.[42]

Great reliance is placed on treaties as a source of international law. The International Court of Justice, whose function it is to adjudicate upon disputes of an international character between states, applies as a source of law international conventions which establish rules that are expressly recognized by the states involved in a dispute.[43] The Court also has jurisdiction to interpret a treaty at the request of a state.[44]

The Vienna Convention on the Law of Treaties,[45] while recognizing treaties as a source of law, accepts free consent, good faith and the *pacta sunt servanda* as universally recognized elements of a treaty.[46] Article 11 of the Vienna Convention provides that the consent of a state to be bound by a treaty may be expressed by signature, exchange of instruments constituting a treaty, ratification, acceptance, approval or accession, or by any other means agreed upon. 'Ratification', 'acceptance', 'approval' and 'accession' generally mean the same thing: that in each case the international act so named indicates that the state performing such act is establishing on the international plane its consent to be bound by a treaty. A state demonstrates its adherence to a treaty by means of the *pacta sunt servanda*, which is reflected in article 26 of the Vienna Convention in that every treaty in force is binding upon the parties and must be performed by them in good faith. The validity of a treaty or of the consent of a state to be bound by a treaty may be impeached only through the application of the Vienna Convention,[47] which generally requires that a treaty could be derogated upon only in circumstances which the treaty in question so specifies;[48] when a later treaty abrogates the treaty in question;[49] there is a breach of the treaty;[50] a *novus actus interveniens* or supervening act which makes the performance of the treaty impossible;[51] and the invocation by a state of the *Clausula Rebus Sic Stantibus*,[52] wherein a fundamental change of circumstances (when such circumstances constituted an essential basis of the consent of the parties to be bound by the treaty) which has occurred with regard to those existing at the time of the conclusion of the treaty, and which was not foreseen by the parties, radically changes or transforms the extent of obligations of a state. A state may not invoke the fact that its consent to be bound by a treaty has been expressed in violation of a provision of its internal law regarding competence to conclude treaties and seeks to invalidate its consent unless such violation was manifest and concerned a rule of its internal law of fundamental importance.[53]

States or international organizations which are parties to such treaties have to apply the treaties they have signed and therefore have to interpret them. Although the conclusion of a treaty is generally governed by international customary law to accord with accepted rules and practices of national constitutional law of the signatory states, the application of treaties is governed by principles of international law. If, however, the application or performance of a requirement in an international treaty poses problems to a state, the constitutional law of that state would be applied by courts of that state to settle the problem. Although article 27 of the Vienna Convention requires states not to invoke provisions of their internal laws as justification for failure to comply with the provisions of a treaty, states are free to choose the means of implementation they see fit according to their traditions and political organization.[54] The overriding rule is that treaties are juristic acts and have to be performed.

Every international treaty is affected by the fundamental dichotomy where, on the one hand, the question arises whether provisions of a treaty are enforceable at law and, on the other, whether the principles of state sovereignty, which is *jus cogens* or mandatory law, would pre-empt the provisions of a treaty from being considered by states as enforceable. Article 53 of the Vienna Convention addresses this question and provides that treaties, which at the time of their conclusion conflict with a peremptory norm of general international law or *jus cogens*, are void. A peremptory norm of general international law is a norm accepted and recognized by the international community of states as a whole as a norm from which no derogation is permitted and which can be modified only by a subsequent norm of general international law having the same character. The use of the words 'as a whole' in article 53 effectively precludes individual states from considering, on a subjective basis, particular norms as acceptable to the international community.[55] Therefore, according to this provision, the outer space treaties discussed above could not have derogated from principles of accepted international legal norms when they were being concluded. The Vienna Convention has, by this provision, implicitly ensured the legal legitimacy of international treaties, and established the principle that treaties are in fact *jus cogens* and therefore are instruments containing provisions the compliance with which is mandatory.

Treaties and the International Court of Justice

In international law, although there is a distinction between formal and material sources, it is often difficult to maintain. What matters really is that sources, of whatever nature they may be, are the important reflectors of evidence of the existence of consensus among states concerning certain rules, regulations and practices that would obtain at international law. Ian Brownlie is of the view that

> decisions of the International Court, resolutions of the General Assembly of the United Nations, and 'law making' multilateral treaties are very material evidence of the attitude of States toward particular rules, and the presence or absence of consensus. Moreover, there is a process of interaction which gives these evidences a status somewhat higher than mere 'material sources'. Thus neither an unratified treaty nor a report of the International Law Commission to the General Assembly has any binding force either in the law of treaties or otherwise. However, such instruments stand as candidates for public reaction, approving or not, as the case may be: they may stand for a threshold of consensus and confront states in a significant way.[56]

The law of treaties, on the one hand, addresses questions relating to the content of obligations between states and, on the other, relates to the incidence of obligations resulting from express agreement by and between states. Treaties are usually considered as falling under two headings: treaties which incorporate particular international law and those which incorporate general international law. If one were to analyse finely the distinction between these two treaties one could assume that, while the former binds a few states, the latter is more multilateral and would be considered as treaties which make law on a general basis. There is, however, no fundamental difference between the two categories as both types of treaties bind the states parties to obligations stipulated therein.

Article 38.1 of the Statute of the International Court of Justice (ICJ) provides that the ICJ, in settling international disputes, will apply international conventions, whether general or particular, international custom, the general principles of law as recognized by civilized nations, and judicial decisions and the teachings of the most highly qualified publicists of the various nations, as subsidiary means for the determination of the rules of law. As far as judicial decisions are concerned as binding precedents, the ICJ is constrained by article 59 of its own statute which stipulates that the decision of the Court has no binding force except between the parties and in respect of a particular case.

Although the provisions in article 38.1 are expressed in terms of the function of the Court, and the elements therein are by no means explicitly referred to as sources, article 38 is generally considered as a statement comprising sources of international law. Brownlie observes that these sources are not stated to represent a hierarchy, but the draftsmen intended to give an order and in one draft the word 'successively' appeared.[57] Brownlie concludes that in general article 38 does not rest upon a distinction between formal and material sources, and a system of priority application depends simply on the order (a) to (d) in all cases.[58]

The recent ICJ hearing of the *PAN AM* case is of particular relevance to the subject of the effect of ICJ decisions on air law. It is relevant at this stage to examine the general position of the ICJ *vis-à-vis* the Security Council, as both are primary organs of the United Nations, and a certain clash of interests between the two organs can be perceived in the ICJ's judicial consideration of Security Council decisions.

The International Court of Justice is the principal judicial organ of the United Nations and, therefore, it is incontrovertible that the ICJ cannot be considered subservient or subsidiary to any other organ of the United Nations.[59] The logical conclusion that would follow from this premise is that the ICJ would have principal jurisdiction or authority over judicial issues and other organs would have principal authority over political and administrative issues. Therefore, if the ICJ should be considered in its role as the principal judicial authority of the United Nations system, then its judicial character and integrity, as well as the integrity of the judicial system it portrays, must be preserved at all costs. It is submitted that the fundamental argument in this issue should be based on the very nature of international law that the ICJ represents and uses in its adjudicatory process. If one were to impute a certain moral flavour to international law and therefore to the ICJ, one would be impelled to treat the ICJ as the exclusive authority which administers public international law to the parties which come before it.

There is no presumption in international law that the Security Council and the ICJ cannot concurrently address an issue which is before them. In fact, the two organs did just that in the *Iran Hostages* case.[60] In this case, consequent upon the ICJ entertaining a request from one of the parties to the action, the Security Council adopted a resolution of which the preamble took into consideration the order of the ICJ. The Court observed:

> it does not seem to have occurred to any member of the Council that there was or could be anything irregular in the simultaneous exercise of their respective functions by the Court and the Security Council. Whereas Article 12 of the Charter expressly forbids the General Assembly to make any recommendation with regard to a dispute or situation while the Security Council is exercising its functions in respect of that dispute or situation, no such restriction is placed on the functioning of the Court. The reasons are clear. It is for the Court, the principal judicial organ of the United Nations, to resolve any legal questions that may be in issue between parties to a dispute; and the resolution of such questions by the Court may be an important, and sometimes decisive, factor in promoting the peaceful settlement of the dispute.[61]

The Court also addressed the compelling question of statutory provision on the subject, where article 36 of the United Nations Charter, in paragraph 3, provides expressly that the Security Council should also take into consideration that legal disputes should, as a general rule, be referred by parties to the ICJ in accordance with the provisions of the statute of that court. However, the practical applicability of this principle may become an issue in some instances. Judge Bedjaoui in the *PAN AM* case observed:

> if the concomitant exercise of concurrent but not exclusive powers has thus far not given rise to serious problems, the present case, by contrast, presents the Court not only with the grave question of the possible influence of the decisions of a principal organ on the consideration of the same question by another principal organ, but also, more fundamentally, with the question of the possible inconsistency between the decisions of the two organs and how to deal with so delicate a situation.[62]

Be that as it may, on an overall assessment of the subject, it would not be illogical to conclude that the ICJ could determine legal disputes that are part of a political issue that is addressed concurrently by the Security Council.

There is no room for doubt that, in the formulation of space law as a new legal regime, the international community has paid attention to the most significant influence over this discipline of the two superpowers which existed at the time. The two great power blocs, the United States of America and the Union of Soviet Socialist Republics, were then the main protagonists (supported by their allies and a few neutral European states and the Third World). This polarization created an environment whereby an ideological balance was required to counter the possibility of encroachment by Realist thought which was calculated to establish an outer space legal regime that would have admitted of the creation of real property rights by one power bloc over the other in outer space, to the detriment of humankind in general.

The detriment envisaged was not only in its physical attributes and apprehension for the physical welfare of humanity, but also in the economic imbalance a Realist approach to space law would have brought to bear. The segmentation of space law into municipal regimes would have resulted in the inexorable endorsement of Realist theory, that states are egotistical utility enhancers and that the freedom of internal legislation would have given states a legal licence to maximize their freedom of outer space activities, thereby obviating any possibility of cooperation with other states. The inevitable corollary to this scenario would have been the avoidance of spreading the benefits of outer space exploration and exploitation over the world.

The general delineation of outer space as a common area rather than as an area which could be conquered therefore rested on the more traditional ground of international cooperation. However, the reason for the two power blocs to settle on commonality rather than on appropriation as the basis for the philosophy of space law is by no means the result of hard bargaining. It was the preferred choice of both parties. History records that there was no coercion or imposition of one system over another at the time of law making. One commentator says: 'it resulted from a process of weighing competing proposals based on different analogies and converging on the view that one of the underlying analogies was better than the other'.[63] Be that as it may, it is not possible to dismiss the pervasive influence exerted by the international legal order in the late 1950s, when space law was being promulgated. It was this influence which made it possible for the philosophy of space law to be primarily founded upon the concept that, unlike the situation in the formulation of air law in 1944, where states were aware of the economic and technical implications of a tried and tested product, outer space was an unknown quantity, controlled exclusively at that time by two power blocs who had ominous war power, and therefore its philosophy was destined to spread across the globe equally, ensuring commonality and responsibility.

NOTES

1 See R.I.R. Abeyratne, 'The Philosophy of Air Law', 37 *Am. J. Jurisprudence* (1992) 135–44.
2 H. Lauterpacht, *International Law*, 8th edn (1955) p.11.
3 See *National Geographic*, March 1981, p.317.
4 Karl-Heinz Böckstiegel, 'Prospects of Future Development in the Law of Outer Space', *Annals of Air and Space Law*, vol. VIII (1983) p.305.
5 Ibid., p.314.
6 UNGA Resolution 1348 (XII), 13 December 1958.
7 Treaty on Principles Governing the Activities of States in the Exploration and Use of Outer Space, Including the Moon and Other Celestial Bodies, opened for signature at Moscow, London and Washington on 27 January 1967, 610 UNTS 205.
8 D. Goedhuis, 'Some Substantive and Procedural Issues Presently at Stake in Space Legislation', 25 *Zeitschrift für Luft-und Weltraumrecht – German Journal of Air and Space Law* (1976), 198–9; also Bin Cheng, 'The 1967 Space Treaty', 95 *Journal du Droit International* (1968) 578.
9 M.G. Markoff, 'Disarmament and "Peaceful Purposes" Provisions in the 1967 Outer Space Treaty', 4 *Journal of Space Law* (1976) 3. Also N.M. Matte, 'Aerospace Law: Telecommunications Satellites', 166 *Recueil des Cours* (1980) 1, 147; R.S. Jakhu, in Girardot *et al.* (eds), *Developing Countries and the Fundamental Principles of International Space Law*, 351; C.Q. Christol, *The Jus Cogens Principle and International Space Law XXVI Colloquium* (1983) 1.
10 *ICJ Reports* (1970) 32.
11 The Vienna Convention on the Law of Treaties will be discussed later in this chapter.
12 *Barcelona Traction, Light and Power Company Limited, ICJ Reports* (1974) 269–70.
13 *Yearbook of International Law Commission* (1976), vol. II, pt One, p.29.
14 *ICJ Reports* (1970) 32.
15 Convention on Registration of Objects Launched into Outer Space, adopted by the General Assembly of the United Nations, New York, 12 November 1974, 1023 UNTS 15.
16 Manfred Lachs, *The Law of Outer Space, An Experience in Contemporary Law Making* (1972) p.70.

17 Ibid.
18 Treaty on Principles Governing the Activities of States in the Exploration and Use of Outer Space, including the Moon and Other Celestial Bodies, opened for signature at Moscow, London and Washington, 27 January 1967, 610 UNTS 205.
19 Ibid., article IX.
20 Ibid.
21 Agreement Governing the Activities of States on the Moon and other Celestial Bodies, signed on 5 December 1979, UN Doc A/RES/34/68 of 5/12/1979.
22 Ibid., article 7.
23 Convention on International Liability for Damage Caused by Space Objects, 29 March 1972, 24 U.S.T. 2389, T.I.A.S. No. 7762.
24 Article II(a) defines damage as including loss of life, personal injury or other impairment of health; or loss or damage to property of states or of persons natural or juridical, or property of international governmental organizations.
25 Stephen Gorove, 'Liability in Space Law: An Overview', *Annals of Air and Space Law*, vol. VIII (1983) p.373.
26 Ian Brownlie, *Principles of Public International Law*, 4th edn (1990) p.433.
27 1925 RIAA ii, 641.
28 Resolution 1721 (XVI) adopted on 20 December 1961. See also article 3 of the Outer Space Treaty.
29 *In Re.Chorzow Factory (Jurisdiction) Case* (1927) PCIJ, Ser. A, no. 9, at 21.
30 *ICJ Reports* (1949) 23.
31 Carl Q. Christol, *Space Law Past, Present and Future* (1991), p.231.
32 (1927) *PCIJ* Ser. A, No. 9 at 18.
33 Article 24 of the United Nations Charter provides that the members of the United Nations confer on the Security Council primary responsibility for the maintenance of international peace and security and recognizes that the Security Council would act on behalf of all member states of the United Nations. Article 23 of the Charter provides that the Security Council shall consist of 15 members of the United Nations. The Republic of China, France, the Russian Federation (then USSR), the United Kingdom of Great Britain and Northern Ireland and the USA are permanent members. Article 25 provides that members of the United Nations agree and accept to carry out the decisions of the Security Council in accordance with the provisions of the Charter.
34 *ICJ Reports* (1949) 174.
35 See Charter of the United Nations and Statute of the International Court of Justice, United Nations, New York, Article 13.1(*a*).
36 Article 2 of the Draft Code, pp.64–5.
37 Report of the International Law Commission to the General Assembly on the Work of the 1st Session, A/CN.4/13, 9 June 1949, p.21.
38 Vienna Convention on the Law of Treaties, United Nations General Assembly Document A/CONF.39/27, 23 May 1969.
39 There are instances where states may record their reservation on particular provisions of a convention while signing the document as a whole. The International Court of Justice in its examination of the Genocide Convention has ruled: 'The object and purpose of the Convention … limit both the freedom of making reservations and that of objecting to them. It follows that it is the compatibility of a reservation with the object

and purpose of the Convention that must furnish the criterion for the attitude of a State in objecting to the reservation' (1 *ICJ Rep.* 1951, at 15).

40 Georg Schwarzenberger and E.D. Brown, *A Manual of International Law*, 6th edn (1976) p.118.

41 The Preamble to the Outer Space Treaty states: 'The States Parties to this Treaty … Convinced that a treaty on principles governing the activities of States in the exploration and use of outer space, including the Moon and other Celestial Bodies, will further the principles of the Charter of the United Nations.'

42 D.W. Greig, *International Law*, 2nd edn (1976) p.8.

43 Charter of the United Nations and Statute of the International Court of Justice, United Nations, New York, article 38.1 (*a*).

44 Ibid., article 36.2(*a*).

45 Vienna Convention on the Law of Treaties, UN Doc A/CONF.39/27, 23 May 1969.

46 Ibid., Preamble.

47 Ibid., article 42.1.

48 Ibid., article 57.

49 Ibid., article 59.

50 Ibid., article 60.

51 Ibid., article 61.

52 Ibid., article 62.

53 Ibid., article 46.

54 Paul Reuter, *Introduction to the Law of Treaties* (1989) p.16.

55 See Frans G. von der Dunk, 'Jus Cogens Sive Lex Ferenda: Jus Cogendum', *Air and Space Law: De Lege Ferenda*, Essays in Honour of Henri A. Wassenbergh, edited by Tanja L. Masson-Zwaan and Pablo M.J. Mendes De Leon (1992) pp.223–4.

56 Ian Brownlie, *Principles of Public International Law*, 4th edn (1990) p.2.

57 Ibid., p.3.

58 Ibid., p.4; see also *Right of Passage Case*, *ICJ Reports* (1960), 90.

59 See Shabtai Rosenne, *The World Court*, 4th edn (1989) p.28.

60 *Case Concerning United States Diplomatic and Consular Staff in Tehran (United States of America* v. *Iran*) [1980] *ICJ Rep.* 3.

61 Ibid., 21–2.

62 *Libyan Arab Jamahiriya* v. *United States of America; Libyan Arab Jamahiriya* v. *United Kingdom*, Provisional Measures, Order of Apr.14 1992 [1992] *ICJ Rep.* 114 at 143.

63 M.J. Peterson, 'The Use of Analogies in Developing Outer Space Law', 51 *International Organization* (1997) 2, Spring, 266.

Chapter 2

Space Law Issues

1 THE AEROSPACE PLANE: FRONTIERS BETWEEN AIR LAW AND SPACE LAW

Introduction

The space shuttle was initially described as a space-faring cargo ship and corresponded to the generally accepted definitions of a spacecraft, that is, a rocket-propelled vehicle designed to move in Earth orbit or outer space. Together with these physical propensities, the space shuttle also showed characteristics of an aircraft. It had the capacity to re-enter the atmosphere and land like an aircraft. The space shuttle therefore created problems of jurisdiction for space law with questions such as 'what legal regime should govern the operation of the space shuttle?' and 'at what point would the space shuttle be considered an aircraft if at all?' This dilemma was succinctly identified by two commentators in 1982:

> A quarter century ago, in the early period of space activity, there appeared to be a straightforward distinction between 'aircraft' and 'spacecraft' in terms of the means by which the two types of vehicles were supported in space. 'Aircraft' were deemed to 'fly', being supported aerodynamically on wings, whereas 'spacecraft' were maintained in orbit due to their momentum by the grace of 'orbital mechanics'... Various forms of 'near earth surface' vehicles are now possible which support themselves above ground without resort to aerodynamic means. These range from magnetic levitation vehicles, through VTOL vehicles relying on the reaction thrust of jet or rocket engines, to one-man jet or rocket propulsion gear. More significantly the clearly successful 'shuttle' hybrid vehicle is an early precursor of what may likely develop into the dominant form of 'near-space vehicle'. Clearly the seemingly obvious distinction has disappeared and will likely be considered merely an anachronism in the future.[1]

Since the existing treaties and other rules of space law have mainly been formulated against this background and with the intention of exploratory space activities, new regulatory attempts will have to take into account, to the extent possible, the economic and technical environment of the commercialization of space activities, if real progress in the development and formulation of space law is to attain fruition.

This chapter will examine the effect the aerospace plane will have on the already contentious issue of air traffic rights, given the highly commercial flavour which the air transport industry has been tainted with in modern times, particularly in the face of modern commercial tools such as alliances between mega carriers and code-sharing agreements. Although, admittedly, the aerospace plane will not become an operational reality in the near future, its advent nevertheless promises to introduce some radical challenges to the present structure of air services agreements.

The aerospace plane

An aerospace plane is a hypersonic single stage to orbit reusable vehicle that takes off and lands horizontally on a conventional runway.[2] This is a broad definition, and may be used as a working hypothesis which various technical configurations of different models of aerospace planes could accord with. The aerospace plane will be constructed with the use of aeronautical and space technologies and would be capable and, indeed, required to fly both in airspace and in outer space. In these circumstances, the most fundamental issue at hand is the applicability of laws appropriate to the space plane's activities.

At an open forum discussion held on 6 April 1989 during the annual meeting of the American Society of International Law in Chicago,[3] the legal and policy issues of the aerospace plane were brought into focus and, on the subject of delimitation of applicable laws, a view was expressed by academics of McGill University's Institute of Air and Space Law that the activities of the aerospace plane as a space-traversing device used for point-to-point Earth transport could be governed by air law. It was the view of these academics that, should the principle of air law apply, it was necessary for bilateral agreements to be signed between states prior to an international flight by the aerospace plane. Professor Christol, on the other hand, believes that enormous benefit can be derived through the application of either the air or the space law regime,[4] leaving some to believe that the dilemma could best be left alone for the present since it is premature to speak of an autonomous law for space planes.

Vereschetin adopts a logical approach:

> As to 'ordinary' space planes, if their *raison d'être* is the delivery of cargo or persons to and from space, they should be treated, in principle, from the very beginning until the end of their mission as 'space objects' within the meaning given to this term in space law. Conversely, if any are destined for Earth-to-Earth transportation and, if during their operation they only traverse the fringes of outer space, these vehicles should be legally treated as aircraft.[5]

Tanja Masson-Zwaan agrees:

> After all, the transit through near space which is involved is *incidental* to the main transit which takes place within the airspace. Generally, the aerospace plane will be subject to the sovereignty of the State whose airspace it is in. It must comply with the rules set by ICAO and, if applicable, the tariff regulations set out by IATA.[6]

Speaking from a purely commercial point of view, it follows logically that the aerospace plane which transports persons and goods between states should be considered an aircraft, even if it traverses space at a given time. However, the two commentators' views above are not clear enough to arrive at an acceptable conclusion. For instance, what does the first commentator mean when he uses the term 'fringes of outer space'? Legally speaking, outer space is outer space and any operation of a flight by a vehicle of any description over and beyond the atmosphere would bring such activity within the purview of the outer space treaties. The second commentator makes it even more confusing when she observes that the aerospace plane will be subject to the sovereignty of the state whose airspace it is in. This is an incontrovertible fact which need not be stated, since any object within the airspace of a territorial state would indeed be subject to that state's sovereignty.

Gorove addresses a compromise which would set the upward limit of national sovereignty at a specific height anywhere between the area where satellites can orbit the Earth and where aircraft can fly and, at the same time, not require special permission from the underlying state to traverse space above this height on the way to and from outer space, or alternatively, to give space-faring nations the right of innocent passage through this area while ascending or descending from outer space. The problem with innocent passage, as Gorove validly points out, is that disputes can arise out of the interpretation of what constitutes innocent passage and also from the determination as to whose interpretation will prevail.[7] Another problem that would have to be addressed if the limit of national sovereignty was extended in this manner would concern the provision of air navigation services while the aerospace plane is in outer space above a particular state which would not be equipped to provide that service.

As the following discussion will demonstrate, there is absolutely no difficulty from a commercial standpoint in applying exclusively principles of air law to the operations of an aerospace plane which carries passengers and goods from one state to another, while traversing outer space in the process. However, the commercial implications of this application are quite considerable and would bring to bear the need to address its effect on current commercial practices with regard to air traffic rights.

The aerospace plane and air traffic rights

The issue of air traffic rights is addressed in the Chicago Convention of 1944,[8] which provides that, where non-scheduled air services are concerned, contracting states agree that aircraft of a state may make flights into or transit non-stop across the territory of other states without obtaining permission from the state flown over.[9] However, scheduled air services can be operated only with the special permission or authorization of the grantor state,[10] requiring a bilateral air services agreement between the two states concerned, or a multilateral air services agreement between states concerned. This has led to a sustained system of negotiations between states for rights of their aircraft to operate commercial scheduled flights into other states.[11]

Of the many considerations which are addressed at air services negotiations between states for air traffic rights of their carriers, perhaps the most contentious, and indeed important from a commercial point of view, is the insistence that there should be fair and equal opportunity for the airlines of each state to operate air services between the territories of those states. In early 2000, there were protests being made by six carriers of the United States to President Clinton calling for the suspension of the open skies negotiations between the United States and the United Kingdom which, if successful, would grant carriers of both states unlimited access to each other's territories in the operation of flights. The carriers alleged that the alliance between British Airways and American Airlines would act to those six carriers' detriment in the face of an operative open skies policy between the two states.[12] At the same time the United States also received notice of rejection from the Japanese authorities of its proposal for an open skies agreement with Japan. Comments of disappointment from the United States more than adequately sum up interests at stake in current air traffic rights negotiations:

> Japan's proposal makes explicit their real intent, which is to offer the U.S. some tightly regulated opportunities to serve Japan from smaller U.S. markets in return for the U.S. surrendering control of the Asian market to Japan's high cost carriers. Japanese negotiators seem more intent on protecting intra-Asian air service markets for Japanese carriers by blocking out U.S. carrier competitors than they are in opening the U.S./Japan aviation market.[13]

Japan has responded with the view that, while under the current bilateral air services agreement between the two countries US carriers have unlimited rights to fly beyond Japan, Japan Airlines, which was the only Japanese airline at the time the agreement was signed, has nothing.[14] By this statement, Japan has brought into focus the fair and equal opportunity principle.

On the other hand, Singapore Airlines has been requesting the air transport industry to consider the open skies concept favourably, calling for open skies between the United States and Asia to match transatlantic agreements.[15] Similarly, Delta Airlines has made a strong plea for open skies between the United States and Europe, entreating the European Union to heed the liberal approach taken by both US and European carriers towards the path of open skies.[16] Maurice Flanagan, group managing director of Emirates, the carrier of Dubai, claims that there is one place worldwide where open skies are granted unconditionally to all carriers – Dubai – and adds that the current international aeropolitical environment indulges and excuses overprotectiveness.[17] There is very little doubt that this over-protectiveness stems from a perceived difference between stronger and weaker air carriers where the weaker carriers jealously invoke the fair and equal opportunity clause seemingly to protect what they identify as their 'market share'.

The question of course arises as to whether there is such a thing as 'market share' in the modern context of alliances, code-sharing agreements and 'block-seat' arrangements. Professor Wassenbergh offers a solution:

> Open skies means free access to foreign air traffic markets. But how to use such free access? Not all air carriers may be able nor be located in a place enabling them to successfully compete. The only way we see for the weaker national air carriers to survive and maintain their effective participation in the international air traffic market is by cross border co-operation with a stronger air carrier.[18]

Wassenbergh concludes that the objective must be to provide the world with an optimum air transport system and network, operated with a minimum of harm to the environment and with an option for every state to participate in the provision of the system, or alternatively in the benefits of operating the system.[19] This is a noble objective, but is still far from being achieved through a workable formula. If, as Wassenbergh correctly states elsewhere, the future of international aviation lies in a group of air carriers that serve whole world regions, bonded together by commercial trade agreements and region-dominating carriers who will replace the national flag carriers that have ruled international skies since the post-World War I era,[20] the aerospace plane, once introduced to the market on a regular commercially operational basis, would further affect the fast disappearing 'fair and equal opportunity' principle.

The aerospace plane, which would drastically reduce flying time between such city-pairs as Los Angeles, on the one hand, and Tokyo and Sydney, on the other, would inevitably create hubs whereby regional carriers would converge with passengers (and cargo to a lesser extent) destined for carriage in the aerospace plane. In the long run this might lead to passengers of conventional aircraft being siphoned off to the aerospace plane. For example, hypothetically, a passenger embarking in Bombay for Tokyo might find that he would save time by travelling to an intermediate point and connecting with the aerospace plane from a point such as Singapore, and such an alternative may deprive airlines which do not use the aerospace plane in their fleet but operate air services between Bombay and Tokyo from losing the custom of that passenger. The use of hubs from which the aerospace plane flies would therefore be in greater focus and there would be more scope for greater and more prolific alliances between carriers to pool their resources in maximizing the carriage of passenger traffic. This scenario adds to the thrust of Wassenbergh's vision of greater emphasis being placed on alliances in the future.

It is incontrovertible that, at least at the introductory stages of the aerospace plane, it would operate on a third and fourth freedom basis; that is, from point to point without fifth freedom traffic being embarked or disembarked on the way, as is being done now. Take, for instance, the example already used of traffic between Los Angeles and Sydney (Australia), where a journey which takes at least 18 hours by a B747 aircraft would be accomplished by the aerospace plane in four hours on a direct flight. If the aerospace plane is large enough (which would not be so at the initial stages) and is designed one day to carry more than 300 passengers in each flight, it would be analogous to a present-day A310, MD11 or even B747 aircraft. Assuming the Americas, Europe and some states in Asia would use the aerospace plane to start with, there would be an exclusive third and fourth freedom traffic rights regime for which air services negotiations would be undertaken by the states which use the aerospace plane. The frequency of operations negotiated for would entirely depend on how dexterous states would be in attracting traffic to their aerospace planes.

Commercial aspects

The aerospace plane is really the third stage of accelerated air transport, the first being the Anglo-French Concorde supersonic aircraft. The second stage – a supersonic successor to Concorde – is now being considered. This successor would form a closer link between subsonic air transport and the aerospace plane.

The Concorde is the only aircraft at present able to cover 6000 kilometres in three hours with one hundred passengers on board. The most sophisticated jet fighters cannot perform this feat without in-flight refuelling. The 25-year-old Concorde, however, has its range circumscribed by its fuel-thirsty engines and is unable to cope with the growing demand for long-range flights, such as the 10 000-kilometre run between Los Angeles and Tokyo.

Concorde's successor will therefore need to cover a range of at least 10 000 kilometres in supersonic cruise mode (possibly even 12 000 kilometres), while carrying 250 to 300 passengers in a three-class configuration. As for fares, they would have to be comparable with existing first class fares or at least business class fares. It would not be illogical to assume that the aerospace plane, to compete with the future Concorde, would have to offer comparable service and fares. It would have to match the Concorde in capacity, which would mean that fuel efficiency would indeed be a key element in the design of the aerospace plane.

Assuming that the aerospace plane can offer comparable features to the Concorde while offering the added advantage of greater speed, it would presumably start by being operated by airlines of a few developed states, thereby attracting a hub-and-spoke type of air transport service. One could therefore envisage a proliferation of feeder services carrying passengers to the hub where the aerospace plane operates. In the face of the present environment of air transport services heading towards liberalization, at least in the context of the aerospace plane, the need for predetermination of capacity of the Bermuda I model of 1946 could be resuscitated[21] in order that the number of feeder services operated into a hub be curtailed.

Practically, such a situation, where third and fourth freedom air traffic rights are once again given prominence under the Bermuda I umbrella, would give rise to a dichotomy. On the one hand, when states negotiate bilaterally for air traffic rights in relation to third and fourth freedom traffic, the airline of the state which has the hub for the aerospace plane may wish to carry as much feeder traffic on its own services. This tug of war for a share of third and fourth freedom feeder traffic may result in a back-to-basics approach where fair and equal opportunity under the Bermuda I canvas was considered to be in relation to sharing air traffic between carriers and not necessarily to competition between carriers. Under such a commercial environment of rigid negotiation, carriers may go back to insisting on fair and equal opportunity to share feeder traffic for the aerospace plane rather than agreeing to have fair and equal opportunity to compete. In any event the aerospace plane will perforce introduce a generic commercial regime that would need careful commercial strategy on the part of both the large carriers and the small carriers.

In their consideration of third and fourth freedom (feeder) traffic, states might find relevant the concept of the 'safety net' which emerged from the International Civil Aviation Organization (ICAO)'s Fourth Worldwide Air Transport Conference held in November–December 1994.[22] The 'safety net' is designed to provide an integrated, interrelated package of provisions that would enable states, compatible with global trends and regulatory practices in other areas of economic relations, to move towards a more open, competitive air transport sector. Under the 'safety net', which would apply to all carriers alike, irrespective of their commercial advantages, each party grants unrestricted basic market access rights to each other party for use by their air carriers for services touching the territories of both parties (without cabotage rights). Optional would be seventh freedom carriage (that is, services touching the territory of the granting party but not that of the designating party) and cabotage rights.

The 'safety net' also enables each party to have the right to impose a capacity freeze. Such a freeze would be implemented *inter alia* only in instances where a rapid and significant decline occurs in a party's participation in a country pair market. It is not an automatic mechanism which comes into play immediately when a market share goes below a certain amount. Instead, it requires the affected party to assess whether or not to initiate the capacity freeze, when, for example, the capacity offered by its carriers falls below one-half that offered by the carriers of the other party, or one-third of the capacity offered. Incontrovertibly, therefore, the invoking of the 'safety net' is based on flights offered in the country pair market by the third and fourth freedom operations. The 'safety net' is being further studied by ICAO's Air Transport Regulation Panel, which is continuing to hold its work sessions.

Another mechanism to emerge from the ICAO Worldwide Air Transport Conference of 1994 which may interest states in the context of feeder traffic in relation to the aerospace plane is 'preferential measures in the economic regulation of international air transport to ensure the effective participation of developing countries in such transport'. Consideration of these preferential measures emerged as a result of the recognition by the Conference that a liberalized regulatory regime would have credibility only if it were based on existing realities and provided for sustained participation by all states, including developing ones. In this context, one of the compelling realities which needs to be addressed is the disparity in the economic development and the competitive situations between the air carrier of many developing countries and those of most developed countries. In recognition by the Conference that these disparities, which may affect the size and competitiveness of air carriers between and among states, could limit the real and effective participation of developing countries in air transport, it was considered that some practical supportive measures in the form of preferences were indeed needed.

Preferential measures, which are quite separate and distinct from the safeguards of the 'safety net', have three basic characteristics. They are usually granted on a non-reciprocal basis and the state granting the preference should not expect reciprocal treatment from the beneficiary state. They are granted to air carriers of developing countries where the disparities in size and competitiveness are such as to warrant special treatment. These measures are externally supportive and are designed to create an operative environment which would enable airlines of a developing country to build up its ability to compete in the air transport market. Above all, these measures are subject to bilateral or multilateral agreement between the states concerned.

The 'safety net' and preferential measures are two mechansims which would warrant closer scrutiny for their commercial relevance, if the hub-and-spoke system were to be made applicable to the commercial regime of the aerospace plane. One is encouraged by the fact that the 'safety net' mechanism will be further developed by ICAO Air Transport Regulation Panel and could well prove to be an effective tool for the attainment of commercial harmony between carriers when they are faced with more efficient and speedier aircraft, such as the aerospace plane, in the future.

Code-sharing agreements

The advent of the aerospace plane will also bring to bear the increased need for airlines to enter into code-sharing agreements with each other. Code sharing between two airlines is essentially two different airlines posing as one, sharing or rotating aircraft crew and responsibility.[23] It has been called a little more than a glorified interline agreement which occurs when one airline operates a flight but both its and another carrier's codes are used.[24] Thus, for example, a passenger who contracts with airline A to travel from Canada to Australia may find himself in the same aircraft with a passenger who contracted with airline B for the same journey.

The United States Department of Transportation (DoT) uses a rather technical definition for code sharing which it calls 'a common airline industry marketing practice where, by mutual agreement between cooperating carriers, at least one of the airline designator codes used on a flight is different from that of the airline operating the flight'.[25] The DoT then classifies code sharing under this definitive structure into two types, the first being the typical international airline operation where two or more airlines each use their own designator codes on the same aircraft operation, and the second enunciating the domestic code shared flight where the code on the passenger's ticket is not that of the operator of the flight, but where the operator does not offer the service in his own name. The DoT goes on to bifurcate international code sharing: in the first category, only one segment of the journey – which usually involves a connection – operates under two different codes, one used by an airline for its local traffic and the other used by its partner for the entire journey; in the second, the entire journey is advertised and displayed under the codes of the two airlines which share the flight concerned.[26]

The marketing benefits of code sharing have been identified as the ability of airlines to coordinate schedules, transfer baggage easily, maintain common marketing activity by the sharing air carriers, use through fares, use single check-ins, share airport lounges, share frequent flyer programmes, and agree upon exactly which airline is legally responsible for the passenger's whole journey by air. American Airlines, one of the early proponents and participants in the code-sharing concept, adds the safeguarding of traffic rights to this list, where it is claimed that a stronger carrier in the market could be forced to code share with a weaker national carrier, thus spreading commercial benefits on a given route among two carriers equitably.

One of the most scathing attacks on code sharing is that it seeks to create the illusion that interline connections between code-sharing partners are the equivalent of on-line connections, which is not so. It is claimed that this alleged illusion is successfully carried out because passengers prefer on-line to interline connections by a ratio of approximately four to one, fooling them into believing that a code share is an on-line service. Robert Crandall, then chairman of American Airlines, was of the view that allowing foreign carriers to deceive consumers into believing that a domestic code-shared service is really an extension of an international service of a foreign carrier effectively precludes genuine carriers from building strong, dependable on-line services.[27] Crandall also believed that code sharing is an anti-consumer marketing activity in that it causes multiple listings of the same flights in computer reservations systems and printed multi-airline schedules, thus debasing the quality of the information available to consumers.[28]

Code sharing really gathered momentum with the introduction of computer reservations systems. Major United States airlines found it attractive to engage in code sharing in relation to computer reservation systems (CRS) as it provided them with a better exposure on the CRS screen. Although a code-shared flight may not yet appear on a computer screen in its pristine form to be identfied as such, code-shared flights now appear in CRS as on-line connections and are thus given priority over interline connections, giving them an overall higher profile in the CRS and making them more likely prospects for booking by a travel agent.[29] These code-shared flights which appear as 'connections with aircraft change' on the screen would enable such flights to appear at least four times on the same screen. Some countries therefore view code-shared agreements as efficacious marketing tools and dissociate the concept entirely from the issue of traffic rights.

In January 1995, United States Secretary of State for Transportation, Fedrico Pena, announced the International Aviation Policy Statement of the United States which primarily endorsed code sharing as a cost-efficient way for carriers to enter new markets and expand their systems.[30] Earlier, in December 1994, the US Department of Transport had released its report on international code sharing which it had commissioned from Gellman Research Associates.[31] Secretary of State Fedrico Pena referred to the study as follows:

> This study fully supports the department's international aviation policy statement. It demonstrates that the movement towards globalization and transnational alliances through code sharing and liberalized bilateral arrangements delivers benefits not only for United States consumers but for the United States airline industry as well.[32]

One of the issues that emerged from the study was that the critical factor in code sharing is not whether it is good or bad, but whether it has certain undesirable effects that need to be addressed by policy makers. Based on an econometric consumer choice model that was applied to certain code-sharing agreements, as against non-code-shared flights, the study concludes that the negative impact on consumers as a result of potential deception is inconsequential as any impact of such misleading practices would be cushioned by existing DoT safety nets. The GRA study's findings were also consistent with the overall DoT perception that all international traffic will ultimately be restructured into long-haul services linking intercontinental hubs, with intraregional spokes feeding traffic, leading to the proliferation of airlines and the expansion of code sharing.[33]

The study concluded that benefits to consumers, estimated at $37.4 million, were minuscule compared to approximately $10 billion that passengers spend each year on transatlantic tickets. Even if one were to assume, as the study suggests, that the number should be doubled, a gain of around $75 million was comparatively inconsequential. Another conclusion was that consumer benefits of code sharing were not so much quantifiable in fiscal terms but rather in terms of higher convenience, higher quality of airline service and time savings generated through the faster elapsed time offered by code-shared flights.

Features of code sharing

A code share means that the flight code for one airline is used on one or more flights operated by another airline. One of the commonest uses of the term 'code sharing' is to signify that two airlines conclude an arrangement according to which two or more connecting flights are offered under a common designator code and flight number or those of both airlines, although individual segments are only operated with aircraft of one airline.

Code-sharing arrangements can form part of larger cooperation arrangements between the parties, including provisions on such issues as revenue or profit sharing, capacity allocation (block spacing), coordination of schedules, baggage handling and usage of nearby gates at the same airport or the same airport in an airport system. While originally code sharing was mainly agreed for air services of carriers in bilateral traffic, now the so-called 'third-country code-sharing' is becoming more and more important. This latter kind of code sharing refers to arrangements between carriers at least one of which does not have the nationality of either of the two countries touched by the service which is the subject of the arrangement. Some aeronautical authorities worldwide consider that such code-sharing arrangements require an authorization. Some consider it a normal cooperation (or marketing) arrangement between airlines requiring no approval at all.

Code sharing has considerable advantages for the two partners of such an arrangement. One of the main advantages is the more efficient and effective use of expensive aircraft. By concluding code-sharing arrangements an airline at the same time is able to reduce the operations of its own aircraft and to offer more flight connections under the airline's own designator code and own flight number. In addition to this, the economic risk of the operation of a route is reduced and handling and air navigation fees are saved. As a result of a code-sharing arrangement, an airline might also find it worthwhile to serve points it had not previously served.

A further potential advantage for the code-sharing partners is the better treatment of these connections in some computer reservation systems (CRS). Many systems outside the European Union and the European Civil Aviation Conference (ECAC) area up to now show code-sharing connections as on-line connections, which means they appear before the other interline connections. Therefore code-sharing connections tend to be booked first. This can create considerable competitive advantages for the code-sharing partners compared to those competitors who have to offer the same connections without a code-sharing partner as regular interline connections. So these competing carriers are potentially at a disadvantage. Code-sharing arrangements also easily lead to a situation where the many possible combinations of the codes of the partners will lead to excessive exposure on CRS displays, thereby forcing competitors out of the first screens. The European CRS rules limit these possibilities. Code sharing can also provide considerable marketing advantages for the partners of such an arrangement. Code-sharing arrangements involving a bigger and a smaller carrier which up to this time was only active in national air traffic can enable this smaller carrier to participate in international air traffic beyond the national framework. This is, in principle, likely to be good for competition.

It is possible that the carriers participating in such a code-sharing arrangement might agree not to start up any new services or to terminate any existing services on the route in question. At the same time they might even refrain from competing with each other over any connecting services. Therefore, code-sharing arrangements – in the extreme – might lead to a restriction of competition. Such an effect is more likely where code-sharing arrangements form part of larger cooperation arrangements between the parties or where code sharing covers non-busy routes.

Code-sharing arrangements result in the number of air services offered to the customers under the designator code of each code-sharing partner being increased. The passenger profits from this situation, because the code-sharing partners, as a rule, coordinate their flight schedules so that connecting destinations which otherwise could only be reached after considerable delays can now, despite a change of airline, be reached after a short interim stop only. The passenger can only very rarely recognize, when he books a flight or from the flight ticket he receives, that on the way he has to change aircraft and, above all, airline. So it can happen to a passenger that, without prior notice, he is carried by an aircraft of a carrier which he has not chosen. Such problems arise, however, only if the passenger has been misled during the booking process, and that disadvantage has to some extent been attenuated in Europe where the CRS are obliged to show the identity of the air carrier actually operating the flight. Furthermore, a condition can be placed on carriers via their operating permits to the effect that they must ensure that passengers are informed of the identity of the carrier performing the particular service in question.

In the best of circumstances code-sharing arrangements lead to a situation where the carriers involved can reduce the use of their own aircraft on certain routes. Combined with this, a reduction in fuel consumption and, therefore, lower air pollution could be achieved, if the aircraft 'saved' in this way are not used for other (additional) flight connections. The saving of aircraft connected with code sharing could also mean that airport slots become free and can be used for other flight connections. In addition, there is the possibility that routes which, up to this time, were served by both partners with their own aircraft from and to the same airport and which might have to be discontinued because of low load factors, can still be served with one aircraft at least through this code-sharing arrangement.

A further advantage could be that airports that at the moment only have a few connections to international destinations are now able to join the international air traffic. This is a profit for the airports as well as for the passengers. On the other hand, code sharing can also lead to a situation where one partner only serves a few, central gateways in the territory of the other partner with its own aircraft, and the other partner operates the national feeder services. This could result in fewer airports handling traffic and, more specifically, fewer movements as segments of long-haul operations. As international passengers would still pass through the airport concerned this could, however, only mean a decline in movements.

The regulatory treatment of code-sharing arrangements may be characterized by two different approaches. On the one hand, code sharing is seen primarily as a mere marketing tool which does not require any prior authorization from the competent authorities (unless required explicitly in any applicable bilateral or multilateral arrangement). This view is essentially based on the argument that code sharing does not imply any additional operations or any increase in capacity but merely improves the marketing possibilities of existing services.

On the other hand, code sharing is seen as an (at least indirect) form of market access for a code-sharing carrier which requires prior authorization on the basis of underlying traffic rights and/or special code-sharing rights. In support of that position, it is usually argued that the code-sharing carrier holds out the service as if it were its own and thus may circumvent agreed frequency and capacity restrictions. Since states enjoy sovereignty over their airspace, the states involved would seem to be able to regulate the matter as they want.

The code-sharing agreements concluded between US and European carriers for routes between the USA and Europe, as well as the exchanges of views among the governments of the ECAC states, have prompted the question of whether or not code sharing can be seen separately from the traffic rights and frequency or capacity framework which are negotiated bilaterally: in other words, whether, on the basis of such cooperation arrangements, services can be operated to points for which no traffic rights exist or for which code-sharing services have not been expressly agreed between the states concerned.

In the light of the above discussion, the following issues may be identified as being worthy of consideration:

1 the impact of code-sharing arrangements on bilaterally agreed frequency and capacity restrictions;
2 the ability of a carrier to be able to show its designator code and its flight number on a segment to be operated by its code-sharing partner, only if it itself also has obtained the traffic rights for that segment but does not operate it;
3 the ostensible need for an agreement between governments that contains regulations on code-sharing rights in addition to the agreed traffic rights, as so-called 'quasi traffic rights' or whether code-sharing arrangements should only be treated as commercial arrangements that require no official approval;
4 the inclusion in any agreement between governments of regulations covering possible competition aspects of code sharing;
5 the usefulness of agreeing on regulations for third-country code sharing on routes via intermediate points, or code sharing between carriers of one party and those of a third state; and
6 the relevance of principles of reciprocity such as that a third country, whose airline concludes a code-sharing arrangement with an airline from one of the two contracting states which concerns services from points in the territory of the other contracting state, should grant similar code-sharing rights to the airlines of the other contracting state.

As a result of the increasing interest of the airlines in code sharing it is possible that a global network of cooperating airlines may develop very quickly in international aviation. Not all states agree as to how code sharing is to be dealt with, but it is clear that code sharing is of current importance.

Commercially speaking, the aerospace plane will be one more feature in the air transport industry which would call for the need for the world to move from total restraint of competition to rational competition. Of course, as Wassenbergh observes, governments must closely control the activities of the air carriers in the markets they serve. However, contrived notions of predetermined capacity should not be a factor in the commercial assessment of the aerospace plane's potential. Rather, the focus should be on commercial cooperation between air carriers when this new phenomenon descends upon us from the fringes of outer space.

2 LIABILITY OF STATES AS PROVIDERS OF SPACE TECHNOLOGY IN THE FIELD OF AIR NAVIGATION

Introduction

In 1983, the Informal Aviation Review Committee (ARC) of the ICAO[34] Council, which was established as a result of the increasing awareness that air navigation systems needed improvements to take civil aviation into the 21st century, recommended in its report to the Council, *inter alia*, that timely studies should be initiated on the policy and institutional implications which might arise from, and consider the arrangements which would be required for, a sharing of satellite systems.[35] Action required by the Council was 'to form a Special Technical Committee with terms of reference … whose task would be the development of an appropriate work programme to be submitted to the Council for approval'.[36] This special committee, called the Future Air Navigation Systems (FANS) Committee, had the following terms of reference:

> to study technical, operational, institutional and economic questions, relating to potential air navigation systems; to identify and assess new concepts and new technology, which may have future benefits for the development of international civil aviation; and to make recommendations thereon for an overall long-term projection for the coordinated evolutionary development of air navigation for international civil aviation over a period of time of the order of twenty-five years.[37]

The FANS Committee, which was to be composed of providers and users of the air navigation system in all parts of the world,[38] was also to be instructed to adopt a systems approach to its work as recommended by the ARC and to consider all available present and developing technology, including satellite technology, to ensure that its projection of air navigation requirements over a period of at least 25 years represented the most cost-effective and efficient solutions for international civil aviation.[39]

The Council, at its 111th Session in March 1984, considered certain proposals contained in a working paper[40] presented by the director, Air Navigation Bureau, wherein it was stated that several contracting states had already evinced interest in the establishment of a FANS Committee.[41] On 16 June 1984, the Secretary General of ICAO issued a State Letter[42] to all contracting states and interested international organizations requesting the views of states in the formation of the FANS Committee. In all, 14 states and three international organizations responded, evincing interest.[43]

Although the expectations of those involved in the FANS concept were to implement an aeronautical satellite system exclusively for civil aviation, the ARC was unable to demonstrate that this was financially or procedurally practicable. Similar difficulties were experienced by the high-frequency data link and the voice system, both of which required advanced technology network principles. Accordingly, the Air Navigation Commission (ANC) considered a proposal for civil aviation to share satellite systems with other modes of communication. The ANC also recognized that sharing satellite systems would entail an in-depth and lengthy study involving the identification of clear parameters regarding relations with other institutions. The FANS Committee was therefore invited to consider how this might best be accomplished.[44]

Implementation of the mandate given to the FANS Committee hinged on the experience of Committee members and the expertise of ICAO staff. The mandate was very wide in scope, making it obvious that the FANS Committee could not restrict its work programme unless absolutely necessary. Basically, the FANS Committee's work was twofold. The Committee was required to develop future air navigation systems,[45] an overall plan for air navigation for the next 25 years in coordination with the existing mechanisms of ICAO.[46] The terms of reference of the FANS Committee were identified on 30 March 1984:

> To study technical, operational, institutional and economic questions, including cost/benefit effects, relating to future potential air navigation systems; to identify and assess new concepts and new technology, including satellite technology, which may have future benefits for the development of international civil aviation including the likely implications they would have for users and providers of such systems; and to make recommendations thereon for an over-all long-term projection for the co-ordinated evolutionary development of air navigation for international civil aviation over a period of the order of twenty-five years. The Committee should avoid duplication of effort and its work should be co-ordinated with that of existing groups in the Organization.[47]

On the basis of its terms of reference, the FANS Committee interpreted its objectives to be the following:

a to help ICAO to examine future needs in a system concept; that is, not only to consider specific new technologies, but to consider them in the context of valid requirements, cost effectiveness, and practical mechanisms for achievement of their capabilities and their benefits;

b to help improve the international aviation support system to better serve the aeronautical users of the system. This includes safety improvements in those geographic areas where services have not been fully implemented, as well as needed efficiency improvements;
c to achieve better international understanding of modernization efforts planned and under way in a number of states and to identify those system elements which may have application beyond national boundaries;
d to identify needs, and subsequently to consider the satisfaction of those needs by systematically
   1 identifying world aviation needs for the next 25 years;
   2 considering potentially applicable technologies which may cost-effectively satisfy the identified needs; and
   3 laying the groundwork for any required international standardization by appropriate bodies of ICAO and other organizations.

The above four objectives were further narrowed by the FANS Committee to include three elements of focus: aeronautical communications (COM), aircraft navigation (NAV) and air traffic surveillance (SURV).[48]

The conclusions of the FANS Committee were as follows:

a the use of satellite technology was the only viable solution that could overcome the shortcomings of the present system and, to that end, FANS developed a satellite communications system that coordinated well with air traffic control systems over land and sea;
b aviation needed a substantial frequency spectrum for satellite services;
c services called Automatic Dependent Surveillance (ADS) and Required Navigation Performance Capability (RNPC) had to be developed, the former which automatically transmitted the position of aircraft by satellite to air traffic control facilities, and the latter which unified different navigation devices hitherto used, by the use of clearly spelled out levels of capability; and,
d the airport capacity problem was acute and should be addressed as a part of the FANS programme, whereby surface surveillance, guidance and control systems could be developed.[49]

Considering the high degree of international cooperative efforts that were necessary between the protagonists of the FANS saga – the various civil aviation administrations, international organizations, service providers and users – a new FANS Phase II Committee was established in 1989, *inter alia* to develop a global plan for the systematic implementation of the FANS systems. This plan, which was completed in September 1993, contains guidelines for implementation of the FANS system.

The pivotal point of the FANS programme, and its proper initiator into the actual use of space technology was the 10th Air Navigation Conference of ICAO, held in

1991. Representatives of 85 nations confirmed at this conference that future air navigation systems would extensively use satellites, plunging the civil aviation world into the regime of outer space. It was recognized at this conference that FANS would develop into a worldwide evolution of communications, navigation and surveillance (CNS) techniques in a largely satellite-based air traffic management (ATM) system.[50] The global CNS/ATM system is designed to facilitate air navigation throughout a unified airspace, and is particularly considered to help Third World air navigation.[51] The new technologies are considered generally easier to operate and maintain than the old technologies, involving minimal training expenditure. In the developed world, both the current United States' Global Positioning System (GPS) and the Russian Global Navigation Satellite System (GLONASS) are well advanced to accommodate the Global Navigation Satellites System (GNSS). Both countries were expected to have full operational configuration of satellites in orbit by 1995 (which goal was attained), probably on a combined GLONASS/GPS basis to fit in with the GNSS concept.[52]

The ICAO CNS/ATM systems mark a significant departure from the present air navigation systems, calling for radical restructuring of global air navigational modes with the use of satellite technology. The use of space technology in air navigation, while bringing together the resources of outer space and airspace, has also generated provocative issues of legal significance, attenuating general legal principles related to the transfer of space technology and the legal liability of the states involved in the transfer of such technology. We will examine these issues and discuss the legal principles involved below.

Regulatory and legal aspects of air navigation

Article 12 of the Chicago Convention[53] stipulates that each contracting state undertakes to adopt measures to ensure that every aircraft flying over the territory of a state or manoeuvring over such territory shall abide by the rules and regulations of that state relating to the flight and manoeuvre of aircraft. This extends the principle of state sovereignty reflected in article 1 of the Convention[54] and accords states an absolute prerogative to establish air navigational rules in their territories whether or not facilities for air navigation are obtained through space technology. States are bound, however, by article 28 of the Convention to provide in their territory, airports, radio services, meteorological services and other air navigational facilities to facilitate international air navigation, in accordance with the Standards and Recommended Practices established from time to time, pursuant to the Convention.[55] The Convention, in turn, empowers ICAO to adopt Standards and Recommended Practices dealing, *inter alia*, with: (a) communications systems and air navigational aids including ground markings;[56] (b) rules of the air and air traffic control practices;[57] (c) collection and exchange of meteorological information;[58] and (d) aeronautical maps and charts.[59]

Contracting states have undertaken in article 37 of the Convention to collaborate in securing the highest practicable degree of uniformity in regulations, standards, procedures and organization, relating to aircraft, that are adopted by ICAO in the above fields. ICAO also derives its mandate to enact standards and recommended practices on air navigational facilities from article 44(*c*) of the Convention which encourages the development of airways, airports and air navigational facilities for international civil aviation.

The ICAO Council is further empowered by the Convention to consult a state (together with other states of the region, if necessary) and make recommendations to improve air navigational facilities in that state, if the Council is of the opinion that the airports and other navigational facilities, including radio and meteorological services in that state, are not adequate for the safe, regular, efficient and economical operations of air services.[60] These recommendations are by no means mandatory and a state is not deemed guilty of an infraction of the Convention if it elects not to follow the recommendations of the Council in this regard.

At the 28th Session of the ICAO Legal Committee held in Montreal (11 to 22 May 1992), the Committee concluded that CNS/ATM systems as developed by ICAO were compatible with the provisions of the Chicago Convention and the regulatory role of ICAO and that there was no legal impediment to the implementation and achievement of the FANS concept.[61] Accordingly, the Legal Committee recommended, *inter alia*, that the ICAO Council approve the following guidelines, which were adopted at the 28th session:

a universal accessibility to air navigation safety services must be available without discrimination;
b the rights and responsibilities of states to control operations of aircraft and enforce safety regulations within their sovereign airspace must not be compromised;
c arrangements must preserve, facilitate and not inhibit ICAO responsibility for the establishment of appropriate Standards, Recommended Practices and Procedures in accordance with article 37 of the Convention on International Civil Aviation;
d arrangements must recognize states' responsibility and authority to enforce safety regulations;
e existing governmental or intergovernmental agencies, modified if necessary, should be used to the extent practicable;
f existing institutional arrangements and legal regulations should be preserved wherever practicable;
g arrangements should provide for the determination of liabilities;
h adequate arrangements should be made for recovery in the event of a significant malfunction or catastrophic failure of the satellite system;
i arrangements must be adequately flexible to accommodate currently defined services and a range of future services;

j arrangements should *allow* the introduction of satellite services on an evolutionary growth basis;
k policies governing charges levied on users must not inhibit or compromise the use of satellite-based safety services;
l institutional arrangements should not prevent competition among different service providers that comply with ICAO Standards and Recommended Practices (SARPS);
m arrangements must ensure the ability to protect safety communications from harmful interference;
n arrangements must retain air traffic services (ATS) authority to coordinate and maintain control, directly or indirectly, over aeronautical mobile-satellite communications according to message priorities established in the International Telecommunication Union (ITU) Radio Regulations (RR);
o arrangements must facilitate the certification by states of those service providers whose services comply with ICAO Standards, Recommended Practices and Procedures for the aeronautical mobile-satellite (R) service (AMS(R)S);
p arrangements must ensure guaranteed priority of aeronautical mobile-satellite safety communications over aeronautical non-safety and non-aeronautical mobile-satellite communications in accordance with ICAO SARPS;
q ICAO's responsibility for coordination and use of AMS(R)S spectrum must continue to be recognized;
r arrangements must be in place so that service providers, operating in the same area, cooperate to ensure that space segment resources are made available to handle AMS(R)S service;
s arrangements should make all four identified satellite services (ATS, AOC, AAC and APC) available through any given satellite in any region of the world;
t arrangements should enable all AMSS functions (ATS, AOC, AAC and APC) to be provided through common avionics equipment in the aircraft;
u states must be assured of the continued availability of the service;
v arrangements must ensure the ability to protect navigation signals and supporting communication signals from harmful interference;
w arrangements must ensure that ATS authorities can coordinate and control the means to derive and distribute information related to integrity, fault warning and augmentation of GNSS in accordance with ICAO Standards;
x arrangements must not preclude the ability of states directly or indirectly to augment GNSS;
y arrangements must ensure performance within the appropriate required navigation performance criteria including integrity, fault warning, reliability, continuity and accuracy for the different phases of flight; and
z arrangements must ensure reasonable allocation of costs between the user states, aviation, and other system users and that GNSS status information is available for distribution to the civil aviation community.[62]

In consideration of the above guidelines and taking into account the overall characteristics that CNS/ATM systems are expected to have, the ICAO Council, on 9 March 1994, approved a Statement of Policy on CNS/ATM Systems which, *inter alia*, accepted the principle of universal acceptability without discrimination to all air navigation services provided by way of the CNS/ATM systems, and confirmed that the implementation and operation of CNS/ATM systems which states undertake to provide in accordance with article 28 of the Chicago Convention shall neither infringe nor impose restrictions upon states' sovereignty, authority or responsibility in the control of air navigation and the promulgation and enforcement of safety regulations.[63] The Statement also pronounced that ICAO shall continue to discharge the responsibility for the adoption and amendment of Standards, Recommended Practices and Procedures governing the CNS/ATM systems and that ICAO shall continue to explore, in consultation with contracting states, airspace users and service providers, the feasibility of achieving a civil, internationally controlled global navigation satellite system (GNSS).[64]

Space technology and air navigation

ICAO's participation in programmes for the exploration and use of outer space was recognized at the 15th Session of its Assembly in June/July 1965 where the Assembly adopted Resolution A15–1 which recognized ICAO's interest in the exploration and use of outer space and directed the Council to carry out a study of those technical aspects of space activities that affect international air navigation.[65]

At the 22nd Session of the ICAO Assembly held in Montreal in September/October 1977, the Assembly adopted Resolution A22–20 which recognized that the exploration and use of outer space for peaceful purposes is of great interest to international civil aviation and affects matters falling within the Organization's competence under the terms of the Chicago Convention and that ICAO is responsible for developing international civil aviation on all matters related to the use of space technology for air navigational purposes. Accordingly, the resolution, *inter alia*, urged contracting states to keep ICAO informed regarding the programmes and the progress achieved in the exploration and uses of outer space that are of interest to international civil aviation.[66]

The contents of this resolution were revised and the resolution was superseded at the 29th Session of the Assembly held in Montreal in September/October 1992 by Resolution A29–11 which, while recognizing that Resolution A22–20 established the responsibility of ICAO for stating the position of international civil aviation on all related outer space matters, resolved that ICAO continues to be responsible for stating the position of international civil aviation on all related outer space matters and monitoring and coordinating the work performed by states on regional and global planning on these matters in order that the introduction of the CNS/ATM systems takes place in an orderly and efficient manner globally and in a balanced way. The resolution also urged contracting states to keep ICAO informed regarding their programmes and the progress achieved in the exploration and use of outer space that are of interest to international civil aviation.[67]

At the Fourth Meeting of the Special Committee for the monitoring and coordination of Development and Transition Planning for the Future Air Navigation Systems (FANS Phase II) held in Montreal in September/October 1993, the Committee endorsed the early implementation of the available technologies in order to accrue early benefits. The Committee recommended that ICAO should encourage the achievement of early benefits through the use of existing technological advances, with early exploitation of the following:

a aeronautical mobile-satellite service (AMSS) through existing available satellites;
b automatic dependent surveillance (ADS) through existing communication media (for example, very high frequency (VHF), satellite communications links;
c global navigation satellite system (GNSS)-type services through use of GPS, GLONASS, overlays, ground augmentations and so on; and
d the aeronautical telecommunications network (ATN) through, for example, use of ARINC Specification 622.[68]

The provision of satellite communications and surveillance services involves many elements, comprising ATS facilities, terrestrial networks, earth stations, spacecraft and airborne facilities. The Committee was of the view that international organizational arrangements should allow these different elements to be provided by different suppliers who could meet ICAO standards, and that in this regard ICAO was the only appropriate body that should establish technical standards for international aeronautical communications, navigation and surveillance services. It was also felt that ICAO was responsible for the coordination of the use of frequencies allocated exclusively to the aeronautical mobile satellite (R) service (AMS(R)S).[69]

The International Maritime Satellite Organization (INMARSAT), which came into existence in 1979,[70] adopted certain amendments at the Fourth Session of its Assembly in October 1985, conferring on INMARSAT the role of provider of aeronautical satellite telecommunications to the world. Article 27 of the INMARSAT Convention[71] requires INMARSAT to cooperate with the United Nations and its bodies dealing with the peaceful uses of outer space. There is no doubt that this provision does not derogate ICAO's competence to adopt Standards and Recommended Practices under the Chicago Convention relating to air navigation, although technological facilities relating to satellite communications would be provided globally to air navigation services by INMARSAT. Dr von Noorden observes:

> nonetheless, ICAO remains the sole international body with the competence to establish international standards and procedures relating to aeronautical satellite telecommunications. It is, furthermore, very much in INMARSAT's interest that ICAO should, in due

> course, establish relevant standards and procedures, because INMARSAT may turn out not to be the only provider of aeronautical satellite telecommunications services. In this event, it would be highly undesirable for the various competing systems to be technically incompatible, so that airborne equipment could operate only to one system.[72]

It is therefore conclusive that ICAO is the ultimate standard-setting organ in regard to the use of space technology in air navigation.

General principles of state responsibility

The first area of state liability that comes to mind involves the use of defective outer space equipment that would give incorrect information to air navigation services. Liability in this instance could ensue if damage to persons or property is caused by the use of such information.

Remote sensing of the Earth's surface is another activity that opens itself to state liability issues.[73] The notion of using devices such as satellites to survey the globe, although incontrovertibly beneficial to the development of cartography, meteorology, geography and oceanography – all of which affect air navigation – would inevitably raise questions of state privacy. Some may even argue that the sharing of satellite resource data may derogate article 2(7) of the United Nations Charter which prohibits state intervention in matters which are essentially within the domestic jurisdiction of any state. The unauthorized space observation of a territory of a state by another has been identified as a deprivation of a right of the observed state, even if no more information is obtained than that which is already available to that state,[74] resulting in the award of pecuniary compensation.[75]

The refusal of a state which holds data obtained from remote sensing of the Earth's surface to provide such information to another state may result in a claim by the latter state that the withholding of such data is an abuse of its rights and that such refusal is calculated to result in such information being used against the requesting state. The aggrieved state may even claim that the state which holds the data would use the information to its advantage, resulting in the unjust enrichment of the state which holds the technology and information at the expense of the other.

The protection of knowledge and communication is another area which requires careful consideration when legal issues relating to the application of space technology to air navigation are considered. These aspects of space technology would be protected under patent laws. While ground-based space technology and communications arising therefrom would be protected by patent laws applicable normally both nationally and internationally, it is arguable that new issues in the realm of patent laws relating to outer space technology may have to be addressed. A critical factor for consideration would be the specific instances where a state would withhold information from air navigational facilities where such information has been obtained through the use of space technology and could affect the security of the state which holds such information. The use of space technology in air navigation is incontrovertibly linked to principles of space law that would admit of such use.

3 THE NEW GLOBAL NAVIGATION SATELLITES SYSTEM

Introduction

The Global Navigation Satellites System (GNSS) is essentially a system of satellite technology which, when applied to aviation, determines the position, velocity and components of an aircraft in flight. GNSS has its origin in the groundbreaking ICAO mechanism devised in 1983 called the Future Air Navigation System (FANS) which paved the way for the highly contemporary air navigation management system called Communications, Navigation, Surveillance/Air Traffic Management (CNS/ATM). GNSS has been aptly described as the most exciting technological shopping trip of the century that will provide many safety and efficiency 'specials' to both the developed and developing world.[76] Some of the safety and efficiency features promised by GNSS are advanced screening of mountainous regions in countries such as Japan, New Zealand and Nepal (which are currently finding it difficult with available radar screening technology) and visual surveillance of vast desert areas of the Middle East and countries such as Australia and the United States.[77]

Ever mindful of the legal implications that such a gigantic stride in satellite technology may bring the world of civil aviation, ICAO has prepared a draft charter setting out the legal issues of GNSS. The document, developed through a panel of legal and technical experts, embodies the fundamental postulates driving the implementation and operation of GNSS within the parameters of certain accepted international law norms such as sovereignty of states and international accord through cooperation. The main thrust of the GNSS mechanism is of course the ensuring of safety in aviation through precision in CNS/ATM which is the pre-eminent consideration of international civil aviation at the present time.

At ICAO's first-ever worldwide CNS/ATM Systems Implementation Conference, held in Rio de Janeiro from 11 to 15 May 1998, the Conference considered the above-mentioned ICAO draft charter[78] on the Rights and Obligations of States Relating to Global Navigation Satellite Systems as an interim legal framework for CNS/ATM systems. The Rio Conference, which was identified by the President of the ICAO Council, Dr Assad Kotaite, as one which succeeded in focusing the attention of the world aviation community on key issues of financing and management of CNS/ATM systems and crystallized the needs and available resources for the safe and orderly growth of civil aviation into the next millennium,[79] expressed its support for the adoption of the draft charter.

The draft charter embodies the most compelling elements that would affect the operation of GNSS, such as aviation safety, global accessibility by users of GNSS, accuracy, reliability, continuity, availability and integrity of GNSS, sovereignty, and compatibility with relevant global planning and implementation. Of these elements, the issue of sovereignty is the most fundamental and essential. It is the core issue which reaches the philosophy of GNSS, unlike the other elements which are technical and procedural.

The draft charter, presented to the 32nd Session of the ICAO Assembly in September/October 1998, states that it is driven by the need to ensure safety in aviation in the context of the use and operation of GNSS and the underlying principle, *inter alia*, that every state preserves its authority and responsibility to control operations of aircraft and to enforce safety and other regulations within its sovereign airspace. It further elaborates that the implementation and operation of GNSS shall neither infringe nor impose restrictions upon states' sovereignty, authority or responsibility in the control of air navigation and the promulgation and enforcement of safety regulations.

Whatever may be the contribution of ICAO and the rest of the global aviation community towards successfully implementing GNSS, ultimately the overall responsibility of implementing GNSS falls on states themselves. The genesis of state responsibility lies in article 28 of the Chicago Convention,[80] which states, *inter alia*, that each contracting state undertakes, to the extent practicable, to provide in its territory, airports, radio services, meteorological services and other air navigation facilities to facilitate international air navigation, in accordance with the standards and practices recommended or established from time to time, pursuant to the Convention. This provision incontrovertibly brings to bear the need for states not only to take all practicable measures to provide air navigation facilities in their respective territories but also to be associated with implementation of GNSS through standards and recommended practices adopted under the umbrella of the Chicago Convention. Article 28 also imputes to states the responsibility of international cooperation in this regard and their attendant responsibility of ensuring the success of that implementation.

Principles of legal liability of states in the operation of GNSS have been discussed earlier[81] and it is not the intent of this chapter to re-examine them. Instead, we will examine the fundamental principles of state responsibility under article 28 of the Chicago Convention and build on the significant observation made by the President of the ICAO Council on this subject:

> The activities of non-governmental entities in outer space shall require authorization and continuing supervision by the appropriate State. The implications of this provision, which has been regarded as a part of general international law, will have to be studied in the context of GNSS. While an air law instrument may impose responsibility directly on non-governmental service providers of GNSS in the sense of private law, the general responsibility of the relevant States in the sense of public law has not been obviated.[82]

GNSS, which comes within the purview of aerospace law, will command a place in the law of outer space which is perhaps the most dramatic example of new international law. There is no doubt that GNSS will involve part option, part practice and part treaty in space law practice, defying orthodox and dogmatic classification. By its very nature, and being a product of new economic and technological pressures, GNSS will demand a stringent test of the elasticity of international and municipal law, requiring a harmonious blend between the two legal systems and making their boundaries less clearly defined. The use of the common term 'transnational law', which is now freely used to define this grey area, is a good example of a possible jurisprudential approach to GNSS.

The 1989 British case involving the International Tin Council[83] stressed the importance of international law and its application on a community basis. Lord Oliver observed:

> A rule of international law becomes a rule – whether accepted into domestic law or not – only when it is certain and is accepted generally by the body of civilized nations; and it is for those who assert the rule to demonstrate it, if necessary before the International Court of Justice. It is certainly not for a domestic tribunal in effect to legislate a rule into existence for the purposes of domestic law and on the basis of material that is wholly indeterminate.[84]

The thrust of Lord Oliver's observation is that a municipal tribunal, when it is confronted with the need to apply a principle of international law, should determine whether such a principle has been widely accepted by the international community. A municipal tribunal certainly does not possess the jurisdiction to impose an international norm which it creates for the purpose, even if such a fictitious principle is to apply only domestically.

In order to examine the principles of state responsibility, we will address the most fundamental postulates of jurisprudence at air and space law which establish such responsibility. If it can be accepted that a principle of *jus cogens* creates obligations *erga omnes*, it becomes an undeniable fact that article 1(1) of the Outer Space Treaty could be considered a peremptory norm or *jus cogens,* since it generates obligations towards the international community as a whole. Christol observes:

> Article 1 Paragraph 1 of the Space Treaty, with its adoption of the common benefits and interests guarantee, can be supported (as an example of peremptory norms) because the provisions conform to moral law in the sense that all humankind is to benefit unconditionally, and because the terms are consistent with the spirit and the purposes identified in Article 1 Pars. 1 through 3 and Article 2 pars 1 through 4 of the UN Charter, as well as with complementary international agreements of lesser authority. To the extent that the terms are beneficial to individuals, the larger community, and States, and when the provisions are found on the fundamental moral principles contained in the foregoing paragraphs of Article 1 and 2 of the UN Charter, such basic principles qualify for the status of peremptory norms of general international law.[85]

The effect of this observation is that the content and nature of article 1(1) confirms that it is a *jus cogens*. There is seemingly no reason why the international community should not give such recognition to the 'common interest' principle as enshrined in article 1(1) which is aimed at the protection of the interests of the international community as a whole. *A fortiori*, on the same basis, article IX of the Outer Space Treaty which requires that states should avoid harmful contamination and adverse change in the environment of the Earth which may result from the exploration of outer space would incontrovertibly be considered *jus cogens*.

The provision and use of GNSS by states within their territories carries with it the fundamental responsibility not to cause damage to international users of such services. This raises the delicate issue of *culpa* or fault on the part of the state concerned and whether knowledge of the damage can be imputed to the provider state even in instances where knowledge cannot be clearly established. In the *Corfu Channel Case*,[86] which involved damage to British vessels in Albanian waters caused by mine laying by Albania, the Court said:

> it cannot be concluded from the mere fact of the control exercised by a State over its territory and waters that that State necessarily knew, or ought to have known, of any unlawful act perpetrated therein, nor yet that it necessarily knew, or should have known, the authors. This fact, by itself and apart from other circumstances, neither involves *prima facie* responsibility nor shifts the burden of proof.
>
> On the other hand, the fact of this exclusive territorial control exercised by a State within its frontiers has a bearing upon the methods of proof available to establish the knowledge of that State as to such events. By reason of this exclusive control, the other State, the victim of a breach of international law, is often unable to furnish direct proof of facts giving rise to responsibility. Such a State should be allowed a more liberal recourse to inferences of fact and circumstantial evidence …
>
> The Court must examine therefore whether it has been established by means of indirect evidence that Albania has knowledge of mine-laying in her territorial waters independently of any connivance on her part in this operation. The proof may be drawn from inferences of fact, provided they leave *no room* for reasonable doubt. The elements of fact on which these inferences can be based may differ from those which are relevant to the question of connivance.[87]

There is also explicit recognition that principles of international law apply to space law. The General Assembly of the United Nations in 1961 adopted the view that international law, including the Charter of the United Nations, applies to outer space and celestial bodies.[88] It is also now recognized as a principle of international law that the breach of a duty involves an obligation to make reparation appropriately and adequately.

Principles of state responsibility at air law

Inherent in the GNSS mechanism is the critical role played by air traffic management which is not regulated by international convention owing to the permeating influence of the principles of state sovereignty. Therefore responsibility of states for their air traffic management rests heavily on the concept of sovereignty upon which air law has built its formation. Air law is based entirely on the concept of state sovereignty in air space and is essentially related to land. The concept dates back to early Roman times when: 'States claimed, held, and in fact exercised sovereignty in the air space above their national territories … and [therefore] the recognition of an existing territorial airspace of States by the Paris Convention of 1919[89] was well founded in law and history.[90]

The Roman state adopted an all-embracing approach in ensuring the protection of private and public rights of its citizens. It could not have assumed full jurisdiction to lay down rules for its citizenry unless it exercised rights of sovereignty in airspace as well as on land. The genesis of the concept of sovereignty in airspace is traced to Justinian's *Corpus Juris Civilis*,[91] where the concept seemed rather to be the work of some gloss upon a passage in the Digest.

Accordingly, airspace at that time became, in international law, a contentious issue when it came to justifying the removal of projections from adjoining property over a place of burial.[92] Bouve added the view that airspace was new space added to accommodate man's ability to fly.[93] Thus the right bestowed by the private law maxim, *Cujus est Solum, Ejus est Usque ad Coelum*, was firmly entrenched as an absolute right of a person under ancient Roman law. This maxim, which means that a right of land ownership brings with it rights of ownership of airspace above the land, was later found to be unacceptable as an absolute rule. Blacklisted as a 'product of some black letter lawyer',[94] the rule was later adapted to mean that no nation acquired any domain in what was known as navigable airspace until such domain was needed to protect subjacent territory.[95]

The doctrine of sovereignty was introduced to the Western world by the French philosopher Bodin. At a time when political attitudes were in transition from the dominance of the universal church to a universal legal order, Bodin introduced sovereignty as a supreme power over citizens and subjects that was not itself bound by laws.[96] He elaborated the principle that every independent community had to consider that, while acknowledging the authority of the law, a state was above the law if it wished to govern successfully. Other jurists who supported the theory of exclusive sovereignty were Hugo Grotius, who maintained that sovereign states were independent of foreign control, and Thomas Hobbes, who said that sovereignty was absolute and its misuse was unthinkable. John Locke attempted to compromise the absolute quality of sovereignty by opining that sovereignty was not absolute and unquestionable in that it was an exchange of social trust between the government and the people. Accordingly, there was an inarticulate premise that a breach of the social trust between the two parties would erode the concept of sovereignty. John

Austin, in his *Province of Jurisprudence Determined* (1892) defined sovereignty to emanate from a person when 'a determinate human superior not in the habit of obedience to a like superior, receives habitual obedience from the bulk of a given society, that determinate superior is sovereign in society and that society is therefore sovereign and independent'.[97]

The important question is, how is sovereignty determined? Both juristic and judicial opinion favour the view that sovereignty of airspace should be determined on the role played by the importance of subjacent airspace in its relation to land and sea. In other words, a symbolic possession of the airspace is necessary in order that states can claim sovereignty over their airspace. Therefore the concept of sovereignty becomes compatible with the concept of ownership of property with possession by the owner, to the exclusion of others. To determine sovereignty in airspace, three elements would have to be resolved: the use of airspace, the nature of its possession and the nature of its control to the exclusion of others.

The use of airspace is inextricably linked to the social needs that the airspace in question would subserve. Roscoe Pound envisaged that one of the fundamental bases for the control and use of property was its sociological importance.[98] There is no difficulty in establishing a nexus between the sociological value of territorial land and sea and the protection offered to them by the subjacent airspace of a country. The next element – symbolic possession – has its roots in the early Roman law concept of *traditio longa manu*,[99] where possession was transferred by a symbolic act such as the handing over of a key to a premises when continued and consistent access was impracticable. Savigny elaborates on this classical theory by infusing three elements into the concept of possession: detention with *animus domini* or the will to hold as owner, *animus possidendi* or the will to exclude others from one's property, and *animus rem sibi habendi* or the will to hold for oneself. Savigny's concept of the need to blend detention with *animus* (intention) for the establishment of possession is satisfied by the modern concept of sovereignty in airspace, since all these elements can be seen in a state's claim to sovereignty over airspace where the three elements impute the physical fact of *de facto dominium* to the intention to retain possession of the object.[100] Jhering went a step further by claiming that detention was not necessary; only the will of the possessor was. Weber and Erlich both contended that the law is not a formal set of rules but a prime method of establishing order in society and accordingly required a person merely to show incontrovertible reason for the need to possess property. The final element – the nature of control of airspace – can be subsumed in modern juristic thought: that the modern interpretation of the concept of sovereignty is not the ability to make war or to exploit others, but to legislate over a given state or community.[101]

Perhaps the most convincing justification for the acceptance of sovereignty in airspace as the fundamental legal norm in air law is seen in Hans Kelsen's pure theory of the law.[102] Kelsen considered that all international laws derived their basis from a *grundnorm* or a basic legal postulate derived purely from law and not from morality. This basic norm was international custom. In this context, the philosophy of air law is founded on the concept of sovereignty in airspace and would sustain its credibility through this customary concept. The idea of sovereignty is then taken to its final conclusion and ultimate justification by Pound, when he states:

> Men must be able to assume in civilized society that they may control, for purposes beneficial to themselves, what they have created by their own labour and what they have acquired under existing social and economic order. This is a final postulate of civilized society.[103]

If Pound's view – that man must control what he has created for his benefit, under the existing social and economic order – were to prevail, it is logical to say that the element of control that man exercises as 'sovereignty' must essentially be viewed on a collective basis, and that the interest of the world community must necessarily be considered.

Judicial decisions and academic views on sovereignty

The linkage between the use of airspace and the protection of a subjacent territory was supported by American and English decisions[104] where the *ad Coelum* maxim was called 'a fanciful phrase … a glittering generality which has not arisen out of contested law suits and not therefore received close judicial scrutiny'.[105] American judicial opinion is exemplified in the decision in *Hinman* v. *Pacific Air Transport*,[106] where the court said: 'Title to the airspace unconnected with the use of land is inconceivable. Such a right has never been asserted. It is a thing not known to the law.'[107]

The court in this instance applied the overall doctrine as modified and ruled that the plaintiff, who claimed ownership of 150 feet above his land, had no rights in superjacent airspace over the defendant who operated his plane 100 feet above the plaintiff's land. The *ad Coelum* maxim was therefore no longer regarded as the law. On the one hand, the formula that it extended from the centre of the Earth to the skies was judicially tenuous. On the other, the fact that a landowner had unlimited rights relating to the airspace above his land was considered retrogressive and indefinable. There was no evidence of customary acceptance of the maxim for jurists to consider it as a scholastic doctrine of practical acceptance.

The *ad Coelum* formula therefore became a figurative phrase, never to be taken literally but used to express complete ownership of land, and the right to superjacent airspace only to the extent as was necessary or convenient to the enjoyment of land. The owner of land owns as much of the airspace above him as he uses, but only so long as he uses it.

By the end of the 19th century, the private law concept of absolute ownership of airspace over land was antiquated. The beginning of the 20th century saw the emergence of states' sovereignty in airspace. The impetus for public international law to take over the issue of rights over airspace was given by the August 1904 aerial incident, when Russian guards shot down the German balloon *Tschudi* when it was flying outside Russian territory, and the two unrelated but similar incidents that occurred in 1908 and 1910.[108] The French government hastened to call a conference of European powers in 1910. For the first time, participating states at this conference recognized airspace belonging to individual states on the basis that 'The upper air is a national heritage common to all of the people, and its reasonable use ought not to be hampered by an ancient artificial maxim of law.'[109]

The consensus of opinion of the European states in 1910 followed the landmark US decision of *Erickson* v. *Crookston*,[110] decided in 1907, where the court said: 'Common law rules are sufficiently flexible to adapt themselves to new conditions arising out of modern progress, and it is within the legitimate province of the courts to so construe and apply them.'[111] World War I decided the issue of public rights over airspace when Germany alleged that the *casus belli* was the penetration of German airspace by French aviators. The experience of the war (1914–1918) strongly reinforced the view of the British delegation (supported by Holland, Denmark and Switzerland) at the European Air Law Conference of 1910 that states' sovereignty extended *Usque ad Coelum* and that belligerent aircraft cannot go over the territory of another at will.[112] By the end of the war, air law was regarded as a discipline that accepted air as a free commodity except when it was connected to owned property (subjacent airspace) and seen to be used to protect that property.[113]

Professor Bin Cheng addresses the principles governing post-World War II sovereignty over airspace as enunciated in article 1 of the Chicago Convention[114] and concludes:

> The now firmly established rule of international law that each State possesses complete and exclusive sovereignty over the airspace above its territory means that international civil aviation today rests on the tacit acquiescence or express agreement of States flown over.[115]

Shawcross and Beaumont define sovereignty in international law as the right to exercise the functions of a state to the exclusion of all other states in regard to a certain area of the world.[116] In international aviation the concept of sovereignty is the fundamental postulate upon which other norms and virtually all air law are based.[117] Post-1944 attitudes towards the concept of sovereignty in airspace and the philosophy of air law range between the unlimited public law right of a state to exercise sovereignty over its airspace and the idea of free movement of air traffic. Professor Goedhuis identifies the idea of 'free traffic' as opposed to the exclusivity of the sovereignty principle as being considered by jurists as a constructive element of aviation which furthers life and raises it to a higher level.[118] This view is supported by the claim that general principles of international law demand that sovereignty of states be limited by the principle of freedom of peaceful traffic.[119]

Be that as it may, a view advocating the free use of airspace of a country by aircraft of foreign nationalities would give rise to a dichotomy: that there should be freedom of aviation with a minimum of restrictions or none at all, or that international air traffic should be firmly regulated. Professor Lissitzyn analyses the concept of sovereignty in its modern development as having three basic principles: that each state has exclusive sovereignty over its airspace; each state has complete discretion as to the admission of any aircraft into its airspace; and that airspace over the high seas and other areas not subject to a state's jurisdiction is *res nullius* and is free to the aircraft of all states.[120]

H.A. Wassenbergh lists seven objectives of a state's policy in respect of modern civil aviation:

a to contribute to the functioning of the international community of states as a total legal order by upholding and further developing the rule of international law;
b to protect the integrity and identity of the national society;
c to promote the nation's participation in man's activities in the air and space;
d to create the best possible conditions and opportunities for use by the public of aviation and space activities;
e to increase the benefits to be derived from the use of the air and outer space for its nationals;
f to promote the further development of technology and the knowledge of man;
g to cooperate with other states on the basis of equal rights in order to bridge conflicting national interests and achieve the aims mentioned above.[121]

Paul Steven Dempsey attributes the insistence of man on sovereignty to the fact that the human being is a territorial beast whose primordial imperative was to satisfy his thirst for control over a given area.[122] This view seems compatible with the early trends where the Paris Convention[123] provided that each state enjoys complete and exclusive sovereignty over the airspace above its territory.[124] Accordingly, from 1919, transit and landing rights for airlines became notionally subject to the explicit or tacit approval of the state in which the aircraft landed. Later, in August 1945, at the first meeting of the Opening Session of the Interim Council of the Provisional International Civil Aviation Organization (PICAO), the Hon. C.D. Howe, Minister of Reconstruction, Canada said: 'We (Canada) believe that there must be greater freedom for development of international air transport and that this freedom may best be obtained within a framework which provides equality of opportunity and rewards for efficiency'.[125]

Edward Warner, Representative of the United States of America (later the first President of the ICAO Council) said at the same meeting:

> Our first purpose will be to smooth the paths for civil flying wherever we are able. We shall seek to make it physically easier, safer, more reliable, more pleasant; but I believe it

> will be agreed also that we should maintain the constant goal that civil aviation should contribute to international harmony. The civil use of aircraft must so develop as to bring the peoples closer together, letting nation speak more understandingly unto nation.[126]

Dr Warner had notably stressed the purpose of civil aviation as being the promotion of international harmony and dialogue between nations. He had also made it clear that the seminal task of civil aviation is to bring the people of the world together through understanding and interaction. It is clear that, at this stage at least, civil aviation was recognized more as a social necessity than as a mere economic factor.

In addition, through the statements of Minister Howe and Dr Warner, one can glean the attitude of the international community towards aviation at that time: (a) that civil aviation was based on equality of opportunity, and (b) that it was a social need rather than a fiscal tool.

Jurisprudential aspects of state responsibility for ensuring that there is no damage or loss to others caused by the use and operation of GNSS lie essentially in the importance one could place in the thrust of public international law principles of international cooperation and comity, on the one hand, and municipal law which may be calculated to obviate such obligations, on the other. The theoretical dichotomy is well reflected in the clash of ideology between dualism and monism.

Dualism (or pluralism) recognizes that international law and municipal law are two distinct forces: one representing law between sovereign states, and the other representing the internal or domestic law of a state whereby relations between citizens and between citizens and the executive of the state concerned are determined. Typical dualist theory leaves the two regimes severely alone, holding that, while municipal law may decree certain international laws to be part of municipal law, it is certainly not a rule-of-thumb issue to make international law part of municipal law. Based on this logic, dualist doctrine would expect municipal courts to apply municipal law.

Monism, on the other hand, accepts unreservedly the supremacy of international law and bases itself on its distrust of the state in its role of protector of human rights. At least in the context of the relation between obligations of states and municipal law, monism is given more credibility than dualism, in that a state cannot plead provisions of its own laws or inadequacies in its laws as its response to a breach of its obligations imposed by international law. Jurisprudence supporting this premise is monotonously consistent, as is reflected in the *Free Zones Case*,[127] where the Provisional Court of International Justice (PCIJ) ruled that France was precluded from using its own legislation to desist from performing its international obligations. In the earlier case of *Polish Nations in Danzig*,[128] the PCIJ held:

> It should … be observed that … a State cannot adduce as against another State its own Constitution with a view to evading obligations incumbent upon it under international law or treaties in force. Applying these principles to the present case, it results that the question of the treatment of Polish nationals or other Persons of Polish origin or speech

must be settled exclusively on the basis of the rules of international law and the treaty provisions in force between Poland and Danzig.[129]

There is a compelling school of thought which is consistent with the above judicial theory and holds that there is a general duty incumbent upon all states to bring their internal laws into conformity with obligations and responsibilities imposed by international law.[130]

If the concept of state sovereignty were still to preclude consensus on international accord with regard to state responsibility for air traffic control services provided within states' territories, one could expect that the responsibility of states in this field would have to be determined by the principles of public international law.

State responsibility at air law would not only be restricted to the instance of provision of air traffic control services but also to other aspects which involve GNSS. In all such instances both air law and space law are inextricably interwoven by the principle of state responsibility *erga omnes* enumerated in the *Barcelona Traction* case, which Professor Brownlie elaborates as a general principle of international law and Justice Huber identifies as the necessary corollary of a right.

In the ultimate analysis, therefore, one could only agree with Wassenbergh when he said that one of the seven objectives of a state's policy with regard to modern civil aviation is to cooperate with other states on the basis of equal rights in order to bridge conflicting national interests. GNSS should form no exception to this thinking process.

NOTES

1 S. Mishra and T. Pavlasisk, 'On the lack of physical bases for defining a boundary between air space and outer space', *Annals of Air and Space Law*, vol. VII (1982), p.409.

2 Razanowski, Moleff and Smith, 'The U.S. National Aero-Space Plane: A Comparison with Aero-Space Programs in Other Countries and Future U.S. Options', CRS-3, Congressional Research Service, Library of Congress, Washington, DC (1989).

3 Among the issues discussed at this conference were the application of law, the status of passengers as 'astronauts', registration and liability. See 17 *Journal of Space Law*, 1 (1989), 73–4.

4 C.Q. Christol, 'The Aerospace Plane, its Legal and Political Future', 9 *Space Policy* (1993), 35.

5 V.S. Vereschetin, 'Next Steps in International Space Law', *Perspectives on International Law* (ed. Nandasiri Jasentuliyana) (1995), pp.463–70.

6 Tanja L. Masson-Zwaan, 'The Aerospace Plane: an Object at the Cross-Roads between Air and Space Law', *Air and Space Law De Lege Ferenda*, Essays in Honour of Henri A. Wassenbergh (1992), pp.257–8.

7 Stephen Gorove, 'Legal and Policy Issues of the Aerospace Plane', 16 *Journal of Space Law*, 2 (1988) 150.

8 Convention on International Civil Aviation, ICAO doc 7300/6, 6th edn (1980).
9 Ibid., article 5.
10 Ibid., article 6.
11 For a detailed discussion on the current global situation of air traffic rights, see R.I.R. Abeyratne, 'The Air Traffic Rights Debate – a Legal Study', *Annals of Air and Space Law*, vol. XVIII 1 (1993), 3; and 'The Worldwide Air Transport Conference and Air Traffic Rights – a Commentary', *European Transport Law*, vol. XXX, 2 (1995), pp.131–47.
12 U.S. Airlines Urge Halt to UK Open Sky Talks', *The Air Letter*, Thursday 25 July 1996, p.3. See also 'Fly America equals U.S. Protectionism?', *The Avmark Aviation Economist*, April/May, 1996, pp.3–6.
13 'No Surprises in Japan's Rejection of Open Skies', *Aviation Daily*, 28 June 1996, p.529.
14 'U.S.–Japan: Fair Play Comes First', *Airlines International*, January/February, 1996, p.7.
15 'SIA Chief Seeks Open Skies between U.S. and Asia', *The Air Letter*, Monday 24 June 1996, p.3.
16 'Delta Calls for Open Skies with Europe', *The Air Letter*, Friday 24 May 1996, p.1.
17 Maurice Flanagan, 'Open Skies and the Survival of the Fittest', *Aerospace*, August 1996, 16.
18 Henri Wassenbergh, 'De-regulation of Competition in International Air Transport', *Air and Space Law*, vol. XXI, 2 (1996) 83.
19 Ibid., 89.
20 'New Economic Forces Reshape Global Aviation', *Aviation Daily*, 20 November 1995, p.283.
21 For a discussion on predetermination of capacity and its commercial implications, see Henri Wassenbergh, *supra*, note 21, 80–89.
22 For a detailed discussion and analysis of the Conference, see R.I.R. Abeyratne, 'The Worldwide Air Transport Conference and Air Traffic Rights – A commentary', *supra*, note 14. See also, by the same author, 'The Air Traffic Rights Debate – where does Everyone Stand?', 14 *Lloyds Aviation Law*, 17, 1 September 1995, pp.1–6. A commentary on the Conference is also contained in B.D.K. Henaku, 'ICAO: Fourth Air Transport Conference', *Zeitschrift für Luft-und Weltraumrecht*, (German Journal of Air and Space Law), September 1994, 247–56.
23 'Code Sharing: If It's Tuesday, This Must be Aeroflot', *Airways*, January/February 1995, 19. See also 'Is Airline's Gain, Consumer's Loss?', *The Avmark Aviation Economist*, vol. II, 8, October 1994, 13.
24 'Coded Warnings', *Airline Business*, January 1995, 26.
25 *The Avmark Aviation Economist*, October 1994, 16, *supra* note 26.
26 Ibid.
27 See Robert Crandall, 'Chicago's Legacy, Barriers to Multilateral Liberalization', 2 *Viewpoint*, 1, at 12. Crandall cites the example of the British Airways–USAir code-sharing agreement which allegedly allows British Airways access to nearly six times as many world city-pair markets as are available to American Airlines. He further claims that, since British Airways now has the ability to gather passengers from almost anywhere in the United States and fly them across the Atlantic, and since it has created pseudo-hubs in the United States to connect with its real hub at London

Heathrow, neither the British government nor British Airways would have any incentive to let American Airlines or any other US carrier compete with British Airways for any substantial portion of the traffic flowing across Heathrow from countries around the world to and from the United States.

28 Ibid.

29 See Jan Ernest C. de Groot, 'Code Sharing – U.S. Policies and Lessons for Europe', *Annals of Air and Space Law*, vol. XIX, 2 (1994), p.64.

30 'Coded Warnings', *Airline Business*, January 1995, 26.

31 The objectives of the study were to develop a methodology to assess the effects of code sharing on the level and distribution of traffic among carriers, with the capability to measure the effect of future code-sharing agreements; to examine the effects of code sharing on the costs and profitability of airlines; to assess the effects of code sharing on consumers of airline services; and to project the future use and impact of code sharing over the next 20 years.

32 'GRA Report Sanctifies DoT Policy', *The Avmark Aviation Economist*, December 1994, 2.

33 Ibid.

34 The International Civil Aviation Organization (ICAO) was created in 1944 to promote the safe and orderly development of civil aviation in the world. A specialized agency of the United Nations, it sets international standards and regulations necessary for the safety, security, efficiency and regularity of air transport and serves as the medium for cooperation in all fields of civil aviation among its 183 contracting states.

35 C-WP/7678, 16/6/83, '1800th Report to the Council by the President of the Air Navigation Commission', 3. In 1968, the Panel on Application of Space Techniques Relating to Aviation (ASTRA) appointed by the ICAO Air Navigation Commission identified the principal functions listed for an aeronautical satellite system as air traffic services/ground voice communications; air traffic services/ground data transmission; company operational control air/ground voice communications; company operational control air/ground data transmission; and air traffic services monitoring of flight progress and of separation between aircraft. See C.C.E. Bellringer, 'Aeronautical Satellite Promises Many Improvements in International Civil Aviation Operations', *ICAO Bulletin*, March 1971, 10.

36 Ibid., 8, item 7.1(c). The Special Technical Committee derived its *raison d'être* from the Second United Nations Conference on the Exploration of Peaceful Uses of Outer Space in 1981 which emphasized 'that ICAO is responsible for developing the position of international civil aviation on all matters related to the study of the questions involving the use of space technology for air navigation purposes, including the determination of international civil aviation's particular requests in respect of space technology' (International Civil Aviation Organization Second United Nations Conference on the Exploration and Peaceful Uses of Outer Space, 'Report on the Civil Aviation Interests in the Use of Outer Space', Background Paper A/CONF. 101/ BP. IGO/1 (1981)).

37 Ibid., 13 (Appendix C). The main benefits to air navigation resulting from satellite technology have been listed under three headings: radiocommunication – which promises increased reliability and availability, increased communication capability between pilot and air traffic control and increased airline operational control capability; radiodetermination – which aims at reduction in aircraft separation standards with an

equal or higher safety level, leading to reduction in the direct operational costs of aircraft, improved payload economies and savings on passenger time; and changes in infrastructure – leading to decommissioning (in due time) of certain conventional high frequency (HF) and very high frequency (VHF) aeronautical mobile installations and the consolidation of some oceanic control areas with consequential reduction in the number of control centres. See Bellringer, *supra*, note 38, 9.

38 The representation of the FANS Committee was composed of 19 states and four international organizations, as follows: Argentina, Australia, Brazil, Canada, Denmark, France, Germany, Iceland, India, Iraq, Italy, Japan, Kingdom of the Netherlands, Saudi Arabia, Spain, Russian Federation, United Kingdom, United Republic of Tanzania, United States; International Air Transport Association (IATA), International Council of Aircraft Owner and Pilot Associations (ICAOPA), International Federation of Airline Pilots' Associations (IFALPA) and International Federation of Air Traffic Controllers' Associations (IFATCA).

39 See C-WP/7749, 9/11/83, Appendix A, which gives draft terms of reference of the FANS Committee. The Council later added to these terms the requirement that the Committee should avoid duplication of effort and its work should be coordinated with that of existing groups in the Organization. See C-Dec. 110/9, 28/11/83 at 1.

40 C/WP 7821.

41 See C. Min. 111/18 (Council 111th Session, 18th Meeting, 30/3/84) reprinted in Council Minutes, 111th Session 1984:ICAO, 194–6.

42 AN 1/16-84/6, dated 16 June 1984.

43 See C-WP/7821, 19/3/84. See also C-Min. 110/8 Subject No. 45, and Council Minutes, 110th Session 1983, 83.

44 See FANS/1-WP/7, 1984 05 22 at 2.

45 *Air navigation* has been discussed above to encompass all facilities which may be used in air navigation. *Systems* would refer *in limine* to article 28 of the Chicago Convention to include air navigation facilities and standard systems: airports, radio services, meteorological services and other air navigation facilities as well as standard systems of communications procedure, codes, markings, lighting and other operational practices and rules (see FANS/1-WP/8 1984 06 04 at 1). To better relate to what was being asked of the FANS Committee, the Air Navigation Commission (ANC) decided to establish a description of the term 'systems approach' based on knowledge and experience of ICAO's functions. A description was therefore agreed upon, as follows: 'In using the term "systems approach", a broad concept is intended which will consider the inter-action, interdependence, and inter-relationship of all elements of the international civil aviation system. In this context the "international civil aviation system" is taken to be a universal system which includes, as elements, all things, persons, organizations, activities and documentation that contribute to international civil aviation.

46 FANS/1-WP/8, 1984 06 04 at 2.

47 FANS/1-WP/9, 1984 10 05 at 17.

48 The following timetable was envisaged by the FANS Committee as reflecting its projected achievements: (a) 1991–7, development, trials and demonstrations; (b) 1993–2000, gradual implementation and use of elements of the system by some aircraft and CAAs; (c) 2000–2005, full FANS services available in parallel with existing systems; (d) 2005–10, progressive dismantling of terrestrial systems not required by FANS;

and (e) 2010, FANS to be fully and exclusively operative. See 24 *Aeronautical Satellite News* (ASA), October–November 1991, 10.

49 'Special Committee Reports on Future Air Navigation Systems (FANS)', 5 *Airport Forum*, October 1988, 10.

50 *Flight International*, 9–15 October 1991, 26. See also *Aviation Week and Space Technology*, October 14 1991, 36.

51 Ibid. The Asia/Pacific region has already devised a plan to replace archaic ATM concepts with those of FANS. This programme is being handled in Bangkok through an ICAO-controlled body, Asia Pacific Air Navigation Planning and Implementation Regional Group (APANPIRG). APANPIRG was charged with monitoring and identifying shortcomings in the development of the Asia/Pacific region's FANS programme and its transition to the CNS/ATM system at least by 1994. See *Jane's Airport Review*, November 1992, vol. 4 (9), 45.

52 Charles D. LaFond, 'ICAO Looks to Space', *Air Transport World*, December 1991, 97. See also Brian O'Keefe, 'Our Future Air Navigation System Embodies Global Concept', *ICAO Bulletin*, vol. 44 (9), September 1989, 17.

53 Convention on International Civil Aviation, signed at Chicago on 7 December 1944 (hereafter the Chicago Convention). See ICAO Doc 7300/8, 8th edition (2000).

54 Article 1 provides: 'The contracting States recognize that every State has complete and exclusive sovereignty over the airspace above its territory'.

55 Chicago Convention, *supra*, note 56, article 28(*a*).

56 Ibid., article 37(*a*).

57 Ibid., article 37(*c*).

58 Ibid., article 37(*g*).

59 Ibid., article 37(*i*).

60 Ibid., article 69.

61 ICAO Assembly, 29th Session, Executive Committee, Technical, Economic and Legal Commissions, A 29–WP/42, EX/10, TE/5, EC/9, LE/6, 17/8/92 at 6–7.

62 ICAO Doc 9588–LC/188, 3–13 to 3–15.

63 Legal Committee, 29th Session (Montreal, 4–15 July 1994, LC/29–WP/3–2, 28/3/94).

64 Ibid., 1–2.

65 Resolutions adopted by the Assembly and Index to Documentation, Doc 8528, A 15–P/6, at 23.

66 Assembly Resolutions in Force (as of October 1989), Doc 9558, 1–29.

67 Assembly 29th Session, Montreal 22 September–8 October 1992, Resolutions Adopted by the Assembly and Index to Documentation, Doc 9600, A-29 RES, 70–72.

68 FANS (II)/4–WP/82, 30/9/193, Recommendation 8/3 at 8–5.

69 Ibid., 8A–19.

70 The purpose of INMARSAT is to make provision for the space segment necessary for improving maritime communications, thereby assisting in improving distress and safety of life at sea communications, efficacy and management of ships, maritime public correspondence and radio determinate capabilities.

71 International Conference on the Establishment of an International Maritime Satellite System, 1975–1976 (1976) p.38.

72 Wolf von Noorden, 'Space Communications to Aircraft: A New Development in International Space Law (Part II)', 15 *Journal of Space Law* (1987) 2, 155.

73 The United Nations General Assembly in 1970 stated that potential benefits from technological developments in remote sensing of the Earth from space platforms could be extremely meaningful for the economic development of all countries and for the preservation of the global environment. See UNGA Resolution 2733C (XXV), 16 December 1970.
74 M. McDougal, H. Lasswell and I.A. Vlasic, *Law and Public Order in Space* (1963) p.540.
75 Ibid., p.541.
76 Rosalind Dubs, 'Selection of GNSS Solutions for Australia and the Region', *Journal of Air Traffic Control*, July–September 1996, p.64.
77 See Anne Paylor, 'Asia Prepares for GNSS', *Airports International*, May 1994, pp.33–5.
78 See ICAO working paper WW/IMP-WP/10, 11/5/98, Item 5, Appendix.
79 See 'ICAO World-wide Conference Produces Strong Recommendations for Financing and Managing CNS/ATM Systems Implementation', *ICAO News Release,* PIO 3/98 at p.1.
80 Convention on International Civil Aviation, signed at Chicago on 7 December 1944, Doc 7300/7, 7th edn (1997) ICAO, Montreal.
81 See B.D. Kofi Henaku, 'International Liability of the GNSS Space Segment Provider', *Annals of Air and Space Law*, vol. XXI, pt I (1996) pp.143–79; also Assad Kotaite, 'ICAO's Role with Respect to the Institutional Arrangements and Legal Framework of Global Navigation Satellite Systems (GNSS) Planning Implementation', *Annals of Air and Space Law*, vol. XXI, pt II (1996) pp.202–3.
82 Kotaite, *supra*, note 84, p.203.
83 [1989] 3 W.L.R. 969 (H.L.).
84 Ibid., 1014.
85 Christol, *supra* note 7.
86 *ICJ Reports* (1949) 4.
87 Ibid., 18.
88 Resolution 1721 (XVI) adopted on 20 December 1961. See also article 3 of the Outer Space Treaty.
89 The Paris Convention of 1919 will be referred to later in this chapter.
90 John Cobb Cooper, 'Roman Law and the Maxim "*Cujus Est Solum*" in International Law', cited in 55 *Explorations in Aerospace Law* (1968) 102.
91 42 tit. 24, pr 22 S.4.
92 A.K. Kuhn, 'Beginnings of an Aerial Law', 4 *Am. J. Int. Law* (1910) 123.
93 Bouve, 'The Development of International Rules of Conduct in Air Navigation', 1 *Air Law Rev.* (1930) 6.
94 S.E. Baldwin, 'The Law of the Airship', 4 *Am. J. Int. Law* (1910) 97.
95 John Cobb Cooper, *supra*, note 93, 29.
96 C.B. Weeramantry, *An Invitation to the Law* (1982) p.175.
97 Ibid., p.176.
98 Roscoe Pound, *Introduction to the Philosophy of the Law* (1961) p.114.
99 Weeramantry, *supra*, note 99, 165.
100 Roscoe Pound, *Jurisprudence*, vol. V, pt 8 (1959) p.95.
101 Dennis Lloyd, *The Idea of the Law* (1964) p.171.
102 See Leon L. Fuller, *The Problems of Jurisprudence* (1949).

103 Roscoe Pound, *An Introduction to the Philosophy of Law* (1922), pp.192–3.
104 *United States* v. *Curtiss-Wright Export Corp et. al* 299 US 3904 (1936), *United States* v. *State of California* 322 US 19 (1947); for English law, see *Wandsworth Board of Works* v. *United Telephone Company* 13 Q.B. 904. See also Robert R. Right, *The Law of Airspace* (1968) p.65 for comments on the *ad Coelum* principle as used in the USA and UK. In English law the *ad Coelum* principle at private law can be traced to Lord Cooke (Liber 1, S.1 p.4). This doctrine was approved in *Fay* v. *Prentice* (1845) 1 CB 827, *Corbett* v. *Hill* (1874) 9 L.R. Eq 671 and *Ellis* v. *Loftus* (1874) L.R. 10, C.P. 10.
105 *Wandsworth Board of Works* v. *United Telephone Company, supra*, note 107, 905.
106 84 F. 2d. 411 (2d Cir 1937).
107 Ibid., 417.
108 Visty C. Gunatilaka, 'Problems of Airspace Sovereignty in the Seventies', LLM thesis, May 1972, Institute of Air and Space Law, McGill University, Montreal, p.5.
109 W. Jefferson Davis, *Aeronautical Law* (1930) p.30.
110 100 Minn. 481 (1907).
111 Ibid., 484.
112 N.H. Mollere, *The Law of Civil Aviation* (1963) p.4.
113 Carl Zollman, *Law of the Air* (1927) p.3.
114 *Supra.*
115 Bin Cheng, *The Law of International Air Transport* (1962) p.3; see also ibid. pp.3–17 for a discussion on the manner in which air rights devolve upon air carriers under the sovereignty doctrine of the Chicago Convention.
116 Shawcross and Beaumont, *Air Law* (1977) p.15.
117 Ibid.
118 D. Goedhuis, *Idea and Interests in International Aviation* (1947), quoted in Z. Joseph Gertler, 'Order in the Air and the Problem of Real and False Options', *Annals of Air and Space Law*, vol. IV (1979) p.100.
119 Ibid.
120 O.J. Lissitzyn, *International Air Transport and National Policy* (1983) p.365.
121 H.A. Wassenbergh, 'Reality and Value of Air and Space Law', *Annals of Air and Space Law*, vol III (1978) p.352.
122 Paul Steven Dempsey, *Law and Foreign Policy in International Aviation* (1987) p.7.
123 Convention Relating to the Regulation of Aerial Navigation, signed, 13 October 1919 (hereafter Paris Convention).
124 Paris Convention, article 1.
125 *PICAO Documents*, Montreal, 1945, vol. 1, Doc. 1, 3.
126 Ibid., Doc 2, at 2.
127 (1932) PCIJ, Ser. A/B No. 46 . 46 at 167.
128 (1931) PCIJ, Ser. A/B No. 44 at 20.
129 Ibid., at 24.
130 See Fitzmaurice, 92 *Hague Recueil*, II (1957) 89.

Chapter 3

Space Law: Emergent Trends

1 LIABILITY FOR ACTS OF PROFESSIONAL NEGLIGENCE AND CRIMINALITY COMMITTED IN OUTER SPACE

Introduction

In space law, there is no such being as a 'person' in outer space. There are only astronauts and personnel.[1] The 1967 Outer Space Treaty stipulates that state parties to the treaty shall regard astronauts as envoys of mankind in outer space and shall render to them all possible assistance in the event of accident, distress or emergency landing on the territory of another state party or on the high seas.[2] The provision also requires state parties to return astronauts under the above circumstances safely and promptly to the state of registry of their space vehicle.[3]

The treaty provision is a reproduction *verbatim* of paragraph 9 of United Nations General Assembly Resolution XVIII of 1962.[4] Although, initially, the world's 'envoys of mankind' seemingly created some apprehension in the international community as to whether such phraseology connoted diplomatic immunity to astronauts, Bin Cheng clears up this ambivalence by concluding that it was only a figure of speech which has not been repeated in any United Nations documentation as yet.[5] The perceived inadequacy of definitive identification at international law of an astronaut and his conduct in outer space retains three postulates as guidance in the determination of an astronaut's conduct. They are that international law is incontrovertibly applicable to outer space activities, and outer space, including the moon and other celestial bodies, is totally independent of appropriation by states or individuals, leading to the inevitable conclusion that outer space would be analogous at international law to the high seas.

Jurisdictionally, astronauts are clearly within the purview of the state on whose territory they are or above whose territory and in the airspace of the state concerned. Generally, in outer space, this status quo changes, and astronauts become liable under the laws of the state of registry or the state which launches their spacecraft for travel and work in outer space.[6] This is brought to bear by article VIII of the Outer Space Treaty which provides:

> A State party to the Treaty on whose registry an object launched into outer space is carried shall retain jurisdiction and control over such object, and over any personnel thereof, while in outer space or on a celestial body.[7]

However, as Bin Cheng validly points out,[8] the interpretation of article VIII could well result in ambivalence and confusion. The 'object' and 'personnel' referred to in the treaty provision do not adequately cover persons who are not 'personnel', such as passengers in a spacecraft. Of course, as Cheng maintains, the quasi jurisdiction of the state of registry of the spacecraft can apply both in the instance of conduct in the spacecraft as well as outside the spacecraft on the basis that the astronaut concerned would be deemed to belong to the spacecraft at all times in outer space. Logically, therefore, such jurisdiction could be imputed to passengers, visitors and guests by linking them to the spacecraft in which they travelled. This far-reaching generalization would then cover the conduct of an astronaut or other persons while walking on the moon, Mars or other celestial body, as well as such persons who go on space walks outside the spacecraft in which they travelled.

Another provision which sheds some light on past attempts by the international community to identify liability and jurisdictional issues relating to astronauts is article 12 of the Moon Treaty of 1979,[9] which provides: 'States Parties shall retain jurisdiction and control over their personnel, space vehicles, equipment facilities, stations and installations on the moon.' It is presumed that the legal link between the personnel and the spacecraft they travel in under the circumstances are imputed to the state of registry of the said craft. If this were not the case, and such a link cannot be established, the provision itself would become meaningless and destitute of effect.

The above provisions, although seemingly adequate for an incipient world space programme, do not adequately address modern exigencies of outer space activity such as collaboration in space stations where repair missions and salvage activities may call for multinational crews, joint space exploration calling for multiple space technology, and even transport to outer space of passengers (the last of which, although futuristic, is nonetheless a possibility in the relatively near future). This chapter will examine the legal principles of general international law which would form at least a useful analogy to the conduct of persons in outer space and celestial bodies in instances which are not covered by current principles of law obtaining in the law of outer space.

Legal initiatives at treaty making

The recognition that the scope of manned space flight is being expanded (at least in theory at the present time) from the flight of astronauts to other persons such as repair crew and passengers, is becoming evident. In an attempt in 1988 at drafting a Convention on manned space flight, a team of draftsmen comprising a distinguished cluster of experts[10] in space law from Germany, the Russian Federation and the United States succeeded in a sustained attempt at producing a draft legal instrument which covers certain exigencies of personal conduct in space travel. The most significant thrust of this draft Convention is that it blends harmoniously the essential qualities of scholarship and practicality. The draft Convention has been published[11] in order to draw the attention of the world community of space lawyers and seek comments. The draft Convention effectively conveys the fundamental postulate that manned space flight is the cornerstone of exploration of outer space and therefore its development requires guidelines on international cooperation and liability.

The draft Convention, in article III, links itself to the Outer Space Treaty principle of awarding jurisdiction in relation to a manned space object and person therein to the state of registry in relation to occurrences in outer space or in a celestial body or on or in the high seas or any other place beyond the jurisdiction of any state. Article IV of the draft Convention devolves responsibility and authority over a manned space flight, the space object involved in such flight, and all persons on board, on the commander of the space object. The commander is given sole authority throughout the flight to use any reasonable and necessary means to achieve this end. The same provision makes both the commander and all members of the crew answerable to a person identified as the Director of Manned Space Flight Operations, who is defined by the draft Convention as a person who is designated by the state exercising jurisdiction and control over the space object to be in charge of a particular manned space flight. By this measure, the draft Convention skilfully and unequivocally identifies the chain of command, giving the commander absolute authority on the spot over all those in the space object during the flight, while making him answerable to a person designated as Director of Manned Space Flight Operations, who presumably will be on the ground and in mission control.

The draft Convention also ensures safety of persons involved in a manned space flight whether they be crew, passengers or any other category of persons affected by such flight. One of the strengths of the draft Convention is its provision with regard to environmental pollution or other harm caused to the environment by a manned space flight, where the instrument lays responsibility on states whose manned space exploration may jeopardize an existing environmental balance. The draft Convention also provides for assistance to be given by persons in a manned space flight to others in distress in outer space and prescribes international responsibility on states, whether the space flights in question are carried out by governmental or non-governmental entities.

Of direct analogy to this instrument are three Conventions and a Declaration at air law which lay down principles of law with regard to criminal conduct of persons on board aircraft. Of course, understandably, given the fact that crimes on board aircraft have been prolific over the past years, in comparison, these instruments are somewhat more evolved than the space law initiative and have concentrated on such offences as hijacking and other terrorist acts. But they also provide for sanctions against general criminal conduct and therefore would form a useful paradigm for future space law initiatives, particularly on the subject of terrorism in outer space and celestial bodies. The Tokyo Convention of 1963, on Offences and Certain Other Acts Committed on Board Aircraft,[12] refers to any offence committed or act done by a person on board any aircraft registered in a contracting state, while the aircraft is in flight or on the surface of the high seas or of any other area outside the territory of such state.[13] The aircraft is considered to be in flight from the moment power is applied for the purpose of take-off until the moment when the landing run ends.[14] In addition, the Tokyo Convention mentions acts of interference, seizure of or other wrongful exercise of control of an aircraft, implying its concern over hijacking.[15]

The Hague Convention of 1970,[16] in article 1, identifies any person who, on board an aircraft in flight, unlawfully by force or threat or by any other form of intimidation seizes or takes control of such aircraft, or even attempts to perform such an act, as an offender.[17] Anyone who aids such an act is an accomplice, and is included in the category of the former.[18]

It is clear that the Hague Convention by this provision has neither deviated from article 11 of the Tokyo Convention nor offered a clear definition of the offence of hijacking. It merely sets out the ingredients of the offence: the unlawful use of force, threat or any other form of intimidation and taking control of the aircraft. The use of physical force, weapons or firearms or the threat to use such modes of force are imputed to the offence in this provision. The words 'force', 'threat' or 'intimidation' indicate that the element of fear would be instilled in the victim. It is an interesting question whether these words would cover an instance where the use of fear as an implement to execute the offence of hijacking covers non-coercive measures such as the drugging of food or beverages taken by the passengers or crew. The Hague Convention does not ostensibly cover such instances. In this context, many recommendations have been made to extend the scope of its article 1.[19] It is also interesting that the Convention does not envisage an instance where the offender is not on board the aircraft but remains on the ground and directs operations therefrom after planting a dangerous object in the aircraft. According to article 1, the offence has to be devoid of a lawful basis, albeit that the legality or illegality of an act is not clearly defined in the Convention.

It is also a precondition in article 1 that the offence has to be committed in flight, that is while all external doors of the aircraft are closed after the embarkation of the passengers and crew.[20] The mobility of the aircraft is immaterial. Furthermore, article 1 is rendered destitute of effect if an offence is committed while the doors of the aircraft are left open.

The Convention for the Suppression of Unlawful Acts Against The Safety of Civil Aviation, signed at Montreal on 23 September 1971,[21] also fails to define, in specific terms, the offence of hijacking, although it circumvents barriers placed by article 1 of the Hague Convention.[22] For instance: it encircles instances where an offender need not be physically present in an aircraft; includes instances where an aircraft is immobile, its doors open; and even draws into its net any person who disseminates false information which could endanger an aircraft in flight.[23] None of the three conventions, however, has succeeded in identifying the offence of hijacking or advocating preventive measures against the offence itself.

The Tokyo Convention was perhaps the first major attempt at curtailing the menace of hijacking. Not only did it deal solely with jurisdiction over offences committed in an aircraft in flight, but it also did not exclude any criminal jurisdiction which would have been exercised according to the provisions of any law.[24] The element of nationality underlines the parochial nature of the treatment of the offence and the obstinate refusal of the international community to infuse a universality into the treatment of the offence. Perhaps, as one commentator observed,[25] the international community was not prepared in 1963 to address this problem on a collective basis.

The subsequent Hague Convention emphasizes that each contracting state undertakes to impose severe penalties, without defining what these penalties should be.[26] Furthermore, the geographic limitations set out in article 1 significantly curtail the punitive measures recommended in the Convention. The Convention makes a further serious omission in stating that it applies only if the place of take-off and place of landing are outside the state of registration of the aircraft.[27] This gives rise to a serious anomaly, in that, if an aircraft with a destination outside its territory of nationality is seized in mid-air prior to leaving its airspace and brought back to the place of take-off, the Convention would not apply even to scheduled flights.

The Montreal Convention, which followed in 1971, although extending the period in which the offence would be committed to a period beginning at pre-flight preparation and ending 24 hours after landing, does not cover acts of sabotage, destruction or any damage effected before the above period starts after 24 hours after landing. The Montreal Convention, however, is the best attempt so far at attempting to control or curb the offence of hijacking on an international level. Even so, the three attempts so far at international accord fail to cover certain gaps which still exist in this area of prevention and control of hijacking:

1 the Conventions do not provide for and guarantee the trial of an offender and do not specify adequate punitive measures;
2 no obligation is cast on contracting states for the extradition of an offender;
3 no provision is made for the universal adoption of standards of precaution and safety; and
4 the initial attempt, albeit somewhat unsophisticated, of the Tokyo Convention at a remedial approach has been thwarted by the repressive attitude of the two subsequent Conventions.

The Bonn Declaration of 1978 was yet another attempt by the international community to combat terrorism related to international civil aviation. The major economic powers, Canada, France, the Federal Republic of Germany (as it then was), Italy, Japan, the UK and the USA, collaborated to intensify efforts to combat terrorism. The seven signatory states pledged to take immediate action to cease all flights to a country which refuses to extradite hijackers or return hijacked aircraft, and to halt all incoming aircraft from that country or from any airlines of that country.

However, the view has been put forward that, under the principles of the Bonn Declaration, retaliatory action in the nature of self-preservation by third states against an offending state is subjectively assessed, and that action taken should be commensurate with the gravity of the infringement of the provisions of the Declaration.[28] Be that as it may, the Bonn Declaration was a clear demonstration that positive action can be taken against the threat of interference with international civil aviation if there is international cooperation. The signatories to the Bonn Declaration were the largest manufacturers of aircraft and their airlines covered more than half the world's scheduled passenger kilometres. They obviated the insurmountable difficulty of obtaining all the signatures of the ICAO contracting states while amply demonstrating that agreements of this nature are effective tools against the terrorist.

Comparison between space law and maritime law

Outer space and celestial bodies can be used for the common heritage of mankind but are *res extra commercium* like the high seas.[29] However, here the distinction ends, in that, unlike the high seas, which can be appropriated in certain circumstances, such as through acquiescence by one state of appropriation of an area of the high seas by another, outer space or celestial bodies cannot be appropriated under any circumstances. In the *Fisheries* case,[30] the International Court of Justice adopted the view that a consistent course of action on the part of fishermen of Norwegian vessels had established a pattern of fishing in a certain area over a period of time, which had been tacitly acquiesced by the British (who were contesting the right of Norway to fish in the area on the grounds that it was beyond the designated baseline of Norwegian waters) and that therefore Norway had established its right to continue the practice under the application of the general principles of international law to the specific case. The Court held (referring to Norway's practice of fishing in the disputed area): 'In this connection, the practice of States does not justify the formulation of any general rule of law … all that the court can see therein is the application of general international law to a specific case.'[31]

It is not possible to apply this principle to the conduct of crews or other persons in outer space. One cannot establish a pattern of conduct as a prescriptive right in outer space because there are no territorial limits demarcated by and between individual states in outer space. *A fortiori*, outer space has been identified as one composite area which cannot be appropriated by one particular state to the exclusion of others by treaty provision.

Freedom of outer space, which lays the foundation for conduct of persons in outer space, is enshrined in article 1 of the Outer Space Treaty of 1967, which stipulates that the exploration and use of outer space, including the moon and other celestial bodies, shall be carried out for the benefit and in the interests of all countries, irrespective of their degree of economic or scientific development, and shall be the province of all mankind. The provision also requires outer space to be free for exploration and use by all states without discrimination of any kind, on a basis of equality and in accordance with international law. Finally, the provision grants free access to all states in relation to all areas of celestial bodies.

Freedom of the high seas is contained in article 2 of the Convention on the High Seas of 1958 which provides that, since the high seas are open to all nations, no state may validly purport to subject any part of them to its sovereignty. Freedom of the high seas comprises the freedom of navigation, the freedom of fishing, the freedom to lay submarine cables and pipelines and the freedom to fly over the high seas. These freedoms are recognized by the principles of public international law.

On a purely superficial comparison of the freedoms of outer space and the high seas, one can notice a general similarity, in that both areas are open to mankind equally. However, the purposes for which the areas can be used are intrinsically different. For example, space law is all-encompassing on the subject of the conduct of humans in outer space and celestial bodies. The Outer Space Treaty makes the sweeping statement that outer space and celestial bodies shall be open for exploration by mankind, which includes, *inter alia*, the freedom to conduct research, experiments and other forms of exploration. The Convention on the High Seas, on the other hand, is inclusive and therefore restrictive in forming areas of specific activity. The Convention on the Law of the Sea of 1982 has somewhat remedied this *lacuna* by adding, in article 87(1), the freedom of scientific research *inter alia* to the already existing four freedoms.

Criminal conduct is an area where the principles of international law applicable to the high seas lend themselves as a useful analogy to space law. Of course, the offence of piracy cannot be committed by astronauts who are sent to outer space in spacecraft belonging to a state. The offence has to be committed for private ends by persons in a private ship or craft. The offence of piracy in the high seas would nonetheless apply as an analogy to a similar offence committed by private individuals in outer space who do not represent a state as official crew members. This would cover the improbable but nonetheless possible events of the future such as a mutiny on board a commercial spacecraft carrying passengers (which is an analogy derived from shipping law). Piracy in outer space may also occur in instances where personnel of a space craft could act on the orders of a recognized government which is in gross breach of international law and which show a criminal disregard for human life.

The offence of piracy at sea and its consequences were succinctly defined by Judge Moore in his dissenting judgment in the *Lotus* case.[32]

> In the case of what is known as piracy by law of nations, there has been conceded a universal jurisdiction, under which the person charged with the offence may be tried and punished by any nation into whose jurisdiction he may come. I say 'piracy by law of nations', because the municipal laws of many States denominate and punish as 'piracy' numerous acts which do not constitute piracy by law of nations, and which therefore are

> not of universal cognizance, so as to be punishable by all nations. Piracy by law of nations, in its jurisdictional aspects, is *sui generis*. Though statutes may provide for its punishment, it is an offence against the law of nations; and as the scene of the pirate's operations is the high seas, which it is not the right or duty of any nation to police, he is denied the protection of the flag which he may carry, and is treated as an outlaw, as the enemy of all mankind – *hostis humani generis* – whom any nation may in the interest of all capture and punish.[33]

Article 15 of the Convention on the High Seas of 1958 defines the offence of piracy as the following:

> 5 Any illegal acts of violence, detention or any act of depredation, committed for private ends by the crew or the passengers of a private ship or a private aircraft, and directed:
> 6 On the high seas, against another ship or aircraft, or against persons or property on board such ship or aircraft;
> 7 Against a ship, aircraft, persons or property in a place outside the jurisdiction of any State.
> 8 Any act of voluntary participation in the operation of a ship or of an aircraft with knowledge of facts making it a pirate ship or aircraft;
> 9 Any act of inciting or of intentionally facilitating an act described in sub-paragraph (1) or sub-paragraph (2) of this Article.

Mutatis mutandis, this provision would serve well as an analogy and persuasive authority in the event that a similar offence committed in outer space or celestial body is examined by a competent court of any jurisdiction.

The Convention restricts the application of the offence of piracy to acts on the high seas or 'any place outside the territorial jurisdiction of any state', which means essentially *in contextu* an island or '*terra nullius*' (no man's land). The latter is a fitting analogy for outer space or celestial body which is outside the jurisdiction of any state.

Article 19 of the Convention on the High Seas provides for remedial action and grants the right to any state on the high seas, or in any other place outside the jurisdiction of that state, to seize a pirate ship or aircraft, or a ship taken by piracy and under the control of pirates, and arrest the persons and seize the property on board. The courts of the state which carried out the seizure may decide upon the penalties to be imposed, and may also determine the action to be taken with regard to the ships, aircraft or property, subject to the rights of third parties acting in good faith.

The significance of the provisions of the Convention with regard to the offence of piracy, when related to similar offences which may be committed in outer space, lies in the universal application of the various limits of the offence itself. For example, the offence of piracy includes acts of violence, detention or any act of depredation. This effectively brings to bear its relevance to instances such as the takeover, detention or illegal deviation of a spacecraft and therefore is quite useful as paradigm legislation for space law.

With regard to principles of tortious liability, space law and shipping law have a common thread of international responsibility of states. Space law, by virtue of the principle that a state of registry retains jurisdiction in its space object, imputes territoriality to a state in relation to its space craft, space station or other space object. Therefore any act committed by one state or individual representing a state which would adversely affect such space object would be comparable with an instance where the act of one state affects another in its territorial waters.

Principles of state responsibility for negligent acts leading to reparation are concomitants of substantive public international law. International responsibility relates both to breaches of treaty provisions to which states are bound and also to other infringements of legal duty. Brownlie makes bold to assert that there is no harm in using the term 'international tort' to describe the breach of a duty which results in a loss to another state.[34] Judge Huber, in the *Spanish Zone of Morocco Claims* case observed: 'Responsibility is the necessary corollary of a right. All rights of an international character involve international responsibility. If the obligation in question is not met, responsibility entails the duty to make reparation.'[35]

In the celebrated *Corfu Channel* case,[36] which involved the liability of Albania for mine laying in her international waters which caused damage to British minesweepers, the Court held:

> These grave omissions involve the international responsibility of Albania. The Court therefore reaches the conclusion that Albania is responsible under international law for the explosions which occurred … and for the damage and loss of human life which resulted from them.[37]

The above principle will incontrovertibly apply equally to space law, for two reasons: both space law and the law related to the sea are grounded in the principles of public international law; and principles of state responsibility are universal and cannot be applied on different bases with regard to species of international law.

The responsibility of states for the negligent acts of their agents in outer space would be based on the concept of objective responsibility: responsibility of states for those acts committed by their officials or their organs and which acts such officials are bound to perform in the course of their duties. The elements of *faute* or fault on the part of the officials is irrelevant. Tortious liability of the state concerned and responsibility therefor would also ensue in instances where the officials or state agencies act beyond their competence. The only necessary element for the imposition of state responsibility is the establishment of the fact that such persons acted with authority derived from the state concerned when the tortious act was performed.

Although the nature of outer space and the high seas, and the uses they are put to, are different, the underlying principles with regard to the conduct of persons in the two geographic areas are similar, if not identical. Treaty provisions with regard to the use of both are certainly comparable, and to this extent space law could alternate principles from the law of the sea when necessary.

As has been already discussed in this chapter, proponents of space law should now address the broader issue of persons other than astronauts being involved in space travel in the future. Preparation for this eventuality should be made not only technologically but also intellectually.

2 ENVIRONMENTAL PROTECTION AND THE USE OF NUCLEAR POWER SOURCES IN OUTER SPACE

Introduction

The COSMOS 954 incident of January 1978 – where a Soviet satellite disintegrated over Northern Canada – brought to bear the relevance of environmental protection as a corollary to the exploration of outer space. The accident scattered debris, most of which was found to be radioactive, over 600 kilometres of Canadian territory. Two subsequent incidents, the first relating to the re-entry of COSMOS 1402 into the Earth's atmosphere in early 1983 and the second relating to COSMOS 1960 in 1988, endorsed the concern of the world community on environmental issues which are related to the exploration of outer space.[38] These incidents also underscored the fact that the primary pollutant in activities related to nuclear power sources in outer space is radioactivity caused by nuclear waste which is released both in outer space and in the environment.

The limited Nuclear Test Ban Treaty,[39] which is the seminal document that provides for environmental protection against radioactivity caused by nuclear waste, provides in its article 1 that states parties to the treaty undertake to prohibit, to prevent and not carry out any nuclear weapon test explosion, or any other nuclear explosion, at any place under its jurisdiction or control or *inter alia* in outer space or in any other environment if such explosion causes radioactive debris to be present outside the territorial limits of the state under whose jurisdiction or control such explosion is conducted.[40] The treaty further provides that no state party may collaborate with or encourage such activity.[41]

The Outer Space Treaty,[42] while expostulating the fundamental principle in its article I that the exploration and use of outer space, including the moon and other celestial bodies, shall be carried out for the benefit and in the interests of all countries, explicitly imposes in article VII international liability and responsibility on each state party to the treaty, for damage caused to another state party or to its populace (whether national or juridical) by the launch or procurement of launch of an object into outer space. In its preceding provisions the treaty imposes international responsibility on states parties for national activities conducted in outer space. The treaty also requires its states parties to be guided by the principle of cooperation and mutual assistance in the conduct of all their activities in outer space.[43] This overall principle is further elucidated in the same provision:

> States Parties to the Treaty shall pursue studies of outer space, including the moon and other celestial bodies, and conduct exploration of them so as to avoid harmful contamination and also adverse changes in the environment of the Earth resulting from the introduction of extra terrestrial matter.[44]

The Moon Agreement[45] of 1979 provides that, in the exploration and use of the moon, states parties shall take measures *inter alia* to avoid harmfully affecting the environment of the Earth through the introduction of extraterrestrial matter or otherwise.[46] The United Nations Conference on the Human Environment, held in Stockholm in June 1972,[47] while recognizing that states have, in accordance with the Charter of the United Nations and the principles of international law, the sovereign right to exploit their own resources pursuant to their own environmental policies,[48] require states to cooperate in the further development of international law regarding liability and compensation for the victims of pollution and other environmental damage caused by activities within the jurisdiction or control of states to areas beyond their jurisdiction.

Application of international environmental law to outer space exploration

Justice Manfred Lachs was of the view:

> if all activities connected with outer space are to be conducted for the benefit of all and to the detriment of none, international co-operation is essential, and if all the possibilities opened up are to be used in a responsible manner, the conduct of States in regard to outer space must be submitted to the rule of law.[49]

Although Judge Lachs' observation was indubitably meant to convey the need for global cooperation in issues of outer space exploration in the broadest possible sense, it is relevant in the present context that this visionary statement could be segmented to apply to corollaries of outer space activities as well, such as the environmental impact of nuclear power sources in outer space. In a determination of this narrow area, the emergence of environmental law as a necessary adjunct to the burgeoning world order of today becomes a compelling issue.

It is indeed inevitable that advances in space technology and cooperation in outer space exploration will raise issues regarding the environmental impact of these developments. At the same time, it is fortunate that an international order governing environmental protection has emerged to offer solutions to the problems that may arise from those activities. The effectiveness of international environmental law as it applies to outer space exploration therefore becomes the pivotal consideration.

The application of environmental law to outer space activities lies in the fundamental postulate that outer space is free for exploration and use by all states without discrimination of any kind and on a basis of equality.[50] This principle lays down the freedom of action for all states on the basis of the prohibition of discrimination; the recognition of equality of all states; and the requirement that the activities be conducted in accordance with international law.[51] The last element – accordance with international law – derives its validity from the 1963 Declaration of Legal Principles Governing the Activities of States in the Exploration and Use of Outer Space wherein states parties declared in unequivocal terms that their governments would respect the principles of the declaration,[52] which essentially established the general principle of international cooperation and adherence to customary international law in outer space exploration. This leaves no room for doubt that international environmental law, like the space treaties discussed above, would be inextricably applicable to space law.

In December 1992, the United Nations General Assembly adopted resolution 47/68,[53] which provides that activities involving the use of nuclear power sources in outer space shall be carried out in accordance with international law, including in principle the charter of the United Nations and the Outer Space Treaty. The treaty also provides that, in order to minimize the quantity of radioactive material in space and the risks involved, the use of nuclear power sources in outer space shall be restricted to those space missions which cannot be operated by non-nuclear sources in a reasonable way. Among the more notable provisions of the treaty are those providing for assistance to states, whereby all states possessing space monitoring and tracking facilities are to communicate to the Secretary General of the United Nations and the states concerned information on space objects with a nuclear power source entering the atmosphere; with international responsibility of states for national activities in outer space involving nuclear power sources and liability and compensation.

The cornerstone of international environmental law is the Rio Declaration,[54] which is a statement of basic principles emanating from the United Nations Conference on Environmental Development held in Rio de Janeiro in June 1992. The Rio Declaration endorses and updates principle 21 of the Stockholm Declaration, which provides a delicate but harmonious balance of recognizing the inalienable rights of all states to exploit their own resources pursuant to their own environmental and developmental policies while at the same time recognizing their responsibility to ensure that activities within their jurisdiction and control do not cause damage to the environment of other states or of areas beyond the limits of national jurisdiction.[55]

The Rio Declaration explicitly places common but differentiated responsibilities on states on the subject of environmental protection by exhorting developed countries to be internationally responsible in their international pursuit of sustainable development in view of the pressures their societies place on the global environment and of the technologies and financial resources they command.[56] The Rio Declaration also calls for the application of the 'polluter pays' principle,[57] and, *inter alia*, obliges states to undertake environmental impact assessment.[58] Nanda observes:

> International environmental law has become probably the most vigorously evolving chapter in international law, in the form of global, regional and bilateral treaties; in the form of rapidly developing customary law; in the form of supernational directives (in the EU); and even more, in the form of various types of soft law.[59]

Therefore, as outer space exploration evolves with its characteristic rapidity, the need for international law to address specific issues becomes compelling. Environmental protection is one such issue, which requires urgent and short-term attention.

It has been said that three of the most important space law issues that the international community will have to deal with relate to manned space flights, future aerospace planes and the protection of the space environment.[60] Of these, space environment is arguably the most contentious, at least if one were to judge from the proliferation of legal material that has emanated from scholars on the subject of contamination of the environment by by-products of space exploration.

The central treaty provision which refers to space environment is article IX of the Outer Space Treaty, which entreats states to avoid harmful contamination of the environment of the Earth and also to ensure that there are no adverse changes in the environment as a result of their activities in outer space. As a 'stand alone' provision, article IX is impotent, in that it fails definitively to set standards or at the least to leave room for a regulatory body to set standards in the field of space environment. For instance, article IX provides that states shall, 'where necessary, adopt measures' for the above purpose. One has to go a bit further than this blanket statement if one is to ensure global cooperation in matters of space environment. Jasentuliyana draws the analogy of the annexes to the Chicago Convention in the field of regulation by ICAO in matters related to civil aviation:

> the technical Annexes to the Chicago Convention are one reason why ICAO has been so successful in international law making. Through the use of these Annexes, the Organization has been able to separate the political and technical facets of international civil aviation. To a large degree, uniformity in all technical and navigational aspects of international civil aviation has been achieved.[61]

Jasentuliyana takes his statement a step further when he recommends that the United Nations develop a treaty with broad and general guidance for this purpose, leaving it to an international technical body to establish standards and recommended practices for states to follow.[62] This is a sound recommendation, not only because the commentator has chosen the closely related field of aviation as an analogy, but also because the annexes to the Chicago Convention have demonstrated their efficacy over the years as instruments of regulation. It must be noted that, within the United Nations law-making system, not only the adoption of a treaty, but also its subsequent development, have been proved to be important. Of course, such a project should be embarked upon after a carefully thought out assessment of the likelihood of success of such a treaty, which will depend on (1) the technical difficulty of the project and resolution of the scientific, technical, economic and other problems that may accompany it; and (2) the acceptability of the treaty to the organizations of states parties and its effectiveness in implementation of its provisions.

Although several specialized agencies of the United Nations system have procedures that modify, without eliminating, the positivist principle that states are normally bound only by international rules to which they have consented,[63] ICAO provides the best example of treaty development. The Chicago Convention authorizes the ICAO Council to adopt international standards and recommended practices (SARPS) as annexes to the Convention. These SARPS have bestowed on the ICAO Council at least a quasi-legislative function and are highly authoritative in practice. They ensure safety and efficiency in air travel and are used widely by states, particularly in the context of Annex 2, which provides for rules of the air.

Therefore, although the analogy of the annexes to the Chicago Convention is not necessarily a panacea to the perceived lacuna in the field of regulation of environmental protection in outer space exploration, it may well be a suitable starting point.

3 LIABILITY OF STATES FOR COLLUSION WITH EXTRATERRESTRIAL INTELLIGENCE IN THE SHARING AND USE OF SPACE TECHNOLOGY

The phenomenon of extraterrestrial intelligence

Although the title of this section is purely conjectural, its contents – in the eventuality of the occurrence suggested therein becoming real – bring to bear the need to reflect on principles of state liability under international law within the framework of existing norms relating to the use of advanced technology for peaceful uses of outer space.

American geneticist Joshua Lederberg introduced to the world the science of exobiology (or astrobiology), a branch of biology which deals with the search for extraterrestrial life, especially intelligent life, outside the solar system. Although remote astronomical observations of a planet or other celestial body provide information about its physical environment, the determination of the presence of life on these bodies is more difficult. Exobiological techniques are designed to detect life forms, artifacts produced by intelligent life, waste products of metabolic reactions, remnants of former life, prebiological molecules that may reflect early evolutionary stages or substances such as carbon or combination of hydrogen and oxygen forming water that are necessary for the sustenance of life as it is experienced on Earth.

In 1948, the US Air Force commenced maintaining a file of reports relating to extraterrestrial phenomena, called 'Project Blue Book'. In July 1952, the US government established a panel of scientists including engineers, meteorologists, physicists and an astronomer to investigate a series of radar detection coincident with visual sightings near the national airport in Washington, DC. The panel was organized by the Central Intelligence Agency, which underscores the thrust of public and government concern and interest at the time.[64]

The concern was based on US military activities and intelligence and the fact that the panel's report was originally classified 'Secret'. Later declassified, the report revealed that 90 per cent of UFO sightings could be readily identified with astronomical and meteorological phenomena (for example, bright planets, meteors, auroras, ion clouds) or with aircraft, birds, balloons, searchlights, hot gases and other phenomena, sometimes complicated by unusual meteorological conditions.

The publicity given to early sightings in the press undoubtedly helped stimulate further sightings not only in the United States but also in Western Europe, the Soviet Union, Australia and elsewhere. A second panel, established in February 1966, reached conclusions similar to those of its predecessor. This left a number of sightings admittedly unexplained, and in the mid-1960s a few scientists and engineers, notably James E. McDonald, a University of Arizona meteorologist, and J. Allen Hynek, a Northwestern University astronomer, concluded that a small percentage of the most reliable UFO reports gave definite indications of the presence of extraterrestrial visitors.

This sensational hypothesis, promoted in newspaper and magazine articles, met with prompt resistance from other scientists. The continuing controversy led in 1968 to the sponsorship by the US Air Force of a study at the University of Colorado under the direction of E.U. Condon, a noted physicist. The Condon Report, 'A Scientific Study of UFOs' was reviewed by a special committee of the National Academy of Sciences and released in early 1969. A total of 37 scientists wrote chapters or parts of chapters for the report, which covered investigations of 59 UFO sightings in detail, analysed public opinion polls and reviewed the capabilities of radar and photography. Condon's own 'Conclusions and Recommendations' firmly rejected ETH – the extraterrestrial hypothesis – and declared that no further investigation was needed.

This left a wide variety of opinions on UFOs. A large fraction of the US public, and a few scientists and engineers, continued to support ETH. A middle group of scientists felt that the possibility of extraterrestrial visitation, however slight, justified continued investigation, and still another group favoured continuing investigation on the grounds that UFO reports are useful in sociopsychological studies. These varying views and attitudes were expressed at a symposium held by the American Association for the Advancement of Science, in December 1969. Several years later, in 1973, a group of US scientists organized the Center for UFO Studies in Northfield, Illinois, to conduct further work.

Scientific aspects

On 24 June 1947, American pilot Kenneth Arnold described some unusual flying craft he had seen over the mountains off the west coast of the United States. In his words, 'they flew like a saucer would if you skipped it across water'.[65] Newspapers applied his phrase to the craft themselves, and the misleading label 'flying saucer' has followed the phenomenon of the unidentified flying object (UFO) ever since.

The word 'UFO' officially means simply something that has not been, or cannot be, accounted for by any of the known laws of physics. But the seemingly rational behaviour reported in many UFO sightings, as well as the accounts of meetings with humanoids, has led to the speculation that UFOs are, in fact, spacecraft bringing creatures from outer space.

If this is so, the spaceships must be able to cover immense distances. People who claim to have had contact with extraterrestrials often say they have spoken with Venusians. But Venus is highly unlikely to be inhabited. Any intelligent life forms must be coming from still further away and, even assuming that lifespans of creatures from other planets may be much longer than our own, it is clear that UFOs must be able to travel very fast indeed if they are not to take hundreds of years to travel between inhabited planets.

Reports of the movement of UFOs are remarkably consistent. Most people describe them as hovering and then taking off at very high speed, often executing manoeuvres that would be impossible in conventional aircraft. Even allowing for exaggeration by excited witnesses, the consistency of the reports suggests the UFOs use a very powerful force to produce dramatic accelerations.

None of the rocket fuels we use at present can produce either the speed or the acceleration observed in the UFOs, because they store only a small amount of energy for a given mass. Right from the beginning, rocket travel has been faced with the problem of enabling the rocket to carry enough fuel for its journey; it must lift the fuel, which can be very heavy if the journey is long, as well as itself and its occupants. The solution has been the multi-stage rocket: the initial acceleration is given by a rocket that is jettisoned when its fuel is used up and a second rocket takes over.

Space flights have always stretched our rocket technology to its limits and, as everyone knows, our rockets and spacecraft do not accelerate very briskly away from the Earth. Although they eventually reach quite high speeds, they are nowhere near fast enough to reach planets outside our solar system within a human lifetime. If we assume UFOs are subject to the same laws of physics as we are, then, to operate on and near the Earth with the rapid accelerations and manoeuvres at high speeds that are often reported, they must be using a different source of energy from conventional chemical fuels. Their fuel must be highly compact, with a high energy yield for a small mass: the obvious source is nuclear fuel.

As long ago as 1958 – just after Yuri Gagarin had become the first man ever to orbit the Earth in space – Freeman Dyson, a theoretical physicist, embarked on a plan for a nuclear-powered spaceship. He had previously worked on the development of the atom bomb and had a comprehensive understanding of nuclear power. He assembled a group of scientists at La Jolla, Southern California, to work with him; he called his scheme 'Project Orion'. Project Orion was a serious attempt to build a spacecraft powered by nuclear explosions, and was intended as an alternative to the multi-stage rockets that Werner von Braun was proposing for space travel. Freeman Dyson's ultimate aim was to build a spacecraft the size of a small city that would take a group of people to a distant comet on the edge of the solar system, where they would settle. This may have been only a pipe-dream, but the design was real enough.

The spacecraft was to be powered by hydrogen bombs. Essentially, his idea was to carry a number of hydrogen bombs aboard the spacecraft; these would be moved, one by one, to a position underneath the craft where they would be exploded. The base of the spacecraft would absorb the shock and the craft would be driven along. Obviously the spacecraft and the bomb system would have to be designed so that the craft was propelled along and not simply blown apart, but – in principle, at least – this was straightforward. However, Dyson was never able to test his ideas: he was prevented by public concern about the pollution of the atmosphere by radioactive fallout.

UFOs are often reported as disappearing rapidly, going off 'like a television set', and reappearing just as quickly. This aspect of the phenomenon has puzzled scientists for a long time and has led to suggestions that UFOs use some kind of 'anti-optic device' to prevent their being seen. There are, however, some simpler explanations that account for the majority of reports. UFOs 'disappearing' in the night could do so by simply switching off their lights; daytime discs could appear to vanish if they turn themselves sideways-on to the observer: it would be very difficult to pick out the thin edge of a disc against the sky. These explanations do not, of course, account for radar-visual sightings that suddenly vanish. But if a UFO disappeared behind a patch of disturbed air, a mirage-like effect could easily screen it both from sight and from radar detectors.

There are, however, cases on file for which none of these explanations seem credible. It seems that the phenomena involved can only be explained as products of a technology much further advanced than our own. By far the majority of UFO reports describe the strange objects as disc- or cigar-shaped and it could be that most UFOs reported as cigar-shaped are in fact discs. Whether or not this is actually the case, the number of reports of saucer-shaped UFOs is overwhelming. There has been a great deal of speculation as to why this should be so – some people have suggested the mystical significance of the circle may have something to do with it – but there is a simple explanation.

On long interstellar voyages, a spacecraft will pass through vast regions of empty space, far from the regions of gravitational attraction of any major objects, where there is no wind resistance, no up or down, no east or west; nothing. The most logical shape for a vessel travelling in these circumstances is circular, for a circle is symmetrical about an infinite number of axes. The fact that most UFOs are disc-shaped rather than spherical can be explained as a design feature that allows spacecraft to operate at high speeds once they have entered the atmosphere of planets: by flying with their edges into the wind, they can cut down the effect of air resistance almost to zero.

Whether or not UFOs existed in the past, there is no doubt that UFO sightings have proliferated in astonishing numbers over the past 30 years. This fact seems to be in some way linked to man's first steps towards exploring space, and this connection is undoubtedly an important clue in trying to explain the UFO. Estimates of the total number of UFO sightings vary so widely as to be meaningless; more helpful figures are provided by the catalogues of reported sightings prepared by individual investigative organizations. In the 1960s, a French team catalogued more than 600 encounter cases in France alone, each vouched for by responsible investigators. In the early 1970s, UFO investigators made lists of all reported landing cases for particular countries: 923 were recorded in the United States, 200 in Spain.

Are UFOs real in the sense that, say, spacecraft are real? The surest proof would be actually to get hold of one, and there are persistent rumours that certain governments, notably that of the United States, have indeed obtained a UFO, which is kept in total secrecy. However, this remains mere conjecture, despite the sworn affidavits of alleged witnesses. Indeed, the whole matter of governmental involvement – or the lack of it – is a further and fascinating aspect of the UFO controversy.

In the absence of a real UFO that we can touch and examine, there is a great deal of evidence of the phenomenon in the form of a mass of photographs and a handful of movies. The majority are undoubtedly fakes. Those with good credentials are so blurred, so distant or so ambiguous that they simply add a further dimension to the problem: why, if UFOs exist, and in an age when many people carry cameras with them most of the time, have we not obtained better photographic evidence?

Perhaps the strongest evidence we have is from the effects caused by UFOs on surrounding objects, particularly machinery. In November 1967, a truck and a car approaching each other on a New Hampshire road in the United States in the early hours of the morning simultaneously suffered engine failure when a large egg-shaped object crossed the road between them. The police, and subsequently the Ministry of Defence, investigated the incident, but no official explanation was ever issued. Such a case may leave investigators puzzled, but it makes one thing certain: if they can cause physical effects, UFOs must be physically real.

If they are physical objects, UFOs must originate from somewhere. When the first UFOs of the current era were seen, back in the 1940s, it was assumed they came from somewhere on Earth. The Americans suspected they were a Russian secret device, perhaps developed using the expertise of German scientists captured at the end of World War II. But as more reports came in it became clear that no nation on Earth could be responsible. Nor was there sufficient evidence to support other ingenious theories: that they came from the Himalayas, long a favoured source of secret wisdom, or Antarctica, where unexplored tracts of land and climatic anomalies provide a shaky foundation for speculation. Instead, ufologists began to look beyond the Earth, encouraged by the fact that our own space explorations programme was just beginning. We were starting to take an active interest in worlds beyond, and it seemed reasonable that other civilizations might have a similar interest in us.

However, although the number of potential sources of life in the universe is virtually infinite, the probability of any civilization being at a stage of development appropriate for space travel is very small. They fact that no solid evidence has been found for the extraterrestrial hypothesis is discouraging. Although it is the best available explanation, it remains no more than speculation.

Close encounters

Established science has always tended to view the UFO phenomenon with scepticism. In his book, *The UFO Experience*,[66] Dr J. Allen Hynek, who was astronomical consultant to Project Blue Book (the US Air Force investigation into UFOs), tells the story of an event at an evening reception held in 1968 in Victoria, British Columbia, at which a number of astronomers were present. During the evening it was announced that strange lights, possibly UFOs, had been spotted outside. Dr Hynek continues: 'The news was met by casual banter and the giggling sound that often accompanies an embarrassing situation.' And, he reports, not a single astronomer went outside to look.

Even Project Blue Book attempted to explain away every reported sighting in terms of conventional science. It soon began to earn itself a bad name because many of its explanations were impossible to believe. In 1966, the US Air Force set up a two-year research project – to investigate, in effect, its own investigations! Dr Hynek, while acting as a consultant to Project Blue Book, developed a system of classification of UFO 'types', which has become standard. He divided UFO reports according to the distance, greater or less than 500 feet (150 metres), at which the UFO was observed, and subdivided each of these two sections into three, giving six categories altogether.

The commonest sightings are of the 'distant' type. *Nocturnal lights* are strange lights seen at a distance in the night sky, often with unusual features such as variations in the intensity of light or colour and sudden, remarkable changes of speed and direction of movement. *Daylight discs* are distant objects seen against the sky during the daytime. The shapes vary considerably: cigars, spheres, eggs, ovals and pinpoints as small as discs are often reported. *Radar-visuals* are distant UFOs recorded simultaneously on radar and visually with good agreement between the two reports. Hynek excluded 'sightings' made solely by radar since false traces can result from a number of natural factors such as ground scatter – the signal is reflected from high ground – temperature inversions and even thick banks of cloud or flocks of birds. Radar-visual sightings are the most important categories of UFO reports as they give independent instrumental evidence of the sighting; unfortunately, they are very rare.

Reports of UFOs seen at close range are the most interesting, and often spectacular; these are the famous 'close encounters'. *Close encounters of the first kind* are simple observations of phenomena where there is no physical interaction between the phenomena and the environment. *Close encounters of the second kind* are similar to the first kind, except that physical effects on both animate and inanimate matter are observed. Vegetation may be scorched or flattened, tree branches broken, animals frightened or car headlights, engines and radios doused. In cases of electrical failure, the equipment usually begins to work normally again once the UFO has disappeared. *Close encounters of the third kind* occur when 'occupants' are reported in or around the UFO. Hynek generally ruled out so-called 'contactee' cases in which the reporter claimed to have had intelligent communication with the 'occupants', arguing that such reports were almost invariably made by pseudo-religious fanatics and never by 'ostensibly sensible, rational and reputable persons'. But even these cases occasionally have to be taken seriously by scientists.

Applicable space law principles

In a purely forensic sense, the fundamental postulate of space law, which devolves upon states the responsibility to explore and use outer space for peaceful purposes, is pivotal to the conjecture of extraterrestrial intelligence. Two United Nations General Assembly resolutions on the subject are now current. Resolution 49/34,[67] which *inter alia* covered international cooperation in the peaceful uses of outer space, links the importance of international cooperation to the development of the rule of law, including the relevant norms of space law and their important role in international cooperation for the exploration and use of outer space for peaceful purposes. The Resolution also expresses *inter alia* the concern of the General Assembly of the United Nations with regard to the possibility of an arms race in outer space and urges the United Nations Committee on the Peaceful Uses of Outer Space (UNCOPUOS) to continue its consideration of the legal aspects related to the application of the principle that the exploration and utilization of outer space should be carried out for the benefit and in the interests of all states, taking into particular account the needs of developing countries.[68] The Committee is also requested to continue to consider, as a matter or priority, ways and means of maintaining outer space for peaceful purposes and to report thereon to the General Assembly.[69]

The operative criterion for the adoption of the above aims, as used by the resolution, lies in the endorsement that they should be achieved through international cooperation in the development of the role of law. The resolution therefore brings to bear the ineluctable and compelling need for the application of existing principles of international law as a means towards this end.

On 5 February 1996, the General Assembly of the United Nations adopted Resolution 56/27,[70] relating to international cooperation in the peaceful uses of outer space. This resolution broadly reaffirmed the principles of Resolution 49/34. Having considered the report of UNCOPUOS on the work of its 38th session, the General Assembly endorsed the Committee's recommendation that the Committee should, through its Scientific and Technical Sub-Committee, *inter alia*, consider the use of nuclear power sources in outer space and questions relating to space transport systems and their implications for future activities in space.[71] Matters relating to life sciences, space medicine and astronomy were some of the areas that were focused on for further consideration in the resolution.[72]

The mandate which UNCOPUOS has received from the United Nations General Assembly includes the task of studying the nature of legal problems which may arise from the exploration of outer space. Other international bodies, such as the International Telecommunications Union (ITU) and the International Atomic Energy Agency (IAEA) – the latter being interested in environmental problems and questions relating to nuclear energy – are also involved in the corollaries to the peaceful use of outer space as they affect the human being.

Peaceful uses of outer space

There is no known principle or pronouncement of law which mentions 'extraterrestrial intelligence'. Therefore, *ex facie*, no existing norm of international law prohibits social intercourse in outer space between humans and extraterrestrial beings (if such were to exist). The only prohibition which will obtain at international law would be if such intercourse leads to the 'non-peaceful' use of outer space by states. It is incontrovertible that the absence of peaceful use of outer space (when states indulge in activities in outer space) would inevitably mean warlike or aggressive use of outer space. Accordingly, such action would perforce form 'use of force' by such states on other states or persons affected by these actions.

Arguably, the oldest forensic regulatory material which would apply to the subject of aggression is contained in the work of the International Law Commission, which became functional in April 1949 and submitted a Draft Code of Offences against the Peace and Security of Mankind in 1951. At the request of the Soviet Union, the Commission, in 1954, submitted to the General Assembly of the United Nations the following definition of the concept of aggression, whereby the Commission recognized that the following acts are offences against the peace and security of mankind:

a any act of aggression, including the employment by the authorities of a state of armed forces against another state for any purpose other than national or collective self-defence or in pursuance of a decision or recommendation of a competent organ of the United Nations;

b any threat by the authorities of a state to resort to an act of aggression against another state.[73]

This seminal definition, with its far-reaching implications, has not been adopted formally by the United Nations General Assembly. However, the definition itself lends itself to offering, in approximate terms, a statement that defines 'non-peaceful' conduct or a 'breach of the peace'.

The 'law' on the use of force that has developed through the United Nations is substantial. As article 1, paragraphs 1 and 2, of the UN Charter suggest, the primary purposes of the United Nations are: '(1) To maintain international peace and security, and to that end: to take effective collective measures for the prevention and removal of threats to the peace, and for the suppression of acts of aggression or other breaches of the peace, and to bring about by peaceful means, and in conformity with the principles of justice and international law, adjustment or settlement of international disputes or situations which might lead to a breach of the peace'; and '(2) To develop friendly relations among nations based on respect for the principle of equal rights and self-determination of peoples, and to take other appropriate measures to strengthen universal peace.'

The United Nations Charter contains numerous provisions which are relevant to the use of force. Several General Assembly resolutions, adopted without dissent or with near unanimity, have restated, amplified and clarified the meaning of these charter provisions. Possibly the most relevant and authoritative is the 1970 Declaration on Principles of International Law Concerning Friendly Relations and Co-operation Among States in Accordance with the Charter of the United Nations (Friendly Relations Declaration).[74] Although some dispute exists in regard to the precise legal status of the Friendly Relations Declaration, it is generally regarded as an authoritative interpretation of broad principles of international law expressed in the charter.[75] Another, and more controversial, example is the General Assembly's 'Definition of Aggression' resolution.[76]

The UN Charter does not directly address the question of intervention by states; rather, under article 2(7) it precludes the organization itself from intervening 'in matters which are essentially within the domestic jurisdiction of any state'. Hence the General Assembly's Declaration on the Inadmissibility of Intervention in the Domestic Affairs of States and the Protection of Their Independence and Sovereignty,[77] adopted in 1965 by a vote of 109 to none, with one abstention,[78] takes on special legal significance. The declaration, *inter alia*, provides:

> no State has the right to intervene, directly or indirectly, for any reason whatever, in the internal or external affairs of any other State. Consequently, armed intervention and all other forms of interference or attempted threats against the personality of the State or against its political, economic and cultural elements are condemned.[79]

The declaration further provides: 'no State shall organize, assist, foment, finance, incite or tolerate subversive, terrorist or armed activities directed towards the violent overthrow of the regime of another State, or interfere in civil strife in another State'.[80]

The Security Council and the General Assembly are the primary organs of the United Nations that have responsibility under the charter to regulate the use of force. Sharp debate has arisen over the precise allocation of authority in this area between the Council and the Assembly, and a focal point of this debate has been the Assembly's 'Uniting for Peace' resolution,[81] whereby the Assembly claims the authority to recommend collective measures in situations where the Council is unable to deal with a breach of the peace or act of aggression in the face of a veto. A useful source which reflects the charter's allocation of powers between the Assembly and the Council is the International Court of Justice's advisory opinion in the *Certain Expenses* case,[82] which, while not directly addressing the legality of the Uniting for Peace resolution, contains dicta relevant to this issue and generally constitutes an authoritative discussion of the charter's allocation of powers between the Council and the Assembly. Similarly, the Court's advisory opinion in the *Namibia* case[83] extensively discusses the scope of decision-making authority in both organs. Even when Council and Assembly decisions are not regarded as binding, they may be considered as interpretations of the charter entitled to some weight.

The 'case law' of the United Nations on the use of force consists primarily of Security Council resolutions. In such cases as Korea, Rhodesia, South Africa and Iraq, among others, Security Council resolutions have developed the law of the charter.

Certain interpretations or legal opinions by the Secretary-General on the use of force also may carry some weight. As the chief administrative officer of the United Nations,[84] the secretary-general is perforce obliged to carry out functions assigned him by the principal organs of the organization, including the General Assembly and the Security Council.[85] He has no independent law-making authority. His responsibility is rather to implement resolutions of the deliberate organs pursuant to their terms, which, however, may at times be cast in the most general language. In such cases the secretary-general must interpret the resolution himself. Secretary-General Dag Hammarskjold, for example, in implementing Security Council resolutions that authorized him to provide the government of the Congo with military assistance, created considerable controversy with his interpretations of the authority conferred upon him by these resolutions. In defending these interpretations Hammarskjold later wrote:

> Is he [the secretary-general] entitled to refuse to carry out the decision properly reached by the organs on the ground that the specific implementation would be opposed to positions some Member States might wish to take as indicated, perhaps, by an earlier minority vote? Of course, the political organs may always entrust him to discontinue the

> implementation of a resolution, but when they do not instruct him and the resolution remains in effect, is the Secretary-General legally and morally free to take no action, particularly in a matter considered to affect international peace and security? Should he, for example, have abandoned the operation in the Congo because almost any decision he made as to the composition of the force or its role would have been contrary to the attitudes of some Members as reflected in debates and maybe even in votes, although not in decisions?
>
> The answers seem clear enough in law; the responsibilities of the Secretary-General under the Charter cannot be laid aside merely because the execution of decisions by him is likely to be politically controversial. The Secretary-General remains under the obligation to carry out the policies as adopted by the organs. The essential requirement is that he does this on the basis of his exclusively international responsibility and not in the interest of any particular State or group of States.[86]

Several decisions and advisory opinions of the International Court of Justice bring to bear their relevance to the use of force. Although the doctrine of *stare decisis* does not apply to ICJ decisions, and such decisions do not create law in the common law sense, they nonetheless constitute an authoritative statement of the law and are a crucially important part of the international legal process.

A significant factor in the development of United Nations law on the use of force is the practice of states within and outside the organization. This state practice consists of the conclusion of treaties – the North Atlantic Treaty Organization (NATO) treaty and several non-aggression pacts, for example – and claims and counterclaims in diplomatic intercourse regarding the content of applicable norms. Some contend that votes in United Nations organs constitute state practice, although this proposition is controversial. At a minimum these votes may constitute evidence of *opinion juris*; that is, that states are engaging in the practice under a sense of legal obligation.

Articles 2(4) and 51

The visionaries who drafted the UN Charter undoubtedly sought to obviate the use of the word 'war' in the charter. However, because the terms 'aggression' and 'war' (emphasized in the Covenant of the League of Nations) had caused problems of interpretation for the League in practice, it is apparent that the drafters of the United Nations Charter decided on a different approach. Article 2, paragraph 4 of the charter provides that 'All Members shall refrain in their international relations from the threat or use of force against the territorial integrity or political independence of any state, or in any other manner inconsistent with the Purposes of the United Nations.'

This notwithstanding, the overall approach was not uniformly followed elsewhere in the charter, and this has raised confusion as to the proper interpretation and application of article 2(4). For example, article 1 proclaims the primary purpose to be the maintenance of international peace and security by taking effective collective measures to prevent or remove 'threats to the peace' and to suppress 'acts of aggression or other breaches of the peace'. It does not use the words 'force' or 'threat of force'. The application of the qualifying words 'in conformity with the principles of justice and international law' to the organization's first purpose, moreover, has led some to claim that, as long as law and justice are served, recourse to force may be justified. Similarly, the principle of self-determination in article 1(2) has been cited to support the contention that force can be used on behalf of 'wars of national liberation'. Also, as discussed later, the Security Council is directed

> to determine the existence of any threat to the peace, breach of the peace, or act of aggression and to make recommendations or decide on measures to restore international peace and security. This means that there is 'no necessary identity between what is legally prohibited by Article 2(4) and what the Council seeks to control in the discharge of its responsibilities'.[87]

Those who favour limited constraints on the right of states to use armed force have relied on textual analysis to interpret article 2(4) as authorizing a number of exceptions to that article's prohibition against the 'threat or use of force'. Oscar Schachter observes:

> A more basic question of interpretation [than that concerning the meaning of 'force' and 'threat of force'] is presented by the peculiar structure of the article. It is generally assumed that the prohibition was intended to preclude all use of force except that allowed as self-defense or authorized by the Security Council under chapter VII of the Charter. Yet the article was not drafted that way. The last twenty-three words contain qualifications. The article requires states to refrain from force or threat of force only when that is 'against the territorial integrity or political independence of any state' or 'inconsistent with the purposes of the United Nations'. If these words are not redundant, they must qualify the all-inclusive prohibition against force. Just how far they do qualify the prohibition is difficult to determine from a textual analysis alone.[88]

Some have claimed that these words greatly qualify the prohibition against force. The qualifying language, for example, would allow the use of force solely to vindicate or secure a legal right, that is, an exercise in self-help. As Schachter has observed, this argument has enjoyed little governmental or scholarly support.

Similar textual arguments have been made to support the use of force by states to take territory they consider rightfully theirs (for example, Argentina and the Malvinas/ Falkland Islands, Iraq and Kuwait), or a right of 'humanitarian intervention', and the right to self-determination (including, in its most recent manifestation, a claim of right to overthrow a repressive or tyrannical government, as well as to achieve freedom from foreign domination). Schachter examined each of these arguments in detail in recent writings[89] and has concluded:

> Many governments attach importance to the principle that any forcible incursion into the territory of another state is a derogation of that state's territorial sovereignty and political independence, irrespective of the motive for such intervention or its long-term consequences. Accordingly, they tend to hold to the sweeping article 2(4) prohibition against the use or threat of force, except where self-defense or Security Council enforcement action is involved.[90]

In addition to these textual arguments, commentators have argued that recent developments in international relations have significantly altered the conditions on which the restrictive rules were based.[91] The developments most often cited are widespread violations of article 2(4)[92] and the failure of the United Nations system of collective security.[93] Widespread violations of article 2(4), some contend, constitute state practice that has superseded the charter provision and its customary law analogue. This argument has several flaws. First, there are relatively few blatant violations of article 2(4). Moreover, almost every clearly illegal use of armed force has been condemned by large numbers of states and by the political organs of the United Nations. Most important, this argument has not been accepted by states. On the contrary, many states, including the United States, have taken the legal position that article 2(4) is a peremptory norm *(jus cogens).* Also the argument was expressly rejected by the International Court of Justice in *Nicaragua* v. *United States.*[94] There, the Court stated:

> It is not to be expected that in the practice of States the application of the rules in question should have been perfect, in the sense that States should have refrained, with complete consistency, from the use of force or from intervention in each other's internal affairs. The Court does not consider that, for a rule to be established as customary, the corresponding practice must be in absolutely rigorous conformity with the rule. In order to deduce the existence of customary rules, the Court deems it sufficient that the conduct of States should, in general, be consistent with such rules, and that instances of State conduct inconsistent with a given rule should generally have been treated as breaches of that rule, not as indications of the recognition of a new rule. If a State acts in a way prima facie incompatible with a recognition of a new rule, but defends its conduct by appealing to exceptions or justifications contained within the rule itself, then whether or not the State's conduct is in fact justifiable on that basis, the significance of that attitude is to confirm rather than to weaken the rule.[95]

As to the failure of the United Nations collective security system, the legislative history of article 2(4) lends no support to the thesis that the effective functioning of a system of collective security is regarded as a condition of the continuing validity of the article's severe constraints on the use of force.[96] Moreover, recent developments may have given new life to the charter's concept of collective security.

A variant of this changed circumstances argument relies on the concept of reciprocity: widespread violations of law by some states should release others from the obligation to comply, an argument by analogy to the right of one treaty party to suspend the treaty between it and a violator for a violation especially affecting that party.[97] Several problems are inherent in this argument. First, as has been discussed, article 2(4), in addition to being a treaty provision, is widely regarded as an archetypal peremptory norm from which no derogation is permitted. Second, and significantly, the reciprocity thesis finds no support in state practice: no state has cited another state's violation of article 2(4) as a basis to suspend that provision's obligations in relations between it and the violator. Third, the charter permits a variety of responses to a breach of article 2(4): the right to self-defence in the event of an armed attack; recourse to the Security Council or the General Assembly; and, if a jurisdictional basis is available under its statute, recourse to the International Court of Justice.[98]

The justification for recourse to armed force most often cited by states is, of course, the right to self-defence. Article 51 provides:

> Nothing in the present Charter shall impair the inherent right of individual or collective self-defense if an armed attack occurs against a Member of the United Nations, until the Security Council has taken measures necessary to maintain international peace and security. Measures taken by Members in the exercise of this right of self-defence shall be immediately reported to the Security Council and shall not in any way affect the authority and responsibility of the Security Council under the present chapter to take at any time such action as it deems necessary in order to maintain or restore international peace and security.

4 TRADE SECRETS IN THE OUTER SPACE EXPLORATION INDUSTRY

Introduction

The outer space exploration industry is heavily permeated by information technology. Foremost among the areas which use computer software is the spacecraft manufacturing industry and marketing divisions of aerospace equipment producers. There is no doubt that, among the software used in space, some may be considered by the owners of such information as trade secrets. This being the case, owners of information technology cannot avoid their employees, particularly those who are employed in the technological and scientific aspects of such information, acquiring intimate knowledge and know-how of the technology involved in such instances. It is only possible, therefore, that such information may be leaked in certain circumstances by the employers concerned or any other person who may acquire knowledge of the technology through partnerships and other collaborative relationships with the owner of the technology. Employees, in particular, may become dangerous competitors of their employer once their employment ceases, thus becoming a potential threat to the latter in his endeavour to safeguard his information.

In the landmark 1987 case of *Ticketnet Corp* v. *Air Canada*,[99] which established the principle of sanctity of information in software, the Ontario High Court found that, if parties concerned envisioned a contractual relationship *in futuro* between them, their conduct should necessarily reflect a mutual duty of confidence in that one party must not reveal information technology gathered from the other party in the process of negotiations. In the *Air Canada* case, the plaintiff *Ticketnet Corp* was the originator of a concept in developing a software product which created a system of making reservations for theatrical and other entertainment. The defendant, Air Canada, when approached by the plaintiff, expressed its intent to be associated with the projects. In the lengthy process of negotiations, much information relating to the information technology of the project was exchanged between the parties. Both parties had made known to each other their intent to be in a contractual relationship with each other, whereby Ticketnet would retain ownership of the software while granting certain rights to Air Canada. Although the parties had never reached *consensus ad idem* and there was no binding contract between them, they had reached an understanding of collaboration involving information technology sharing. While negotiations were in progress, Ticketnet had disclosed information relating to the intended project to American Airlines, which can be regarded as a competitor and business rival of Air Canada. Air Canada pleaded in the Ontario High Court for an interlocutory injunction which would restrain Ticketnet from releasing information relating to the Air Canada–Ticketnet project to third parties. White J granted the injunction, on the basis that Air Canada could reasonably have expected that a contract would come into being and negotiations were in progress. His honour therefore concluded that Ticketnet was under a duty at law not to divulge information relating to an ongoing contractual process until and unless that process came to an incontrovertible end.[100]

This section will examine the general principles of common law which apply to the exchange of trade secrets in the outer space exploration industry, with particular emphasis on trade secrets related to information technology.

Legal principles

The incidence of trade secrets being exchanged in the business world has reached such substantial proportions as to make it an inarticulate premise that competition from former employees is presumptive evidence of dishonesty. There is, of course, a thin line between the genuine skill acquired by a technical person through years of experience which he takes with him to a new employer and a specific detailed revelation by him of a subjective piece of information technology used by specified parties exclusively, such as in the Air Canada–Ticknet relationship. In general terms, a spacecraft manufacturer or airline marketing division cannot allege that a former employee has misused information gathered during his work with them if he legitimately uses the knowledge and skills gained in a general way for the execution of his work with his new employer. As was stated by Hoffman J in the British case of *Lock International Plc* v. *Beswick*,[101] courts are at a disadvantage when trying to determine a difference between a genuine use of acquired skill and the release of trade secrets by a technical expert and it may well turn out that what may appear to be information specific to one business enterprise is really a general practice used by many in the relevant field.[102]

However, if, as in the case of *Telex corp* v. *IBM Corp*,[103] there is a manifest and overt attempt by an employer to extract detailed confidential and trade information from its employees who had brought such information from their work at a former employer, the courts would find it easy to distinguish such an instance as a conscious and knowing exchange of trade secrets.

Decided instances of common law are numerous,[104] where employees have terminated their employment with one employer in order to gain more lucrative employment elsewhere by using as a tool the intimate knowledge of their employers' information technology secrets in order to convince their new employer of their worth.

A salutary principle obtaining at common law with regard to the safeguard of trade secrets is the fiduciary relationship principle which *in limine* precludes a party in contractual relationship with another to form a contractual relationship with a business competitor of the latter, particularly if certain information of a confidential nature has been exchanged between the parties. It need not necessarily be that the confidential information may be used in the contract. For instance, if A enters into contract with spacecraft manufacturer B for the provision of computer software to the latter, and in the process B reveals confidential information including B's system requirements to A, A cannot enter into a contract with spacecraft manufacturer C for the reason that A is already privy to confidential information belonging to B which may be of use to C. The relationship between A and B has been judicially identified as a fiduciary one.[105] The 1988 British House of Lords' decision in *A.G.* v. *Guardian Newspapers Ltd.*[106] has extended this principle to provide relief even where no fiduciary relationship exists between parties who enter into an arm's-length contract with each other, if one party believes that the other has been provided with what the former considers to be confidential information.

Courts have been mindful of the extremity of legal principles which protect or safeguard trade secrets at common law and which may sometimes genuinely restrain open competition and business opportunity. To this end, covenants in restraint of trade are considered *prima facie* illegal and therefore unenforceable and this principle can be rebutted only when a covenant is drawn up reasonably and is calculated to protect the intellectual property of an employer. Although, in *Herbert Morris Ltd.* v. *Saxelby*,[107] the House of Lords established the non-competition rule as above, which has since been embellished to the extent that the rule cannot be construed as one restraining an employee from making genuine use of his knowledge, experience and skill or one being injurious to the public.[108]

On the reverse side of the coin lies a situation where an employee who developed an information software package for his former employer while he served for him as an independent contractor may find his software package being used by the former employer after his departure. The fact that the person who developed the software package did so as an independent contractor imputes a copyright to him which the former employer cannot use unless otherwise agreed to between the parties. In the modern commercial context, where 'outsourcing' is gaining ground as a business practice, it would not be uncommon to find spacecraft manufacturers, airlines and travel agents contracting services of computer experts to develop software packages for their business. In such a situation the expert would function as an independent contractor and consequently might have more independence in the use of information technology developed by him during a previous contractual relationship.

In the 1991 United States decision of *MacLean Associates* v. *Wm. M. Mercer-Meidlinger-Hansen Inc.*,[109] the Court of Appeals held that, if work involved the development of information technology produced by a worker outside the scope of employment, such work would not belong to the employer. However, any work done within the employee's scope of employment would be 'work for hire' and come under the ownership of the employer. The courts viewed with favour the earlier Supreme Court decision in *Community for Creative non-Violence* v. *Reid*[110] which held that the Copyright Act of 1976 provides that copyright ownership vests initially with the author of a work concerned – the author being the person who creates the work and therefore owns it. The court in the *Reid* case found that the Copyright Act made exception in instances of hire or employment where the employer or person for whom the work is prepared becomes the author *ipso facto* and is considered the owner of the work. The Court of Appeals in the *MacLean* case attenuated the basic principle of 'work for hire' as enunciated in the *Reid* case and added that factors such as the skill required in carrying out the work, the tools used, the location of the work, and the duration of the relationship between the parties *inter alia* would be persuasive and determinative of authorship of the work concerned.

In the regulatory field, article 6 of the World Intellectual Property Organization (WIPO) Copyright Treaty, adopted by the Diplomatic Conference on 20 December 1996, grants authors of literary and artistic works the exclusive right of authorizing or making available to the public the original copies of their works and further provides that such unfettered right does not derogate the right of parties to determine contractual terms that would affect such author's rights in the case of a valid contract at law. The IPO Copyright Treaty, which is a special agreement between parties to the Berne Convention of 1971,[111] protects computer programs in article 4 by providing that computer programs are protected within the meaning of article 2 of the Berne Convention, which establishes copyright of authors of literary works and artistic material.

Copyright and trade secrets in outer space

The first instance of a trade secret dispute related to flying arose with the first-ever flight by the Wright Brothers in Kitty Hawk, North Carolina. The brothers discovered that the problem of lateral stability which was so important to flight could be solved by following the flight of buzzards. Watching the gliding birds, the Wright Brothers mimicked the wing twisting of the birds by constructing a mechanism that warped the horizontal plane of an aeroplane's wings at either side in opposite directions. After patenting this mechanism as applying to any system that varied the lateral margins in opposite directions, the brothers applied it to their inaugural flight in 1903.

Ironically, at the same time as the Wright Brothers were perfecting their mechanism, a young building apprentice by the name of Curtiss was working as a member of Alexander Graham Bell's team of experts conducting flying experiments. Curtiss developed 'wing flaps' in the nature of ailerons by using the Wright Brothers' 'wing twist' method and applied for a patent that recognized the wing flap mechanism. By 1915, the wing flap method had obviated the Wrights' wing twist method and all planes were using it. The Wright Brothers sued Curtiss for infringement of patent in 1909, on the grounds that their method also applied to wing flaps. They won the case.[112]

The *Wrights* v. *Curtiss* dispute was the genesis in the United States of the 'Cross Licencing' Agreement, where manufacturers of spacecraft formed an association in 1917 which entitled each member to grant all its spacecraft patents to all other members. However, the United States government in 1972 claimed that the 'Cross Licencing Agreement' hampered competition in research and development and succeeded in dismantling the Agreement in 1975 by common decree.

The *Wrights–Curtiss* case was preceded in 1879 by the seminal case of *Baker* v. *Selden*,[113] where the United States Supreme Court grappled with the question as to whether copyright protects an idea or concept. The answer was in the negative, and the Supreme Court concluded that copyright applied to the expression of an idea rather than the idea itself. The *Baker* decision, which concerned the ruled lines and headings of a ledger used by Selden which were allegedly used in the same form by Baker, forms a sound analogy to trade secrets in outer space, in the context of the principle that blank account books do not form the subject matter of copyright protection.[114] The blank account book in the *Baker* decision could well be a user interface for spacecraft design or format for an airline computer reservation system.

Trade secrets in the field of outer space activities could well be regarded by courts of common law jurisdiction as those that can be used with flexibility and changed, unlike musical recordings and radio programmes, which have to be copied exactly as the original arrangement.[115] For example, a computer program's expression, which is accompanied by screen displays in the instance of computer reservations systems, could come under the protection of copyright since it can be duplicated by several different computing methods which may slightly alter the user interface.

Although the early decision in the *Baker* case held that blank layouts, if not accompanied by expression, cannot claim protection under copyright law, this principle seems to be questionable in the light of the later decisions. The 1986 decision of *Broderbund Software Inc.* v. *Unison World Inc.*[116] held that display screens, even though they do not convey specific identifiable and unique expressions, are protectable under copyright laws. The court established that the structure, sequence and organization of a display screen is *per se* copyrightable, together with the text and artwork of their displays. However, the later decision handed down in 1987 in the case of *Digital Communications Assocs* v. *Softclone Distributor Corporation*[117] held that copyright does not extend to screen displays, disputing the practice at that time that screen displays were copyrightable. In the context of airline computer reservation systems, the *Softclone* decision would impose the need to bring under copyright the design and structural organization of a computer display screen of a particular CRS system.

Fortunately, the confusion caused by the polarization between the *Broderbund* decision and the *Softclone* decision seems to have been settled rationally by the United States Supreme Court decision, in 1993, in *Apple Computer* v. *Microsoft and Hewlett-Packard*,[118] where the court held that, to establish a *prima facie* case of copyright infringement, the plaintiff must prove that the works at issue are substantially similar, if not identical, in both ideas and expression.[119] This broad principle would apply equally to spacecraft manufacturing designs as well as to airline computer reservation systems and any other software designed for the space industry.

Under English law, although trade secrets are recognized as being vital to the sustenance of a business, stealing trade secrets does not mean that the person who commits the offence can be prosecuted for the offence of theft. The Data Protection Act of 1984, in section 5(2) provides, *inter alia*, that a person who has access to a data entry in a computer shall not obtain the data from any source not described in the data entry and use the data for any purpose other than the one specified in the entry. He shall also not transfer the data directly or indirectly to a source other than one described in the entry.

In the 1996 case of *R.* v. *Brown*,[120] the defendant, a onetime police officer having access to data stored in the police national register on persons, divulged information thereof to his friend, a debt collector, for the latter's professional benefit. The purpose for which the defendant was given access to the data was for policing, and it was found by a jury that the defendant was guilty on two counts under section 5(2) of the Data Protection Act of 1984, and fined £500 on each count. On appeal, the Court of Appeal quashed the defendant's conviction on both counts, on the grounds that the word 'use' in section 5(2) meant that the offender has to do something to the data once he accesses it, in order for it to be construed that he 'used' the data. In the defendant's case, the Court of Appeal contended that the defendant had done nothing to the data once he had accessed it, other than to give the information contained in the data to his friend.

In the House of Lords, which heard the appeal of the prosecution against the Court of Appeal's finding, Lord Goff of Chieveley disagreed with the construction placed on the word 'use' by the Court of Appeal, stating:

> I approach the matter as follows. I accept that, since the word 'use' is not defined in the Act, it must be given its natural and ordinary meaning. Synonyms of the word 'use' are to 'make use of' or to 'employ for a purpose'.[121]

His Lordship applied the above interpretation in relation to 'data' accessed through a computer, conceding that data are actually information recorded in a computer-readable form which can be made use of by the mere act of reading them and relaying their contents to a third party who is not supposed to read them.

Lord Griffiths, in concurring with Lord Goff of Chieveley, observed that, once information is made public through a computer system, the only protection that the data reflecting that information have is through legislation such as the Data Protection Act, and that the purpose of the offence created by section 5(2) was essentially to protect the value and integrity of the information.[122]

If the *Brown* decision were to be applied to the general common law principles obtaining in the area of trade secrets, one could conclude incontrovertibly that the mere 'use' of a trade secret, or, in other words, a mere disclosure of data information displayed on a computer screen by one to another, would constitute the exchange of that trade secret.

In the space industry, the most critical business tools at the present time are information and technology. These tools become more important in the context of the acute competition seen both in the spacecraft manufacturing industry and in the air transport industry. Protection of trade secrets, whether they are client lists or manufacturing designs, becomes of critical importance to the space industry.

In order to establish that given material is a trade secret, the owner must have shown that he took the necessary precautions of keeping such material away from his competitors. Some reasonable measures that have been taken by spacecraft manufacturers and the outer space exploration industry are the installation of alarm systems, card access readers, surveillance cameras and electrified fences. 'Firewalls' on computers such as access codes have also proved to be significant deterrents.

Courts may look at numerous factors to determine whether or not a given piece of information could be regarded as a trade secret. For example, if the information was already known outside the owner's business, he cannot reasonably expect a court of common law jurisdiction to consider his information a trade secret. The courts would also obviously examine the protective measures used by the owner to keep his information from being released to the world. Another compelling factor would be the actual value of the information to the competitor.

Curiously, it is generally recognized at law that a trade secret should not be an absolute secret which is kept hidden by the owner. If such were the case, it could not be used or exploited to its full potential. To be useful, any information has to be shared with some who could contribute to its proper use. Therefore a trade secret can be released with controlled access. Controlled access of trade information can best be illustrated by the subject of the use of the airline product and its distribution over the Internet.[123] While airline reservation systems and related material should not be readily available to the world on the Web, they should nonetheless be made available to interested parties through an access code.

One must also be mindful of the proliferation of economic intelligence gathering going on in the commercial world today. Economic intelligence gathering, as against industrial espionage or the blatant theft of trade secrets, is the lawful practice of seeking, researching and collecting useful information without violating existing laws. It is based on the recovery of legally available data. This practice paves the way for the information gatherer to gain commercial power and therefore all reasonably effective measures have to be taken by the owner of information if he is to protect information which he considers trade secrets. The space industry is no exception.

5 TRADEMARKS IN THE OUTER SPACE INDUSTRY

Introduction

Branding is a major management tool in modern commercial marketing. Needless to say, the outer space exploration industry relies heavily upon its trademarks. Furthermore, as in every other competitive business, the outer space exploration industry has its own catchphrases for advertising its product, which have been the cornerstone of their business development. Since all trademarks used by the outer space exploration industry are distinctive, they have an inherent legal right to consider them exclusive and to bring an action in a common law court if any person were to copy their trademark or to introduce similarity with intent to confuse the consumer into believing a link to exist between the original trademark holder and the person who borrows the idea.

The extent to which common law courts would enforce trademark rights is clearly demonstrated in the 1992 decision of *Two Pesos, Inc.* v. *Taco Cabana Inc.*,[124] where the United States Court of Appeals for the Fifth Circuit held that a trade dress which is inherently distinctive and is capable of identifying products or services comes from a specific source. Although this case involved an operator of a Mexican restaurant who sued an operator of a similar chain of restaurants for introducing a dress for the staff which was similar to the former's staff dress, a distinct analogy can be drawn between the *Two Pesos* case and one that would involve an airline and another business enterprise faced with the same problem.

This section will examine the common law principles applicable to a spacecraft manufacturer's protection of its trademarks in the context of the international nature of business operations of the outer space exploration industry.

Trademarks

A trademark is defined in the United States as 'Any word, name, symbol or device or any combination thereof, adopted and used by a manufacturer or merchant to identify its goods and distinguish them from those manufactured or sold by others.'[125] A trademark serves the initial purpose of identifying the source or origin of goods or services, whether or not that source is not familiar to the potential customer. It also symbolizes goodwill by identifying a particular characteristic to potential customers, thereby accomplishing the most important task of commercial enterprise – offering a warranty of quality.

In general terms, a trademark by its very nature goes to the root of the philosophy behind intellectual property, which is that intellectual property, of which trademarks is a species, is the product of human thinking and therefore cannot be restricted to parochial visual parameters. For example, to be illegally used by one, a trademark need not necessarily be an identical reproduction. All that a trademark needs to have is what is known as 'secondary meaning' or any characteristic which is unique. In this sense even a particular blend of colour, such as gold and green, would entitle the original user to protection under trademark law. In the 1995 decision of *Qualitex Co.* v. *Jacobson Products Co. Ltd*,[126] the United States Court of Appeals for the Ninth Circuit held that a mere colour combination, if it reflects secondary meaning, would be protected under trademark law in the United States. In the *Qualitex* case, the petitioner Qualitex Company had for years coloured the dry cleaning press pads it manufactures with a special shade of green gold. After respondent Jacobson Products (a Qualitex rival) began to use a similar shade on its own press pads, Qualitex registered its colour as a trademark and added a trademark infringement count to the suit it had previously filed, challenging Jacobson's use of the green gold colour. Qualitex won in the District Court, but the Ninth Circuit set aside the judgment on the infringement claim because, in its view, the Langham Trademark Act of 1946 which applied to this case did not permit registration of colour alone as a trademark.

On further appeal, the United States Supreme Court held that colour alone can meet the basic legal requirements for use as a trademark as it is demonstrated both by the language of the Act, which describes the universe of things that can qualify as a trademark in the broadest of terms, and by the underlying principles of trademark law, including the requirements that the mark 'identify and distinguish [the seller's] goods … from those manufactured or sold by others and to indicate [their] source', and that it not be functional.[127] The Supreme Court further held that the District Court's findings (accepted by the Ninth Circuit and here undisputed) showed Qualitex's green gold colour had met these requirements. The court further held that the colour acted as a symbol, as customers would identify the colour with Qualitex. Therefore it was the court's view that the colour had developed secondary meaning.

A person using a trademark which is not registered is legally entitled under common law to stop another from using a confusing trademark with intent to pass off his goods or services as those of the user of the original trademark. Such an act would come within the purview of the tort of passing-off,[128] which in essence prevents unfair competition by which one sells one's goods or services as being those of another supplier. The plaintiff, or person who alleges the tort, has to show that the defendant, or person who faces the civil suit, created actual confusion with the use of his trademark. The plaintiff has also to prove that he had built sufficient reputation in the market place and that a regular customer would have been sufficiently confused by the defendant's act to believe that the defendant's product was actually that of the plaintiff.

The above principle could not, however, derogate the fact that a long-term non-user of a registered trademark would be in jeopardy of losing its link with the person who registered such trademark. In the case of *Perfumes Nautee, Ltd.* v. *American Int'l Industries*,[129] decided in 1992, the Trademark Trial and Appeal Board held that the user of a trademark 'Naughty' for a perfume had lost his rights to the trademark owing to his non-user for two years, causing abandonment of the trademark. A subsequent purchase of the trademark in question by another trader was held to be valid and effectual at law.

In certain instances, criminal liability is imposed upon a person who may deface or alter a trademark. This has now become a common offence with the advent of the computer. For example, a person who defaces a trademark placed on the Internet by an airline would be found criminally liable, as in the 1985 Canadian case of *R.* v. *Locquet*,[130] where the accused was convicted under sections 406 to 412 of the Canadian Criminal Code for falsifying a trademark on a computer program. In view of the importance of this case, some trademark issues addressed below will have specific reference to Canadian law.

The outer space exploration industry would find it relevant that the most fundamental principle in trademark law is that mere creation of a trademark does not create a right towards it. The famous *Exxon Case*[131] of 1981 established the seminal principle that only use, or its surrogates, that is public recognition that a trademark relates to a person, or an intention by that person to use such trademark, creates a valid legal right. The *Exxon Case* also held that it is not the creator of the trademark who obtains the right but the person who registers the trademark as its user.

Once a trademark is registered and it is clear to the world that the person who registers it is already using it or intends to use it, the most significant factor which would apply towards the protection of the trademark is its use by another, or, as is seen more often in commercial practice, the act of passing-off, which was referred to earlier. The legal entitlement to a trademark would enable a person, in such an instance, to challenge the practice by another, on proof of the following:

1 a reputation or goodwill accruing to the holder of the trademark through a business name, work or other trading symbol;
2 a misrepresentation by the person who is passing off his goods or services as the trademark holder, calculated to confuse the customers as to the true identity

of his product and thereby linking his product with that represented by the genuine trademark;

3 the cause of actual or likely damage to the trademark holder; and
4 public policy which would support a remedy against the act of passing-off.

In addition to the above, the following characteristics of registration and passing-off enable one to compare the two areas.

a Passing-off usually requires a symbol both to be used and to have gained a market reputation before protection can be claimed. By contrast, an application to register a mark can be filed well before use. Use must still be proved before registration, but no market reputation need normally be shown to derive from the use.
b Passing-off will protect a symbol only in the locality of its reputation. By contrast, a registration is usually Canada-wide. It can also be used as the basis for corresponding applications for similar protection in most other countries in the world.
c Passing-off requires proof that a defendant misrepresented its products, service, or business as, or connected with, the plaintiff's. It also requires proof of consequential injury to the claimant's relations with those who do business with it (that is, its 'goodwill'). A registration, by contrast, may protect the mark for the whole range of goods or services for which it is registered, without proof of damage. The registrant can also stop the use of different, but confusingly similar, marks for different businesses, even if the defendant prominently disclaims any connection between the two businesses.
d Passing-off requires the plaintiff to prove the existence and extent of its reputation each time an action is brought. By contrast, a registration is, until expunged, presumed valid for Canada for all the wares and services for which it is registered. Protection continues, though the mark is little used or known.
e Passing-off does not prevent a mark's image from being diluted or tarnished. A misrepresentation of trade source must first still be shown, although this concept is sometimes stretched to breaking point. By contrast, a registration (controversially) directly protects a mark from any depreciation of its goodwill, even without any misrepresentation.

The tort of passing-off may be maintainable even if a trademark holder's licence to hold such trademark is inoperable or has expired.

International perspectives

Inasmuch as domestic jurisdiction is significant for a discussion on the subject of trademarks, so is international adjudication, if an overall perspective on the legal issues dealing with trademarks is to be obtained. Furthermore, the issue of internationality in trademark cases concerning spacecraft would be particularly relevant in instances where substantive ownership and effective control of such spacecraft would vest in a state.[132]

The issue of dispute resolution in a commercial activity is addressed as a primary concern in the drafting of legal instruments relating to that activity. Transactions involving Trade-related Intellectual Property Rights (TRIPS) form a much-evolved commercial process which stands today as one of the most prolific financial activities of the commercial world. It comes within the purview of the General Agreement on Tariffs and Trade (GATT) and it therefore owes its genesis to the Marrakesh Declaration of 15 April 1994, which heralded the conclusion of the Uruguay Round of Multilateral Trade Negotiations and established the World Trade Organization (WTO).[133] Therefore, although TRIPS has its own dispute settlement provisions under its own agreement under the WTO umbrella, the TRIPS dispute settlement mechanism may well end up within the WTO dispute settlement arena and, therefore, it would be useful to examine the overall WTO dispute resolution principles in this regard.

The WTO dispute settlement principles

The Marrakesh Agreement (hereafter the Agreement) ushered in a new era of global economic cooperation, reflecting the widespread desire to operate in a fairer and more open multilateral trading system for the benefit and welfare of its member states.[134] A critical issue that emerged from this legal instrument was the function of the WTO as a forum for negotiations among its members concerning their multilateral trade relations in matters which are dealt with under the agreements in the annexes to the Agreement. The WTO may also provide a forum for further negotiations among its members concerning their multilateral trade relations, and a framework for the implementation of the results of such negotiations, as may be decided by the Ministerial Conference.[135] The WTO also administers the Understanding on Rules and Procedures Governing the Settlement of Disputes (hereafter referred to as the Dispute Settlement Understanding, or DSU) in Annex 2 to the Agreement.[136] Annex 2 underscores the philosophy of dispute settlement reflected in the Agreement as being to strengthen the multilateral system of trade relations that the WTO represents.

Article 23 of Annex 2 provides that, when members seek the redress of a violation of obligations or other nullification or impairment of benefits under the covered agreements or an impediment to the attainment of any objective of the covered agreements, they shall have recourse to, and abide by, the rules and procedures of the Understanding. In such cases, members are required to abstain from making a determination to the effect that a violation has occurred, that benefits have been nullified or impaired or that the attainment of any objective of the covered agreements has been impeded, except through recourse to dispute settlement in accordance with the rules and procedures of the Understanding.[137] Members are also required to follow the procedures set forth in article 21, which call for prompt compliance with recommendations of the dispute settlement body, with particular attention being given to developing-country members with respect to measures which are subject to dispute settlement. This measure has been taken to determine the reasonable period of time for the member concerned to implement the recommendations and rulings,[138] and follow the procedures set forth in article 22. Article 22 provides for international conditions for compensation and the suspension of concessions, in order to determine the level of suspension of concessions or other obligations and obtain authorization from the dispute resolution body before suspending concessions or other obligations in response to the failure of the member concerned to implement the recommendations and rulings within that reasonable period of time.

There is also provision in Annex 2 for particular consideration to be given to a least developed country member in the dispute resolution process under the WTO umbrella. Members are required in this regard to exercise due restraint in raising matters under the procedures of the Marrakesh Agreement when a least-developed country member is involved in a dispute. If nullification or impairment is found to result from a measure taken by a least-developed country member, complaining parties should exercise due restraint in asking for compensation or seeking authorization to suspend the application of concessions or other obligations pursuant to procedures prescribed by the Agreement.[139]

Annex 2 of the Agreement contains principles relating to the DSU. These principles have attempted to rectify some of the perceived inadequacies of the GATT system which prevailed prior to the adoption of the Marrakesh Agreement. Some reasons for dissatisfaction with the GATT procedures for dispute settlement[140] have been identified in the past as the lack of automatic access to panels, delays in appointing them, lack of terms of reference of panels, slow and inexpedient consideration of the cases owing to the lack of strict adherence to time limits for procedural discipline, inadequate panel selection process, and poor quality panel reports. Furthermore, the practice of GATT has been to focus more on conciliation and negotiated settlements than on the recognition and enforcement of obligations. Under this system, recommendations were made only in instances where the parties were unable to reach a mutually acceptable solution to their dispute. The much-needed practical implementation of recommendations and rulings of the GATT dispute resolution system and the absence of recourse to the losing party were not addressed in the GATT system. The early system of GATT dispute resolution was accused of lacking legalistic procedures which were formulated through a cohesive system of rules and more precise decisions which were taken on the merits of the disputes. GATT's preference for negotiated settlements – which were accused of favouring member countries with political and economic leverage over less able nations – has also been criticized.

Instead, an adjudicative system has been recommended as the most expedient and fair manner in which the settlement of disputes could be effected through GATT. Some of the suggestions that were made to improve the GATT system were development of a mechanism for early warning; notification to the Council of mutually agreed solutions where any GATT member could address and raise matters relating to such solutions; provisions for approaching the Council direct and gaining access thereto; mediation by the director general of GATT in certain circumstances; the establishment of panels by the Council within specified and strict time limits; the establishment of a group of legal experts devoted exclusively to dispute settlement; the standardization of terms of reference of panels; the establishment of and insistence on time limits on the work of panels and the examination of the findings of the panels by the Council; expansion of the role of the legal staff of the GATT secretariat in dispute settlement; and a better-quality government participation in the settlement process. It was also felt that there was a compelling need for special and more favourable treatment to be accorded to developing countries, such treatment to include specialized legal aid, training courses and post-consultation review by the Council. The last concern in particular was addressed by the Uruguay Round and provision has been made for more favourable treatment to be given to least-developed countries.

It is now evident that the careful consideration given by the Uruguay Round of Negotiations to the compelling issue of dispute resolution in multilateral trade has resulted in the Understanding, as reflected in Annex 2 of the Agreement being structured in such a detailed manner. The rules and procedures of the Understanding apply to disputes brought pursuant to the consultation and dispute settlement provisions of the agreements (referred to in the Understanding as 'covered agreements'), of which trade in civil aircraft is one.[141] The rules and procedures of the Understanding also apply to consultations and the settlement of disputes between members concerning their rights and obligations under the provisions of the Marrakesh Agreement which established the WTO.

The Dispute Settlement Body (DSB) which is established under the Council for Trade in Services, which is in turn established under the General Council of the WTO, was set up to administer the rules and procedures in the annex and, except as otherwise provided in a covered agreement, the consultation and dispute settlement provisions of the covered agreements. Accordingly, the DSB has the authority to establish panels, adopt panel and appellate body reports, maintain surveillance of implementation of rulings and recommendations, and authorize suspension of concessions and other obligations under the covered agreements.[142] The DSB is required to inform the relevant WTO councils and committees of any developments in disputes related to provisions of the respective covered agreements.[143] Under article 3 of the annex, members affirm their adherence to the principles of the management of disputes heretofore applied under articles XXII and XXIII of GATT 1947, and the rules and procedures as further elaborated and modified in the annex.[144] This means that, effectively, trade in civil aircraft and services related thereto would be governed by the initial structural format of the 1947 rules as amended. Emphasis is placed on the prompt settlement of situations in which a member considers that any benefits accruing to it directly or indirectly under the covered agreements are being impaired by measures taken by another member. The effective functioning of the WTO and the maintenance of a proper balance between the rights and obligations of members have been identified as critical in the dispute settlement process, which is required to be expedient.[145]

Recommendations or rulings made by the DSB are calculated to aim at achieving a satisfactory settlement of the matter in accordance with the rights and obligations under the Understanding and under the covered agreements.[146] The annex also insists that all solutions to matters formally raised under the consultation and dispute settlement provisions of the covered agreements are consistent with those agreements and that they should not nullify or impair benefits accruing to any member under those agreements or impede the attainment of any objective of those agreements.[147] Before bringing a case before the DSB, a member has to exercise judgment as to whether action under the procedures of the Agreement would be fruitful. Therefore a solution which is mutually acceptable to the parties to a dispute and consistent with the covered agreements is clearly preferred. In the absence of a mutually agreed solution, the first objective to be achieved under the Agreement would be to secure the withdrawal of the measures concerned if these are considered to be inconsistent with the provisions of any of the covered agreements.[148] The Understanding further prescribes that the provision of compensation should be resorted to only if the immediate withdrawal of the measure is impracticable, and as a temporary measure pending the withdrawal of the measure which is so inconsistent.[149] An infringement of the obligations assumed under a covered agreement is *prima facie* considered to constitute a case of nullification or impairment. In such cases there is normally a presumption that a breach of the rules has an adverse impact on other members of that covered agreement, and in such instances, the member against whom the charge is laid is required to rebut the charge.[150]

One of the fundamental principles of the Understanding is that requests for conciliation and the use of the dispute resolution procedures should not be intended or considered as contentious acts. If a dispute arises, all members are required to be involved in the procedures in good faith in an effort to resolve the dispute. Furthermore, complaints and counter-complaints in regard to distinct matters should not be linked.[151]

The Understanding is applied only with respect to new requests for consultations under the consultation provisions of the covered agreements made on or after the date of entry into force of the Agreement. Developing member countries are given the benefit of invoking certain provisions of the Agreement that are calculated to be to their benefit, in instances where complaints or charges are brought by developing member countries under the rules of the Agreement.[152] If a request for consultations is made pursuant to a covered agreement, the member to whom the request is made is required to reply to the request within ten days of its receipt and enter into consultation in good faith within a period of no more than 30 days of receipt of such request, with a view to reaching a satisfactory solution, unless otherwise mutually agreed upon.[153] Consultations are confidential and held without prejudice to the rights of any member in any further proceedings.[154]

As discussed earlier, the WTO dispute settlement structure encourages conciliation and mediation under procedures that are undertaken voluntarily if the parties to the dispute so agree.[155] Any party to a dispute may, at any time, request good offices, conciliation and mediation. They may begin at any time and be terminated at any time. Once procedures for good offices, conciliation or mediation are terminated, a complaining party may then proceed toward the establishment of a panel. At the request of the complaining party, a panel is established under the Agreement latest by/at the DSB meeting following that at which the request first appears as an item on the agenda of the DSB, unless of course, the DSB decides not to establish a panel at its meeting.[156] A panel is composed of well-qualified governmental and/or non-governmental individuals, including persons who have served on or presented a case to a panel; served as a representative of a member, or if a contracting party to GATT 1947; or as a representative to the council or committee of any covered agreement or its predecessor agreement, or in the secretariat; has taught or published on international trade law or policy; or served as a senior trade policy official or member.[157] They are selected in such as way as to ensure the independence of the members and to give the panel a diverse selection of individuals with a wide spectrum of experience and exposure.[158] To this end, the WTO secretariat maintains an indicative list of governmental and non-governmental individuals possessing the qualifications to assist in the selection of panellists as required.[159]

The function of panels is to assist the DSB in discharging its responsibilities under the Understanding and the covered agreements. Accordingly, a panel is required to make an objective assessment of the matter before it.[160] While the reports of the panels are not considered by the DSB until 20 days after the date they are circulated to members,[161] objections filed by members to these reports have to be filed with the DSB at least ten days prior to the DSB meeting that would discuss such objections.[162] The parties to a dispute have a right to participate in DSB hearings concerning their dispute. The reports are adopted by the DSB within 60 days of their circulation by a panel, unless otherwise decided.[163]

For the purpose of hearing appeals from the dispute resolution process of panels, a standing appellate body is established by the DSB. Such body is composed of seven persons, for a four-year term, three of whom will hear any one case. The appellate body comprises persons of recognized authority, with demonstrated expertise in law, international trade and the subject matter of the covered agreements generally. They are not affiliated to any government and their membership is generally indicative of that of the WTO.

Where a panel or the appellate body concludes that a measure is inconsistent with a covered agreement, such body will recommend to the member concerned to bring the measure into conformity with the Agreement. In addition, the panel or appellate body may suggest ways in which the member concerned could implement the recommendations.[164] The time frame for a decision of the DSB to be taken conclusively is set as nine months from the date of establishment of the panel by the DSB until the DSB considers the report of the panel or appellate body for adoption.[165] Prompt compliance with the rulings or recommendations of the DSB is mandatory. Any member who is so obligated shall convey his intention to comply with such ruling or recommendation to the DSB at a meeting of the DSB held within 30 days of the adoption of the report of the panel or appellate body affecting such member.[166] A reasonable period of time is granted to a member who is unable to comply with such rules or recommendations.[167]

The TRIPS dispute settlement system

TRIPs has certainly introduced a new dimension to legal issues that may arise as a result of the exercise of intellectual property rights. The TRIPS Agreement, which is formally called the WTO Agreement on Trade-Related Aspects of Intellectual Property Rights, is the only agreement under the WTO umbrella which requires member states of the WTO to incorporate into their domestic legislation substantive legal matters of a complex nature, both for domestic and imported goods and services. The TRIPS Agreement makes copious cross references to treaties other than the WTO and stipulates minimum standards applicable for the enforcement of the provisions of the Agreement. The Agreement also prescribes that any state may seek settlement of an allegation of inadequate implementation of the TRIPS Agreement by another state, by bringing its case before the WTO DSB.

The TRIPS dispute settlement system operates on a co-dependent basis, by anchoring itself to the WTO Dispute Settlement Understanding.[168] While Article 64 of the TRIPS Agreement settles the issue of dispute settlement, Article 68 stipulates that the TRIPs Council shall provide assistance as requested by WTO members on dispute settlement, to the WTO secretariat, director-general and its secretariat with respect to dispute settlement panels and their composition. The TRIPS Council has the authority, under this provision, to recommend experts to the panel as required.

The World Intellectual Property Organization (WIPO) which administers several multilateral conventions on intellectual property rights, has been included in the TRIPS Agreement to the extent that the Agreement carries several substantive provisions of WIPO treaties.[169] This notwithstanding, the WIPO secretariat does not receive an automatic mandate to sit in on TRIPS adjudication panels, although it may render an interpretation of a state's observation or position on a dispute settlement issue relating to WIPO rules.

The TRIPS Agreement essentially carries rights for the acquiring and maintaining of intellectual property rights, guaranteeing them in the process. It also offers relief by way of prescribing effective means of enforcing such rights. However, the

Agreement does not contain a guarantee of market access for goods developed through the intellectual property rights process, thereby raising a doubt as to whether the TRIPS Agreement could entertain complaints against violation of TRIPS under its article 64.3.

Articles 20 and 21 on the use of trademarks explicitly protect the rights holder of a trademark in furthering his rights under his trademark and therefore can be considered to be among the rare TRIPS provisions which may offer relief in dispute settlement.

The outer space exploration industry is fast becoming one of the largest global commercial undertakings, and it is not uncommon to see within it particular characteristics recognized as being distinctive to particular members of that industry. In this context, those institutions which have established a name of repute would have to zealously guard their trademarks. Although, as discussed earlier, common law courts have set up stringent standards of conduct, and international regulation in this regard is fast moving to provide a comprehensive system of adjudication, the outer space exploration industry has resorted to its own tools of commercial management to obviate the inconvenience of trademark infringement by offering attractive franchising agreements to those who wish to use the names of reputed carriers. The franchise agreement in the outer space exploration industry has proved so far to be an ethical and expeditious implement of commercial management[170] and can indeed be considered a viable alternative to the tedious process of adjudication on trademark infringement.

6 CYBER TERRORISM AND OUTER SPACE

Introduction

In March 1998, the website of the National Aeronautics and Space Administration (NASA) of the United States received a 'denial of service' attack, calculated to affect Microsoft Windows NT and Windows 95 operating systems. These attacks prevented servers from answering network connections and crashed computers, causing a blue screen to appear on the computers. The attacked systems were revived, but this attack was a follow-up of one in February of the same year, when, for two weeks the US Defense Department had unclassified networks penetrated, where hackers accessed personnel and payroll information.

Cyber terrorism has the advantage of anonymity, which enables the hacker to obviate checkpoints or any physical evidence being traceable to him or her. It is a low-budget form of terrorism where the only costs entailed in interfering with the computer programs of a space programme would be those pertaining to the right computer equipment. Any interference with a space programme of a nation, which would be inextricably linked to peaceful uses of outer space, would be tantamount to an act of terrorism performed against international peace.

The maintenance of international peace and security is an important objective of the United Nations,[171] which recognizes one of its purposes as being:

> To maintain international peace and security, and to that end: take effective collective measures for the prevention and removal of threats to the peace, and for the suppression of acts of aggression or other breaches of peace, and to bring about by peaceful means, and in conformity with the principles of justice and international law, adjustment or settlement of international disputes or situations which might lead to a breach of the peace.[172]

It is thus clear that the United Nations has recognized the application of the principles of international law as an integral part of maintaining international peace and security and avoiding situations which may lead to a breach of the peace.[173]

Under general legal principles, 'unlawful interference' with legitimate outer space activity can be regarded as a crime. A crime has been identified as 'a wrong which affects the security or well-being of the public generally so that the public has an interest in its suppression'.[174] The word 'wrong' in this definition could be considered as presupposing an act that is perpetrated against the law. Since interference with civil aviation is in itself a wrong, and therefore definitively against the law, the question arises whether the word 'unlawful' is tautologous. Tautology in the phrase 'unlawful interference' was judicially discussed in England in 1981, in a case which involved indecent assault on a mental patient. Hodgson J observed:

> it does not seem to me that the element of unlawfulness can properly be regarded as part of the definitional element of the offence. In defining a criminal offence the word 'unlawful' is surely tautologous and can add nothing to its essential ingredients.[175]

Lord Justice Lawton, in a later case, analysed Justice Hodgson's reasoning and observed:

> We have found difficulty in agreeing with this reasoning, even though the judge seems to be accepting that belief in consent does entitle a defendant to an acquittal on a charge of assault. We cannot accept that the word 'unlawful' when used in a definition of an offence is to be regarded as tautologous. In our judgment the word 'unlawful' does import an essential element into the offence. If it were not there, social life would be unreasonable.[176]

Lord Lane CJ, in the 1987 case of *R.* v. *Williams*,[177] citing with approval Lord Justice Lawton's analysis, went on to say: 'the mental element necessary to constitute guilt is the intent to apply unlawful force to the victim. We do not believe that the mental element can be substantiated by simply showing an intent to apply force and no more'.[178] Lord Lane CJ seems to impute to the defendant a knowledge of going against applicable law, making the word 'unlawful' *sui generis* and mutually exclusive from the term 'interference'.

This line of cases seems to suggest by analogy that 'unlawful interference' constitutes an act whereby the perpetrator knows that his interference with an activity is clearly contrary to the law. Unlawful interference with outer space activities forms no conceivable exception to this logicality.

Another significant fact emerges from the judgment of Lord Lane CJ when his lordship said:

> What then is the situation of the defendant in labouring under a mistake of fact as to the circumstances? What if he believes, but believes mistakenly, that the victim is consenting, or that it is necessary to defend himself, or that a crime is being committed which he intends to prevent? He must then be judged against the mistaken facts or circumstances and if the prosecution fails to establish his guilt, then he is entitled to an acquittal.[179]

By analogy, therefore, if a person interferes with outer space activities performed legitimately by a recognized state, but does not believe he is contravening the law, he is not guilty of an offence and the mental element in an offence becomes as important as the physical element of the offence of unlawful interference with civil aviation. The criminal element[180] that is thus infused into the offence of unlawful interference makes the offence, like any other, hinge on the criminal policy that is created in the jurisdiction to which it applies. In other words, an act of interference would be considered unlawful and thereby an offence only in jurisdictions whose criminal policies determine such acts to be unlawful. Although a crime has so far not been coherently defined by any writer,[181] the characteristics of a crime, that is the *actus reus* (physical act forbidden by law) and the *mens rea* (the intention to commit the act and to understand the reasonable and natural consequences of the act), have been identified.[182] The identification of these elements has given rise to the maxim *Actus non facit reum (hominem) nisi mens sit rea*, meaning that, whatever deed a man may have done, it cannot make him criminally punishable unless his doing of it was activated by a legally blameworthy attitude of mind. Usually, each prohibited deed is legally specified and defined and the legal definition identifies the essential facts which must be present to constitute the forbidden deed.

The manipulation of computer data by hackers is analogous to a robbery in one's house. In the Canadian case of *R. McLaughlin*,[183] when a student of a university hacked his way into a computer, the Supreme Court of Canada decided that a computer is not a telecommunications facility but a data-processing device the abuse of which should be an indictable offence. This decision made the Canadian legislature amend its laws accordingly.[184]

The United Nations Charter

Although the charter contains no provision which deals directly with the security of outer space exploration, it is one of the most salutary international legal documents in the area of outer space security. The preamble to the charter stipulates that citizens of the member states of the United Nations will practise tolerance and live together in peace with one another as good neighbours. The principle of security is embodied in several articles of the charter. Article 1(2) provides that the purpose of the United Nations is to pursue the development of friendly relations among nations based on respect for the principle of equal rights and self-determination of peoples, and to take other appropriate measures to strengthen universal peace.

As spacecraft are presumed to be used at the present time to transport crews for purposes of space exploration, and they will, in the future, be used to transport civilians, both the Outer Space Treaty and the Liability Convention should ensure the protection of civilians and their property from dangers affecting spacecraft in flight. The United Nations Charter can therefore be regarded as imputing to the international community a duty to protect the human being and his property in relation to flight:

> There is a mandatory obligation implied in article 55 of the Charter that the United Nations 'shall promote respect for, and observance of, human rights and fundamental freedoms'; or, in terms of article 13, that the Assembly shall make recommendations for the purpose of assisting in the realization of human rights and freedoms. There is a distinct element of legal duty in the understanding expressed in article 56 in which all members pledge themselves to take joint and separate action in co-operation with the organization for the achievement of the purpose set forth in article 55.[185]

A spacecraft cannot be attacked, whether by physical military means or by sabotaging communication means used. The United Nations Charter opposes the use of force against outer space exploration. Article 2(4) of the charter prohibits the use of force in any manner inconsistent with the purposes of the charter. There is also provision for the settlement of disputes by peaceful means.[186]

Any attack against a spacecraft or space station, however founded, is a special kind of aggression and is protected by the right of self-defence which is recognized against such an attack, by article 51 of the charter. This provision narrows the field of the exercise of self-defence to circumstances involving an armed attack. Although no authoritative definition of an armed attack has ever been adopted internationally, it is generally presumed that an armed attack against space exploration would constitute belligerence endangering the safety of those affected by such attack when it is carried out by an offender or offenders wielding weapons. This analogy is true of cyber crime against the use of outer space.

The Geneva Convention on the High Seas (1958)

Transport systems have often attracted terrorist attacks and the international community has come to terms with the vulnerability of modern aviation, taking sustained steps towards its protection.

The earliest form of terrorism against international transportation was piracy. Pirates are considered by international law as common enemies of all mankind. The world naturally has an interest in the punishment of offenders and is justified in adopting international measures for the application of universal rules regarding the control of terrorism. The common understanding between states has been that pirates should be lawfully captured on the high seas by an armed vessel of any particular state, and brought within its territorial jurisdiction for trial and punishment. Lauterpacht wrote:

> Before international law in the modern sense of the term was in existence, a pirate was already considered an outlaw, a hostis humani generis. According to the Law of Nations, the act of piracy makes the pirate lose the protection of his home State, and thereby his national character. Piracy is a so-called international crime, the pirate is considered enemy of all States and can be brought to justice anywhere.[187]

It is worthy of note that, under the rules of customary international law, the international community had no difficulty in dealing with acts of terrorism which form the offence of sea piracy. Owing to the seriousness of the offence and the serious terroristic acts involved, the offence was met with the most severe punishment available – death. The universal condemnation of the offence is reflected in the statement: 'In the former times it was said to be a customary rule of international law that, after the seizure, pirates could at once be hanged or drowned by the captor.'

The laws dealing with the offence of piracy went through a sustained process of evolution. In 1956, while considering legal matters pertaining to the law of the sea, the International Law Association addressed the offence of piracy and recommended that the subject of piracy at sea be incorporated in the Draft Convention of the Law of the Sea. This was followed by the United Nations General Assembly Resolution (Resolution No. 1105 (XI) in 1957, which called for the convening of a diplomatic conference to further evaluate the Law of the Sea). Accordingly, the Convention on the High Seas was adopted in 1958 and came into force in September 1962.

The Geneva Convention on the High Seas of 1958[188] was the first attempt at international accord to harmonize the application of rules to piracy both at sea and in air. The Convention adopted authoritative legal statements on civil aviation security, as it touched on piracy over the high seas.[189] Article 5 of the Convention inclusively defines piracy as follows:

> Piracy consists of any of the following acts:
>
> 1) Any illegal acts of violence, detention or any act of depredation, committed for private ends by the crew or the passenger of a private ship or a private aircraft, and directed:
>   a) on the high seas, against another ship or aircraft, or against persons or property on board such ship or aircraft;

b) against a ship, aircraft, persons, or property in a place outside the jurisdiction of any state;

2) Any act of voluntary participation in the operation of a ship or of an aircraft with knowledge of facts making it a pirate ship or aircraft;

3) Any act of inciting or of internationally facilitating an act described in sub-paragraph 1 or sub-paragraph 2 of this article.

As provided for by Article 14 of the Convention, there is incumbent on all states a general duty to 'cooperate' to the fullest extent in the repression of piracy as defined by the Convention. One commentator has observed,

> The International Law Commission in its 1956 report, however, deemed it desirable to enjoin cooperation in the repression of piracy, to define the act to include piracy by aircraft, as set forth in the repressive measures that may justifiably be taken. The United Nations conference on the Law of the Sea in Geneva in 1958 accordingly incorporated these adjustments of the law to modern times in its convention on the High Seas.[190]

Article 14 seemingly makes it a duty incumbent upon every state to take necessary measures to combat piracy by either prosecuting the pirate or extraditing him to the state which might be in a better position to undertake such prosecution. The Convention, in Article 19, gives all states universal jurisdiction under which the person charged with the offence of aerial or sea piracy may be tried and punished by any state into whose jurisdiction he may come. This measure is a proactive one in that it eliminates any boundaries that a state may have which would preclude the extradition or trial in that state of an offender. Universal jurisdiction was conferred upon the states by the Convention also to solve the somewhat complex problem of jurisdiction which often arose under municipal law where the crime was committed outside the territorial jurisdiction of the particular state seeking to prosecute an offender. The underlying salutary effect of universal jurisdiction in cases of piracy and hijacking which was emphasized by the Convention, is discussed in the following manner:

> the absence of universal jurisdiction in relation to a given offence means that, if a particular State has no jurisdiction either on the basis of territoriality or protection, or on the personality principle, whether passive or active, it will not be authorized to put the offender on trial, even if he is to be found within the territorial boundaries of the State.[191]

The inclusion of the offence of 'piracy' in the Convention brings to bear the glaring fact that the crime is international in nature, giving the international community the right to take appropriate measures to combat or at least control the occurrence of the offence. The general Convention by its very nature and adoption has demonstrably conveyed the message that piracy is a heinous crime which requires severe punishment. The Convention also calls for solidarity and collectivity on the part of nations in combating the offence in the interests of all nations concerned.[192]

Notwithstanding the above, it is worthy of note that the phenomenon of hijacking as it exists today need not necessarily fall within the definition of piracy as referred in article 15 of the High Seas Convention (1958). Although there exists a marked similarity between the offences of unlawful seizure of aircraft and acts of piracy directed against ships on the high seas, in that, in both cases, the mode of transport is threatened and abused and the safety of the passengers, crew members and the craft itself is endangered by the unlawful use of force or threat, there may still be a subtle difference that may exist between the offence as applying to sea transport and to air transport.

Whilst, admittedly, there are similarities between the acts of piracy against ships and those against aircraft, the legal differences that may exist should be determined in order to inquire whether aircraft hijacking amounts to piracy as defined by the Convention.

The essential features of the definition of piracy as incorporated in the Geneva Convention are as follows: (1) the pirate must be motivated by 'private' as opposed to 'public' ends; (2) the act of piracy involves action affecting a ship, an aircraft; (3) the acts of violence, detention and depredation take place outside the jurisdiction of any state, meaning both territorial jurisdiction and airspace above the state; (4) acts committed on board a ship or aircraft, by the crew or passengers of such ship or aircraft and directed against the ship or aircraft itself, or against persons or property, do not constitute the offence of piracy.

Upon close examination, it appears that the definition of piracy does not apply to the phenomenon of aerial piracy or hijacking. Firstly, it is a fact that most hijackings are not carried out in pursuance of private ends. INTERPOL[193] reported in 1977 that the percentage of cases in which political motives had impelled the offender was 64.4 per cent. Hijacking of aircraft for political motives would thus not relate to article 15(1) of the Convention on the High Seas (1958) since acts solely inspired by political motives are excluded from the notion *piracy jure gentium*. Sami Shubber has observed of the 1958 Convention that its inapplicability to the notion of aerial piracy may lie in the fact that private ends do not necessarily mean that they can affect private groups, acting in pursuance either of their political aims, or of gain. The fact that it is not always possible to distinguish between private ends and public ends in defiance of the political regime of the flag state may be said to be covered by article 15(1) of the Convention.[194] The reasons given by Shubber were that 'private ends' do not necessarily mean private gain.

Under the definition, the act of illegal violence or detention must be directed on the high seas, against another ship or aircraft. It is obvious therefore that this interpretation does not apply to hijacking since the offence of hijacking is committed by the offender who travels in the aircraft. It is hard to imagine that an offender could enter an aircraft from outside while the aircraft is in flight. The Convention also excludes acts committed on board a ship by the crew or passenger and directed against the ship itself, or against persons or property on the ship, from the scope of piracy,[195] which will also make the definition inconsistent with the exigencies related to the offence of aerial piracy.

Piracy, according to the Convention, must be committed on the 'high seas', which is a direct analogy to cyber piracy in outer space or no man's land. Furthermore, piracy under article 15 of the Convention must involve acts of violence, detention or depredation. Instances of sabotage through cyber terrorism may be direct, or through threats, and may even be carried out through a variety of means other than those involving violence or force.

It is therefore reasonable to conclude that cyber terrorism would necessarily draw a direct analogy with and bring to bear the relevance of the Geneva Convention on the High Seas. In this context, the Convention is not without value to the present, and indeed the future, context of space travel.

Jurisdictional issues

Perhaps the single most important issue in cyber conduct is that which pertains to jurisdiction. Given the worldwide web and its global application, the most compelling question in this regard would pertain to the transboundary applicability of an Internet contract. In this regard, the most convenient analogy comes from the two jurisdictions of Canada and the United States. Would a hacker in Canada, who interferes with computer programming over the Internet in Toronto and Miami, be liable to be charged for his crime in the United States by the aggrieved company which has its home base in Florida? In a case decided in 1952[196] in Canada, where the plaintiff brought a case to the Ontario High Court against an American radio broadcasting station which was broadcasting, from across the border, allegedly libellous statements which could be heard over the air waves in Canada, the defendant radio station brought up a motion of dismissal, alleging that the Ontario Court in Canada had no jurisdiction to hear a case against a party to the action which was an enterprise based in the United States. The court disagreed, and held:

> A person may utter all the defamatory words he wishes without incurring any civil liability unless they are heard and understood by a third person. I think it a 'startling proposition' to say that one may, while standing south of the border or cruising in an aeroplane south of the border, through the medium of modern sound amplification, utter defamatory matter which is heard in a Province in Canada north of the border, and not be said to have published a slander in the Province in which it is heard and understood. I cannot see what difference it makes whether the person is made to understand by means of the written word, sound-waves or ether-waves in so far as the matter of proof of publication is concerned. The tort consists in making a third person understand actionable defamatory matter.[197]

In the more recent case of *Pindling* v. *National Broadcasting Corporation*,[198] in respect of an American television broadcast received in Canada, the Ontario High

Court held that the Prime Minister of the Bahamas was held entitled to bring the case to Canada, instead of the United States. The *Pindling* decision illustrates well the principle of 'forum shopping' which can be culled from the television context and be held applicable to the analogous situation of a contract transacted over the Internet.

The above principle may be derogated only in an instance where the Court seized of the case could invoke the principle of 'forum non conveniens' which allows the transfer of a suit from an originally filed jurisdiction to some other jurisdiction which is better placed to hear the case concerned. In the 1996 case of *National Bank of Canada* v. *Clifford Chance*,[199] the Canadian courts, which were charged with hearing a case where a Toronto-based firm had contracted with a law firm in the United Kingdom, transferred the case to the United Kingdom although the contract was concluded in Toronto, on the grounds that the contract concerned a UK-based project and the legal advice obtained had been UK law given by lawyers in the United Kingdom. Based on the *Clifford Chance* principle, it would not be unusual for a common law court to determine that, in an auction for an airline seat, where the offer emanates from, say, Canada over the Internet for a seat out of the United Kingdom on a UK-based carrier, the applicable jurisdiction would lie with the courts in the United Kingdom, although the contract itself may have been concluded in Canada.

There is a dichotomy in the judicial thinking with regard to cases involving contracts concluded over the Internet. On the one hand, courts are refusing to bring a person into a jurisdiction purely because he contracted with a business entity which is based in that jurisdiction. This approach is illustrated by the 1994 US decision in the case of *Pres-Kap, Inc.* v. *System One, Direct Access Inc.,*[200] where the court refused to grant jurisdiction to Florida where a resident in New York had used a Florida-based online network information service merely to gain access to a database. Similarly, the court in the famous 1997 *SunAmerica* case[201] refused to find jurisdiction in a trademark case solely on the basis of the defendant's operation of a general access web site:

> Plaintiffs ask this Court to hold that any defendant who advertises nationally or on the Internet is subject to its jurisdiction. It cannot plausibly be argued that any defendant who advertises nationally could expect to be haled into Court in *any* state, for a cause of action that does not relate to the advertisements. Such general advertising is not the type of 'purposeful activity related to the forum that would make the exercise of jurisdiction fair, just or reasonable'.[202]

Similarly, in another 1997 case, *Hearst Corporation* v. Goldberger,[203] the defendant operated a passive general access web site, the courts were of the view that to open worldwide jurisdiction merely because the Internet offered worldwide access would be iniquitous:

> Where, as here, defendant has not contracted to sell or actually sold any goods or services to New Yorkers, a finding of personal jurisdiction in New York based on an Internet website would mean that there would be nationwide (indeed, worldwide) personal jurisdiction over anyone and everyone who establishes an Internet web site. Such nationwide jurisdiction is not consistent with traditional personal jurisdiction case law nor acceptable to the Court as a matter of policy.[204]

The *Hearst Corporation* decision seems to have followed the observation of a case[205] decided one year earlier, where the court held:

> Because the Web enables easy worldwide access, allowing computer interaction via the Web to supply sufficient contacts to establish jurisdiction would eviscerate the personal jurisdiction requirement as it currently exists; the Court is not willing to take this step. Thus, the fact that Fallon has a Web site used by Californians cannot establish jurisdiction by itself.[206]

The second line of judicial thinking is the converse to the above approach, where courts have imputed to the non-resident defendant the responsibility for complexities brought about by the Internet in its universal applicability. Therefore, in *Compuserv Incorporated* v. *Patterson*,[207] the courts held a Texas-based computer programmer legally responsible for his Ohio-based computer network online service, and found him to be under Ohio Law. Although the defendant had never visited Ohio, he was nevertheless found to be subject to Ohio law on the basis that an electronic contract had been concluded in Ohio where the defendant was distributing his product.

The principle of universal application of jurisdiction has been invoked in other instances, where courts have accepted jurisdiction on the basis of sales made to customers through the defendant's web site,[208] or based on soliciting donations,[209] or based on subscribers signed up by the defendant for services delivered over the Internet,[210] or for having follow-on contacts, negotiations and other dealings in addition to, and often as a result of, the initial Internet-based communication.[211] The common thread which runs through the fabric of judicial thinking in this regard is that parties who avail themselves of technology in order to do business in a distant place should not then be able to escape that place's legal jurisdiction. These cases are all-embracing, from contract breach claims to tort, including trade libel; in several cases, courts have even found jurisdiction in trademark infringement matters merely on the basis of a defendant's general access web site,[212] or linking to a national ATM network through a telephone line indirectly through an independent data processor in a third state.[213]

An overall evaluation of the U.S. civil cases discussed above concludes that, while the general trend is for courts to assert jurisdiction over non-residents based on their Internet activities, there are still a few situations where some courts may not apply jurisdiction.

Although the choice of forum may extend universally, it does not necessarily mean that enforcement from a judgment would automatically follow. In the case of *Bachchan*

v. *India Abroad Publications Incorporated*,[214] the plaintiff, who was a national of India who had won the right to have his case heard in the United Kingdom, was unable to enforce judgment in New York. The New York courts held that the United Kingdom law applicable to the case did not accord with United States law and therefore the decision could not be recognized as enforceable in the United States.

An insurmountable problem in international criminal justice is the question, 'before what court and according to what law should an individual who has committed an international crime be tried?' There are two possibilities: (a) an individual criminal may remain at large and unpunished; and (b) an international criminal may be tried by the court of any state which can bring him physically within its jurisdiction. The former reflects the present ludicrous state of international criminal law. The latter brings to bear the reversal of established international law, as was seen in the dangerous precedent created in the extradition from Argentina to Israel of war criminal Eichmann and his trial in Israel for international crimes.[215] This would doubtless create international 'vigilantes'.

The inherent defect in the application of municipal law to international crimes lies in the fact that a host of municipal courts, adjudicating on different or separate instances of criminality, may find difficulties in maintaining uniformity in application and interpretation. Uniformity of formulation could only be achieved if states followed an authoritative text when incorporating international criminal law into their municipal systems. Although this may be possible, it would certainly be a tedious and devious process. A more expedient method would be for states to accept such a text in the form of an international code or convention, to be administered by one international body on the principle of international citizenship of people, irrespective of their nationality. To achieve this goal, the concept of state sovereignty as it exists today has to be revisited along the lines of the foregoing discussion.

Another factor that has to be taken into account in the creation of an international court of criminal justice is that, as a condition precedent, states should form a consensus on definitions relating to critical terminology. For instance, an international crime would have to be clearly defined and universally agreed upon. The word 'aggression' would also have to be clearly spelled out.

During World War II the idea of an international criminal court gained increasing significance and it is often not realized how much effort was devoted to the practicalities of the creation and organization of such a court. The work of a number of official and unofficial bodies[216] paved the way for the deliberations of the International Conference on Military Trials which resulted in the establishment of the International Military Tribunal at Nuremberg.[217]

Although the International Military Tribunal, *functus officio*, ceased to exist, the question of the creation of an international criminal court was actively taken up by the United Nations. It was raised in connection with the formulation of the Nuremberg principles in 1948[218] and with the Genocide Convention.[219] The General Assembly eventually invited the International Law Commission to investigate the desirability and possibility of the creation of an international criminal court.[220] Although this task was successfully completed, the matter went no further. In 1954, the General Assembly resolved that, considering the relationship between the question of the definition of aggression, the draft code of offences against the peace and security of mankind and the creation of an international criminal court, further discussion of the latter should be deferred until the other two matters had been settled. The General Assembly reaffirmed this view in 1957. This ambivalence on the part of the United Nations reflects the fact that, as long as the solution of the problem of defining aggression remains a condition precedent to the creation of an international criminal court, no further progress will be made.

The formation of an international court may be based on the simplistic truism that, as there are international crimes, so there should be an international court of justice to adjudicate on those crimes. States should, in this context, adopt a more universal attitude that recognizes the following premise: 'international law pierces national sovereignty and presupposes that statesmen of the several States have a responsibility for international peace and order as well as their responsibilities to their own States'.[221]

The fact that the successful formation of such a court is possible may be attenuated from the existence of the International Court of Justice and the successful conclusion of the Nuremberg trials at the Nuremberg Tribunal. It cannot be denied that, at Nuremberg, agreement was reached by lawyers from nations whose legal systems, philosophies and traditions differed widely. They circumvented technical difficulties at the trials with 'a minimum of goodwill and common sense'.[222]

The philosophy of the court should be totally flavoured by international interests, as opposed to national interests. Therefore prosecution should not be relegated to a national entity or authority. It should be left to an international authority such as the United Nations.

Judges of the court should be selected from jurists worldwide, as in the procedure followed in the election of judges to the International Court of Justice. A rigid screening system would have to be built into the rules of court to obviate adjudication of issues which are of a tendentiously political nature. An international convention or code should govern such principles as custody of offenders pending trial, whereby contracting states would guarantee to arrest criminals and deliver them up for trial.

An international convention or code

One of the responsibilities that would devolve upon the international community towards developing an international convention or code would be to set precise laws with regard to addressing pertinent issues involved. States should endeavour:

a to refuse to support states which do not take stringent action with regard to their communication laws on terrorism;

b to enforce stringent limits on activities and size of diplomatic and consular missions and other official bodies overseas of states which engage in or condone cyber criminal activities; and
c to introduce stringent and improved extradition procedures within the process of law for bringing to trial those who have perpetrated acts of cyber terrorism.

The Convention or code should, in addition, enforce the following:

a introduction and implementation of strict visa and immigration requirements and procedure in respect of materials of states which support, sponsor or condone terrorism;
b monitoring all persons, including those of the diplomatic corps, who have been expelled or excluded from states on suspicion of involvement in international terrorism and refusing to let them enter those states;
c establishing multilateral, plurilateral and bilateral liaison and cooperation of police authorities, security and military authorities of states;
d in the light of the COPUOS role in peaceful uses of outer space activities, strengthening the role of this Committee's regulatory role in the promulgation and disseminating of Standards and Recommended Practices (SARPs) and requiring states' compliance therewith; and
e providing adequate sanctions against states who fail to comply with the above SARPs.

The offences related to cyber terrorism should be addressed on the basis that individuals have international duties which transcend the national obligations of obedience imposed by an individual state. By the same token, it must also mean that individual states owe their citizens and the world at large a responsibility for maintaining world security. The philosophy of these two premises has to be vigorously employed in bringing to fruition the above measures. It is only then that a substantial legal contribution could be made to the controlling of this offence.

Dispute resolution in the United Nations system

The question as to whether there is an existing system of dispute resolution at aerospace law is an interesting one. The International Court of Justice remains the formal judicial organ of the United Nations. There is of course the authority of the Security Council of the United Nations which is empowered to pass resolutions on any matter pertaining to world security.

The International Court of Justice (ICJ) was created to perform a dual function: as an agency of the United Nations and as an organ of international law. In its latter manifestation, the court renders judgments; in its former, it gives advisory opinions to the international community through the United Nations. Presumably, when the

ICJ was established, it was not envisaged that these dual functions would cause a conflict of interest between the status of the court as an independent judicial organ and its role as a component of the United Nations. In any event, its predecessor, the Permanent Court of International Justice, seemingly had no problems in rendering advisory opinions to the League of Nations and pronouncing judgments in contentious litigation between states. During the past few decades, however, relations between the United Nations and the ICJ have become increasingly close, creating a certain arcane ambivalence between the two functions of the court, which some would call an organic overlap of interests.

There are three possible ways in which the perceived conflict of interests could be approached. Firstly, the international community could 'live with' the present ambivalence; secondly, it could always rigidly demarcate clearly the two functions; and, thirdly, the ICJ could become a United Nations court. A common denominator which binds these three approaches is the way in which principles of public international law that may apply to the status of the ICJ are interpreted. There are two alternative ways in which international law could be interpreted to underscore the role of the ICJ within the UN system. The first alternative would be to favour a flexible, extensive interpretation and the second would be to adopt a strict and restrictive interpretation. In formal politicolegal terminology this dichotomy may be identified as a conflict between judicial conservatism and abstention, on the one hand, and judicial liberalism and involvement, on the other. Practically, these two alternatives of approach will involve, on the one hand, the application, in contentious cases, of laws applicable to the United Nations system on the basis that cases heard by the court are United Nations cases; and, on the other, the non-traditional approach of application of principles of international law to disputes between states, without regard to United Nations law.

Admittedly, the ICJ is constituted by article 7 of the United Nations Charter as a principal organ of the United Nations and by article 92 of the charter as the principal judicial organ of the United Nations. Therefore, one might argue, *ipso facto*, that the ICJ is a court of the United Nations and, as such, should apply United Nations law. The statute of the International Court of Justice, however, in article 38 provides that a court shall apply international conventions; international custom, as evidence of a general practice accepted as law; the general principles of law recognized by civilized nations; and judicial decisions and teachings of highly qualified jurists of the various nations. This provision seemingly veers the court away to a system which brings to bear the need for the court to apply principles of public international law which are independent of the rest of the United Nations system, thus casting a shadow over the initial premise set by article 7 of the United Nations Charter. *A fortiori*, article 36 of the ICJ statute provides that state parties to the statute may at any time declare that they recognize as compulsory, *ipso facto*, and without special agreement, in relation to any other state accepting the same obligation, the jurisdiction of the court in all legal disputes concerning, *inter alia*, any question of international law. Although, incontrovertibly, article 7 of the United

Nations Charter espouses judicial conservatism and articles 36 and 38 of the ICJ statute entrench judicial liberalism within the ICJ, confusion is further confounded by the fact that article 92 of the United Nations Charter identifies the ICJ statute as an 'integral part' of the charter but nowhere is it stated that the charter is part of the statute.[223]

Another contentious area which compounds the conflict of interests between the ICJ and the UN is reflected in article 25 of the charter which provides that members of the United Nations agree to accept and carry out decisions of the Security Council in accordance with the charter. Taken as an isolated provision, article 25 reads fine, but unfortunately, when read with articles 36 and 38 of the ICJ statute – which bestows upon the court a certain degree of uniformity in the application of international law to disputes between states – the issue becomes shrouded in rhetoric, and raises the issue as to whether states would be effectively precluded from seeking redress from the ICJ in the first place in instances where a Security Council decision explicitly pronounces upon the subject of a dispute. Moreover, it begs the question whether the ICJ would be constrained in applying principles of international law to a dispute where the Security Council has pronounced upon its issues.

The South West African cases (1966)

Arguably, the emergence of the conflict of interests between judicial conservatism and liberalism in the face of the ICJ's position as a judicial organ of the United Nations was first seen in the South West African cases of 1966. These cases, involving *Ethiopia* v. *South Africa* and *Liberia* v. *South West Africa*,[224] questioned the continued existence of the Mandate for South West Africa and duties and performance of the Union and brought into question the validity of a previous advisory opinion given in 1950 and a judgment in 1962 with regard to the same issue. One of the questions that were addressed by the court in this instance was whether the validity of the earlier opinion and judgment could be invoked by the ICJ as binding. Judge Padilla Nervo, in his dissenting judgment, supported the view that 'The Court, being a Court of Justice, cannot, even in giving advisory opinions, depart from the essential rules guiding their activity as a court.'[225] This view vehemently maintains that the functions of the ICJ, be it in its advisory capacity or in its adjudicatory role, are essentially judicial and that, implicitly, no external influence should affect them. This position is supported by Justice Jessup, in his dissenting judgment, when he observes: 'If the opinions are treated as mere utterances and freely discarded, they will inevitably bring the Court into disrepute … the Court must, in view of its high mission, attribute to them great legal value and a moral authority.'[226]

Justice Jessup also endorsed the view that the practical differences between the binding force of a judgment, which derives from specific provisions of the charter and statute apart from the authority of the court, and the authoritative nature of an advisory opinion possessed of that same authority, are not significant. It was his honour's contention, therefore, that in using judicial decisions as a source of law as provided for in article 38(1)(*d*) of the statute, no distinction at all is made between judicial decisions given in the form of a judgment, and judicial decisions given in the form of an advisory opinion.[227]

Justice Jessup also noted that, in the statute, the words 'decision' and 'judgment' are used interchangeably and that there was no clear distinction between them. One of the most compelling statements made in support of the binding nature of judgments of the ICJ was the recognition by his honour of the application of the rule of *res judicata* to ICJ judgments. The rule recognizes that previous decisions are binding on subsequent ones and relates exclusively to courts of law. Justice Jessup, citing article 60 of the statute which provides that the judgment of the court is final and without appeal, went on to support the view: 'I do not mean that only what is written in the operation part (dispositif) [of the judgment] constitutes the Court's decision. On the contrary, it is certain that it is almost always necessary to refer to the statement of reasons to understand clearly the operative part and above all to ascertain the *causa petendi*.'[228]

It is also interesting that the dissenting judgment of Justice Forster in the South West African cases is significant in its assertion that the ICJ was 'the final bulwark of protection' as recourse against possible breaches and abuses of the law.

The above observations, made in 1966 by members of the ICJ, created a stronger awareness of the role of the court as an adjudicating body having binding force on states parties. Furthermore, this new awareness brought to bear the reality that the ICJ, although the organ of the United Nations, is also a judicial organ which may exercise independent authority over states through its judgments. The only obstacle to this judicial exuberance was the overriding gloom that was portended by article 25 of the charter: that members of the United Nations agree to abide by decisions of the United Nations Security Council. This provision effectively empowers states to decide in the Security Council what they should be doing, thus seemingly precluding themselves from having recourse to judicial intervention by the ICJ.

Post-South West African trends

The South West African cases, particularly the 1966 decision, brought out the fact that the ICJ was reluctant to accept that humanitarian considerations are sufficient *per se* to guarantee legal rights and obligations, and that the court could and should proceed accordingly. Judge Arrêt, in his judgment, was of the following view:

> It [the ICJ] is a Court of Law and can take account of moral principals only insofar as these are given a sufficient expression in legal form. Law exists, it is said, to serve a

> social need; but precisely for that reason it can do so only through and within the limits of its own discipline. Otherwise, it is not a legal service that would be rendered.[229]

This conservative pronouncement drew the attention of the United Nations to the fact that the ICJ, being an organ of the United Nations, should conduct itself as a judicial body of the United Nations, consequently taking into consideration such United Nations legal instruments as General Assembly resolutions and Security Council resolutions, along with principles of international law in formulating its decisions.

The representative of Pakistan represented the following view, which was shared in one way or another by many members:

> The insensitivity of these judges to current international standards or legal norms, their disregard of the mode of generation of customary international law, their refusal to apply, in performance of their functions in accordance with Article 38 of the Statute, directives manifested in the resolutions of the General Assembly, are things which are bound to perturb enlightened public opinion throughout the world.[230]

Many delegations accordingly advocated a change in the composition of the court. To cite one example, the representative of Upper Volta said: 'Created at a time when the world was altogether different from that of today, the International Court of justice is not attuned, in its present composition, to today's realities. A change in its composition would be to the advantage of this Organization.'[231] Once again, therefore, tables were turned, and the United Nations settled itself comfortably to considering the ICJ as its judicial organ which dispensed justice primarily according to United Nations law.

Another measure adopted by the General Assembly in drawing the ICJ closer to it was to respond to the emerging trend of conservatism of the ICJ by adopting resolutions with respect to South Africa. It even approved a resolution which had, and probably was intended to have, a most direct bearing on one of the points essential to the case of the applicants whose appeal was rejected by the ICJ. According to article 7, paragraph 2, of the Mandate for South West Africa, the court had jurisdiction in any dispute arising between the mandatory and another member of the League of Nations relating to the interpretation or application of the Mandate 'if it cannot be settled by negotiation'. On 18 December 1960, after rejecting South Africa's *sub judice* plea, the Assembly adopted resolution 1560 (XV) in which it concluded 'that the dispute which has arisen between Ethiopia, Liberia and other Member States on the one hand, and the Union of South Africa on the other, relating to the interpretation and application of the Mandate, has not been and cannot be settled by negotiation'.[232] The applicants referred to the first part of this conclusion in support of their propositions that a 'dispute' existed and that it 'cannot be settled by negotiation'. In fact, it constitutes the whole of their argument on this vital condition of the jurisdiction of the court. [233]

In concluding this discussion relating to the 'arcane' link between the United Nations and the court, several observations may be made. The court has been integrated into an organization which in its day-to-day political activities accords only a marginal place to law, whereas its predecessor – the Permanent Court – was loosely linked to the league which showed a keen and fairly consistent commitment to law and the procedures of law. Allowing for the fact that the founders of the United Nations could not anticipate the political climate in which the organization would function and the pervasive East–West, North–South and decolonization tensions, it is still true, it is submitted, that while the integration between the Permanent Court and the league might have been useful but was in fact not necessary, the integration of the International Court into the United Nations was neither necessary nor useful. It was not necessary because the success of the Permanent Court showed that the court, even though only administratively connected with the league,[234] could function effectively, as indicated by the volume of contentious cases and, particularly, the number of advisory opinions which it handled. The experience of the Permanent Court proved conclusively that an organic connection with the parent organization was not necessary. The next question then would be, 'has institutional integration been beneficial to the International Court?'

To answer the above question, it is necessary to consider the influence of the proliferation of United Nations laws which have been introduced in recent times, primarily in the form of General Assembly resolutions and international treaties which are designed to address topical world issues. These laws obviously form an integral part of modern international political intercourse and are compelling in themselves.

In addition, the Security Council has been energetically considering recent issues of critical importance to world peace, which again brings the relevance of the United Nations triangle of the Security Council, General Assembly and the ICJ into focus. Under these circumstances, there is no room for doubt that the ICJ and United Nations law are inextricably linked, now more than ever before.

The effect of United Nations law on the ICJ

The Charter of the United Nations is the seminal document which creates international obligations of states. Articles 1 and 2 of the charter accomplish this task eminently, the former by defining, in general but precise terms, the purposes for which the United Nations was set up, and the latter by stipulating a list of principles in accordance with which the organization and its member states have to act in pursuit of the purposes. The charter has also set up the ICJ which manifestly is the judicial organ that is capable of inducing compliance by states with their legal obligations under the United Nations umbrella. The statute of the court, which is an integral component of the charter, invests the ICJ with inherent powers to decide on legal disputes between states. It is significant, however, that the statute does not give the court absolute power, but, rather, reposes a discretion on states to accept or reject the pronouncement of the court on the basis of inviolability of state sovereignty. The General Assembly and the Security Council have the right to seek advisory opinion of the court 'on any legal question' under article 96 of the charter. These advisory opinions could be used as effective means of inducing compliance by member states under the charter. Article 94 cements this process by giving the Security Council the competence to recommend or decide on measures to be taken to give effect to the judgment. This is an effective provision so far not used in practice, which successfully induces compliance, backed by a legal obligation flowing from the charter.[235] This notwithstanding, it is fair to say that neither the United Nations nor any of its specialized agencies were conceived as legislative bodies and the existence of legal provisions both in theory and in practice to coerce enforcement and inducement of compliance does not make the United Nations a world government. It is essentially an intergovernmental organization and therefore United Nations law remains the law of nations and should be considered as such by the ICJ.

Early statements by the ICJ regarding its status

As early as 1950, the court addressed the issue of its status as a judicial organ of the UN in several pronouncements which indicated its perception of its role or roles in relation to the dual function conferred upon it, and also – in general terms – the limits which its judicial character, its statute and international law impose upon it when acting in either capacity. Accordingly, the court has referred to itself as an 'organ of the United Nations',[236] as the principal judicial organ,[237] as an organ of international law,[238] and as a court of law.[239] The first two descriptions can be related to the court's advisory and the latter two descriptions to the contentious function.

In the *Peace Treaties* (First Phase) case the court gave an indication of its conception of its role as an organ of the United Nations. In that case the position was taken by the court that its status was different from that of its predecessor which was only loosely connected with the League of Nations.[240] The court made five statements: first, it declared that 'the reply of the Court, itself an "organ of the United Nations" represents its participation in the activities of the Organization'; secondly, that the reply 'in principle, shall not be refused'; thirdly, that the reply 'is only of an advisory character: as such it has no binding force'; fourthly, 'it follows' said the court, 'that the State, whether a Member or not, cannot prevent the giving of an Advisory Opinion which the United Nations considers to be desirable in order to obtain enlightenment as to the course of action which it should take'; and fifthly, that while 'the consent of States, parties to a dispute, is the basis of the Court's jurisdiction in contentious cases', the situation 'is different in regard to advisory proceedings even where the request for an opinion relates to a legal question actually pending between States'.[241] In addition, the court, in the *Membership* case, declared that it could 'not' attribute a political character to a request which, framed in abstract terms, invites it to undertake an essentially judicial task, 'the interpretation of a treaty provision' and that it was 'not concerned with the motives which may have inspired this request'.[242]

The institutional link between the ICJ and the UN brings to bear certain basic principles which in turn establish a conceptual nexus between the two bodies. The court, a principal and a judicial organ, participates in the activities of the United Nations, that is, in its political and highly politicized activities. Thus its opinions serve as a stage in the action to be taken by the United Nations. For this reason no consent of the state or states concerned in the dispute or in the subject-matter of the request is necessary. In addition, the opinion has no binding effect and in this context, it has been suggested, no legal force, nor in principle should a request for an opinion be refused. The court has reiterated the last proposition several times,[243] but it should be noted that it underscores the positive aspect of the discretion vested in the court by article 65(1) of the statute, which merely says that the court 'may' give an advisory opinion. Furthermore, it will be noted that, as a consequence of the elimination of consent of the state or states concerned, such states may or may not – in the *Peace Treaties* case some of them did not – participate in the proceedings. The court does not seem to consider in such cases the principle *audiatur et altera pars* essential.

Fundamentally, and in almost every respect, the perception of the court differs from that of its predecessor. For instance, in the *Eastern Carelia* case, the Permanent Court, although it was also called upon to discharge two functions, conceived its role in unitary terms: 'the Court, being a Court of justice, cannot, even in giving advisory opinions, depart from the essential rules guiding their (*sic*) activity as a Court'.[244] This one-sided view was reflected in the assimilation of the procedure between the two functions which were inherited by the present court (articles 82 to 85 of the Rules of the Court) and in the assimilation of the legal effect of opinions and judgments. In the words of the Permanent Court: 'Answering the questions would be substantially equivalent to deciding the dispute between the parties.'[245]

The court has not been ambivalent in the area of its 'legal functions as a principal judicial organ' in that it has indicated that there are some limits imposed upon its cooperation with the United Nations. Thus the court may refuse to give an opinion if the question is not a legal one and even refuse to give an opinion if the question is a legal one if 'the circumstances of the case are of such a character as should lead it to decline to answer the request'.[246] On the other hand, the court also declared, presumably having in mind its dual role as a principal organ and as a judicial organ, that only 'compelling reasons' should lead it to refuse to comply with a request.[247] The court, as indicated above, is bound by its statute and international law as well as considerations of judicial propriety. However, it is interesting to note that the court has not yet been faced with a request with which for 'compelling reasons' it would have had to refuse to comply, but that in one contentious case, the *Cameroons* case, it decided to decline to render a judgment on grounds of judicial propriety.[248]

Individual members of the court also stressed the new role of the court and its limitations. To give some examples: Judge Azevedo considered that the court 'has been *raised* to the status of a principal organ and thus more clearly geared to the mechanism of the United Nations Organization' and that it 'must do its utmost to co-operate with the other organs with a view to attaining the aims and principles that have been set forth'. On the other hand, he emphasized that there are 'certain limits which a judicial court may not overstep, even in the exercise of an advisory function assigned to it as a *subsidiary* activity'. He regarded absence of consent as one of those limits.[249]

Judge Winiarski was of the opinion that, while the court 'has no doubt the duty to give the opinions which are requested of it, for this is one of the two purposes for which it has been constituted ... there may be important legal grounds for not giving an opinion'.[250] In his view 'the Court has its own responsibility which cannot disappear behind that of the Assembly'.[251]

A seemingly inconsequential observation of Judge *ad hoc* Dr Ecer in the *Corfu Channel* case, which contended that the task of the court 'as the judicial instrument of the United Nations' was:

> to help to strengthen the cohesion of the international community. The instrument of cohesion of the international community is the United Nations Charter. It is true international law, with its source in the new requirements of international life and the juridical conscience of its peoples. The authority of the Judgment and that of the Court as judicial organ of the United Nations would be strengthened by a reference to the provisions of the Charter.[252]

This observation is significant, in that it draws a nexus between the charter and the court itself, bringing to bear the inextricable link between the UN and the ICJ.

One of the significant observations as to the status of the court emerged in the South West African cases when Ernest A. Gross, agent of the applicants, observed:

> Such an approval [to regard the international consensus[253] as a general principle of law recognized by civilized nations everywhere in the world] would view the interpretation of the subdivisions of Article 38 in light of the needs of the developing international legal order, giving to Article 38 a dynamic content, and thereby giving full scope to the fact that the Statute of the Court is an integral part of the Charter ... and is itself capable of, and entitled to, the same flexible principles of interpretation as have been applied to the remaining provisions of the Charter itself. This of course applies with even greater force to the Mandate instrument and international régime. The Statute of the Court, as an integral portion of the Charter, underscores the point that this Court itself is formally constituted as an international component of the organized community, thereby making it highly appropriate to give effect to the law-creating processes active in other segments of this same international community, of which the Court is the high judicial tribunal.[254]

The doctrine tends to agree with the perception of the role of the court as developed in the *Peace Treaties* case and to stress, on the one hand, its duty to take part in the political activities of the political organs of the United Nations and, on the other, as the court has done, to emphasize that this duty is not unlimited and that the court must preserve its character as a court. Lauterpacht expressed the view that 'the tendency to caution in matters of jurisdiction is – and ought to be – mitigated in the case of advisory opinions by the specific character of that function of the Court, namely that it is essentially advisory in nature. In addition, in relation to the international Court of Justice – as distinguished from the Permanent Court of International Justice – there is the further consideration that the Court is expressly described as the judicial organ of the United Nations and that its resulting obligations and powers must ... be deemed to modify to some extent the previous position on the subject'.[255] De Visscher is of the opinion that, while the court as the principal judicial organ should in principle reply to every request for an opinion, it should decline to do so if it were in the guise of an opinion to decide the merits of a dispute without the consent of the states concerned.[256] In Hudson's view, the court, being 'a part of the General Assembly ... would seem to be bound to pay attention to the course of the United Nations'.[257] In strongest language, Rosenne expressed the view that, 'in its capacity of a principal organ of the United Nations ... subject to overriding considerations of law (including judicial propriety), the Court must co-operate in the attainment of the aims of the Organization and to strive to give effect to the decisions of the Principal organs, and not to achieve results which would render them nugatory'.[258] Adverting to the sources of decision which the court should apply, Rosenne on the one hand contends that the court must not reach its decisions 'on opportunistic grounds or those of expediency' but, on the other hand, this does not mean that 'the members of the International Court, as the judges of any domestic court, are expected to remain indifferent to prevailing trends and requirements of the society which has charged them with judicial functions'. Nevertheless, 'the principal objective of the political function of adjudication, and hence of the Court as an institution for that purpose, is to meet the desire for completely non-political treatment of a matter, and its solution on the basis of law'.[259]

These observations merely reflect the general parameters within which general judicial activities are carried out and should not be considered as conclusive guidelines in determining the mandatory factors of the ICJ in carrying out its judicial functions.

The effect of Security Council decisions on the International Court of Justice: the Lockerbie example

On 20 July 1992, the Libyan Arab Jamahiriya submitted a working paper[260] to the 29th Session of the ICAO[261] Assembly under Agenda Item 13 on aviation security. The paper quotes the preamble to the Chicago Convention which claims *inter alia* that 'the development of international civil aviation can greatly help to create and preserve friendship and understanding among the nations and peoples of the world'. Alleging that political aspects and considerations of international relations have eroded the role played by international law, Libya invited the Assembly

a to reaffirm the role and importance of civil aviation in creating and preserving friendship and understanding among the nations and peoples of the world;
b to affirm its adherence to the legal mechanism that has been established by the international civil aviation community to handle civil aviation matters, considering that such mechanism solely is qualified to deal with such issues, thus ensuring the progress of civil aviation and the protection of its further development;
c to reaffirm the dignity of civil aviation and the need to dissociate it from political considerations, and to keep the legal and political matters related thereto away from such considerations, so that such matters may be dealt with by the international and regional civil aviation organizations.

The main allegation of Libya was against the alleged interference of politics in the administration of justice and the adjudication of disputes in international civil aviation. This case is therefore a good example through which to examine the status of international law and determine the role played by the United Nations (with its many limbs such as the International Court of Justice and the Security Council) as the principal collective body of states in the maintaining of peace.

There are many observations in the opinions of the judges of the International Court of Justice in the *Lockerbie* case[262] that shed light on this study. Before examining the various judicial opinions and the views of scholars that support them, it would be appropriate to identify the two issues that were highlighted in the adjudication that proved to be relevant in the determination of international law:

a whether the International Court of Justice, the principal function of which is to dispense justice, is constrained in the examining of legal issues if such had earlier been examined by the Security Council;
b whether international law is *jus cogens* or compulsory law in practicality as against being *jus dispositivum* or law, the adherence to which has been left to the moral discretion of states.

The United States, in its submission to the International Court of Justice in the *Lockerbie* case, contended that the Security Council was actively seised of the situation which was the subject of the application of Libya and that therefore the court should not indicate provisional measures as requested.[263] Judge Oda, Acting President of the Court, observing that Libya instituted proceedings against the United States in respect of the interpretation and application of the Montreal Convention of 1972, which provides for punitive measures against crimes related to civil aviation, noted that it was a general principle of international law that no state could be compelled to extradite its nationals and that the state concerned held the prerogative of trying the accused of a crime in its own territory. Judge Oda seems to recognize two principles in his opinion: (1) while any state can request extradition, no state can coerce extradition of nationals of another state; (2) whether or not a state can compel extradition is a matter for resolution by the general principles of international law and not necessarily those stipulated in the Montreal Convention.

It appears that the question in Judge Oda's mind was therefore whether the Security Council, by its resolution 748 (1992) which required Libya to extradite its nationals either to the United States or to the United Kingdom, had the authority to override an established principle of international law. The answer to this question was, in Judge Oda's view, in the affirmative, when he opined:

> I do not deny that under the positive law of the United Nations Charter a resolution of the Security Council may have binding force, irrespective of the question whether it is consonant with international law derived from other sources. There is certainly nothing to oblige the Security Council, acting within its terms of reference, to carry out a full evaluation of the possibly relevant rules and circumstances before proceeding to the decisions it deems necessary. The Council appears, in fact, to have been acting within its competence when it discerned a threat against international peace and security in Libya's refusal to deliver up the two Libyan accused. Since, as I understand the matter, a decision of the Security Council, properly taken in the exercise of its competence, cannot be summarily reopened and since it is apparent that resolution 748 (1992) embodies such a decision, the Court has at present no choice but to acknowledge the pre-eminence of that resolution.[264]

Judge Oda was emphatic that the Security Council resolution had overriding effect over any principle of international law. He observed, however, that, if the court appeared to have *prima facie* jurisdiction over a legal issue that was the subject of its consideration, the court was not precluded from indicating provisional measures applied for, merely because of the absolute pre-emptive powers of the Security Council Resolution. The learned judge concluded that, in this case, the application of the Libyan government would have been rejected by the court in any case, as the application was based on the Montreal Convention and not on the general customary international law principle *aut didere aut judicare*, which calls for the extradition of an offender to an appropriate jurisdiction if a state concerned cannot or refuses to judge him. Judge Oda was also unequivocal in his view that the Security Council Resolution would prevail over any established rule of international law.

Judge Ne, on the other hand, in his opinion, observed that the Security Council and the International Court of Justice could simultaneously exercise their respective functions without being excluded by each other. Citing the arbitration that came up before the ICJ in respect of the United States diplomatic consular staff in Teheran, Judge Ne quoted from that judgment:

it is for the Court, the principal judicial organ of the United Nations, to resolve any legal questions that may be in issue between parties to a dispute; and the resolution of such legal questions by the Court may be an important, and sometimes decisive, factor in promoting the peaceful settlement of the dispute.

This is indeed recognized by article 36 of the charter, paragraph 3 of which specifically provides that:

In making recommendations under this Article the Security Council should also take into consideration that legal disputes should as a general rule be referred by the parties to the International Court of Justice in accordance with the provisions of the Statute of the Court.[265]

Judge Ne also analysed article 24 of the United Nations Charter which provides: 'In order to ensure prompt and effective action by the United Nations, its members confer on the Security Council *primary* responsibility for the maintenance of international peace and security'. The learned judge reasoned that the charter did not confer exclusive responsibility upon the Security Council and observed that the Council has functions of a political nature assigned to it, whereas the court exercised purely judicial functions. According to Judge Ne, therefore, both organs could perform their separate but complementary functions with respect to the same events. On the above reasoning, Judge Ne concluded that, since the court held independent jurisdiction, it could interpret the applicable law, which in this case was article 14(1) of the Montreal Convention. The ICJ could therefore, according to Judge Ne, by no means be pre-empted by a Security Council resolution, in its exercise of jurisdiction and application of the principles of international law.

Judges Evensen, Tarassov, Guillaume and Aguila Mawdsley expressed their collective opinion that, prior to the adoption by the Security Council of resolution 748 (1992), the United States and the United Kingdom, although having the right to request extradition, could only take measures towards ensuring such extradition that were consistent with the principles of international law. With the resolution in force, however, the judges concluded that the court was precluded from indicating provisional measures against the United States.

Judge Lachs, who, although in a separate opinion, declared that the ICJ was bound to respect the binding decisions of the Security Council, seems to have recognized the coexistence of the two institutions, and the right of the court to render its opinion irrespective of the application of Security Council resolutions. Judge Lachs said:

The framers of the Charter, in providing for the existence of several main organs, did not effect a complete separation of powers, nor indeed is one to suppose that such was their aim. Although each organ has been allotted its own Chapter or Chapters, the functions of two of them, namely the General Assembly and the Security Council, also pervade other Chapters other than their own. Even the International Court of Justice receives, outside

> its own Chapter, a number of mentions which tend to confirm its role as the general guardian of legality within the system. In fact the Court is the Guardian of legality for the international community as a whole, both within and without the United Nations. One may therefore legitimately suppose that the intention of the founders was not to encourage a blinkered parallelism of functions but a fruitful interaction.

Two main organs of the United Nations have the delivery of binding decisions explicitly included in their powers under the charter: the Security Council and the International Court of Justice. There is no doubt that the court's task is 'to ensure respect for international law' (*ICJ Reports* (1949) 35). It is its principal guardian. Now, it has become clear that the dividing line between political and legal disputes is blurred, as law becomes ever more frequently an integral element of international controversies. The court, for reasons well known so frequently shunned in the past, is thus called upon to play an even greater role. Hence it is important for the purposes and principles of the United Nations that the two main organs with specific powers of binding decision act in harmony – though not, of course, in concert – and that each should perform its functions with respect to a situation or dispute, different aspects of which appear on the agenda of each, without prejudicing the exercise of the other's powers. In the present case the court was faced by a new situation which allowed no room for further analysis or the indication of effective interim measures. The order made should not, therefore, be seen as an abdication of the court's powers; it is rather a reflection of the system within which the court is called upon to render justice.[266]

Judge Shahabuddeen, recognizing that there is no superior authority to that of the Security Council, added in his opinion that treaty obligations can be overridden by a decision of the Security Council's sanctions. Addressing the critical question whether a decision of the Security Council may override the legal rights of states, Judge Shahabuddeen did not attempt an answer, but merely concluded that such a decision may stand in the way of the legal rights of a state or its subjects being judicially scrutinized. Judge Bedjaoui, in his opinion, added to the opinion of Judge Shahabuddeen, saying that, as a rule, the International Court of Justice does not exercise appellate jurisdiction over the Security Council.[267] Judge Bedjaoui, however, strongly dissented from the views of his colleagues which recognized that a Security Council resolution completely pre-empted the jurisdiction of the International Court of Justice and effectively precluded the latter from performing its judicial functions. The learned judge stringently maintained that there were two aspects to the problem between Libya and the United States on this issue – political and judicial. In his view, although it was not possible for the court to override the Security Council resolution, the court was by no means precluded from declaring provisional measures, as applied for by Libya, even if such a declaration by the court was rendered destitute of effect by the Security Council resolution.[268]

Judge Weeramantry, concurring with Judge Bedjaoui, conceded that, although article 25 of the United Nations Charter required member states of the United

Nations to accept and carry out decisions of the Security Council, the court was not deprived of its jurisdiction in issuing provisional measures as applied for by Libya. Adding that the International Court of Justice and the Security Council were created by the same charter to fulfil the common purposes and principles of the United Nations, Judge Weeramantry concluded that the two agencies are complementary to each other, each performing a special role assigned to it. The court, however, unlike most courts that were vested with domestic jurisdictions, was not enabled to sit in review of the executive (which in this context was the Security Council).

The dichotomy arose, in Judge Weeramantry's mind, when the principal judicial organ of the United Nations was restrained by decisions of its executive arm when deciding, according to the principles of international law, disputes that are submitted to it. The conclusions reached by Judge Weeramantry were based on the Kelsenian observation that the Security Council and the General Assembly were only quasi-judicial organs of the United Nations and that the Security Council was by no means a judicial organ since its members were not independent;[269] and the court ought to *collaborate* with the Security Council if the circumstances so require.[270] Judge Weeramantry therefore emphasized that the court must at all times preserve its independence, particularly in view of the fact that article 24(2) of the charter provides that the Security Council shall act in accordance with the purposes and principles of the United Nations, which are set out in article 1(1) of the charter as being those aims to settle international disputes and situations that might lead to breaches of the peace, according to the principles of justice and international law. The conclusion of the opinion of Judge Weeramantry is particularly relevant:

> A great judge once observed that the laws are not silent amidst the clash of arms. In our age we need also to assert that the laws are not powerless to prevent the clash of arms. The entire law of the United Nations has been built up around the notion of peace and the prevention of conflict. The Court, in an appropriate case, where possible conflict threatens rights that are being litigated before it, is not powerless to issue provisional measures conserving those rights by restraining an escalation of the dispute and the possible resort to force. That would be entirely within its mandate and in total conformity with the Purposes and Principles of the United Nations and international law. Particularly, when situations are tense, with danger signals flashing all around, it seems that this Court should make a positive response with such measures as are within its jurisdiction. If the conservation of rights which are *sub judice* comes within the jurisdiction of the Court, as I have no doubt it does, an order restraining damage to those rights through conflict must also lie within that province. If international law is to grow and serve the cause of peace as it is meant to do, the Court cannot avoid the responsibility in an appropriate case.
>
> I would indicate provisional measures *proprio motu* against both parties preventing such aggravation or extension of the dispute as might result in the use of force by either or both parties. Such measures do not conflict with any decision the Security Council has

made under Chapter VII, nor with any obligation arising under Article 25, nor with the principle underlying Article 103. The way towards a peaceful resolution of the dispute may thus be preserved before the parties find themselves on paths from which there may be no return. This action is based on Article 41 of the Statute of the Court and Articles 73, 74 and 75 of the Rules of Court.

Scholastic views

The status of the International Court of Justice as an organ of the United Nations that dispenses justice and hence has full capacity to examine and determine legal issues stands clear in the minds of legal scholars. Hans Kelsen, analysing article 92 of the United Nations Charter which provides that the International Court of Justice shall be the principal judicial organ of the United Nations, observes:

> if the term judicial organ in Article 92 means 'tribunal' the International Court of Justice is not only the 'principal' but also the only judicial organ of the Organization, at least, the only tribunal established directly by the Charter as an organ of the United Nations.[271]

The word 'tribunal' generally means a 'place of judgment' or decision and specifically means a court of justice[272] when it exercises judicial powers. Therefore Kelsen's analysis admits of no other conclusion than that the ICJ is the only judicial organ of the United Nations as, in Kelsen's words, 'the Security Council is not a judicial organ because its members are not independent'.[273]

Kelsen's claim is further buttressed by the provisions of the United Nations Charter themselves. According to article 36(1) of the charter, the ICJ has jurisdiction to hear all cases referred to it by the states parties, and according to article 36(2), that jurisdiction extends to determining questions of international law and interpretation of treaties. The disconcerting dichotomy is that, while article 25 of the charter obligates member states to adhere to or abide by decisions of the Security Council, article 36 grants the court jurisdiction to hear and decide issues *inter alia* on questions of international law or interpretation of treaties and their nature and reparation to be made in cases of breaches of the peace. In addition, article 38 of the charter allows the court to apply, *inter alia*, international convention and international custom in the reaching of its decision. According to these principles, the court could have decided on the legal issues of the Libyan application by considering the customary rule of international law, *aut didere aut judicare*, and interpreted the Montreal Convention and delivered its opinion on the legal status of Libya and the United States. At least, by doing so, the ICJ could have fulfilled its role as the primary judicial body of the United Nations, irrespective of whether, under article 25 of the charter, Security Council resolutions were mandatory. What is expected of the ICJ by the charter includes the performance of its judicial role of interpreting the law irrespective of adherence to its findings by member states. In this perspective, the ICJ is truly complementary to the Security Council and need not necessarily give way to Security Council resolutions without making its observations known.

The eleven to five majority decision in the Libyan application which was based almost entirely on article 25 of the charter, and its peremptory requirement that state should follow the decisions of the Security Council and article 103 which pre-empted treaty provisions from creating obligations on member states, has therefore made the ICJ seemingly disregard its role as the primary, if not the sole, judicial body of the United Nations which was empowered to consider questions of law by the charter.

The above facts do not incontrovertibly suggest that the ICJ is unduly constrained by the United Nations Security Council. Nor does it by any means suggest that the ICJ is required by the United Nations to deliver judgments in favour of Security Council resolutions. To the writer's best knowledge and recollection, there have been no overt or covert attempts by the Security Council to exert pressure on the court either collectively or through national interests. Similarly, there has been no recorded instance of the ICJ paying lip service to the interests of international organizations. The court has always acted independently, and without any influence from states parties or the Security Council, within the parameters of its statute and the charter of the United Nations. The difficulty seems to lie in the inescapable and indisputable inviolability of the Security Council (which, after all, is a group of sovereign states) and the position of the court as a creature of the United Nations. In such a circumstance, the traditional concept of independence of the judiciary cannot, and indeed should not, be exercised blindly to the exclusion of the rights of the international organization which has overall power to consider international issues. The ICJ, however, would not, and should not, be fettered in its pronouncements of legal principles which may be applicable to individual cases, within the parameters established in its statute.

Problems faced by international law

The next question to be determined and answered is whether international law now permits the intervention of the United Nations in general and the Security Council in particular in adopting resolutions which disregard customary principles of international law such as those relating to extradition and state sovereignty.

Traditionally, under English common law, the Crown could not surrender an alleged criminal even if the Crown wished to do so, unless the surrender was authorized by legislation.[274] The international law principle *aut didere aut judicare* emanated from this custom. Sovereignty of a state is also a fundamental principle of international law denoting the physical and social manifestation of the primary type of international legal person – the state – whose independence from the outside world extends to self-government, self-legislation and the governance of its subjects.[275] The purpose of the United Nations, as discussed above, is to maintain international peace and security in conformity with the principles of international law,[276] based on the principle of the sovereign equality of all its members.[277] If, then, article 24(2) of the charter obligates the Security Council to act according to the above purpose of the United Nations, why would it disregard the inherent customary principle of international law relating to state sovereignty and extradition and order Libya to extradite its nationals to the United States? The answer lies in the place occupied by international law in the international community.

At the cornerstone of international law lies the concept of state sovereignty which Jean Bodin defined as the absolute and perpetual power within a state.[278] Sovereignty, according to Bodin, therefore is the highest power wielded over citizens of a state and was exercised by a state on its subjects and anyone else who was present in the state's territory at the time in question. This power also included a state's authority and power to make laws. Bodin, however, believed that sovereignty of a state was subject to divine laws (presumably, religious tenets) and laws of nature. He also believed that the sovereignty of a state was subservient to certain human laws common to all nations.[279] The idea that a law of nations, common to all mankind, was at least theoretically applicable to all sovereign states was thus conceived.

The International Court of Justice in 1970 judicially recognized this principle in the *Barcelona Traction* case when it recognized that international law places certain obligations upon states, *erga omnes*; that is, obligations owed to the international community as a whole. The court opined: 'such obligations derive, for example, in contemporary international law from the outlawing of acts of aggression, and of genocide, as also from the principles and rules concerning the basic rights of the human person, including protection from slavery and racial discrimination'.[280]

International law anchors its validity on two elements: the sources of international law and the general principles of law applicable to treaties.[281] The sources of international law are reflected in article 38 of the Statute of the International Court of Justice which provides that, when the court exercises its jurisdiction to adjudicate upon disputes according to the principles of international law, the court shall apply:

a international conventions, whether general or particular, establishing rules expressly recognized by the contracting states;
b international custom, as evidence of a general practice accepted by law;
c the general principles of law recognized by civilized nations; and
d subject to the provisions of article 59,[282] judicial decisions and teachings of the most highly qualified publicists of the various nations, as subsidiary means for the determination of rules of law.

There are certain fundamental inconsistencies that are identifiable with the sources of international law when they are applied practically. Firstly, the basic techniques that are applied to any system of law in order to establish its compelling and binding nature tend to be left confused in the realm of international law. These techniques are (1) *lex superior derogat inferiori*: rules derived from one source prevail over rules derived from another, (2) *lex posterior derogat priori*: later rules prevail over earlier ones, and (3) *lex specialis derogat generali*: a particular or special rule prevails over a general rule. The problem with the application of these techniques to international law is that sources such as international custom and the general principles of international law as recognized by civilized nations cannot be determined in a chronological sense to accord with the above, since custom and the acceptance of legal principles as universal law take time and hence would be indeterminable as applicable law at a given time.[283]

The next problem to be considered is the application by the ICJ of the 'general principles of law recognized by civilized nations' as provided for in article 38(*c*) of the statute of the International Court. Are the general principles of law 'recognized' by the civilized nations the same as those that are developed and codified as principles of international law, initiated by the United Nations General Assembly by the United Nations Charter? The General Assembly does not have full and universal legislative powers,[284] and any codification of the principles of international law that emanates from being initiated by the United Nations General Assembly would only be persuasive. In this environment, it would remain increasingly difficult for the ICJ to determine as to what laws are 'recognized' by civilized nations as the general principles of law.[285]

Over and above the customary and other principles of international law which may be considered as the 'recognized' principles of international law, there is also the *jus cogens* or 'compelling law' which takes precedence in the realm of international law.[286] Article 53 of the Vienna Convention on the Law of Treaties, which was adopted on 23 May 1969 (hereafter referred to as the Vienna Convention)[287] provides that treaties conflicting with a peremptory norm of general international law (*jus cogens*) would be void. The article states:

> A treaty is void, if, at the time of its conclusion, it conflicts with a peremptory norm of general international law. For the purpose of the present Convention, a peremptory norm of general international law is a norm accepted and recognized by the international community of States as a whole as a norm from which no derogation is permitted and which can be modified only by a subsequent norm of general international law having the same character.

Article 64 of the Vienna Convention runs as follows: 'If a new peremptory norm of international law emerges, any existing treaty which is in conflict with that norm becomes void and terminates.' The *jus cogens* therefore admits of no derogation by the will of the contracting parties whether in the drafting of the treaty provisions or in interpretation thereof. It is also generally accepted that the *jus cogens* principle as enunciated in the Vienna Convention and accepted as a general principle of international law applies only to treaties and not to unilateral acts by states such as those that may commonly be seen in instances of extradition and violation of security of one state by another.[288] This would then imply that a peremptory norm of international law or the *jus cogens*, if violated by the act of a state, does not stand void *ab initio* at international law but, rather, requires individual action by states so that the *status quo ante* is restored. In such instances, logically, the ICJ would, when adjudicating upon breaches of international law and consequent action by states, treat the *jus cogens* as a principle of international law under article 36(1) of the United Nations Charter. This would, in turn, render the *jus cogens* destitute of its compelling effect on the conduct of nations and relegate it to the same level as any other norm of international law when a unilateral action of a state is adjudicated upon.

A peremptory norm of international law is presumed to be based on morality. Therefore *jus cogens* would essentially have its origins in moral tenets, such as the right of a state to its security and self-determination, *inter alia*. There are also, in close juxtaposition to these moral principles, certain compelling concepts of customary international law such as state sovereignty which in turn are sufficiently peremptory to be considered a form of *jus cogens*. Where, then, is one to draw the line between *jus cogens* and customary international law? As one legal commentator observes:

> *Jus cogens* is something of a *contradictio in terminis* as far as international law is concerned. For how can *jus cogens*, as a concept introducing morals into international law, be reconciled with the age-old basis of international law, called sovereignty? It can be argued that the principle of sovereignty, which by definition has to be an absolute one in the sense of being 'in principle not being accountable in law to any other authority', itself is a rule of *jus cogens* in its purest form; thus, in a way, it is a problem that bites itself in its tail.[289]

To make matters worse, the Vienna Convention in its article 53 stipulates that a peremptory norm of general international law (*jus cogens*) is a norm accepted and recognized by the international community of states as a norm from which no derogation is permitted and which can be modified only by a subsequent norm of general international law having the same character. This could only mean that there are norms of international law that can be changed and, indeed, can be derogated from. Called *jus dispositivum*, these norms can be derogated from by mutual consent between states. In this sense, principles of state sovereignty may become *jus dispositivum*, although the very essence of international law, and indeed air law, is based on this premise of state sovereignty. Although therefore *jus cogens* has priority over *jus dispositivum*, it does not make sense, since the concept of state sovereignty which is the fundamental norm cannot be logically overridden by *jus cogens*, which arrives on the scene later.

It is time that a clearer view of the status of the ICJ be made known to the international community. This could be achieved by a well-thought-out research study by a collection of jurists such as the International Law Commission. The confusion that has been created by the various types of concepts permeating international law seriously affects the development of clear principles and functional parameters of international law and organization. These concepts should be reconciled though a more cogent system of international law, thereby giving new meaning to the legal protection of the international community and drawing a line between international organization and international justice.

NOTES

1 Treaty on Principles Governing the Activities of States in the Exploration and Use of Outer Space, Including the Moon and Other Celestial Bodies, opened for signature at Moscow, London and Washington on 27 January 1967, 610 UNTS 205.
2 Ibid., article V.
3 Ibid.
4 UNGA Resolution 1962 (XVIII) Declaration of Legal Principles Governing the Activities of States in the Exploration and Use of Outer Space.
5 Bin Cheng, *Studies in International Space Law*, Oxford: Clarendon Press, 1997, pp.259 and 460.
6 Ibid., 458.
7 Like the earlier cited treaty provision, this provision is derived from United Nations documentation and has been reproduced almost verbatim from paragraph 7 of the 1963 General Assembly Declaration appearing in Resolution 1962 (XVIII). The treaty provision extends the scope of application of the provision to conduct of astronauts both inside and outside the spacecraft.
8 Bin Cheng, *supra*, note 5 p.459.
9 Agreement Governing the Activities of States on the Moon and other Celestial Bodies, UN Doc A/RES/34/68 of 5 December 1979.
10 Professor Karl-Heinz Böckstiegel of Germany, Professor Vladen Vereschetin of the Russian Federation and Professor Stephen Gorove of the United States.
11 See *Journal of Space Law*, 18 (2), 1990, 209–20.
12 Hereafter referred to as the Tokyo Convention.
13 Tokyo Convention, ch.1, art. 1(2).
14 Ibid., ch. 1, art. 1(3).
15 Ibid., ch. 4, art. 11.
16 Convention for the Suppression of Unlawful Seizure of Aircraft, the Hague, 16 December 1970, hereafter referred to as the Hague Convention.
17 Ibid., art. 1(*a*).
18 Ibid., art. 1(*b*).
19 See S. Shubber, 'Aircraft Hijacking Under the Hague Convention 1970 – A New Regime?', *International and Comp. Law Quarterly*, 22, 1973, 692.
20 Hague Convention, art. 3, para. 1.
21 Hereafter referred to as the Montreal Convention.
22 Montreal Convention, art. 1.
23 Ibid.
24 Tokyo Convention, art. 3(3).

25 A.F. Lowenfeld, *Aviation Law, Cases and Materials*, New York: M. Bender, 1972, p.87.
26 Hague Convention, art. 2.
27 Ibid., arts 1(4), 3, 4 and 7.
28 Walter Schwenk, 'The Bonn Declaration in Hijacking', *Annals of Air and Space Law*, IV, 1979, 321.
29 Traditionally, the term 'high seas' encompasses all parts of the sea that are not included in the territorial sea or in the internal waters of a state. See Convention on the High Seas, 1958, art. 1. This Convention entered into force on 30 September 1962. It must also be noted that the Convention on the Law of the Sea of 1982 provides that Part VII (High Seas) apply to all parts of the sea that are not included in the exclusive economic zone, the territorial sea or internal waters of a state or in the archipelagic waters of an archipelagic state (see article 86). Brownlie suggests that this provision invites two conclusions: that the exclusive economic zone and designators thereof are optional on the part of a state and, to a large extent, the freedoms applicable to the high seas would also apply to designated zones of the seas such as contiguous and exclusive economic zones. See Ian Brownlie, *Principles of Public International Law*, 4th edn, Oxford: Clarendon Press, 1990, p.232. Therefore, it would not be incorrect to assume that the laws of the high seas are generally universally applicable to all portions of the seas beyond the territorial waters of a state traditionally designated by customary international law, and that, analogically, the principles of the laws of the high seas would apply to outer space and celestial bodies in the instance of the conduct of astronauts.
30 *ICJ Reports* (1951) 116.
31 Ibid., 133.
32 PCIJ, ser A, no. 10 (1927).
33 Ibid., at 70.
34 Brownlie, *supra*, note 29, p.434.
35 RIAA ii 615, at 641.
36 *ICJ Reports* (1949), 23
37 Ibid.
38 For a detailed discussion of these incidents, see 'International Space Law in the Making', *Forum for Air and Space* Law, eds Marietta Benko and Kai-Uwe Schrogl, Paris: Editions Frontières, 1993, pp.19–22.
39 Treaty Banning Nuclear Weapon Tests in the Atmosphere, in Outer Space and Over Water, signed at Moscow on 5 August 1963; UN Treaty Series, vol. 480, United Nations, 1965, 45.
40 Ibid., art. 1(*a*) and (*b*).
41 Ibid., art. 2.
42 Treaty on Principles Governing the Activities of States in the Exploration and Use of Outer Space, including the Moon and Other Celestial Bodies, opened for signature at Moscow, London and Washington, 27 January 1967, 610 UNTS 205.
43 Ibid., art. IX.
44 Ibid.
45 Agreement Governing the Activities of States on the Moon and other Celestial Bodies, signed on 5 December 1979, UN Doc A/RES/34/68 of 5 December 1979.
46 Ibid., art. 7.

47 The United Nations Conference on the Human Environment, adopted on 16 June 1972; see UN Doc A/CONF.48/14 and Corr. 1 reported in *Int. Legal Materials*, XI (6), November 1972, 1416.
48 Ibid., principle 21.
49 Manfred Lachs, *The Law of Outer Space: An Experience in Contemporary Law Making*, Leiden: Martinus Nijhoff, 1989, pp.6–7.
50 See Moon Treaty, *supra*, note 45, art. 1, para. 2.
51 Manfred Lachs, *supra*, note 49, pp.44–5.
52 Ibid., p.138.
53 UNGA 47/68, Principles Relevant to the Use of Nuclear Power Sources in Outer Space, UN Press Release GA/8470, 1 February 1993, 148. See also Marrietta Banko and Kai-Owe Schrogl, *supra*, note 38, 98–110.
54 21 *Int. L. M.* 876 (1992). See also United Nations, *The Global Partnership for Environment and Development: A Guide to Agenda 21*, New York: UN, 1992, pp.1–4.
55 Principle 2 of the Rio Declaration, reprinted in 21 *Int. L. M.* 876 (1992).
56 Ibid., principle 7, 877.
57 Ibid., principle 16.
58 Ibid., principle 17.
59 V. Nanda, 'International Environmental Law and Policy', *Perspectives in International Law*, N. Jasentuliyana, ed., Dordrecht: Kluwer, 1995, p.101.
60 V.S. Vereschetin, 'Next Steps in International Space Law', *Perspectives in International Law*, *supra*, note 44, p.477.
61 Nandasiri Jasentuliyana, 'Celebrating Fifty Years of the Chicago Convention Twenty-Five Years after the Moon Landing: Lessons for Space Law', *Annals of Air and Space Law*, XIX, (II), 1994, p.444.
62 Nandasiri Jasentuliyana, 'A Survey of Space Law as Developed by the United Nations', *supra*, note 60, p.378.
63 See Frederic L. Kirgis, 'Specialized Law Making Processes', *United Nations Legal Order*, vol. 1 (O. Schachter and C.C. Joyner, eds), Cambridge: Cambridge University Press, pp.121–35, for details of regulation by United Nations specialized agencies.
64 See *The New Encyclopaedia Britannica*, vol. 12, Micropaedia, 15th edn, Chicago: Encyclopaedia Britannica Inc 1990, p.129.
65 Kenneth Arnold and Roy Palmer, *The Coming of the Saucers*, New York: 1952, p.3.
66 J. Allen Hynek, *The UFO Experience*, Chicago: H. Regnery Co., 1972, p.12.
67 See UNGA Res 49/34 of 9 December 1994, Official Records of the General Assembly, 49th Session, p.91.
68 Ibid., para. 4(*c*).
69 Ibid., para. 38.
70 UNGA A/RES/50/27, 5 February 1996, Official Records of the General Assembly, 50th Session, 96–76447.
71 Ibid., para. 17(*a*)(iv), 17(*b*)(I).
72 Ibid., para. 17(*b*)(iii) and (vi).
73 Leo Gross, *Selected Essays on International Law and Organization*, New York: Transnational Publishers, 1992, p.51.
74 GA Res. 2625, UN GAOR, 26th Sess., Supp. No. 28, at 121, UN Doc. A/8028 (1971).
75 See R. Rosenstock, 'The Declaration of Principles of International Law Concerning Friendly Relations: A Survey', 65 *AJIL* 713, 714 (1971).

76 GA Res. 3314, UN GAOR, 29th Sess., Supp. No. 31, at 142, UN Doc. A/0631 (1975).
77 GA Res. 2131, UN GAOR, 20th Sess., Supp. No. 14, at 11, UN Doc. A/6014 (1966).
78 The United Kingdom, see UN GAOR, 20th Sess., First Comm., at 430–31, UN Doc. A/C.1/SR 1422 (20 December, 1965).
79 Declaration on the Inadmissibility of Intervention in the Domestic Affairs of States and the Protection of Their Independence and Sovereignty, *supra*, note 77, an.1.
80 Ibid., art. 2.
81 GA Res. 337A, UN GAOR, 5th Sess., Supp. No. 20, at 10, UN Doc. A/1775 (1951).
82 Certain Expenses of the United Nations, 1962 ICJ 151 (Advisory Opinion).
83 Advisory Opinion of the Continued Presence of South Africa in Namibia (South West Africa), 1971 ICJ 16.
84 See UN Charter, art. 97.
85 UN Charter, art. 98.
86 D. Hammarskjold, 'The International Civil Servant in Law and in Fact', United Nations Press Release SG/1035, at 17, quoted in Elarably, 'The Office of the Secretary General and the Maintenance of International Peace and Security', in *United Nations and the Maintenance of International Peace and Security* (1987), 177, 184–95.
87 L. M. Goodrich, E. Hambro and A. Simons, *Charter of the United Nations*, New York: Transnational Publishers, 1969, 46 (hereinafter Goodrich).
88 O. Schachter, 'The Right of States to Use Armed Force', 82 *Mich. L.R.* (1984), 1625.
89 Ibid. Also see O. Schachter, 'In Defense of International Rules on the Use of Force', 53 *U. Chi L Rev.* (1986), 113 (hereinafter Schachter, 'Use of Force'); and O. Schachter, 'Self-Defense and the Rule of Law', 83 *AJIL* (1989), 259.
90 Schachter, 'Use of Force', *supra*, note 89, 1632.
91 As reported in Schachter, 'Use of Force', *supra*, note 89, 124–5.
92 See T. Franck, 'Who Killed Article 2(4)? On Changing Norms Governing the Use of Force by States', 64 *AJIL* (1970), 809; E. Rostow, 'The Legality of the International Use of Force by and from States', 10 *Yale J. Intl L.* (1985), 286.
93 A.V. Thomas and A.J. Thomas, Jr, *Non-Intervention* (1956), 209.
94 Military and Paramilitary Activities in and against Nicaragua (*Nicar.* v. *US)* 1986 *ICJ Rep.* 14, 98 (Judgment of 27 June).
95 Ibid., 98.
96 See, for example, D. Noncic, *The Problem of Sovereignty in the Charter and in the Practice of the United Nations*, New York: UN 1970, 72, 76–7 (guarantees of territorial integrity in art. 2(4) were not intended to limit the article's broad prohibition of self-help measures), cited in Schachter, 'Use of Force', *supra*, note 89, 125–6, n.56.
97 See Address by Ambassador Jeanne Kirkpatrick, 'Law and Reciprocity', reprinted in *Proc. of the 78th Ann. Meeting of the Am. Soc'y of Int'l L*, (1984), 59, 67.
98 See Schachter, 'Use of Force', *supra*, note 89, 129–30.
99 (1987) 21 C.P.C. (2d) 38 (Ont. H.C.).
100 Ibid., at 43.
101 [1989] 3 All. E.R. 373.
102 Ibid., at 383–4.
103 510 F.2d. 894 (10th Cir. 1975).
104 See *DCF Systems Ltd.* v. *Gelman* (1978) 41 C.P.R. (2d) 145 (Ont. H.C.); *Gemologists International Inc.* v. *GemScan International Inc.* (1986) 7 C.I.P.R. 225 (Ont. H.C.);

Geac Canada Ltd. v. *Prologic Computer Corp* B.C.S.C. 6. A.C.W.S. (3d) 320, 1987; *Godin* v. *Gary Abraham Consultants Inc* (1986) 2. Q.A.C. 317 (Que. C.A.); *Marque d'Or Inc* v. *Clayman* (1988) 21 C.P.R. (3d) 490 (Que. S.C.); and *Software Solutions Associates* v. *Depou* (1989) 25 C.P.R. (3d) (N.B. Q.B.).

105 See *Computer Workshops Ltd.* v. *Banner Capitol Market Brokers Ltd.* (1988) 64 O.R. (2d) 266 (Ont. H.C.).

106 [1988] 3All. E.R. 545 (H.L.).

107 [1916] 1. A.C. 688 (H.L.).

108 *Quantum Management Services Ltd.* v. *Hann* (1989) 25 C.P.R. (3d) 218 (Ont. H.L.).

109 952 F.2d 769.

110 490 U.S. 730 (1989).

111 Berne Convention for the Protection of Literary and Artistic Works, 24 July 1971. See United Nations Treaty Series, vol. 828, New York, 1977, no. 11850.

112 For the details, see George Bittlingmayer, 'Property Rights, Progress and the Aircraft Patent Agreement', *The Journal of Law and Economics*, XXXI (1), April 1988, 227–48.

113 101 U.S. 99 (1879).

114 The *Baker* rule has been incorporated in section 102(*b*) of the US Copyright Act of 1976, 17 U.S.C. which states: 'In no case does copyright protection for an original work of authorship extend to any idea, procedure, process, system, method of operation, concept, principle or discovery, regardless of the form in which it is described, explained, illustrated or embodied in such work.'

115 Although in *Motown Record Corp* v. *George A. Hormel & Co.* 657 F Supp. 1236 (D.C. Cal 1987) the Court held that a song or musical composition could be considered under copyright since the original music sheet of that composition would have been under copyright, this may not be logical reasoning, since a song would be duplicated only if the same musical notes were prepared under the same musical arrangement as in the original composition.

116 648 F. Supp 1127 (N.D. Cal. 1986).

117 659 F. Supp 449 (N.D. Ga. 1987).

118 821 F. Supp 616 (N.D. Cal. 1993).

119 Ibid., at 628.

120 [1996] A.C. 543 (H.L.).

121 Ibid., at 548.

122 Ibid., at 556.

123 See Ruwantissa I.R. Abeyratne, 'Infringement of Copyright in Airline Product Distribution Over the Internet', *The Journal of World Intellectual Property*, 1(1), January 1998, 139–52.

124 505 U.S. 763 (1992). See also *Laureyssens* v. *Idea Group, Inc.* 964 F.2d 131 (1992). In the case of *George Basch Co., Inc.* v. *Blue Coral Inc.* 968 F.2d 1532 (1992), the United States Court of Appeal in the Second Circuit held that, in order to be awarded compensation, a plaintiff has a legal obligation to establish that the defendant engaged in wilful deception.

125 15 U.S.C. § 1121. The North American Free Trade Agreement (NAFTA) definition encompasses 'any sign or any combination of signs … including personal names, designs, letters, numerals, colours and figurative elements': NAFTA, 12 December 1992 (Ottawa: Supply and Services, 1993) at art. 1708(1). The case of *Pizza Pizza*

Ltd. v. *Canada (Registrar of Trade Marks)* [1989] 3 F.C. 379 (C.A.) established that even a phone number could be a trademark.

126 Case No. 93-1577, argued on 9 January 1995 and decided on 25 March 1995. See also *Cooper Industries* v. *Channellock, Inc.* 788 F. Supp 873 (1992). The Canadian case of *Smith, Kline & French Canada Ltd.* v. *Registrar of Trade Marks* (No. 2) [1987] 2 F.C. 633 (T.D.) is also a good analogy for a colour being established as a trademark. In this case the medical drug *Tagamet* was found to be identifiable by its pale green colour as its trademark.

127 *Inwood Laboratories, Inc.* v. *Ives Laboratories, Inc.* 456 U.S. 844, at 850.

128 See *Enterprise Rent-A-Car Co.* v. *Singer* (1996), 66 C.P.R. (3d) 453 (F.C.T.D.). See also *Consumers Distributing Company Limited* v. *Seiko Time Canada Ltd.* [1984] 1 S.C.R. 583 [*Seiko*], where adequate notice posted to buyers at the point of sale regarding the differences in services offered with a product precluded a finding of passing-off; and George S. Takach, 'Passing-Off, Trade Mark Protection and Parallel Imports After *Consumers Distributing* v. *Seiko*' (1985) 63 *Can. Bar Rev.* 645. The *Seiko* case may be of important precedent value to certain suppliers in the computer industry.

129 22. U.S. P.Q. 2d 1306 (TTAB 1992).

130 (1985) S.C.P.R. (3d) 173.

131 *Exxon Corp.* v. *Exxon Insurance Consultants International Limited* (1981) 119 (C.A.).

132 For registration laws pertaining to spacecraft, see Convention on Registration of Objects Launched into Outer Space, adopted by the General Assembly of the United Nations, at New York on 12 November 1974, 1023 UNTS 15. If one takes the analogy of airlines, the Convention on International Civil Aviation provides that an aircraft shall bear the nationality of the state in which it is registered. See Convention on International Civil Aviation, signed on 7 December 1944, ICAO Doc 7300/7, 7th edn, 1997, art. 17. Most bilateral air services agreements signed between states for the operation of air services between their territories still contain a provision that substantial ownership and effective control must vest in the state, if such are to be considered that state's national airline for the purpose.

133 The WTO comprises a Ministerial Conference composed of representatives of all member countries and meets at least once every two years. The Ministerial Conference carries out the functions of the WTO and takes necessary action to this effect. There is also, within the WTO structure, a General Council composed of representatives of all member countries, and this council meets as deemed appropriate. As necessary, the General Council conducts the functions of the Ministerial Conference when the latter does not meet. It also carries out its functions as assigned by the Agreement. Furthermore, the General Council also discharges the responsibilities of the Dispute Settlement Body (DSB) under the Dispute Settlement Understanding (DSU). The Dispute Settlement Body may have its own chairman and will establish such rules of procedure as it deems necessary for the fulfilment of those responsibilities. See Marrakesh Agreement, *infra*, note 134, art. IV 1, 2 and 3.

134 Marrakesh Declaration of 15 April 1994, para. 2. The Marrakesh Agreement came into being with the Marrakesh Declaration and is an integral part, therefore, of the Marrakesh Declaration. See *The Results of the Uruguay Round of Multilateral Trade Negotiations, The Legal Texts*, Geneva: GATT Secretariat, 1994, for the text of the Declaration.

135 Marrakesh Declaration, art. III.2. The Ministerial Conference also has the authority to take decisions on all matters under any multilateral trade agreements if so requested by a member, in accordance with the specific requirements for decision making in the Marrakesh Agreement and in the relevant multilateral trade agreement. See art. IV. 1. *Ibid*.

136 Ibid., art. III.3. Annex 2 to the Agreement will be discussed in some detail later in this chapter.

137 Annex 2, art. 23(*a*).

138 Annex 2, art. 23(*b*).

139 Ibid., art. 24.1.

140 See K.R. Symonds and B.H. Hill, *Law and Practice Under GATT* (1988); W.J. Davey, 'Dispute Settlement in GATT', 11, *Fordham Int. L.J.* 51 (1987); R.E. Hudec, *The GATT Legal System and World Trade Diplomacy* (1975), *Adjudication of International Trade Disputes* (1978) and 'GATT Dispute Settlement After Tokyo Round: An Unfinished Business', 13 *Cornell Int. L.J.* (1980), 145. See also J.C. Bliss, 'GATT Dispute Settlement Reform in the Uruguay Round: Problems and Prospects', *Stan. J. Int. L.* (1987), 31; E. McGovern, *International Trade Regulation: GATT, the United States and The European Community* (1986); and K. Dam, *The GATT: Law and International Economic Organization* (1970).

141 Marrakesh Declaration, *supra*, note 134, Appendix 1 to Annex 2.

142 Annex 2, art. 2.1.

143 Annex 2, art. 2.2.

144 Annex 2, art. 3.2.

145 Annex 2, art. 3.3.

146 Annex 2, art. 3.4.

147 Annex 2, art. 3.5.

148 Annex 2, art. 3.7.

149 Ibid.

150 Annex 2, art. 3.8.

151 Annex 2, art. 3.10.

152 Annex 2, art. 3.12.

153 Annex 2, art. 4.3.

154 Annex 2, art. 4.6.

155 Annex 2, art. 5.1.

156 Annex 2, art. 6.1.

157 Annex 2, art. 8.1.

158 Annex 2, art. 8.2.

159 Annex 2, art. 8.4.

160 Annex 2, art. 11.

161 Annex 2, art. 16.1.

162 Annex 2, art. 16.2.

163 Annex 2, art. 16.4.

164 Annex 2, art. 19.1.

165 Annex 2, art. 20.

166 Annex 2, art. 21.

167 Ibid.

168 See Article I, para. I of the WTO Dispute Settlement Understanding.

169 See TRIPS Agreement articles 1, 2, 3, 4, 5, 9, 10, 14, 15, 16, 22, 35 and 39.

170 For a detailed discussion of franchising in the airline business, see R.I.R. Abeyratne, 'Franchising in the Airline Industry, Some Implications at Common Law', *Air and Space Law*, XXII (6), December 1997, 284–90.

171 Charter of the United Nations and Statute of the International Court of Justice, Department of Public Information, United Nations, New York, DPI/511 – 40108 (3–90), 100M at 1.

172 Ibid., 3.

173 On 17 November 1989 the United Nations General Assembly adopted Resolution 44/23 which declared that the period 1990–99 be designated as the United Nations Decade of International Law. The main purposes of the decade have been identified *inter alia* as:

(a) the promotion of the acceptance of the principles of international law and respect therefor;
(b) the promotion of the means and methods for the peaceful settlement of disputes between states, including resort to the International Court of Justice with full respect therefor;
(c) the full encouragement of the progressive development of international law and its codification;
(d) the encouragement of the teaching, studying, dissemination and wider appreciation of international law.

The four tasks of the resolution have been predicated upon the fact that the purpose of the United Nations is to maintain peace and security. See 'Resolutions and Decisions Adopted by the General Assembly During its Forty Fourth Session', vol. 1, 19 September–29 December 1989, *General Assembly Official Records: Forty Fourth Session*, Supplement No. 49 (A/44/49), United Nations, New York, 1990, 31. For a detailed discussion on Resolution 44/23, see R.I.R. Abeyratne, 'The United Nations Decade of International Law', *International Journal of Politics, Culture and Society*, 5(3), New York: Human Sciences Press, 1992, pp.511–23.

174 *Halsbury's Laws of England*, 4th edn Reissue, vol. II (1), London: Butterworths, 1990, para. 1, p.16.

175 *D.P.P.* v. *Morgan* [1981] All E.R. 628, at 639.

176 *R.* v. *Kimber* [1983] 3 All E.R. 316 at 320.

177 [1987] 3 All E.R. 411 (CA).

178 Ibid., at 414. See also *R.* v. *Abraham* [1973] 3 All E.R. 694 at 696.

179 Ibid.

180 See *Halsbury's Laws of England*, *supra*, note 174, vol. II (1) paras 4–9.

181 C.K. Allen, *Legal Duties*, Oxford: The Clarendon Press, 1931, p.230; also *Kenny's Outlines of Criminal Law*, 18th edn, J.W. Cecil Turner, ed., Cambridge: Cambridge University Press, 1962, section 1. See also *Proprietary Articles Trade Association* v. *A.G. of Canada* [1931] A.C. 310 at 324, where it was held that the domain of criminal jurisprudence can only be ascertained by examining what acts at any particular period are declared by the state to be crimes. A general definition of a crime is that it is 'a violation or neglect of legal duty of so much public importance that the law, either common or statute, takes notice of and punishes it'. See John Wilder May, *The Law of Crimes*, Littleton, Colorado: Fred B. Rothman & Co., 1985, p.1. May goes on to say

that 'intent' to commit a crime should appear either expressly or by implication (ibid., 5). According to this definition and reasoning, the intent has to be unlawful.

182 See, generally, *Russell on Crime*, 12th edn J.W. Cecil Turner, ed., London: Sweet and Maxwell Limited, and Littleton, Colorado: Fred B. Rothman & Co., 1986, vol. 1, pp.24–36.

183 1980 2. S.C.R. 331.

184 See George S. Takach, *Computer Law*, Toronto: Irwing Law, 1998, p.158.

185 H. Lauterpact, *International Law and Human Rights*, Oxford: Oxford University Press, 1950, p.149.

186 Art. 33 of the UN Charter.

187 Cited in Oppenheim, *International Law*, 8th edn, vol. 1, Leiden: Sijthoff, 1950, p.609.

188 The Geneva Convention was opened for signature at Geneva on 16 November 1937. See Hudson, *International Legislation*, vol. VII at 862, UN Doc. A/C.6/418, Annex 1, at 1.

189 League of Nations, *Official Journal*, 1934, 1839.

190 Henry Reiff, *The United States and the Treaty Law of the Sea*, Minneapolis: University of Minnesota Press, 1959, p.86.

191 S.Z. Feller, 'Comment on Criminal Jurisdiction over Aircraft Hijacking', *Israel Law Review*, 7, 1972, 212.

192 Ibid.

193 INTERPOL had submitted to the Legal Committee of ICAO in 1977 that, out of recorded hijackings up to that year, the percentage of instances of hijackings which were motivated politically was 6.2 at a ratio of 64:4. See ICAO Doc 8877-LC/161 at 132.

194 S. Shubber, *Jurisdiction Over Crimes on Board Aircraft*, New York: Random, 1968, p.226.

195 'Aircraft Hijacking', *Harvard International Law Journal*, 12, 1971, 65.

196 *Jenner* v. *Sun Oil Co. Ltd.* (1952) 16 C.P.R. 87 (Ont. H.C.J.).

197 Ibid., at 98–9.

198 (1984) 49 O.R. (Ed) 58 (H.C.J.).

199 (1996) 30 O.R. (3d) 746 (Gen. Div.).

200 636 So. 2d. 1351 (Fla. App. 1994).

201 *IDS Life Insurance Co.* v. *SunAmerica, Inc.*, 958 F. Supp. 1258 (N.D. III. 1997), aff'd in part, vacated in part, 1998 WL 51350 (7th Cir.) (Westlaw).

202 Ibid., at 268.

203 1997 WL 97097 (S.D.N.Y.) (Westlaw).

204 Ibid., para. 1. For a similar result, see *Cybersell, Inc.* v. *Cybersell, Inc.*, 44 U.S.P.Q. 2d 1928 (9th Cir. 1997) and *Blackburn* v. *Walker Oriental Rug Galleries*, No. 97–5704 (E.D. Pa., 7 April 1998), reported in *Computer & Online Industry Litigation Reporter*, 21 April 1998 at 4.

205 *McDonough* v. *Fallon McElligott Inc.*, 40 U.S.P.Q. 2d 1826 (S.D. Cal. 1996).

206 Ibid., at 1828.

207 89 F. 3d. 1257 (6th Cir. 1996).

208 *Digital Equipment Corporation* v. *AltaVista Technology, Inc.* 960 F. Supp. 456 (D. Mass. 1997). See also *Cody* v. *Ward*, 954 F. Supp. 43 (D. Conn. 1997), where a court took jurisdiction based on telephone and e-mail communications that consummated a business relationship begun over *Prodigy's* 'Money talk' discussion forum for financial

matters. In partially justifying this decision, the court noted that the use of fax technology, and even live telephone conferences, can greatly reduce the burden of litigating out-of-state.

209 *Heroes, Inc*. v. *Heroes Foundation*, 958 F. Supp. 1 (D.D.C. 1996).

210 *Zippo Manufacturing Company* v. *Zippo Dot Com, Inc.*, 952 F. Supp. 1119 (W.D. Pa. 1997).

211 *Resuscitation Technologies, Inc*. v. *Continental Health Care Corp.*, 1997 WL 148567 (S.D. Ind.) (Westlaw). The court in this case was not concerned that the defendants had never visited the forum state in person and concluded at para. 5: 'Neither is the matter disposed of by the fact that no defendant ever set foot in Indiana. The "footfalls" were not physical, they were electronic. They were, nonetheless, footfalls. The level of Internet activity in this case was significant.' See also *EDIAS Software International, L.L.C*. v. *BASIS International Ltd.*, 947 F. Supp. 413 (D. Ariz. 1996). In this case the court summed up the essence of many of the Internet jurisdiction cases by stating at 420: 'BASIS [the defendant] should not be permitted to take advantage of modern technology through an Internet Web page and forum and simultaneously escape traditional notions of jurisdiction.' See also *Gary Scott International, Inc*. v. *Baroudi*, 981 F. Supp. 714 (D. Mass. 1997).

212 *Panavision International, L.P.* v. *Toeppen*, 938 F. Supp. 616 (CD- Cal. 1996); *supra*; *Maritz, Inc*. v. *CyberGold, Inc.*, 947 F. Supp. 1328 (E.D. Mo. 1996); *Inset Systems, Inc*. v. *Instruction Set, Inc.*, 937 F. Supp. 161 (D. Conn. 1996). In the latter case the court observed, at 165:

'In the present case, Instruction has directed its advertising activities via the Internet and its toll-free number toward not only the state of Connecticut, but to all States. The Internet as well as toll-free numbers are designed to communicate with people and their businesses in every state. Advertisement on the Internet can reach as many as 10,000 Internet users within Connecticut alone. Further, once posted on the Internet, unlike television and radio advertising, the advertisement is available continuously to any Internet user. ISI has, therefore, purposefully availed itself of the privilege of doing business within Connecticut.

213 *Plus System, Inc*. v. *New England Network, Inc.*, 804 F. Supp. 111 (D. Colo. 1992).

214 585 N.Y.S. 2d. 661 (Supp. 1992).

215 See L.C. Green, 'The Eichman Case', *M.L.R.*, 23, 1968, 507–9.

216 Such as the London International Assembly created in 1941 by Viscount Cecil of Chelwood under the auspices of the League of Nations Union; the International Commission for Penal Reconstruction and Development organized at Cambridge in 1941; and the United Nations War Crimes Commission set up in 1943.

217 See R.H. Jackson, *International Conference on Military Trials*, London: Maxwell, 1945 (U.S. Dept. of State Publication 3080).

218 See *Historical Survey of the Question of International Criminal Jurisdiction* (UN Doc. A/CN.4/7/Rev.1), pp.25 *et seq*.

219 Two draft statutes for courts were produced; see ibid., pp.30–46 and 120–47.

220 Ibid., pp.5, 6, 44–6.

221 R.H. Jackson, *supra*, note 217, p.ix.

222 G. Schwarzenberger, *International Law and Totalitarian Lawlessness*, London: Butterworths, 1943, p.76.

223 Article 1 of the statute provides that the court 'shall be constituted and function in accordance with the provisions of the present statute'. This is consistent with article 92 of the charter which provides that the ICJ shall function in accordance with the annexed statute.

224 See International Court of Justice, *Pleadings, Oral Arguments, Documents, South West African cases*, vol. 1, 1966.

225 See International Court of Justice, *Reports of Judgments, South West African Cases, Second Phase*, judgment, 18 July 1966 at 458.

226 Ibid., at 338.

227 Ibid.

228 Ibid., at 333.

229 Ibid., at 34.

230 Doc. A/PV. 1414, p.37.

231 Doc. A/PV. 1425, p.27. See also the statement of representatives of Czechoslovakia, ibid., pp.43–5 ('it is imperative to change its membership so that it reflects the legal and political realities of the present-day world'); Ireland, A/PV. 1427, p.17 ('I feel sure that all who supported the election of those judges who voted for the decision as men who would give wise, equitable and speedy decisions, must bitterly regret that their confidence was misplaced'); Iran, ibid., pp.53–5; Ivory Coast, A/PV. 1429, p.74; Tunisia, A/PV. 1431, p.12; Jamaica, ibid., p.23; Syria, ibid., p.52; Indonesia, A/PV. 1449, p.53; Guinea, A/PV. 1456, p.21 ('Immediately after the scandalous finding of the International Court of Justice, the Africans and their friends decided to make efforts to ensure that the Court would be a reflection of international realities as they exist today'). These views are generally reflected in Ernest B. Gross, 'The South West Africa Case': What Happened?', *Foreign Affairs*, 45, 1966, 48.

232 GAOR: 15th Session, Supp. No. 16 (A/4684), p.32.

233 Memorial submitted by Ethiopia, International Court of Justice, *Pleadings*, South West Africa, vol I, pp.89 and 93.

234 This did not prevent President Loder, at the inaugural meeting of the court, referring to it as 'one of the principal organs of the League' (quoted in Hudson, *The Permanent Court of International Justice, 1920–1942*, New York: UN, 1969, p.113). Hudson also quotes, ibid., p.111, from the letter of the Council to the Committee of Jurists that the court was 'one of the principal organs of the League'. Hudson himself shared these views and called the court 'the judicial organ of the League' (ibid.). A.P. Fachiri looked upon the court as 'an institution distinct from the League': *The Permanent Court of International Justice*, 2nd edn, 1932, p.330.

235 In April 1993, the Security Council adopted SC Resolution 819 in which it took note 'that the International Court of Justice in its order of 8 April, 1993 in the case concerning application of the Convention on the Prevention and Punishment of the Crime of Genocide (*Bosnia and Herzegovina* v. *Yugoslavia (Serbia and Montenegro)* unanimously indicated as a provisional measure that the Government of the Federal Republic of Yugoslavia (Serbia and Montenegro) should immediately, in pursuance of its undertaking in the Convention on the Prevention and Punishment of the Crime of Genocide of 9 December 1948, take all measures within its power to prevent the commission of the crime of genocide' and reaffirmed its condemnation 'of all violations of international humanitarian law, in particular the practice of "ethnic cleansing"' and reaffirmed 'that those who commit or order the commission of such acts shall be held

individually responsible in respect of such acts.' See SC Res. 819 (16 Apr. 1993). However, as article 94 is drafted in terms of a party to a case failing 'to perform the obligations incumbent upon it under a judgment rendered by the Court' and the court made an order for provisional measures only, SC Res. 819 is probably not a resolution under article 94.

236 *Peace Treaties* (First Phase) *ICJ Reports* (1950) 71.

237 *Admissions, ICJ Reports* (1948) 61; *Peace Treaties* (First Phase), *ICJ Reports* (1950) 71; *Nottebohm* (Jurisdiction), *ICJ Reports* (1953) 119; and *Expenses* cases, *ICJ Reports* (1952) 156.

238 *Corfu Channel Case, ICJ Reports* (1949) 35.

239 *South West Africa* (Second Phase), *ICJ Reports* (1966) 34, 36. In the *Cameroons* case, the court saw itself as a 'Court of justice' (*ICJ Reports* (1963) 29).

240 See G.G. Fitzmaurice, 'The Law and Procedure of the International Court of Justice', *BYIL*, 29, 1952, 45–6.

241 *ICJ Reports* (1950) 65.

242 *ICJ Reports* (1948).

243 See the cases: *Reservations, ICJ Reports* (1951) 19; ILO Administrative Tribunal *ICJ Reports* (1956) 86; and *Expenses, ICJ Reports* (1962) 155.

244 *Eastern Carelia* case, PCIJ, Series B, No. 5, p. 29, quoted by the ICJ in the *Expenses* case, *ICJ Reports* (1962) 155.

245 Ibid. See also separate opinion of Judge Azevedo, and the dissenting opinions of judges Winiarski, Zorocic and Krylov in the *Peace Treaties* (First Phase) case: *ICJ Reports* (1950) 80ff, 89ff, 101, 111.

246 *Expenses* case, *ICJ Reports* (1962) 155, and *Peace Treaties* (First Phase), ibid. (1950) 72.

247 ILO Administrative Tribunal, *ICJ Reports* (1956) 86, and *Expenses* case, ibid. (1962) 155.

248 *ICJ Reports* (1963) 29. The court said: 'There are inherent limitations on the exercise of the judicial function which the Court, as a Court of justice, can never ignore … The Court itself, and not the parties, must be the guardian of the Court's judicial integrity'. See Leo Gross, 'Limitations upon the Judicial Function', *AJIL*, 58, 1964, 415–31.

249 Separate opinion, *Peace Treaties* (First Phase), *ICJ Reports* (1950) 82; original emphasis. Judge Azevedo would not go further than to 'acknowledge the duty of reasonable co-operation with the other organs of the United Nations' (ibid., 88).

250 Dissenting opinion, ibid., at 92.

251 Ibid., at 97. Judge Krylov, in his dissenting opinion, also took exception to the view that the court, in its new capacity of principal judicial organ 'had a lesser degree of autonomy than the Permanent Court' (ibid., p.109).

252 *ICJ Reports* (1949) 130.

253 He was referring to the evidence presented in the Reply, at pp.274–91.

254 Oral Hearings, *South West Africa* cases, Verbatim Records, C.R. 65/35, p.28.

255 *The Development of International Law of the International Court*, New York: UN, 1958, p.109. But see p.250 for a statement of the limits having a legal character.

256 *Aspects récents*, p.41.

257 L.C. Green, 'South West Africa and the World Court', *International Journal*, 22 (Canadian Institute of International Affairs), 1966, 58. When two interpretations are possible the judges are exhorted to 'support the operative interpretation'.

258 *The Law and Practice of the International Court*, New York: UN, 1965, vol. I, p.70.
259 Ibid., pp.90–91. Elsewhere he suggests that the court is primarily concerned, equally, in advisory and contentious procedure, with the application of international law to disputes and not 'with the formulation of legal policy' (ibid., p.77).
260 A 29–WP/28, EX/6, 20 July 1992.
261 The International Civil Aviation Organization (ICAO) was created to promote the safe and orderly development of civil aviation in the world. A specialized agency of the United Nations, it sets international standards and regulations necessary for the safety, security, efficiency and regularity of air transport and serves as the medium for cooperation in all fields of civil aviation among its 185 contracting states.
262 On 3 March 1992, the Registry of the ICJ received an application by the Socialist Peoples' Libyan Arab Jamahiriya (hereafter referred to as Libya), instituting proceedings against the United States of America. The application referred to a dispute between Libya and the United States, which arose as a result of the destruction of PAN AM flight 103 in December 1988 over Lockerbie, Scotland. On 14 November 1991, a Grand Jury of the United States District Court for the District of Columbia, indicted two Libyan nationals, charging *inter alia* that they had caused a bomb to be placed on board PAN AM flight 103, which bomb had exploded causing the aeroplane to crash. Consequently, the British and American governments declared that Libya must surrender for trial all three charged with the crime; and accept responsibility for the actions of Libyan officials; disclose all it knows of this crime, including the names of all those responsible, and allow access to all witnesses, documents and other material evidence, including all the remaining timers; and pay appropriate compensation.
263 *ICJ Reports*, at 122. By letter of 2 April 1992, a copy of which was transmitted to Libya by the Registrar, the Agent of the United States drew the court's attention to the adoption of Security Council Resolution 748 (1992) the text of which he enclosed. In that letter the Agent for the United States stated:

> That resolution, adopted pursuant to Chapter VII of the United Nations Charter, 'decides that the Libyan Government must now comply without any further delay with paragraph 3 of resolution 731 (1992) of 21 January 1992 regarding the requests contained in documents S/23306, S/23308 and S/23309'. It will be recalled that the referenced requests include the request that Libya surrender the two Libyan suspects in the bombing of PAN AM flight 103 to the United States or to the United Kingdom. For this additional reason, the United States maintains its submission of 28 March 1992 that the request of the Government of the Great Socialist Peoples' Libyan Arab Jamahiriya for the indication of provisional measures for protection should be denied, and that no such measures should be indicated. (See *ICJ Reports*, ibid., at 125.)

264 Ibid., at 129.
265 *ICJ Reports* (1980) 22, para. 40.
266 Ibid., at 138–9.
267 Ibid., at 140.
268 Ibid., at 155–6.
269 Hans Kelsen, *The Law of the United Nations*, New York: Praeger, 1951, pp.476–7. See *ICJ Reports*, 167.
270 *ICJ Reports*, 168.

271 Hans Kelsen, *supra*, note 269, p.476.
272 *Shorter Oxford Dictionary on Historical Principles*, vol. 11, Oxford: Clarendon Press, 1980.
273 Hans Kelsen, *supra*, note 269, p.477.
274 Lord McNair, *International Law Opinions, Selected and Annotated*, vol. 11, Cambridge: Cambridge University Press, 1956, p.41.
275 Ian Brownlie, *Principles of Public International Law*, Oxford: Clarendon Press, 1966, pp.98–9.
276 United Nations Charter, art. 1.
277 Ibid., art. 2(1).
278 Jean Bodin, *Six Books of the Commonwealth*, Oxford: B. Blackwell, 1955, pp.25–36.
279 See M.S. Rajan, *United Nations and Domestic Jurisdiction*, Bombay: Orient Longmans, 1958, p.3.
280 *Case Concerning the Barcelona Traction Light and Power Co.*, (*Belgium* v. *Spain*) 1970 *I.C.J.* p.32.
281 Ian Brownlie, *supra*, note 275, p.1.
282 Article 59 provides that the decision of the court has no binding effect except between the parties and in respect of that particular case.
283 Michael Akehurst, 'The Hierarchy of the Sources of International Law', *B.Y.I.L.*, 1974–5, 273.
284 J.E.S. Fawcett, 'The United Nations and International Law', *The Evolving United Nations: A Prospect for Peace* (Kenneth J. Twitchett, ed.), London: Europa Publications, 1971, pp.65–6.
285 Lord Oliver has stated: 'a rule of international law becomes a rule – whether accepted into domestic law or not – only when it is certain and is accepted generally by the body of civilised nations; and it is for those who assert the rule to demonstrate it, if necessary before the International Court of Justice. It is certainly not for a domestic tribunal in effect to legislate a rule into existence for the purposes of domestic law and on the basis of material that is wholly indeterminate' ([1989], 3 W.L.R. 969 H.L). See also generally, Robert Y. Jennings, 'An International Lawyer Takes Stock', *I.C.L.Q.*, 39(3), July 1990, 513–29.
286 Marjorie M. Whiteman, 'Jus Cogens in International Law, With a Projected List', *J.Int'l & Comp. L.*, 7, 1977, 613.
287 Vienna Convention on the Law of Treaties, UN Doc. A/Conf.39/27, 23 May 1969.
288 Jerzy Sztucki, *Jus Cogens and the Vienna Convention on the Law of Treaties – A Critical Appraisal*, Vienna and New York: Springer-Verlag, 1974, p.69.
289 Frans G. von der Dunk, 'Jus Cogens Sive Lege Ferenda: Jus Cogendum?', *Air and Space Law: De Lege Ferenda*, Essays in Honour of Henri A. Wassenbergh, Netherlands: Martinus Nijhoff, 1992, p.219.

Chapter 4

Summary of the Issues

Air law and space law are inevitably heading towards common ground in the new millennium, particularly in the light of boundaries between air space and outer space being obviated by aerospace transport and the inherent nature of the modern spacecraft. Another compelling factor is the new CNS/ATM system of using the Global Navigation Satellite System for air navigation. As such, it can be envisaged that well into the new millennium, the commonalities between air law and space law will be more defined and apparent.

This trend will incontrovertibly bring to bear a compelling need to define a more coherent structure of world governance for aerospace transport. It can be envisaged that the United Nations will forge ahead with cooperation between specialized agencies dealing with civil aviation and outer space exploration and transport, particularly on common ground such as regulating the aerospace plane and the use of extraterrestrial satellites for the purpose of air navigation.

Principles of state responsibility and international cooperation, which are emerging as the cornerstones of public international law beyond the year 2000, will need to be more clearly defined. As one of the foremost authorities on space law in recent times, Judge Manfred Lachs, has said:

> If all the activities connected with outer space are to be conducted for the benefit of all and to the detriment of none, international cooperation is essential, and if all the possibilities opened up are to be used in a responsible manner, the conduct of States in regard to outer space must be submitted to the rule of law.[1]

In order that this be achieved, firstly, a uniform code of conduct should be considered as an enforceable set of rules for both aviation and outer space issues. This code should be applicable to a special court mandated to try crimes and offences against aviation and space exploration on a private basis (as in the case of cyber offenders) as discussed above. Where the conduct of states is concerned, stringent Standards and Recommended Practices should be adopted in both fields and the adjudicatory powers of the International Civil Aviation Organization in matters of civil aviation should be revisited and given more recognition, while a parallel United Nations body for issues arising out of problems in outer space law should be identified as an appropriate adjudicatory body. These two bodies could then act as effective 'courts of first instance' with an appeal process leading up to the International Court of Justice.

At present, the Council of the International Civil Aviation Organization (ICAO) has the power under the Chicago Convention to adjudicate disputes between the member states of ICAO on matters pertaining to international civil aviation. The Council is a permanent body responsible to the ICAO Assembly and is composed of 33 contracting states elected by the Assembly. It has its genesis in the Interim Council of the Provisional International Civil Aviation Organization (PICAO).[2] PICAO occupied such legal capacity as may have been necessary for the performance of its functions and was recognized as having full juridical personality wherever compatible with the constitution and the laws of the state concerned.[3] The definitive word 'juridical' attributed to PICAO a mere judicial function, unequivocally stipulating that the organization and its component bodies, such as the Interim Council, were obligated to remain within the legal parameters allocated to them by the Interim Agreement,[4] and that PICAO was of a purely technical and advisory nature. A legislative or quasi-legislative function could not therefore be imputed to the Interim Council of PICAO. It could mostly study, interpret and advise on standards and procedures,[5] and make recommendations with respect to technical matters through the Committee on Air Navigation.[6] The International Civil Aviation Organization (ICAO) which saw the light of day on 4 April 1947, derived the fundamental postulates of its technical and administrative structure from its progenitor (PICAO) and it would seem reasonable to attribute a certain affinity *ipso facto* between the two organizations and, hence, their councils. One of the council's functions is to consider any matter relating to the Convention which any contracting state refers to it.[7] Since one of the distinctive features of the ICAO Council is its ability to make rules for international civil aviation, it follows incontrovertibly that the council's dispute resolution powers are compelling.

The words 'legislative power' have been legally defined as 'power to prescribe rules of civil conduct',[8] while identifying law as a 'rule of civil conduct'. The word 'quasi' is essentially a term that makes a resemblance to another and classifies it. It is suggestive of comparative analogy and is accepted as 'the conception to which it serves as an index and its connection with the conception with which the comparison is instituted by strong superficial analogy or resemblance'.[9] The question *stricto sensu* according to the above definition is therefore whether the ICAO Council now has power to prescribe rules of civil conduct (legislative power) or at the least a power that resembles by analogy the ability to prescribe rules of conduct (quasi-legislative power). Since legislative power is usually attributed to a state, it would be prudent to inquire, on a general basis, whether the ICAO Council has law-making powers (in a quasi-legislative sense). Therefore all references hereafter that may refer to legislative powers would be reflective of the council's law-making powers in a quasi-legislative sense.

Article 54(1) of the Convention on International Civil Aviation prescribes the adoption of international Standards and Recommended Practices (hereafter, SARPS) and their designation in annexes to the Convention, while notifying all contracting states of the action taken. The adoption of SARPS was considered a priority by the

ICAO Council in its Second Session (2 September–12 December 1947)[10] which attempted to obviate any delays to the adoption of SARPS on air navigation as required by the First Assembly of ICAO.[11] SARPS inevitably take two forms: a negative form such as that states shall not impose more than certain maximum requirements; and a positive form such as that states shall take certain steps as prescribed by the ICAO annexes.[12]

Article 37 of the Convention obtains the undertaking of each contracting state to collaborate in securing the highest practical degree of uniformity in regulations, standards, procedures and organization in relation to international civil aviation in all matters in which such uniformity will facilitate and improve air navigation. Article 38 obligates all contracting states to the Convention to inform ICAO immediately if they are unable to comply with any such international standard or procedure and notify differences between their own practices and those prescribed by ICAO. In the case of amendments to international standards, any state which does not make the appropriate amendment to its own regulations or practices shall give notice to the Council of ICAO within 60 days of the adoption of the said amendment to the international standard or indicate the action which it proposes to take.

The element of compulsion that has been infused by the drafters of the Convention is compatible with the 'power to prescribe rules of civil conduct' on a *stricto sensu* legal definition of the words 'legislative power' as discussed above. There is no room for doubt that the 18 annexes to the Convention or parts thereof lay down rules of conduct both directly and analogically. In fact, although there is a conception based on a foundation of practicality that ICAO's international Standards that are identified by the words 'contracting States shall' have a mandatory flavour (infused by the word 'shall') while Recommended Practices identified by the words 'contracting States may have only an advisory' and recommendatory connotation (infused by the word 'may'), it is interesting that at least one ICAO document requires states, under article 38 of the Convention, to notify ICAO of all significant differences from both Standards and Recommended Practices, thus making all SARPS regulatory in nature.[13]

Another strong factor that reflects the overall ability and power of the Council to prescribe civil rules of conduct (and therefore legislate) on a strict interpretation of the word is that in aArticle 22 of the Convention each contracting state agrees to adopt all practical measures through the issuance of special regulations or otherwise, to facilitate and expedite air navigation. It is clear that this provision can be regarded as an incontrovertible rule of conduct that responds to the requirement in article 54(1) of the Convention. Furthermore, the mandatory nature of article 90 of the Convention – that an Annex or amendment thereto shall become effective within three months of its being submitted by the ICAO Council to contracting states – is yet another pronouncement on the power of the Council to prescribe rules of state conduct in matters of international civil aviation. *A fortiori*, it is arguable that the Council is seen to possess not only the attribute of the term 'jurisfaction' (the power to make rules of conduct) but also that of the term 'jurisaction' (the power to enforce its own rules of conduct). The latter attribute can be seen where the Convention obtains the undertaking of contracting states not to allow airlines to operate through their airspace if the Council decides that the airline concerned is not conforming with a final decision rendered by the Council on a matter that concerns the operation of an international airline.[14] This is particularly applicable when such airline is found not to conform to the provisions of Annex 2 to the Convention that derives its validity from article 12 of the Convention relating to rules of the air.[15] In fact, it is very relevant that Annex 2, the responsibility for the promulgation of which devolves upon the Council by virtue of article 54(1), sets mandatory rules of the air, making the existence of the legislative powers of the Council an unequivocal and irrefutable fact.

Academic and professional opinion also favours the view that, in a practical sense, the ICAO Council does have legislative powers. Professor Michael Milde says:

> The Chicago Convention, as any other legal instrument, provides only a general legal framework which is given true life only in the practical implementation of its provisions. Thus, for example, Article 37 of the Convention relating to the adoption of international standards and recommended procedures would be a very hollow and meaningless provision without active involvement of all contracting States, Panels, Regional and Divisional Meetings, deliberations in the Air Navigation Commission and final adoption of the standards by the Council. Similarly, provisions of Article 12 relating to the rules of the air applicable over the high seas, Articles 17 to 20 on the nationality of aircraft, Article 22 on facilitation, Article 26 on the investigation of accidents, etc., would be meaningless without appropriate implementation in the respective Annexes. On the same level is the provision of the last sentence of Article 77 relating to the determination by the Council in what manner the provisions of the Convention relating to nationality of aircraft shall apply to aircraft operated by international operating agencies.[16]

Professor Milde concludes that ICAO has regulatory and quasi-legislative functions in the technical field and plays a consultative and advisory role in the economic sphere.[17] A similar view had earlier been expressed by Buergenthal, who states:

> the manner in which the International Civil Aviation Organization has exercised its regulatory functions in matters relating to the safety of international air navigation and the facilitation of international air transport provides a fascinating example of international law making … the Organization has consequently not had to contend with any of the post war ideological differences that have impeded international law making on politically sensitive issues.[18]

Paul Stephen Dempsey endorses, in a somewhat conservative manner, the view that ICAO has the ability to make regulations when he states:

> In addition to the comprehensive, but largely dormant adjudicative enforcement held by ICAO under Articles 84–88 of the Chicago Convention, the Agency also has a solid foundation for enhanced participation in economic regulatory aspects of international aviation in Article 44, as well as the Convention's Preamble.[19]

A significant attribute of the legislative capabilities of the ICAO Council is its ability to adopt technical standards as annexes to the Convention without going through a lengthy process of ratification.[20] Eugene Sochor refers to the Council as a powerful and visible body in international aviation.[21] It is interesting, however, to note that although, by definition, the ICAO Council has been considered by some as unable to deal with strictly legal matters, since other important matters come within its purview,[22] this does not derogate the compelling facts that reflect the distinct law-making abilities of ICAO. Should this not be true, the functions that the Convention assigns to ICAO in article 44 – that ICAO's aims and objectives are to 'develop the principles and techniques of international air navigation and to foster the planning and development of international air transport' – would be rendered destitute of effect.

Under the Interim Agreement, the PICAO Council was required to act as an arbitral body on any differences arising among member states relating to matters of international civil aviation which might be submitted to it, wherein the Interim Council of PICAO was empowered to render an advisory report or, if the parties involved so wished, give a decision on the matter before it.[23] The Interim Council, which was the precursor to the ICAO Council, set the stage therefore for providing the Council with unusual arbitral powers which are not attributed to similar organs of the specialized agencies of the United Nations system.[24] *A fortiori*, since the ICAO Council is permanent and is in almost constant session, contracting states could expect any matter of dispute brought by them before the Council to be dealt with, without unreasonable delay.[25]

Chapter XVIII of the Convention formalizes the arbitral powers of the Council by stating:

> If any disagreement between two or more contracting States relating to the interpretation or application of this Convention and its Annexes cannot be settled by negotiation, *it shall*, on the application of any State concerned in the disagreement, be decided by the Council.[26] (Emphasis added)

This provision reflects two significant points: the first is that contracting states should first attempt to resolve their disputes by themselves, through negotiation;[27] the second is that the word *shall* in this provision infuses into the decision-making powers of the Council an unquestionably mandatory character. Furthermore, a decision taken by the Council is juridically dignified by article 86 of the Convention, when the article states that, unless the Council decides otherwise, any decision by the Council on whether an international airline is operating in conformity with the provisions of the Convention shall remain in effect unless reversed in appeal. The

Council also has powers of sanction granted by the Convention, if its decision is not adhered to.[28] Schenkman states: 'The power of sanctions in this field is an entirely new phenomenon, attributed to an aeronautical body … none of the pre-war instruments in the field of aviation had the power of sanctions as a means of enforcement of its decisions.[29]

Most contracting states have, on their own initiative, enacted dispute settlement clauses in their bilateral air services agreements wherein provision is usually made to refer inter-state disputes relating to international civil aviation to the ICAO Council, in accordance with Chapter XVIII of the Convention. In this context, it is also relevant to note that the President of the Council is empowered by the Convention to appoint an arbitrator and an umpire in certain circumstances leading to an appeal from a decision of the Council.[30]

A most interesting aspect of the ICAO Council is that one of its mandatory functions is to consider any subject referred to it by a contracting state for its consideration[31] (or any subject which the President of the Council or the Secretary General of the ICAO Secretariat desires to bring before the Council).[32] Although the Council is bound to consider a matter submitted to it by a contracting state, it can refrain from giving a decision as the Council is only obligated to consider a matter before it.

There seems to be an unfortunate dichotomy in terminology in the Convention since, on the one hand, article 54(*n*) makes it mandatory that the Council shall merely *consider* any matter relating to the Convention which any contracting state refers to it, while, on the other, article 84 categorically states that any disagreement between two or more states relating to the interpretation or application of the Convention and its annexes, that cannot be settled by negotiation shall be decided by the Council. The difficulty arises on a strict interpretation of article 54(*n*) where even a disagreement between two states as envisaged under article 84 could well be considered as 'any matter' under article 54(*n*). In such an instance, the Council could well be faced with the dilemma of choosing between the two provisions. It would not be incorrect for the Council to merely consider a matter placed before it, although a decision is requested by the applicant state, since Article 54(*n*) is perceived to be comprehensive as the operative and controlling provision that lays down mandatory functions of the Council. It is indeed unfortunate that these two provisions obfuscate the issue which otherwise would have given a clear picture of the decision-making powers of the Council. A further thread in the fabric of adjudicatory powers of the Council is found in article 14 of the Rules of Settlement promulgated by the Council in 1957,[33] which allows the Council to request the parties in dispute to engage in direct negotiations at any time.[34] This emphasis on conciliation has prompted the view that the Council, under article 84, would favour the settling of disputes rather than adjudicating them.[35] This view seems compatible with the proposition that the consideration of a matter under article 54(*n*) would be a more attractive approach *in limine* in a matter of dispute between two states.

Dempsey points out, that in the four decades since the promulgation of Chapter XVIII, only three disputes had been submitted to the Council for formal resolution:[36] the first involved a dispute between India and Pakistan (1952), where India complained that Pakistan was in breach of the Convention by not permitting Indian aircraft to overfly Pakistani airspace on their way to Afghanistan; the second was a complaint filed by the United Kingdom against Spain (1969), alleging the violation by Spain of the Convention by the establishment of a prohibited zone over Gibraltar; and the third was a complaint by Pakistan against India (1971), concerning a hijacking of Indian aircraft which landed in Pakistan. India unilaterally suspended Pakistan's overflying privileges five days after the hijacking. The first complaint was amicably resolved by the parties, the second was deferred by the parties *sine die*, and the third was suspended with the formation of the State of Bangladesh in 1972, even though the matter had been processed as an appeal from the Council to the International Court of Justice. Unfortunately, none of these instances was taken to its conclusion so that the world could have had the opportunity to evaluate clearly ICAO's decision-making process.

Professor Milde noted in 1979:

> The Council of ICAO cannot be considered a suitable body for adjudication in the proper sense of the word – *i.e.* settlement of disputes by judges and solely on the basis of respect for law. The Council is composed of States (not independent individuals) and its decisions would always be based on policy and equity considerations rather than on pure legal grounds ... truly legal disputes ... can be settled only by a true judicial body which can bring into the procedure full judicial detachment, independence and expertise. The under-employed ICJ is the most suitable body for such types of disputes.[37]

The perceived inadequacies of the ICAO Council in being ethically unsuitable to decide on disputes between states can only be alleviated by the thought that the members of the Council are presumed to be well versed in matters of international civil aviation and therefore would be deemed to be better equipped to comprehend the issues placed before them than the distinguished members of the International Court of Justice, some of whom may not be experts on international air law. Nonetheless, there is no doubt that the ICAO Council possesses juridical powers[38] and that, as one commentator said, 'If ICAO did not exist, it would have to be invented; otherwise, international civil aviation would not function with the safety, efficiency and regularity that it has achieved today'.[39]

ICAO's legislative and adjudicatory teeth have to be strengthened and a suitable international body to go into outer space disputes would have to be established if the issues of the new millennium pertaining to aerospace are to be faced.

NOTES

1 M. Lachs, *The Law of Outer Space: An Experience in Contemporary Law Making*, Dordrecht: Kluwer, 1972, pp.6–7.
2 Hereafter referred to as PICAO. See Interim Agreement on International Civil Aviation, opened for signature at Chicago, 7 December 1944, article 3. Also Hudson, *International Legislation*, vol. IX, New York: Harvard University Press, 1942–5, p.159.
3 Interim Agreement, article 1, section 4. It is interesting to note that PICAO was established as a provisional organization of a technical and advisory nature for the purpose of collaboration in the field of international civil aviation. See article 1, section 1.
4 Ibid.
5 Interim Agreement, section 6.4.*b*(1).
6 Ibid., section 6.4.*b*(6). See also T. Buergenthal, *Law Making in the International Civil Aviation Organization*, The Hague: UN, 1969, p.4, where the author states that PICAO's functions were merely advisory, which precludes any imputation of legislative or quasi-legislative character to its Interim Council.
7 Chicago Convention, article 54.
8 *Schaake* v. *Dolly* 85 Kan. 590, 118 Pac. 80.
9 *People* v. *Bradley* 60 Ill. 402, at 405. Also *Bouviers Law Dictionary and Concise Encyclopedia*, 3rd edn, vol. 11, New York: Vernon Law Book Co., 1914.
10 Proceedings of the Council, 2nd Session, 2 September–12 December 1947, Doc 7248 – C/839 at 44–5.
11 ICAO Resolutions A-13 and A-33 which resolved that SARPS relating to the efficient and safe regulation of international air navigation be adopted.
12 ICAO Annex 9, *Facilitation*, 9th edn, July 1990, Foreword.
13 The *Aeronautical Information Services Manual*, ICAO Doc 8126 – 0 AN/872/3. ICAO Resolution A 1-31 defines a Standard as any specification for physical characteristics ... the uniform application of which is recognized as *necessary* ... and one that States *will conform to*. The same resolution describes a Recommended Practice as any specification for physical characteristics ... which is recognized as *desirable* ... and one that member states *will endeavour to conform to* (Buergenthal, *supra*, note 6, p.10, also cites the definitions given in ICAO's Annex 9 of SARPS).
14 Article 86 of the Convention.
15 Article 12 stipulates that, over the high seas, the rules in force shall be those established under the Convention, and each contracting state undertakes to ensure the prosecution of all persons violating the applicable regulations.
16 Michael Milde, 'The Chicago Convention – After Forty Years', *Annals of Air and Space Law*, IX at 126. See also Jacob Schenkman, *International Civil Aviation Organization*, Geneva: UN, 1955, p.163.
17 Milde, *supra*, note 16, 122.
18 Buergenthal, *supra*, note 6, p.9.
19 Paul Stephen Dempsey, *Law and Foreign Policy in International Aviation*, Dobbs Ferry, New York: Transnational Publishers Inc., 1987, p.302.
20 Eugene Sochor, *The Politics of International Aviation*, London: Macmillan, 1991, p.58.
21 Ibid.

22 Alexander Tobolewski, 'ICAO's Legal Syndrome', *Annals of Air and Space Law*, IV, 1979, 359.
23 Interim Agreement, article 111, section 6(i).
24 Schenkman, *supra*, note 16, p.160.
25 See statement of R. Kidron, Israeli Head Delegate, Statement of the Second Plenary Meeting of the Seventh Assembly on 17 June 1953, reported in *ICAO Monthly Bulletin*, August–October, 1953, p.8.
26 Article 84.
27 Hingorani, 'Dispute Settlement in International Civil Aviation', *Arb J*, 14, 16, 1959. See also *Rules of Procedure for the Council*, 5th edn, 1980, art. 14.
28 Article 87.
29 Schenkman, *supra*, note 16, p.162.
30 Article 85.
31 Rules of Procedure for the Council, section IV, rule 24(*e*). Also Article 54(*n*) stipulates that one of the mandatory functions of the Council is to consider any matter relating to the Convention which any contracting state refers to it.
32 Rules of Procedure for the Council, section IV, rule 24(*f*). The two additional multilateral agreements stemming from the Convention and providing for the exchange of traffic rights – the Air Services Transit Agreement and the Air Transport Agreement – also contain provisions that empower the ICAO Council to hear disputes and 'make appropriate findings and recommendations' (see Air Services Transit Agreement article 11, section 1, and the Air Transport Agreement, article IV section 2).
33 Rules for the Settlement of Differences, ICAO Doc 7782/2 (2edn 1975).
34 Ibid., article 14(*a*).
35 Buergenthal, *supra*, note 6, p.136.
36 Paul Stephen Dempsey, *supra*, note 19, p.295.
37 Michael Milde, 'Dispute Settlement in the Framework of the International Civil Aviation Organization (ICAO)', *Settlement of Space Law Disputes*, Dordrecht: Kluwer, 1979, p.88.
38 J.C. Sampayo de Lacerda, 'A Study About the Decisions of the ICAO Council', *Annals of Air and Space Law*, III, 1978, 219.
39 Gerald F. Fitzgerald, 'ICAO Now and in the Coming Decades', *International Air Transport Law, Organization and Politics for the Future*, N.M. Matte, ed., Montreal: McGill University Press, 1976, p. 50.

Chapter 5
Air Law Issues

1 AIRCRAFT NOISE

Introduction

The world was first exposed to the magnitude of aircraft noise when the original prototype of the de Havilland Comet flew in July 1949. The Comet, which was the first commercial aircraft to be powered by a jet engine, officially entered service on 2 May 1952. However, it was not until the long-range Boeing 707, which was first delivered in 1958, entered service, followed by the ubiquitous Douglas DC-8 of 1962, that the full impact of aircraft noise became the focus of public attention.

Successive lawsuits in the nature of private actions in nuisance followed, prompting collective international action in the form of an international conference convened in London in 1966 which endorsed the concept of manufacturer control by certification of aircraft for noise levels.[1] In 1969, a special international meeting was held at the International Civil Aviation Organization (ICAO) to address issues pertaining to aircraft noise, resulting in the creation of the ICAO Committee on Aircraft Noise (CAN) which in turn was charged with taking appropriate action on the aircraft noise issue. The work of CAN led to the adoption in 1971 of Annex 16 to the Convention on International Civil Aviation,[2] which contained Standards and Recommended Practices on aircraft noise.

Aircraft noise is generated whenever the passage of air over the structure of the aircraft or through its power plants causes fluctuating pressure disturbances which are transformed into auditory impulses in the human being.[3] Such impulses, called unwanted sound, not desired by the recipient,[4] are measured

> using a logarithmic unit called the decibel (dB) in terms of pressure exerted in the ear.[5] In the case of jet aircraft, two distinct kinds of engine noise affect the human ear adversely, namely the roar of the jet exhaust and the whine of the compressor fan.[6] The roar of the jet exhaust occurs mainly in the take-off phase, where the engines are at maximum power to enable the aircraft to be airborne.[7] The whine of the compressor occurs mainly during the landing approach where interaction of the fan blades with turbulence and wakes results in a whine of high frequency in the compressor of the engine.[8]

There is definite medical evidence to prove that exposure to aerial noise causes deleterious psychological effects. For instance, a study made in relation to admissions to a psychiatric hospital in England draws a distinct relationship between the disturbed mental state of the admitted inmates of the hospital and high intermittent noise levels from Heathrow Airport, to which they were exposed.[9] One writer states that airport and industrial noise is the cause of mental stress and maladjustment, increases in chronic fatigue and neurotic complaints in some cases, although different personalities may underlie individual differences in noise effects.[10]

This section will address legal issues pertaining to aircraft noise as a nuisance. It will also evaluate regulatory issues taken to specify aircraft noise levels and policy pertaining thereto and, finally, discuss some recent developments in the area of aircraft noise.

Legal issues

The term 'noise' has so far not been examined in depth by the courts especially in relation to tolerance levels. It is clear that courts have not had occasion to consider noise as a significant factor in litigation which calls for detailed consideration in terms of medical and scientific pronouncements to ascertain what degree of noise is detrimental to the human being. Courts have not been able to do so because of two significant factors. The first is that the issue of noise as pollution has rarely surfaced. The second is that, even if it did surface, courts have always had to question noise as it is referred to in regulations or municipal by-laws, the validity of which has been the primary factor of consideration. It can be seen that most by-laws refer generally to noise and the prohibition of it. It is not surprising, therefore, that courts have never attempted to define noise empirically or medically and instead preferred to observe the nature of noise on a very general basis.

Howlett v. *McCarthy*[11] is an early case which exemplifies the difficulty faced by the courts in this respect. In this instance, a New South Wales court examined a resolution of a council which ordered the occupiers of premises to cause 'no noise' in the use of such premises, between specified hours. In the context of the phrase 'no noise', it was extremely difficult for Judge Betts, who delivered judgment, to examine whether the sound caused by machinery was noise which would amount to a breach of such by-law. The court cautiously observed that a liberal meaning should be attributed to 'noise', as a strict interpretation of the term would hinder anyone in carrying out a business or industry.[12] Therefore 'noise' was identified as that which would carry beyond the confines of the premises it emanated from to such a degree or of such a nature in quality or volume as to interfere with the life of the residents of normal temperament in the neighbourhood. The interference referred to was further elaborated to be worry, inconvenience, annoyance, discomfort or loss of sleep during the prohibited hours.

Judge Betts faced the dilemma of being confronted by two conflicting interests – that of the plaintiff who alleges the injury or annoyance and of the business man who carries on an industry as a means of livelihood. Eventually, his honour introduced an effective compromise by stating that any sound does not necessarily become noise unless it causes the discomfort specified above, and, if it does, the person who suffers the annoyance is entitled to seek redress in order that the noise be abated by the person who causes it. Although the judgment seems fair and just for the time it was delivered, it does not suffice that such a general observation be applied in the present day, when industry and population grow simultaneously and the consideration of sustainable development has become a pre-eminent factor in human development.

The judgment was fully endorsed by Richardson J in a case decided some 20 years later,[13] where his honour did not deviate from the general stance taken by Judge Betts. The same criteria were used in different terminology to state that noise should be modulated so as not to inconvenience others and cause discomfort[14] and that noise caused by such things as hammers, building implements and loudspeakers should not hinder the comfortable enjoyment of life by neighbours.[15] The judgment was followed verbatim by Manning J in *Bankstown Municipal Council* v. *Berzins*,[16] in which his honour stated that noise is distinguishable from sound, in that noise, unlike sound, materially interferes with the ordinary comfort and convenience of residents of the neighbourhood.[17]

The early attitude towards noise as environmental pollution does not differ in any way from that which was taken by the courts. The courts, too, were faced by the problem of being confronted by inadequately framed by-laws and the paucity of precedent which adequately defined noise. In *Leslie* v. *City of Essendon,*[18] a case decided in Victoria, Australia in 1902, Sholl J dealt casually with noise by calling it 'loud sound',[19] whereas Copell AJ, quoting from the *Oxford English Dictionary*, preferred to expand the definition to a 'loud or harsh sound or any kind of din'.[20] It is not unreasonable to assume that, in the light of the few cases decided, noise was always considered subjectively, which made it difficult for courts to ascertain whether in any given instance a person aggrieved had a cause of action. What was lacking was a definite idea of what the basic human tolerance level was. At that time courts did not even mention the possibility of excessive noise causing injury to the human ear. However, as was shown earlier, the above cases were decided between 1936 and 1962, during which time medical science, though not totally unaware of the detrimental effects of noise on the human ear, had not published sufficient material on the subject.

Although ample evidence was available in the 1960s on noise pollution and human physiology, a case decided in 1967 in Victoria, Australia[21] decided to follow precedent and appeared to agree with the general view that noise becomes intolerable when it causes discomfort.[22] Although the courts only examined the validity of a by-law prohibiting noise on a highway, it did mention noise in general without attempting to assess modern scientific findings on the subject.

The British case of *Regina* v. *Fenny Stratford Justices, ex parte Watney Mann (Midlands) Ltd*,[23] decided in 1976, adopted a more positive attitude, even though it did not consider the effects of noise in terms of scientific findings. Watkins J, expressing his opinion of a jukebox as a modern appliance, was both sincere and unequivocal:

> at any rate it is my opinion that excessive noise is one of the curses of the modern age. One of the reasons why this is so is that somebody invented the amplifier, which serves at least one purpose, namely, very nearly to blast out the eardrums of anyone within its proximity.[24]

This statement is certainly more expressive than those exemplifying the previous attitude, although noise-related discomfort and injury was not dealt with specifically. At least the plaintiff is given the assurance that, even though the courts have still not considered modern medical findings on the subject, they consider any kind of noise with the same apprehension as when they consider any other assault on the human body. In addition, one can be comforted by the thought that it will not be long before the courts take full cognizance of the impact of modern scientific findings.

Pollution has been defined as 'the introduction by man, directly or indirectly, of substances or energy into the environment resulting in deleterious effects of such nature as to endanger human health, harm living resources and ecosystems, and impair or interfere with amenities and other legitimate uses of the environment'.[25] The definition covers human health, which has been a major concern of environmentalists for some time. It also accommodates the role played by the United Nations under its charter. Article 1 of the United Nations Charter identifies as one of the purposes of the United Nations the achievement of international cooperation in solving international problems, *inter alia*, of a human character[26] and charges the General Assembly of the United Nations to promote international cooperation, *inter alia*, in the health fields.[27] Article 55 of the charter requires the United Nations to promote higher standards of living[28] and arrive at solutions concerning, *inter alia*, health problems.[29] For this purpose, the Economic and Social Council of the United Nations (ECOSOC) may make or initiate studies and reports, *inter alia*, with respect to international health matters.[30] The role of the United Nations in preserving the environment is thereby clearly entrenched in its charter. International regulation, as discussed above, are but a corollary to this *status quo*.

The tort of nuisance is caused by an unprivileged interference by a person of another's enjoyment of his or her private property, causing discomfort to the latter, and invariably causing the property to diminish in value.[31] There are two instances, however, where recovery against the tort of nuisance is not possible, namely, where a state can invoke sovereignty and where the defence of pre-emption can be successfully claimed.[32] In all other instances, where nuisance is alleged to have been committed by aircraft noise, particularly where a state-run airport is held answerable, a successful legal approach for the plaintiff would lie in the theory of inverse condemnation. The principle of inverse condemnation has been identified as

> the popular description of a cause against a governmental defendant to recover the value of property which has been taken in fact by the governmental defendant even though no formal exercise of the power of eminent domain has been attempted by taking the agency[33]

and was brought to light by the seminal decision in the case of *United States* v. *Causby*,[34] decided in 1946, which involved repeated flights over the plaintiff's property by military aircraft, which held that there had been a compensable interference with property and consequent reduction of its value which was at variance with the Fifth Amendment of the United States' Constitution.[35]

The 1962 case of *Thornburg* v. *Port of Portland*[36] made a significant deviation from the usual principle that compensation for a nuisance caused by noise produced by aircraft could only be awarded if the aircraft was directly above the property concerned and ruled that a trespass resulting in nuisance could occur even if the noise was coming from an aircraft flying beside the property. The *Thornburg* principle was followed some years later in *Martin* v. *Port of Seattle*,[37] which rejected the rigidity of the principle that, in the words of the court, insisted upon 'the wingtip of the aircraft passing through some fraction of an inch of the airspace directly above the plaintiff's land'.[38]

Issues of sovereignty

International responsibility of a state for noise pollution caused by aircraft registered in that state or leased or chartered by an operator of that state cannot be denied merely on the strength of the claim of that state to sovereignty. Although the Chicago Convention, in article 1, stipulates that the contracting states recognize that every state has complete and exclusive sovereignty over the airspace above its territory, the effect of this provision cannot be extended to apply to state immunity from responsibility to other states. In the *Island of Palmas* case,[39] Professor Huber was of the view that 'Sovereignty in the relations between States signifies independence. Independence in regard to a portion of the globe is the right to exercise therein, to the exclusion of any other State, the functions of a State … Territorial sovereignty … involves the exclusive right to display the activities of a State.'[40] Professor Huber's definition, which is a simple statement of a state's rights, has been qualified by Starke as the residuum of power which a state possesses within the confines of international law.[41] If therefore, aircraft noise adversely affect the territories of states they fly over, the state in which such aircraft are registered or leased or chartered would incur legal liability at international law. Responsibility would also devolve upon a state in whose territory such emissions occur, to other states that are threatened by those emissions, to prevent them from permeating the latter states. The International Court of Justice (ICJ) recognized in the *Corfu Channel* case 'every State's obligation not to allow knowingly its territory to be used for acts contrary to the rights of other States'.[42]

Although this case related to the legal liability of a state carrying out mine-sweeping operations in the territorial waters of another without the latter's consent, it provides an analogy to the question of international pollution. Barros and Johnston are of the view:

> some of the comments of the International Court of Justice in the *Corfu Channel* case (1949) can be interpreted as an important judicial affirmation of State responsibility from which one today can infer the obligation of each State not to allow the nationals of other States to suffer pollution or damage that might reasonably be prevented and the liability of providing appropriate compensation to the injured party when the obligation is violated.[43]

When the liability of a State for transborder pollution is identified, the question arises as to who could decide disputes on the issues. The International Court of Justice is empowered to apply the principles of international law, that is, international conventions, international custom (as evidence of general practice accepted as law), general principles of law as recognized by civilized nations, and judicial decisions and teachings of jurists of various nations.[44] However, there are no international conventions, custom or general principles of law governing pollution caused by international civil aviation. In this scenario, Sharon Williams offers four approaches: (1) the adoption of a multilateral pollution treaty, (2) the adoption of regional treaties on pollution, (3) the creation of a special international tribunal to hear cases of environmental pollution, and (4) the setting up of an institution which would be given the power and legal personality to enter into discussions with national and international agencies, individuals and industry.[45]

Issues at common law

Under the common law, a person who suffers harm due to noise could succeed in trespass, negligence or nuisance. The tort of trespass can be invoked when there is an unauthorized entry upon another's land. Unauthorized entry need not necessarily be actual physical presence of the offender on the complainant's land but would include throwing things into the complainant's land, allowing animals to stray onto that land or even placing the offender's ladder against the complainant's wall.[46] Therefore trespass is a personal encroachment by the defendants. However, private nuisance may be an indirect encroachment, without a positive act which *per se* amounts to physical presence. Therefore, when the complaint is obnoxious noise, which is an indirect encroachment, the best remedy to be sought is private nuisance.

To succeed in negligence, a plaintiff must establish that the defendant owed him a duty to take reasonable care and that this duty has been breached, causing the plaintiff damage as a result. The duty of care is owed only to those persons who are in the area of foreseeable danger. In a Canadian case,[47] a cause of action in negligence for damage by aircraft noise arose. The damage complained of was that the female minks in the plaintiff's farm devoured their young. The court referring to the duty owed by the defendant, stated that there is such a duty only where the circumstances of time, place and person would create, in the mind of a reasonable man in those circumstances, such a probability of harm resulting to other persons, as to require him to take care to avert that probable result.[48] It was held that there was no duty of care on the defendant in respect of any harm to the mink. It is submitted that, on similar facts, a cause of action in nuisance would have succeeded because the plaintiff would not have had to prove that the noise was caused by the defendant's negligence.

Elements of private nuisance

It is apparent from the above discussion that the only common law cause of action which merits detailed discussion in this chapter is nuisance. The word 'nuisance' remains the most uncertain word in legal terminology even though it has been put to diverse use by the judiciary. Its tentacles lie spreadeagled on a multitude of wrongs ranging from the noises made by animals to obnoxious smells. Perhaps the reason for this is the spontaneous human response of identifying any interference, obstruction or damage caused to an individual as a nuisance. In attempting to interpret the word 'nuisance', the judiciary has been in a quandary. The meaning of the word 'nuisance' has been stretched from 'a potential source of annoyance'[49] to 'liability for any act of obstruction of the enjoyment of a legal right'.[50] Though the very concept of nuisance originated as retaliation against offences of a public nature, it has since been categorized into public and private nuisance. English common law rigidly classifies a public nuisance as a crime and a private nuisance as a civil wrong.[51] It is submitted that in the environmental law area it is the concept of private nuisance which is most relevant. The concept of private nuisance can be divided into a wrongful disturbance of land and a wrongful interjection of deleterious matter into land belonging to another. Therefore private nuisance is particularly appropriate to claims founded upon excessive noise because it is directed at the interference with a person's interest in the peaceful use and enjoyment of his property. The basis of this branch of the law is the necessity of maintaining a balance between the right of an occupier to use and enjoy his property and the right of an occupier to be protected from interference or injury.[52] Therefore courts, when adjudicating on environmental disputes and determining whether the tort of private nuisance is present, have to balance the equities between the parties. This section will attempt to trace the manner in which the Anglo-Australian judiciary has dealt with nuisance in noise pollution disputes.

The early English case of *Walter* v. *Selfe*[53] was the *tour de force* in awarding the remedy of private nuisance in the environmental law area. The famous dictum of Knight Bruce VC in this case concerned the test of whether emanations from land constitute a nuisance to persons in possession of other land. The criterion was whether they create: 'an inconvenience materially interfering with the ordinary comfort physically of human existence, not merely according to elegant or dainty modes and habits of living, but according to plain and sober and simple notions among the English people'.[54]

Another early case which is frequently considered as formulating the legal principles on nuisance as it applies to noise pollution is *Gaunt* v. *Fynney*. In this case Lord Selborne LC states:

> A nuisance by noise (supposing malice to be out of the question) is emphatically a question of degree. If my neighbour builds a house against a party-wall, next to my own, and I hear through the wall more than is agreeable to me of the sounds from his nursery or his music room, it does not follow (even if I am nervously sensitive or in infirm health) that I can bring an action or obtain an injunction. Such things, to offend against the law, must be done in a manner which, beyond fair controversy, ought to be regarded as exceptive and unreasonable.[55]

Later cases in determining whether noise amounts to a nuisance have applied these principles. In determining what is a reasonable noise and what are plain, sober and simple notions, the courts have had to consider the general nature of the neighbourhood, the nature of the location at which the alleged nuisance took place, the character, duration of time of occurrence of the noise and the effects of the noise.[56]

In an early case[57] decided by the Supreme Court of Victoria, Australia, the ringing of a church bell in the early morning hours of Sunday and public holidays in such a manner as to disturb persons residing in the neighbourhood was considered a nuisance. The court took into account, among other things, the degree of the disturbance caused. This case could be contrasted with a South Australian case decided a few years later.[58] The plaintiff, who lived 17 feet away from the defendant's premises, claimed an injunction and £500 in damages for depreciation of the value of his house by reason of the noises made by the defendant who conducted religious services on Sundays, commencing at 7 a.m. The noises the plaintiff complained of were singing, band playing, hand clapping and walking about the hall. It was held that singing in a place of religious worship is a sound considered to be ordinarily proceeding from such a place. Although the noises complained of in the two cases are similar, the judges in the South Australian case distinguished that case from the Victorian case on the basis that the necessary inference that can be drawn from the Victorian case is that the ringing of a church bell is not considered part of the service, whereas singing is a necessary part of religious worship. Whether such a distinction is logical is a moot point. Therefore, on similar facts, the judges in the two cases came to different conclusions.

In a New South Wales case[59] decided in 1928, the plaintiff, who was the defendant's neighbour, complained that the carrying on of building operations by the defendants by the use of mechanical drills caused a continuous deafening noise during normal business hours. The plaintiff contended that this noise prevented business being carried on in a building owned by the plaintiff. Despite the protests of the company, no effort had been made by the defendants to conduct their operations during hours when the plaintiff's business would not be affected. The court granted an injunction restraining the defendants from causing the nuisance. It was held that an alternative method of conducting their operations was available to the defendants, even though such method was more costly and time consuming. Long Innes J distinguished this case from an early English case[60] in which, on similar facts, the court held that an alternative method of operation would have endangered the lives of the employees.

However, in the later case of *Painter* v. *Reed*,[61] the Supreme Court of South Australia held that the alterations made by the defendant to make his business as unobjectionable as possible were not sufficient to prevent the plaintiff from succeeding in an action for nuisance. In contrast, a 1953 case[62] determined by the Supreme Court of South Australia found the alterations made by the defendant's operations, which substantially reduced the noise, were sufficient to no longer make the noise an actionable nuisance. In this case the plaintiff complained of the noise (and also the dust and the fumes) from a nearby sportsground which was also used as a speedway. Napier CJ, relying on *Gaunt* v. *Fynney*[63] and *Rushmer* v. *Polsue & Alfieri, Ltd*,[64] took into account the nature of the trades usually carried on in the locality and the benefit to the public from the entertainment provided by the defendant's business. His honour found a considerable interference by the defendant with the peace and comfort of the plaintiffs, but concluded that the nuisance no longer existed thanks to the alterations made by the defendant.

In a later case[65] the court took into account the fact that the plaintiff's sole occupation was poultry farming and that the use of explosives by the defendant to clear his land of stumps, which had adverse effects on the plaintiff's poultry, was a serious nuisance which warranted the granting of an injunction to prevent the nuisance. It was held that the defendant could use as an alternative, a reasonably practicable method of removing the trees, even though such a method would be more expensive. In a recent case determined by the Supreme Court of Western Australia,[66] even though the defendants had taken considerable steps to reduce the noise (and the dust) from their quarrying operations, the plaintiffs succeeded in their action in nuisance as the noise interfered with the use and enjoyment of their land.

In analysing the above cases it is clear that, in *Daily Telegraph Co. Ltd.* v. *Stuart* and in *McMahon* v. *Catanzaro* the courts granted injunctions to restrain the nuisance and ordered the defendants to use alternative methods even though such methods were expensive. In *Field*'s case, an injunction was not granted as the nuisance had already been abated by an alternative method. In all three cases the courts took into consideration the alternative methods of operation that the defendants could use and had used. However, in *Painter* v. *Reed*, although it was held by Richards J that 'the defendant had done very much to make the manner of carrying on his business unobjectionable',[67] this was not considered enough to have abated the nuisance. In

Aldridge v. *Clough*, Burt CJ found that 'each step taken no doubt had some beneficial effect', but his honour too came to the same conclusion as Richards J. Therefore, what is an unreasonable act to the plaintiff in nuisance disputes in the noise pollution area has to be determined according to the facts of each case, following the basic idea given in *Walter* v. *Selfe*. An objective standard cannot be used.

In continuing to analyse the judicial dicta on private nuisance as a remedy for noise pollution, the decision in *Ruthning* v. *Ferguson*[68] took into account the test of whether the noise of the defendants' birds interfered with the ordinary physical comfort of human existence according to the plain, sober and simple notions obtaining among the Australian people. An injunction had been granted restraining the defendant from keeping roosters in such a manner as to cause a nuisance to the plaintiffs. This decision was reversed on appeal because it was found in evidence that the complaints of the plaintiffs were grossly exaggerated.

A case decided in 1937 by the High Court of Australia[69] held that mere competition which is offered by the defendants does not amount to an actionable nuisance. The facts of the case, briefly, were that descriptions of races taking place on the plaintiff's land were broadcast by the defendants on adjoining land, without the plaintiff's permission. As a result of such broadcasting, attendance at the race course diminished. The plaintiff asked for an injunction to restrain such broadcasting as it amounted to a nuisance. It was held that, although the plaintiff suffered a substantial monetary loss due to the defendants' actions, it was not considered an interference with the use and enjoyment of the plaintiff's land.

Spencer v. *Silva*[70] was a case where the plaintiff complained of the noise caused by the defendant's use of saws in his business. Mayo J, in determining whether the noise infringed the plaintiff's right to comfort, considered whether the plaintiff was peculiarly susceptible to noise. His honour held the view that the test of determining such susceptibility is objective, that is, it is to be measured according to the plain, sober and simple notions among ordinary people. However, Mayo J held that, although the measure must be objective, the application of the test is subjective. The test is subjective to the extent that, in some circumstances, which do not include cases where the discomfort is purely personal, only very slight evidence of damage need be proved.[71] Concluding that the plaintiff was entitled to an injunction, his honour said:

> When that noise occurs daily for long periods, I think, it becomes a menace to reasonable comfort. It may be true that some people can readily adapt themselves to it without effort, others can with the exercise of determination accustom themselves to it ... but that does not necessarily mean, because that is so, if it is, that the law requires all persons to enure themselves to the unpleasantness or quit.[72]

In the case of *Dunstan* v. *King*,[73] the prolonged and excessive noise emitted from a sawmill and a diesel engine and the smoke and oil fumes therefrom was the alleged nuisance complained of by the plaintiffs who were four residents of that locality. The court followed the rationale in the earlier case of *Spencer* v. *Silva* and decided that the plaintiffs had truthfully described the effects of the mill upon themselves.

Similarly, a case decided two years later[74] considered whether the plaintiff was peculiarly sensitive to the noise complained of. Roper CJ asked the question: 'Are they fastidious or neurotic or oversensitive to something which according to simple and sober notions is not an annoyance at all, or not an annoyance to any appreciable degree?'[75] and came to the conclusion that the noise of the defendant's pigeons flying over the plaintiff's land would be an intolerable nuisance to reasonable normal people.

In *Clarey* v. *Principal and Council of the Women's College*,[76] the High Court of Australia had to consider whether a landlord who lets a portion of his residence for the accommodation of university students could complain that the conduct of the students in making noises which are incidental to the occupation of premises as a dwelling place such as walking about, having a bath, laughing and talking, constitute a nuisance to adjoining occupiers within the meaning of subsection 41(5)(*d*) of The Landlord and Tenant Acts of 1948 to 1950. The court, using *Pollock on Torts* as an authority, came to the conclusion that the use of a dwelling house in an ordinary and accustomed manner is not a nuisance, though it may produce more or less noise and inconvenience to a neighbour.[77]

In *Munro* v. *Southern Dairies Ltd*,[78] the plaintiff complained of the noise and smell from the defendant's dairy. The court, in determining whether the noise and the smell amounted to a nuisance, took into consideration, *inter alia*, the particular sensitivity, if any, of the plaintiff. Sholl J held that, although a man is not entitled to relief merely because he may happen to be unduly sensitive to noise, yet a man who lives next door to premises from which the noise emanates may get relief when another man some distance away will fail to obtain it.[79]

The American case of *Boomer* v. *Atlantic Cement Company*[80] is an example of a case in which the court was swayed by the economic position of the defendant company.[81] Here the plaintiff alleged property damage caused by the dirt and vibrations resulting from the defendant's industrial complex. The court recognized a substantial interference of the plaintiff's rights. Although the court cites the law in New York, which is to the effect that a nuisance will be found to exist even though there is marked disparity in economic consequence between the effect of the injunction and the effect of the nuisance, yet it strangely decided to ignore it on the basis that the rule should not be followed too 'literally'.[82] The court granted damages to the plaintiff instead of an injunction obviously because they were favourably impressed by the vast wealth of the defendant company and knew that a permanent injunction would have caused a significant loss to the company. The court may have been influenced in its decision by the loss of employment to the 300 workers of the defendant company if the court granted an injunction. However, the ability of the common law in protecting the ordinary citizen is illustrated in the English case of *Halsey* v. *Esso Petroleum Co. Ltd.*[83] The plaintiff in this case lived in an area zoned for residential purposes. The defendant, who was a mammoth oil company, used land on the opposite side as an oil storage depot. The plaintiff alleged nuisance resulting from the noise and smell of the defendant's operations. In this case the court refused to be awed by the economic position of the defendant and seemed to base the judgment on the principle that the standards binding on both parties are those of the ordinary reasonable man. Although the defendant company had taken a number of steps to abate the nuisance, the court found that an actionable nuisance existed and granted an injunction restraining the defendant from carrying on the activities which caused the nuisance. Although in both cases the court held that a nuisance existed, in the English case the court by granting an injunction prevented the recurrence of the nuisance. These two cases illustrate the subjective approach adopted by the judiciary in nuisance disputes. A general principle cannot be culled from these decisions.

The case of *Aldridge* v. *Clough*[84] echoes the time-honoured words in *Walter* v. *Selfe*. Burt CJ considered carefully whether the plaintiffs were especially sensitive to the noise and dust from the quarry. His honour came to the conclusion that the evidence of the plaintiffs was not only honest but also fairly objective. The earlier New South Wales case of *Farley and Lewers Ltd*. v. *Attorney General*[85] was cited as authority for the proposition that the plaintiffs' reaction should represent the reaction of the ordinary person. In the course of his judgment, Burt CJ referred to the Noise Abatement Act of 1972 which attempts to prescribe noise levels which, if exceeded, constitute an offence, and held that, on the evidence of the plaintiffs, the latter had made good the claim in nuisance.[86] Although the judgment is clearly based on the rationale in *Walter* v. *Selfe*, Burt CJ determined the case on the evidence, according to his individual view of what constitutes an interference with 'plain and sober notions among our people'.[87]

Relevance of locality

A frequent factor that courts take into consideration in determining whether a particular activity is a nuisance is the locality of the alleged nuisance. For instance, in *Painter* v. *Reed*,[88] in determining whether the noises caused in the early morning by the movement and stamping of horses which disturbed the sleep of the plaintiff constituted an actionable nuisance and should be restrained by injunction, Richards J considered carefully the locality in which the alleged nuisance occurred. His honour was of the opinion that, although the defendant's business was situated in a very suitable place in the city, yet the noise complained of was not as reasonable as the law would require. In *Dunstan* v. *King*,[89] in coming to the conclusion that the noise amounted to an actionable nuisance, the court considered the type of locality in question. Although it was adduced in evidence that there were other sawmills in the district, the court held that there was no other industrial undertaking within reasonable distance of the particular locality, which had the character of a quiet countryside.[90] In *Munro* v. *Southern Dairies Ltd*,[91] too, in considering whether the noise complained of was characteristic of the particular neighbourhood, Sholl J held that it was not so.[92]

In another case,[93] the defendant was a haulage contractor and the noise and the dust caused by his business constituted a substantial nuisance to the plaintiff. The court cited a great deal of judicial authority in this area of the law. After considering the pecuniary loss resulting to the defendant if the court granted a permanent injunction, the fact that no one else living in the neighbourhood supported the plaintiff and the fact that the plaintiff had a motive for complaining about the noise (there was ill-feeling between the two families), the court came to the conclusion that, in a residential suburb, a man is not at liberty habitually to start a noisy motor vehicle at very early hours of the morning when his neighbours are usually asleep. Upon the defendant undertaking to abate the nuisance, the action was dismissed. This case underscores the preoccupation of judges in considering the locality of the alleged nuisance important, even in circumstances where there is evidence in favour of the defendant.

The relevance of locality has been considered in situations where the defendant avers that the plaintiff came to the nuisance. However, 'coming to the nuisance' is not a defence to an action in nuisance. Certain cases have discussed this non-defence. One of the earliest cases[94] which has done so held that the plaintiff's having come to the nuisance did not disentitle him to equitable relief. In *Barber* v. *Penley*,[95] the offending noise came from the crowd at a theatre in the locality where the plaintiff lived. It was held that a person who deliberately goes next door to a theatre cannot expect to have precisely the same amenities that the lessee of a private house in a street occupied by private houses only in the West End would expect. However, the court held that such a lessee still has the right to expect that no nuisance shall be committed to the prejudice of such person.[96] In the more recent case of *Miller* v. *Jackson*,[97] Geoffrey Lane LJ posed the question: 'can the defendants take advantage of the fact that the plaintiffs have put themselves in such a position by coming to occupy a house on the edge of a small cricket field, with the result that what was not a nuisance in the past now becomes a nuisance?'[98]

His lordship held that, although he was inclined to find for the defendants he could not do so as he was bound by judicial precedent. The case of *Sturges* v. *Bridgman*[99]was cited as authority for the proposition that it is no answer to a claim in nuisance for a defendant to show that the plaintiff brought the trouble upon himself by building and coming to live in a house so close to the defendant's premises that he would inevitably be affected by the defendant's activities.[100] Geoffrey Lane LJ thought that this rule works injustice. He reluctantly held for the plaintiff. His lordship seemed to have been much impressed by the fact that the locality was a country area in which cricket was an important activity. Thus courts throughout the ages have been influenced by the locality in question in considering whether the plaintiff came to the nuisance.

The public benefit criterion

Certain cases have considered whether the benefit to the public by the defendant's activity would override the nuisance such activity would cause to the plaintiff. *Munro* v. *Southern Dairies Ltd*[101] was such a case. In this case, Sholl J cited the early case of *Shelfer* v. *City of London Electric Lighting Company*[102] in support of his contention that the public benefit resulting from the defendant's activity was not sufficient to prevent the plaintiff from succeeding in the nuisance action. In the more recent English case of *Kennaway* v. *Thompson and another*,[103] the Court of Appeal considered the jeopardy caused to the public interest in granting an injunction prohibiting the defendant, a boating club, from carrying on noisy activities which prevented the plaintiff from using and enjoying her land. Lawton LJ held that, although the plaintiff was not entitled to an injunction restraining all of the club's activities because there had to be a reasonable amount of give and take, those activities which caused a serious nuisance to her should be restrained by injunction.[104] His lordship was of the opinion that the public benefit generated by the defendant's activities outweighed the inconvenience to the plaintiff who had to absent herself from her house for many days in order to avoid the noise.[105] In dismissing the case of *Miller* v. *Jackson*[106] as not binding on the present case, his lordship held that the statement of Lord Denning MR in that case, that the public interest should prevail over the private interest, runs counter to the principles enunciated in the early case of *Shelfer* v. *City of London Electric Lighting Company.*[107] *Kennaway* v. *Thompson* reiterated the attitude of the courts in considering a person's right to use and enjoy his land as sacrosanct as opposed to the benefit to the public that may accrue from the defendant's activities.

Remedies for nuisance

Damages and injunctions are the two important remedies[108] granted to a successful plaintiff in a nuisance action. Judges have had difficulty in determining whether damages or injunctions should be granted and, if damages are to be awarded, the test in determining reasonable damages. The loss need not be of a pecuniary nature but must be material or substantial. The loss complained of in most of the cases on nuisance by noise is the interference with the use and enjoyment of the complainant's premises.

The decision of *Oldham* v. *Lawson*[109] examined the question of whether damages should be granted for non-pecuniary loss. Harris J held that, until the 1975 case of *Bone* v. *Seale*,[110] there was no test applicable that would warrant the award of damages in the instance where the nuisance complained of does not affect the plaintiff's property. Harris J relied on the dictum of Scarman LJ in *Bone* v. *Seale*: 'Nuisance is a wrong to property, but it is well recognised that even when there is no physical damage to property it may cause annoyance, inconvenience and discomfort to the occupier of the property in his enjoyment of it.'[111]

Scarman LJ relied on *McGregor on Damages* to buttress his proposition that damages are allowable for non-pecuniary loss caused by nuisance and that such damages should be regarded as part of the normal measure of damages; in determining what the normal measure of damages is, his lordship held that the general principle in cases where there is no financial yardstick in awarding damages were formulated by Lord Morris of Borth-y-Gest in *H. West & Son Ltd.* v. *Shephard*,[112] when his lordship said that all that judges and courts can do is to award sums which must be regarded as giving reasonable compensation.

On the question of what is reasonable, Scarman LJ held that there was very little guidance in the law, which led his lordship to formulate the following principle:

> One must bear in mind also a further general principle, that, when one is removed from the world of pecuniary loss and is attempting to measure damages for non-pecuniary loss, an element in reasonableness is the fairness of the compensation to be awarded. There must be moderation; some attention must be paid to the rights of the offending defendant as well as the rights of the injured plaintiff.[113]

Although Harris J accepted this proposition as an accurate statement of the law, it is submitted that Scarman LJ seemed to have experienced the same difficulty as his predecessors in formulating a test for non-pecuniary damages. His lordship, too, fails to formulate a comprehensive test.

In *Spencer* v. *Silva*[114] Mayo J discussed the instances when damages should be granted in lieu of injunctions.[115] Damages instead of an injunction might be given if the injury to the plaintiff's legal right was small, was capable of being estimated in money, could be adequately compensated by a small money payment or if the injunction would be oppressive to the defendant. Mayo J discusses another instance when damages should be granted instead of an injunction. This is the instance when considerable time has elapsed before the plaintiff instituted legal proceedings.[116] It is submitted that, although such a clear statement of the law has been formulated, judges have persisted in applying subjective criteria in determining whether damages or injunctions should be granted. For instance, in *Boomer* v. *Atlantic Cement Company*,[117] the judge refused to grant an injunction preventing the defendant from continuing his commercial activities which was a considerable nuisance to the plaintiff, because the judge was swayed in his judgment by the wealth of the defendant company.

In *Vincent* v. *Peacock*,[118] the court discussed the instances when an injunction should not be granted. In this regard, the court considered the statement of Lord Evershed MR in *Pride of Derby and Derbyshire Angling Association LD.* v. *British Celanese LD.*[119] important. According to Lord Evershed MR, if A proves that his property rights are being wrongfully interfered with by B, and that B intends to continue his wrong, then A is *prima facie* entitled to an injunction, and he will be deprived of that remedy only if special circumstances exist, including the circumstance that damages are an adequate remedy for the wrong that he has suffered.[120] The court in *Vincent* v. *Peacock* held that instances of special circumstances would be extreme hardship, where the effect of granting an injunction would be to order someone to perform an impossibility or to abstain from doing something which is impossible for him not to do. The Supreme Court overruled the decision of the lower court, which failed to grant an injunction to restrain the defendant's drunken behaviour which prevented the plaintiffs from the reasonable enjoyment of their home. The lower court seemed to have considered the facts that the offensive behaviour occurred only when the defendant was drunk and the admission of the defendant that he was an alcoholic sufficed as special circumstances for an injunction not to be granted.[121] The reasoning of the lower court was based on the premise that it was futile to issue an injunction against an offender who cannot control the commission of the offence, being in a perpetual state of intoxication. It is apparent that these were not special circumstances within the rule mentioned above. Special circumstances could be interpreted by different judges in different ways, as the above case illustrates.

The courts may not only grant a remedy to a plaintiff subsequent to the commission of a nuisance from which he suffers; they may also issue an injunction to prohibit any activity which could cause a nuisance. The latter is called a *quia timet* injunction. This effectively precludes the commission of an act which would result in a nuisance. A *quia timet* injunction should be granted only if three factors are present. First would an act considered in a *quia timet* action, if not prohibited, cause a nuisance to the plaintiff? Second, if it would, how imminent is the nuisance? Finally, would the nuisance caused to the plaintiff result in substantial damage to him?

In determining whether these three factors are present, the onus of proof on the plaintiff was considered to be an important consideration in the case of *Grasso* v. *Love*[122] determined by the Full Court of the Supreme Court of Victoria, Australia. Disapproving of the expression 'moral certainty' used in an earlier case[123] to describe what the plaintiff must prove, as suggesting a criminal onus of proof, the court held that there is no third onus of proof required in *quia timet* injunctions, lying between the civil and criminal onus. It was held by the Full Court that the plaintiff must prove that there is a real probability that the defendants' activities would cause a nuisance.[124] Citing academic authority in support of their view,[125] the judges held that, in determining the real probability of the alleged nuisance, the relevant circumstances of the case should be taken into account, to determine whether the issuance of the injunction would be unfair to either party to the action.[126] For example, in *Grasso* v. *Love*, on an appeal against the granting of an injunction against the construction of a drive-in cinema, the appellants argued mainly on the grounds that evidential facts were insufficiently considered in the court of first instance which resulted in a permanent injunction against them. It was held on appeal that, although the issuance of the injunction was justified to the extent that substantial damage would have been caused to the respondents who resided in a portion of the land had the injunction not been issued, it need not have applied to the entire land as there was insufficient evidence to show that the proposed drive-in cinema would have caused a nuisance to the respondents had it been erected on a portion of the land a considerable distance away from the respondents' home. Therefore the Supreme Court considered the rights of both parties in reaching their decision. However, it could be argued that 'relevant circumstances' is a purely subjective phrase and is dependent on the interpretation given to it by courts.

A historical analysis of the *cursus curiae* in the field of nuisance as a remedy for noise pollution illustrates the fact that judges throughout the ages up to the present time have been influenced by the fundamental legal principle enunciated in the early English case of *Walter* v. *Selfe*. However, the judges in the different cases have given their own interpretation of the rationale in *Walter* v. *Selfe*. Although it could be stated that diversity in judicial opinion leads to independence in judicial thinking and that judges should not be hampered by a comprehensive definition, a strong argument against this type of attitude is that the law would be ambivalent when there were a multitude of judicial opinions on one point, out of which no general principle could be culled. It is this vagueness which has led to the common law of nuisance being to a large extent replaced by an array of statutory provisions which have been designed to control environmental damage.

Regulatory issues

The Chicago Convention[127] is the fundamental source which grants regulatory powers to the international community on matters relating to international civil aviation. The Convention in its preamble proclaims that the governments that are parties to it agree on certain principles and arrangements in order that international civil aviation may be developed in a safe and orderly manner. Public safety is a feature of major concern to the Convention, which requires that

> Each contracting State may, for reasons of military necessity or public safety, restrict or prohibit uniformly the aircraft of other States from flying over certain areas of its territory … Such prohibited areas shall be of reasonable extent and location so as not to interfere unnecessarily with air navigation. Descriptions of such prohibited areas in the territory of a contracting State, as well as any subsequent alterations therein, shall be communicated as soon as possible to the other contracting States and to the International Civil Aviation Organization.[128]

The Convention also established the International Civil Aviation Organization, which is required as one of its objectives to foster the planning and development of international air transport so as, *inter alia*, to ensure the safe and orderly growth of international civil aviation throughout the world,[129] to meet the needs of the people of the world for safe, regular, efficient and economic air transport,[130] to promote safety of flight in international air navigation,[131] and to promote generally the development of all aspects of international civil aviation.[132] To this end, ICAO is mandated by the Convention to adopt and amend from time to time as may be necessary, international Standards and Recommended Practices (SARPS) dealing, *inter alia*, with characteristics of airports and landing areas and such matters concerned with the safety, regularity and efficiency of air navigation as may from time to time be appropriate.[133] Each contracting state has undertaken to collaborate in securing the highest practicable degree of uniformity in the above regulations, standards and procedures of the organization.

In order to carry out its policies in environmental issues related to civil aviation, ICAO established the Committee on Aviation Environmental Protection (CAEP) in 1983.[134] CAEP is a technical committee reporting to the ICAO Council and consisting of 14 members nominated by their states. The members are experts in the field of aviation and the environment. The Committee is charged with addressing the main environmental problems involving civil aviation, which are pollution caused by aircraft engine emissions and aircraft noise. The three main approaches adopted by CAEP in its work on aircraft noise concern reduction of noise at source, use of noise abatement operating measures, and land use planning. One of the CAEP's positive contributions to ICAO's environmental programme has been the development of a new chapter for Volume 1 of Annex 16, which contains a noise certification scheme for light helicopters as well as a number of modifications to the technical specifications of the annex. CAEP believes that, although ICAO initiatives on Chapter 2 aircraft (aircraft referred to in Chapter 2 of Annex 16) withdrawal will ameliorate the problem of noise near airports, it will be short-lived, as the rapidly increasing proportions of international air travel in the next few years will render the benefits brought about by the initiative nugatory.

At its Fourth Meeting, held in April 1998, CAEP focused, *inter alia*, on the subject of nuisance and noise from light aircraft and recommended that pilots and operators be aware of the nuisance their operations may cause and take steps to minimize noise levels of their aircraft. In the light of developments concerning the replacement of Chapter 2 aircraft wholly by Chapter 3 aircraft, CAEP has been charged with an extension to its mandate, to undertake additional work on reviewing Chapter 3 noise standards with a view to identifying a standard even more stringent than the Chapter 3 representation.[135] The Noise Scenarios Group was established within CAEP for the purpose of addressing increased options for possible aircraft noise restriction levels.[136]

ICAO's active involvement in aviation-related environmental issues is not without good reason, as nine of the 27 principles contained in the Declaration of the United Nations Conference on Environment and Development (UNCED) – also known as the 'Earth Summit' – held in Rio de Janeiro in June 1992.

1 'States have … the responsibility to ensure that activities within their jurisdiction or control do not cause damage to the environment of other States or of areas beyond the limits of national jurisdiction.' (Principle 2)
2 'The special situation and needs of developing countries, particularly the least

developed … shall be given special priority. International actions in the field of environment and development should also address the interests and needs of all countries.' (Principle 6)

3 'In view of the different contributions to global environmental degradation, States have common but differentiated responsibilities. The developed countries acknowledge the responsibility that they bear in the international pursuit of sustainable development in view of the pressures their societies place on the global environment and of the technologies and financial resources they command.' (Principle 7)

4 'To achieve sustainable development and a higher quality of life for all people, States should reduce and eliminate unsustainable patterns of production and consumption … ' (Principle 8)

5 'States shall enact effective environmental legislation. Environmental standards, management objectives and priorities should reflect the environmental and developmental context to which they apply. Standards applied by some countries may be inappropriate and of unwarranted economic and social cost to other countries, in particular developing countries.' (Principle 11)

6 'Environmental measures addressing trans-boundary or global environmental problems should, as far as possible, be based on an international consensus.' (Principle 12)

7 'In order to protect the environment, the precautionary approach shall be widely applied by States according to their capabilities. Where there are threats of serious or irreversible damage, lack of full scientific certainty shall not be used as a reason for postponing cost-effective measures to prevent environmental degradation.' (Principle 15)

8 'National authorities should endeavour to promote the internalization of environmental costs and the use of economic instruments, taking into account the approach that the polluter should, in principle, bear the cost of pollution.' (Principle 16)

9 'Environmental impact assessment, as a national instrument, shall be undertaken for proposed activities that are likely to have a significant adverse impact on the environment and are subject to a decision of a competent national authority.' (Principle 17)

Standards and Recommended Practices for aircraft noise were first adopted by ICAO on 2 April 1971 and designated as Annex 16 to the Convention. The development of the annex originated in September 1968 at the 16th Session of the ICAO Assembly which adopted Resolution A16-3 which recognized that the problem of aircraft noise was so serious in the vicinity of many of the world's airports that public reaction was mounting to a degree that gave cause for great concern and required urgent solution. The assembly also noted that noise concerned the public and civil aviation and was becoming a matter for concern with the increase in air traffic and that the introduction of future aircraft types could increase and aggravate the problem further unless action was taken to alleviate it. Accordingly, the assembly resolved to instruct the ICAO Council to call an international conference within the machinery of ICAO as soon as possible; to establish international specifications and associated guidance material relating to aircraft noise; and to include, in the appropriate annexes and other relevant ICAO documents and possibly in a separate annex on noise, such material as the description and methods of measurement of aircraft noise and suitable limitations on the noise caused by aircraft that was of concern to communities in the vicinity of airports.

In response to the assembly resolution, a Special Meeting on Aircraft Noise in the Vicinity of Aerodromes was convened in Montreal in November–December 1969 to examine the following aspects related to the problems of aircraft noise:

a procedures for describing and measuring aircraft noise
b human tolerance to aircraft noise,
c aircraft noise certification
d criteria for establishment of aircraft noise abatement operating procedures,
e land use control, and
f ground run-up noise abatement procedures.

Based on the recommendations of the Special Meeting on Aircraft Noise in the Vicinity of Aerodromes, draft International Standards and Recommended Practices for Aircraft Noise were developed and, after amendment following the usual consultation with the contracting states of the organization, were adopted by the council to form the text of Annex 16.

With the development of Standards and Recommended Practices dealing with the control of aircraft engine emissions, it was felt that all provisions relating to environmental aspects of aviation should be included in a single document. Accordingly, Annex 16 was retitled as 'Environmental Protection'. Volume I of the Annex contains the existing provisions relating to aircraft noise and Volume II contains the provisions related to aircraft engine emissions.[137] The much-dreaded sonic boom[138] caused by supersonic aircraft was broadly discussed during the Second Meeting of ICAO's Sonic Boom Committee in Montreal in June 1973.[139] The committee found that the sonic boom had no ill-effects on the human eye and ear. As for psychological effects of the boom, it was noted by the committee that it caused a startle reaction in the human being, in addition to a slight increase in heart rate which returned to normal within a very short period. It was also the committee's view that the startle effects of the Concorde and TU-144 aircraft did not give rise to any significant circulatory effects. With regard to the sociological effects of the sonic boom, the committee considered a study of the Concorde aircraft over Australia in June 1972 and concluded that this aspect should be best studied as both a public and a private law issue by the Legal Committee of ICAO.

The ICAO Assembly has, in addition, adopted several resolutions concerning aviation and the environment. At its 22nd meeting, held in September/October

1977, the ICAO Assembly adopted Resolution A22-12, which recognized, *inter alia*, the following:

1 advancing technology has caused aviation to become a significant influence in the environment;
2 many of the adverse environmental effects of civil aviation activity can be reduced, by the application of integrated measures embracing technological improvements, appropriate noise abatement operating procedures, proper organization of air traffic and the appropriate use of airport planning and land use control mechanisms;
3 other international organizations are becoming involved in activities relating to noise abatement policies;
4 in fulfilling its role, ICAO strives to achieve a balance between the benefit accruing to the world community through civil aviation and the harm caused to the human environment in certain areas through the progressive advancement of civil aviation.

The assembly therefore declared:

1 that ICAO is conscious of the adverse environmental impacts that may be related to aircraft activity and of its responsibility and that of its contracting states to achieve maximum compatibility between the safe and orderly development of civil aviation and the quality of the human environment;
2 that the council should maintain its vigilance in the pursuit of aviation interests related to the human environment and also maintain the initiative in developing policy guidance on all aviation matters related to the human environment, and not leave such initiatives to other organizations.

The assembly also invited states to continue their active support for ICAO's Action Programme Regarding the Environment on all appropriate occasions as their participation in civil aviation's contribution to the United Nations Environment Programme (UNEP) and authorized the ICAO Council, if and when it deems this desirable, to enter into cooperative arrangements with UNEP for the execution of environmental projects financed by the United Nations Environment Fund. The assembly urged states to refrain from unilateral measures that would be harmful to the development of international civil aviation.

At the same session, the assembly adopted Resolution A22–13 on airports and the environment, observing, *inter alia*:

1 the compatibility between the airport and its environment was one of the elements to be taken into account in long-term systems planning;
2 the problem of aircraft noise in the vicinity of many of the world's airports continued to arouse public concern and required appropriate action;

3 the introduction of future aircraft types could increase and aggravate this noise unless action was taken to alleviate the situation.

The assembly therefore requested the council to continue its work on establishing Standards and Recommended Practices relating to the alleviation of the problem and urged contracting states to adopt, where appropriate, the ICAO measures and procedures applicable.

In the following session (September/October 1980), the assembly adopted Resolution A23-10 on aircraft noise and engine emissions from subsonic aircraft and requested contracting states not to allow the operation of foreign-registered subsonic jet planes that did not conform to ICAO's specifications on noise certification standards as specified in Annex 16 until 1 January 1988.[140] At the 28th Assembly Sessions held in October 1990, the ICAO Assembly observed that, while certification standards for subsonic jet aircraft noise levels are specified in Volume I, Chapter 2 and Chapter 3 of Annex 16 and that environmental problems due to aircraft noise continued to exist in the neighbourhood of many international airports, some states were consequently considering restrictions on the operations of aircraft which exceed the noise levels in Volume I, Chapter 3 of Annex 16. The assembly also recognized that the noise standards in Annex 16 were not intended to introduce operating restrictions on aircraft and that operating restrictions on existing aircraft would increase the costs of airlines and would impose a heavy economic burden, particularly on those airlines which do not have the financial resources to re-equip their fleets. Therefore, considering that resolution of problems due to aircraft noise must be based on the mutual recognition of the difficulties encountered by states and a balance among their different concerns, the assembly, by Resolution A28-3, urged states not to introduce any new operating restrictions on aircraft which exceed the noise levels in Volume I, Chapter 3 of Annex 16 before considering

a whether the normal attrition of existing fleets of such aircraft will provide the necessary protection of noise climates around their airports;

b whether the necessary protection can be achieved by regulations preventing their operators from adding such aircraft to their fleets through either purchase or lease/charter/interchange or, alternatively, by incentives to accelerate fleet modernization;

c whether the necessary protection can be achieved through restrictions limited to airports and runways the use of which has been identified and declared by them as generating noise problems and limited to time periods when greater noise disturbance is caused; and,

d the implications of any restrictions for other states concerned, consulting these states, and giving them reasonable notice of intention.

The assembly further urged states

a to frame any restrictions so that Chapter 2-compliant aircraft of an individual operator which are currently operating to their territories may be withdrawn from these operations gradually over a period of not less than seven years;
b not to begin the above phase-in period for any restrictions before 1 April 1995;
c not to restrict before the end of the phase-in period the operations of any aircraft less than 25 years after the date of issue of its first individual certificate of airworthiness;
d not to restrict before the end of the phase-in period the operations of any currently existing wide-body aircraft or of any fitted with high by-pass ratio engines;
e to apply any restrictions consistently with the non-discrimination principle in Article 15 of the Chicago Convention so as to give foreign operators at least as favourable treatment as their own operators at the same airports; and
f to inform the ICAO, as well as the other states concerned, of all restrictions imposed.

The assembly also strongly encouraged states to continue to cooperate bilaterally, regionally and interregionally, with a view to (a) alleviating the noise burden on communities around airports without imposing severe economic hardship on aircraft operators, and (b) taking into account the problems of operators of developing countries with regard to Chapter 2 aircraft currently on their register, where they cannot be replaced before the end of the phase-in period, provided that there is proof of a purchase order or leasing contract placed for a replacement Chapter 3-compliant aircraft and the first date of delivery of the aircraft has been accepted.

The assembly, while urging states, if and when any new noise certification standards are introduced which are more stringent than those in Volume I, Chapter 3 of Annex 16, not to impose any operating restrictions on Chapter 3-compliant aircraft, urged the council to promote and states to develop an integrated approach to the problem of aircraft noise, including land-use planning procedures around international airports, so that any residential, industrial or other land-use that might be adversely affected by aircraft noise is minimal. The assembly further urged states to assist aircraft operators in their efforts to accelerate fleet modernization and thereby prevent obstacles and permit all states to have access to lease or purchase aircraft compliant with Chapter 3, including the provision of multilateral technical assistance where appropriate. This resolution superseded Resolution A23-10, which was discussed above.

Resolution A 28-3 represents a cautious balance between the concerns of the aircraft manufacturers, the airline industry and developing states who do not wish to lose, in the near future, the services of Chapter 2 aircraft which are already in use and service. Although aircraft manufactured prior to October 1977 that are included in Chapter 2 of Annex 16 and called 'Chapter 2 aircraft' are required to be phased out, the compromise in Resolution A28-3 allows states that have noise problems at airports to start phasing out operations by Chapter 2 aircraft from the year 1995 and to have all of them withdrawn by the year 2002, with some exceptions. The resolution envisages that, by the year 2002, only aircraft manufactured after October 1977 and described in Chapter 3 of Annex 16 (called 'Chapter 3 aircraft') would be in operation. Following this resolution, a number of developed states have already started to phase out Chapter 2 aircraft, while giving due recognition to the compromise reached in Resolution A28-3.

At the ICAO's 32nd Assembly, held in September 1998, Assembly Resolution A32-8[141] containing a consolidated statement of continuing ICAO policies and practices related to environmental protection was adopted, making current the regulatory policies relating to aviation and the environment. Appendix B to the resolution cites Annex 16, Volume I as comprising, *inter alia,* noise certification standards for future subsonic aircraft and mentions that aircraft manufacturers and operators need to note that future generations of aircraft have to be so designed as to operate efficiently and with the least possible environmental disturbance. Appendix C calls upon contracting states and international organizations to recognize the leading role of ICAO in dealing with aircraft noise and requests the former to work closely together to ensure the greatest harmonization of work in the area of environmental protection as related to air transport. In Appendix G, which relates to the problem of sonic boom, the assembly reaffirms the importance attached to ameliorating problems caused to the public by sonic boom as a result of supersonic flight and invites states involved in the manufacture of supersonic aircraft to furnish ICAO with proposals that would meet specifications established by ICAO on the subject.

The most topical issue addressed by Resolution A32–8, is in its Appendix D, which, while reiterating the time limits specified for the phasing out of Chapter 2 aircraft and related dates, strongly encourages states to continue to cooperate bilaterally, regionally and interregionally with a view to alleviating the noise burden on communities and also to take into account the problems that may be faced by some operators in phasing out their Chapter 2 aircraft before the end of the period specified. The resolution also urges states, if and when any new noise certification standards are introduced which are more stringent than those in Volume I, Chapter 3 of Annex 16, not to impose any operating restrictions on Chapter 3-compliant aircraft. More importantly, states are urged to assist operators in their efforts at fleet modernization with a view to preventing obstacles and to permit all states to have access to lease or purchase aircraft compliant with Chapter 3.

The qualification in Resolution A32-8 seemingly admits of Chapter 2 aircraft which are converted to be compliant with Chapter 3 noise levels being considered for operation at least until 1 April 2002. The resolution urges states to consider the difficulties faced by operators of Chapter 2 aircraft who are unable to make them Chapter 3-compliant by the given date, implying that it would be in the economic interests of such operators to be given additional time in order to make the necessary replacements. Chapter 2 aircraft could be made Chapter 3-compliant so that the aircraft could be recertified to Chapter 3 standards through re-engining or hush kitting (the technical modification of an aircraft engine to make it less noisy and conform to acceptable noise levels). Chapter 2 aircraft which are likely to be re-engined or hush-kitted are Boeing 727s and 737s, DC-9s, BAC1-11s and some Boeing 747-100s.

There is an attempt on the part of the European Union to limit and eventually eliminate Chapter 3-compliant aircraft from operating within EU countries. This ban would also be calculated to affect the importing of such aircraft into the region. Legislation passed by the Union in April 1999 was intended to bar Chapter 3-compliant aircraft from European registries from 4 May 2000 (originally 1 April 1999, which is three years before the date specified in Resolution A32-8, namely, 1 April 2002) and to prohibit their operation into the countries of the EU after 1 April 2002. Such action has reportedly been criticized by the Air Transport Association which claims that the inflexibility of such a deadline 'will severely undercut – if not destroy entirely – ICAO's efforts to address environmental issues on a uniform international basis'.[142]

The action of the European Union seeks justification on the basis that the exponential air traffic growth in Europe will increase noise around European airports, requiring stringent noise standards. A related fear is reportedly that hush-kitted aircraft, which are rare in Europe, will find a new home in the Continent. Unlike the situation in Europe, airlines in the United States have been somewhat prolific in the use of hush-kits in aircraft[143] and many United States carriers operate Stage 2 hush-kitted aircraft into Europe and even have based equipment in the Continent. In late 1999, although the US State Department had reacted forcefully to the European Union's hush-kitted aircraft ban, the application of which was extended by the Union until May 2000, it was reported that the United States and the European Union were working together on a possible new ICAO Standard (presumably to be called 'Chapter 4').[144]

The issue is a 'double-edged sword' involving two distinct disciplines. As discussed earlier, the European contention is based on the strictly legal issue of noise pollution and overtones of the tort of nuisance committed by operators whose aircraft are not compliant with Chapter 3 standards to the satisfaction of the European Union. Others who oppose what they claim to be a premature enforcement of ICAO standards, as contained in Resolution A32-8, argue that the European hush-kit rule would cost the manufacturing industry significant losses. It is reported that the US industry would lose $2 billion if the ban was enforced in Europe as scheduled.[145]

The aircraft noise issue has entered a phase where trading and environmental issues are at a delicate balance. On the one hand, competition issues pertaining to the sale of hush-kits and other equipment calculated to reduce aircraft engine noise to levels prescribed by ICAO are quite significant from the perspective of international trade, and, on the other hand, environmental issues that have been addressed by the ICAO Council through CAEP and also by the assembly should be given careful consideration. As discussed earlier, ICAO Assembly Resolution A32-8 urges states to give consideration to the economic difficulties that some states may have to face in phasing out Chapter 2 aircraft by the year 2002. However, the resolution does not leave room for states to claim that pure economic factors would effectively preclude them from phasing out Chapter 2 aircraft by the date stipulated in the resolution.

In the context of the competition issue involved, the rules prescribed by the World Trade Organization are indeed applicable and warrant some discussion. WTO seeks to establish a multilateral framework of principles and rules for trade in services with a view to expansion of such trade under conditions of *transparency*,[146] national treatment[147] and *progressive liberalization*. The fundamental principle of GATT is its Most Favoured Nation (MFN) treatment clause whereby each party to the agreement accords immediately and unconditionally, to services and service providers of any other party, treatment no less favourable than that it accords to like services and service providers of any other country.

The genesis of competition law in trade, and, therefore, of WTO rules on competition, may well lie in the United Nations Conference on Trade and Employment, held in Havana in November 1947. This conference laid the ground for the International Trade Organization (ITO), the charter of which had two chapters relating to competition. Chapter III of the Charter of the International Trade Organization provided that no member shall impose unreasonable or unjustifiable impediments that would preclude other members from obtaining, on equitable terms, facilities for economic development. Chapter V, which provided for the elimination of restrictive business practices, requires that each member will take appropriate measures, individually or through collective involvement, to prevent business practices from affecting international trade thereby leading to restrained competition, limited access to markets or fostered monopolistic practices.[148] The ITO competition rules were embellished with controls over price-fixing and other forms of anti-competitive practices endemic to private enterprises. However, the functioning of ITO never attained fruition and these provisions remained academic. A second attempt was made by the United Nations Economic and Social Council (ECOSOC)[149] and this effort too was destined for failure. The third attempt, made by GATT in 1959, also failed to elicit a concrete proposal. Later, the Organization for Economic Cooperation and Development (OECD) established a system of exchange of information and a procedure for consultation of competition rules among enforcement authorities.

WTO was established on 1 January 1995 and will administer the new global trade rules, agreed in the Uruguay Round, which came into effect on the same day. These rules, which are the result of seven years of negotiations among member States of GATT, establish the rule of law in international trade, estimated at $5 trillion in 1995. The WTO involvement in world trade is estimated to raise the fiscal proportions of trade to $500 billion by the year 2005.[150] The WTO has a membership of more than 150 states and is far wider in scope than its predecessor, bringing into the multilateral trading system trade in services, intellectual property protection and investment. Unlike GATT, which was a provisional treaty serviced by an *ad hoc* secretariat, WTO is a full-fledged international organization in its own right and administers a unified package of agreements to which all member states are committed. In other words, it is an improved version of GATT and serves as an effective watchdog of international trade and management consultant. Its economists are required to keep a close watch on the pulse of the global economy and provide studies on the main trade issues of the world.

WTO considers that the following four fundamental factors are shaping the world economy: the broader integration of the world economy; the sharply different trends in the developed and developing countries; the spread of market-oriented reforms; and the end of the cold war.[151] On the subject of market-oriented reforms WTO believes:

> If there are no rules in trade then the resulting anarchy will inevitably lead to conflict. International norms not only ensure freedom for economic agents to operate in their commercial interest across national frontiers. They also enhance the freedom of governments in their trade policy interventions, by defining the scope of actions permissible within the confines of international law. The behaviour of all governments becomes more predictable when all accept the rules of the game.[152]

Obviously, WTO believes that a coherent set of rules followed in conformity with the accepted norms of international law should govern competition. This does not necessarily mean that WTO is against free trade. It merely means that free trade has to be conducted according to accepted universal norms and these norms have been explicitly laid out in the WTO Agreement. The trade in services portion of the agreement carries specific rules of competition. As stated earlier, one of the seminal principles of the agreement requires each member state to accord, immediately and unconditionally to services and service suppliers of any member, treatment no less favourable than that it accords to like services and service suppliers of any other country.[153] Called the Most Favoured Nations treatment (MFN) clause, this provision *in limine* establishes common ground between trading partners and creates certain parameters of activity for partners to follow. The MFN clause is the cornerstone of the WTO principles and acts as the fundamental postulate on which other WTO competition rules are based.

Transparency is another concept which has been recognized for practical applicability in the WTO rules. Accordingly, each member is required to publish promptly and, except in emergency situations, at the latest by the time of their entry into force, all relevant measures of general application which pertain to or affect the operation of the agreement.[154] There is also the requirement of publication of international agreements pertaining to or affecting trade in services to which a member is a signatory.[155] Article XVII of the agreement lays down the principle of national treatment which requires each member to accord to services and service providers of any other member, in respect of all measures affecting the supply of services, treatment no less favourable than it accords to its own like services and service suppliers. This provision is effectively tied up with the principle of elimination of all discrimination from the applicability of the agreement, as reflected in Article V, achieving the dual goal of elimination of existing discriminatory measures and prohibition of new or more discriminatory measures.

It is claimed that, since the primary purpose of the WTO system is to achieve trade among members as liberally and fairly as possible while retaining the essence of non-discrimination in trade practices, the WTO system should guarantee a fair and equitable opportunity to enterprises of members to the national markets of other members. This is done mainly through the removal of governmental barriers to the extent possible and the convergence of national regulatory regimes such as those which relate to intellectual property rights.

One of the most serious challenges faced by WTO in this regard is the claims by some states of 'unfair trade' by others, where the claimant states feel victimized by private business practices of enterprises of other states. The corollaries of anti-dumping is one such example, where the exporter is faced with the situation in which imports to his country are precluded by his country, with a view to compelling the consumption of the exporter's goods within the country of production. This practice often leads to price hiking and protectionism within a market. The WTO rules therefore strive for fair and equal opportunity in competition, the same way the bilateral air services agreement requires.

One of the major considerations of the WTO is the perceived incompatibility between business practices of countries and uniform competition rules which are required to be enforced globally. There is an obvious link between business systems and corporate behaviour on the one hand, and competition rules (or the lack thereof) on the other. There is also probably a functional relationship between them in that competition rules partly reflect existing business systems and corporate behaviour (a regulatory system functions well only if it is fundamentally accepted). Also business systems and corporate behaviour often adjust to, and take advantage of, the possibilities opened by competition rules. To that extent, the disparities between competition rules, on the basis that what is permitted in one state may be prohibited in another, may influence disparities in business systems and corporate behaviour and may constitute an impediment for enterprises which seek entry into another market. Some examples are cited below.

In the European Community where governmental barriers such as tariffs and import restrictions have been removed, competition policy measures play a vital role in ensuring that the common market operates without hindrance by private restrictive business practices. In the EC, the role of competition policy has increased dramatically with the progressive integration of the common market.

In the Structural Impediment Initiative (SII) negotiated between the United States government and the Japanese government in 1989–90, business customs and corporate behaviours were the major issues. The United States government has claimed that restrictive business customs and corporate behaviour were the major impediments which restricted effective market access to the Japanese market by foreign enterprises. In accordance with the SII, both governments have agreed that an increase of competition rules in Japan would increase market access to the Japanese market by foreign enterprises by removing private restrictive business practices. A number of reforms of the Japanese Anti-monopoly Law resulted from this agreement, including an increase of administrative surcharge and criminal fine to be imposed on enterprises when they engage in cartels.[156] This functional relationship between competition rules and business systems and corporate behaviour, rooted as they are in cultural, economic and political traditions, may, however, often place limitations upon possible achievements attained by the applicability of partial harmonization of competition rules. Differences in business systems and corporate behaviour are generally wide-ranging and complex, and the application of competition rules may often fail to bridge the gap between the two elements. This notwithstanding, a vigorous enforcement of competition rules in trading nations may still be able to play a useful role in preparing common rules which could be made applicable to trading nations. The adoption of common rules of conduct for enterprises may well reduce undue imbalances in different business systems and could pave the way for enterprises to compete for roles in markets of trading states outside their own market place.

WTO should also take into consideration the fact that, as globalization of national economies is achieved through the removal of governmental barriers to trade such as tariffs and import restrictions, new trade issues may arise. One such issue is the possible incompatibility between different regulatory/business systems among trading states. Differences in domestic regulatory systems and in business customs and behaviour often emerge as barriers to transnational business activities. These differences may take the form of inconsistencies between technical standards, taxation, environmental protection measures, labour standards and other barriers which hamper enterprises seeking to engage in transboundary trade. Such differences obviously create disparity among the states concerned.

Extraterritoriality is one concept which could affect more than one jurisdiction in the application of domestic trade policy. The United States, the European Community and Germany are proponents of extraterritoriality where competition rules are applied to commercial conduct of foreign enterprises which conduct business in places other than those whose domestic markets are affected by such trade. In the seminal *Alcoa* case[157] of 1945, the United States courts established the 'effects' doctrine whereby commercial conduct carried out overseas but is intended or calculated to affect the United States would be subject to US antitrust laws. This doctrine has been followed by the courts in the United States with an unfailing consistency, culminating in recent guidelines on international commercial operations adopted by the US Justice Department.[158] These guidelines contain principles that give the United States a wide scope of extraterritorial jurisdiction in respect of anti-competitive practices which foreign enterprises follow in countries outside the United States, provided such activities adversely affect the United States' market in that particular commercial activity. One of the most compelling features of this legislation is its emphasis on 'market access' relating to US businesses in foreign countries. A number of hypothetical examples incorporated in these guidelines reflect that the Department of Justice would challenge the conduct of foreign enterprises in foreign countries if such enterprises would hinder US enterprises from using opportunities of exporting goods to a foreign country or investing in a foreign country.

In the famous *Woodpulp* case,[159] the Court of Justice of the European Communities decided that the EC competition rules apply to agreements of foreign enterprises which are entered into outside the European Community as long as they are implemented within the common market.

One cannot deny that in this era of global economy, some degree of extraterritoriality in the enforcement of national competition rules is inevitable. A state would therefore be seen as being justified in applying its competition rules to the conduct of foreign enterprises abroad when conduct which occurs in a foreign country affects its economy adversely, particularly where the state in which such conduct occurs has no competition rules or has no intention to prohibit such conduct. This phenomenon is easily reflected by transnational business entities who may engage in restrictive business practices in a 'twilight zone' where no state can fully exercise jurisdiction and yet harmful effects of such restrictive business practices may be felt in one or more states. To say that there should be no extraterritoriality of any kind in the application of competition rules would mean that such transnational entities can engage in anti-competitive conduct with impunity.

There is of course the consideration that an extraterritorial application of competition rules is a costly business both for the enforcement agency and for the foreign defendants and is often a second-best solution to a problem which essentially inquires as to how to cope with transnational anti-competitive conduct. An extraterritorial application of competition rules is often not as effective as it would be if applied domestically. A state which attempts to apply its anti-competitive laws extraterritorially to a defendant enterprise located abroad could always face difficulties of enforcement and considerations of forum and jurisdiction. There could also be disabling legislation in a foreign state which may effectively preclude extraterritoriality.

The *Watchmakers of Switzerland* case[160] of 1955 exemplifies the essential commercial law principle of the United States, that applicability of antitrust laws on foreign enterprises may often entail conflict with legislation of other states. The court in this case held that a watch repair enterprise, conducted in the United States by two Swiss corporations, could be subjected to the domestic laws of the United States. The court further held that, in order for a foreign corporation to be present within the jurisdiction of a court for purpose of service of process, there must be proof of continuous local activities and a showing that under all circumstances of the case the forum is not unfairly inconvenient. Even though the two Swiss entities had no property in the United States and did not carry out their activities directly (the business activities of the Swiss corporations were carried out by an American corporation in the United States), since the Swiss corporations determined the prices and terms of the business enterprise, the court further held that the Swiss corporations could be subjected to antitrust statutes and tariff laws of the United States.[161]

In the watershed case of *Laker Airways Limited* v. *SABENA Belgian World Airlines*,[162] it was held that territoriality-based jurisdiction allows states in the United States to regulate conduct or status of individuals or property physically situated within a territory even if effects of conduct are felt outside that territory, and conversely, conduct outside a territory, which is calculated to have a substantial effect on that territory, may also be similarly regulated. It was also held that a state has jurisdiction to prescribe law governing conduct of its nationals whether such conduct takes place inside or outside the territory of that state. Accordingly, the plaintiff, Laker Airways Limited, a British corporation seeking remedy in the United States whose activities in question took place in countries other than the United States, was deemed to be subject to US antitrust legislation on the basis that such activities gravely impaired the United States' interests.[163] In deciding upon the contentious question whether the law of the United Kingdom should apply to the plaintiff, the court compared the diametrically opposed antitrust legislation of the United Kingdom and the United States and held:

> We find no indication in either the statutory scheme or prior judicial precedent that jurisdiction (by the United States) should not be exercised. Legitimate United States interests in protecting consumers, providing for vindicating creditors' rights, and regulating economic consequences of those doing substantial business in our country are all advanced under the congressionally prescribed scheme. There are more than sufficient jurisdictional contacts under *United States* v. *Aluminium Co. of America*[164] and subsequent case law to support the exercise of prescriptive jurisdiction in this case.[165]

In the United States, the scope of antitrust legislation and protection thereby extends to those persons who are either directly or indirectly affected adversely by antitrust violations by third parties. The adverse effect on the plaintiff must be one that the laws were written to guard against. An example of this principle can be seen in the *Uranium Antitrust Litigation* of 1979,[166] where a business entity which indulged in a 'tying arrangement'[167] to sell its product was considered a violation of antitrust legislation. The tie-in resulted in a drop in demand for the product concerned, giving way to a drop in prices and adversely affecting other competitors of the product in the market.

The role of WTO in extraterritoriality becomes significant when one considers the eventuality where the extraterritorial application of competition rules becomes too costly or burdensome on states concerned. WTO offers the alternative of its own dispute settlement process and a framework within which members may seek positive comity and a certain convergence or harmonization of competition rules. There have been several proposals for convergence, the most practical and well-thought-out of which is the Draft International Antitrust Code (DIAC) proposed by a group of competition law scholars, called the Munich Group. The DIAC proposes that there should be a comprehensive international antitrust code covering the major areas of competition law such as horizontal agreements, vertical agreements, mergers and acquisitions, the relationship between competition law and industrial policies and others. It also recommends the establishment of an international antitrust agency which shares the responsibility of enforcement of international competition rules with the national governments.

Ideas expressed in the DIAC are similar to Chapter V of the ITO Charter, giving one the impression that the DIAC may well have been drafted along the lines of the schemes of international antitrust enforcement contemplated by the ITO Charter. The DIAC remains the most ambitious of the proposals made so far in recent years.

Another attempt at international antitrust regulations is reflected in the work of a task force established by the American Bar Association which issued a report (ABA Report) advocating an agreement among states with regard to some basic principles on unlawfulness of cartels and unification of filing requirements under the merger laws of various states. The report contains a modest recommendation seeking partial harmonization through an agreement among states on basic principles and does not seek the establishment of a comprehensive international authority to enforce international rules.

Professor Eleanor Fox of New York University Law School has developed the idea of the DIAC further, proposing a scheme in which states would agree on 'a few fundamental world-linking principles' of competition policy such as, *inter alia*, prohibition of cartels and positive comity.[168] Fox's proposal basically requires each state to carry out convergence of competition rules while adopting fundamental principles established in an international agreement.

The advantage of the DIAC approach to establish an international code is that, in such an instrument, rules and obligations of member states would be clear and member states would have a clear goal to achieve. It must be mentioned that a somewhat similar approach has been made within the framework of the WTO, in the area of intellectual property. In the Agreement on Trade-related Intellectual Property Rights (TRIPS), principles with regard to the minimum protection of intellectual property rights and the enforcement of the rights under intellectual property laws are clearly laid out and members are obligated to incorporate these principles in their domestic legislation, while allowing for a grace period in the case of developing countries. It would not be incorrect to say, therefore, that in this respect the DIAC approach already has a precedent in the WTO system.

The disadvantage of a comprehensive international code approach may be that it lacks flexibility. It is often true that, when comprehensive principles are already declared, member states have no choice but to accept them and there may well be justification to consider principles other than those declared in the code which may be more feasible. There could even be possibilities of applying different combinations of such principles.

As mentioned earlier, TRIPS is an attempt to accomplish convergence of intellectual property laws of members. If TRIPS proves to be successful, an international code approach may be a good prospect as a model for international competition laws. Since the TRIPS was formally initiated only at the beginning of 1995, it is premature to predict the prospect of domestic implementation of such a scheme by members at the present time.

Yet another approach is the 'instalment' approach or 'evolutionary' approach, for which there is an important precedent in WTO. This precedent, which is adopted in GATS, provides for a general scheme for future negotiations in the liberalization of trade in services within the general principles of the MFN treatment clause and transparency clause. At the present time, the liberalization of trade in services is largely left to future negotiations and GATS only provides for a scheme of negotiation. This is largely due to the fact that trade in services is a complex field involving complicated and diverse issues. Admittedly, however, it is encouraging that the GATS scheme could be drawn on by members if the need arises in the future.

As to the question whether the GATS negotiating scheme should be adopted with regard to international competition policy, the main consideration should be that, if such is ever considered, it should be contemporaneous with the consideration of a scheme within the WTO for negotiating international antitrust principles. Negotiations may be on a total harmonization or a partial harmonization basis. Such an approach would have the advantage of the possibility of introduction by members of a variety of international competition agreements out of which they could select a suitable one. Also, if this approach is adopted, it would be important for members to have a firm commitment to promote competition law and policy both internationally and domestically. Such commitment should be clearly declared. Also it may be necessary to establish, as in GATS, a time schedule within which negotiations should be carried out.

A declaration of fundamental principles of competition would also be necessary. This declaration should contain provisions analogous to MFN treatment, national treatment and transparency. Consideration should also be given to prohibition in principle of cartels, resale price maintenance, boycotts and others. One should, at the same time, be cautious that, given a wide variety of principles that are followed by members with regard to other areas such as mergers and acquisitions, vertical non-price restraint and predatory pricing, it may be feasible merely to declare general and abstract principles which require members to promote competition policy in such areas.

Although, admittedly, WTO is not the only forum in which a scheme of convergence of competition laws can be accommodated (the OECD for example is, to every purpose, an appropriate forum; also UNCTAD has, through its work, demonstrated that it is another organization that could accommodate this issue) there is compelling reason for such a scheme to be considered under the WTO umbrella owing to the volume of membership that WTO carries. Among the more than 125 states which participated in the Uruguay Round leading to the establishment of the WTO Agreement, not all of them have competition laws and many of them are not ready for them yet. When an international competition code is drafted, it is only logical to expect a certain degree of universality in its principles and such could be accomplished on a wider scale, given WTO's membership.

Petersmann has recommended[169] that an international competition code be accommodated as an agreement of Annex 4 of the WTO Agreement, which contains optional agreements. Petersmann examines the idea of a smaller number of nations entering into such an agreement initially, such as the United States, Japan and members of the European Community, with Canada and Australia joining in. A grace period for developing states to join the agreement has also been addressed. He believes that, at least in the initial stage, an international competition code among a smaller number of members may work more effectively.

Generally, it is felt that the inclusion of an international competition code in the WTO Agreement would have the advantage, in that coordination between competition policy and other policies embodied in WTO agreements such as TRIPS, the Safeguard Agreement and the Antidumping Agreement would be accomplished more easily than it would be if a competition code is established separately from WTO. Another advantage envisaged is that the dispute settlement process incorporated in Annex 2 of the WTO Agreement could be utilized when a dispute arises relating to the enforcement of competition laws.

Comments

There seems to be little doubt that aircraft noise can be a nuisance at law. However, the dichotomy presented by the aircraft noise issue has to be viewed in the broader perspective of trade and the environment. The symbiosis of trade and the environment emerged as a critical issue for trade negotiators in the last stages of the Uruguay Round of discussions. At these discussions the focus remained on two approaches to the issue. The first approach was from the essentially pro-environment groups, who considered that those involved in international trade are primarily interested in the movement of their goods and therefore were not concerned about the environmental implications of their trading activities. The second approach was based on the belief that increased trading activity enhanced possibilities of solving environmental problems. This trend of thinking leaned toward sanctions being introduced against environmentally detrimental trading activity, using GATT (later WTO) as a tool of implementation. The official statement issued in support of the latter approach, which was not supported initially by the majority of states at the Uruguay Round, stated:

> GATT Contracting Parties believe that the successful conclusion of the Uruguay Round was an important step towards creating the conditions for sustainable development. Trade liberalization and the maintenance of an open, non-discriminatory trading system

are key elements of the follow-up to UNCED (United Nations Conference on the Environment).[170]

Developing countries, however, were reluctant to embrace the idea of using trading sanctions towards environmental protection as their main priority remained development, and they were not fully convinced that already scarce resources should be deployed for purposes of protecting the environment. Being a new challenge and still esoteric, environmental protection was viewed in the context of trade liberalization by the developing states in the following manner: 'For developing countries, where poverty is the number one policy preoccupation and the most important obstacle to better environmental protection, global trade liberalization, coupled with financial and technological transfers, is essential for promoting sustainable development.'[171]

Multilateral lending institutions such as the World Bank and the International Monetary Fund are beginning to lay more emphasis on the environmental impact of projects funded by them. However, in the ultimate analysis, both international trade and environmental protection are key issues for development, and they should be viewed as tools that could result in a win–win situation for the parties concerned.

2 MARGINAL COST PRICING OF AIRPORTS AND AIR NAVIGATION SERVICES

Introduction

Air travel has several determinants in regard to demand. Primarily, it is determined by income levels and demographics and the cost of air travel. In the context of cost of air travel, world energy demand, supply and prices are key factors which drive both the profitability of the air carrier and the cost factor involving the use of travel offered by the carrier to the consumer.[172] In the years 1988–99, the total tonne-kilometres performed, or in other words, total scheduled airline traffic, grew at an annual rate of 5.2 per cent.[173] Passenger kilometres growth during this decade was 4.6 per cent and freight tonne-kilometres growth was 6.6 per cent for the same period.[174]

The above figures portend an even more prolific growth rate in the near future, although financial trends in the airline industry are not readily predictable. Therefore total forecasts of revenue generated by airlines are based on assumptions for passenger yields and on passenger forecasts and, on this basis, the International Civil Aviation Organization (ICAO) has forecast that total revenue of airlines worldwide would grow by 3.9 per cent in the year 2000; 4.9 in 2001 and 5 per cent in 2002. These compare with an average rate of 5.6 per cent over the past decade.[175] Although it is still premature to extrapolate an average revenue figure for the decade 1999–2009, it would not be too impractical to note that the cost–price index of airline financing would bring to bear a significant influence in the revenue curve of air carriers of the world over that decade.

The ICAO charges policy

Article 15 of the Convention on International Civil Aviation[176] (hereafter called the Chicago Convention) signed on 7 December 1944, enshrines the basic philosophy of charges on airports and air navigation services. The provision states, *inter alia*, that every airport in a contracting state which is open to public use by its national aircraft shall likewise be open under uniform conditions to the aircraft of all the other contracting states. The like uniform conditions shall apply to the use, by aircraft of every contracting state, of all air navigation facilities, including radio and meteorological services,[177] which may be provided for public use for the safety and expedition of air navigation. Article 15 also provides that any changes that may be imposed or permitted to be imposed by a contracting state for the use of such airports and air navigation facilities by the aircraft of any other contracting state shall not be higher, as to aircraft not engaged in scheduled international air services, than those that would be paid by its national aircraft of the same class engaged in similar operations; and as to aircraft engaged in scheduled international air services, than those that would be paid by its national aircraft engaged in similar international air services.

Article 15 subsumes three fundamental postulates: uniform conditions should apply in the use of facilities provided by airports and air navigation services; aircraft operators should be charged on a non-discriminatory basis; and no charges should be levied for the mere transit over, entry into or exit from a contracting state. The ICAO contracting state which has notified its adherence to the Chicago Convention could exempt itself from article 15, which binds contracting states to adherence under customary international law. The binding force of the Chicago Convention on its contracting states is ensured by the Vienna Convention on the Law of Treaties,[178] which recognizes treaties as a source of law and accepts free consent, good faith and the *pacta sunt servanda* as universally recognized elements of a treaty.[179]

An elaboration of the basic principles of article 15 in the context of airports and air navigation services charges is contained in the *Statements by the Council to Contracting States on Charges for Airports and Air Navigation Services*,[180] which call for an equitable and fair determination and sharing of airport and air navigation services costs – a principle which has had sustained application by contracting states. The Council Statements apply to charges as referred to in the provision of airports and air navigation services within the parameters of articles 15 and 28 of the Chicago Convention. In this context, charges are levies calculated to defray the costs of providing facilities and services for civil aviation. Charges are diametrically opposed in concept to taxes which are levies directed at raising national and local government treasury funds to be used for non-aviation purposes.[181]

In recent years, a compelling need has arisen to address in greater detail the basic principles pertaining to cost recovery applicable to both airports and air navigation services. This is because, primarily, the organizational structure of airports and air navigation services providers have changed in many parts of the globe into autonomous and privatized bodies. Earlier, when the majority of these service providers were instrumentalities of state or branches of government, the charges policies of ICAO, as contained in the Chicago Convention and the Council Statements, could be applied within their basic philosophy.

Now, however, with states having divested themselves of this responsibility and vested the operator of their airports and air navigation services in privatized and other autonomous entities, cost recovery policy may need to be reviewed. With this in view, ICAO suggested to the Conference on the Economics of Airports and Air Navigation Services (ANSConf 2000) held in Montreal on 19–28 June 2000, that the profile of basic cost recovery policy may need to be raised.[182] This measure would still be adopted within the parameters of existing policy calling for revenues from charges levied on international civil aviation and will only be applied towards defraying the costs of facilities and services provided for international civil aviation. It was also recommended that revenues from other sources than charges on air traffic shall be taken into account before the cost basis for charges on air traffic is determined. ICAO also advised ANSConf 2000 that airports and air navigation services may produce sufficient revenues to exceed all operating costs and so provide for a reasonable return on assets to contribute towards necessary capital improvements. Of course, the governing principle would be that consultation with users shall take place before significant changes in charging systems or levels of charges are introduced.[183]

ICAO's recommendations to ANSConf 2000 were both timely and practical, given the evolving fabric of economic forces which now govern airports and air navigation services. The recommendations also stimulate some reflection on the complexities of financing principles now applicable to the services provided by airports and air navigation services providers. In substance, the issue of costing and pricing of services would be dependent upon underlying practices and economic factors such as the bunching of aviation and non-aviation revenues and their effect on the overall pricing policy relating to airports and air navigation services and a significant paradigm shift from article 15 of the Chicago Convention and the Council Statements.[184]

The concept of the single till

At its incipient stage, international civil aviation relegated the airport to the status of a terminus,[185] much the same as a bus terminus of that time, assigning it as the focal geographical point at which people gathered to embark on a plane for a journey by air, or disembark after an air journey. However, airports are now complex industrial enterprises.[186] Quite apart from the essential air side support given by airports to landing and departing aircraft, there are commercial facilities provided for both passengers and the public within the terminal building by concessionaires who are specialists in their own fields of business. The airport authorities collect concession fees (non-aeronautical revenues) from the concessionaires and, in numerous airports around the world, the income derived from such resources is significant, often exceeding traditional income derived through the provision of airport and air navigation services (aeronautical revenues) to incoming and outgoing aircraft.

The 25 largest airports in the world in terms of passenger throughput, 17 of which are located in the United States, handled a combined total of 992 million passengers in 1998.[187] This represented an average per airport of some 109 000 passengers every 24 hours.[188] In 1998 and 1999, the financial situation of airports continued to improve, with a significant number of airports collecting revenues in excess of their costs. Notably, the trend towards higher profitability among airports that operated as commercial (autonomous) entities was highly evident. ICAO records that, particularly in the 1998–9 period, there was a tangible growth in a number of airports in Europe and the Asia Pacific Region, where revenues from non-aeronautical revenues exceeded 50 per cent of the total revenues.[189]

The 'single till' concept, which admits of both aeronautical and non-aeronautical revenues being used for aeronautical purposes, brings to bear the need to determine whether airports, as autonomous business entities, should as of right use non-aeronautical revenues for purposes other than developing airport and air navigation services for the aircraft they serve, or whether both aeronautical and non-aeronautical revenues should be put back into one single till for reducing charges on airports that serve those airports. The cost basis for airport charges setting is set out in ICAO policy as follows:

> The cost to be shared is the full cost of providing the airport and its essential ancillary services, including appropriate amounts for cost of capital and depreciation of assets, as well as the cost of maintenance and operation and management and administration expenses, but allowing for all revenues, aeronautical and non-aeronautical, accruing from the operation of the airport to its operators.[190]

This provision envisages the pooling of airport revenues in one single source or 'till', whether they be aeronautical or non-aeronautical revenues.

The underlying purpose of the 'single till' is to utilize the significant non-aeronautical income such as that derived from retail shops within the terminal building and rentals and parking fees to subsidize costs borne by airports in the provision of airports and air navigation services, thus reducing charges levied on aircraft operators for such services. The operative argument, at least presented implicitly, is that if not for the passengers brought by the airlines into airports, there would be no scope for operating retail shops and parking bays in the airports concerned. In other words, it is imputed that it is the airline passengers and their visitors who are the sole customers of these facilities and, therefore, the airlines which bring in these passengers should benefit from the revenue derived from such facilities. *Ex facie*, this is a sound and incontrovertible premise and it is not the purpose of this section to impugn the compelling nature of the argument. However, it is submitted that a sound legal analysis of the economic concepts underlying the modern airport is a necessity, if a thorough understanding of the subject is to be obtained. Clarification of the various positions of the airlines and airports on this issue would in turn help assess the impact of the 'single till' on commercial competition of airports as autonomous business entities.

An airport, whether publicly owned and operated or privately owned or operated, has to follow a prescribed policy with regard to the recovery of costs incurred in providing airport and air navigation services. This policy is enshrined in article 15 of the Chicago Convention which requires that a state be obligated not to impose higher charges on aircraft of another state engaged in international operations than those paid by its national aircraft engaged in similar international operations. This charges policy is a universal one applying to any type of airport, whether public or private, since the regulation of airports within the territory of a state is usually the responsibility of that state concerned.

Today's airport, in its typical form, is primarily a commercial entity and operates as a business-oriented entity. Most airports provide retail shops and parking facilities, not only for airline passengers and their visitors but also for residents of the area. They are, in this sense, as much profit centres as are such retail outlets as K-Mart and Wal-Mart. In addition, there are also airport free zones which are bonded areas, adjacent to the airport premises which, as the name suggests, are duty-free areas promoting industry and other commercial activity.

The airport, like any other autonomous business enterprise, has to exploit inherent resources optimally, compete with other businesses of the area on quality of services offered, and reinvest funds in developing its business interests. The ICAO Council recognizes the continuing importance to airports of income derived from such sources as concessions, rental of premises and 'free zones'. The council recommends that, with the exception of concessions that are directly associated with the operation of air transport services, such as fuel, in-flight catering and ground handling, the full development of revenues of this kind be encouraged, having regard to the need for moderation in prices to the public, the requirements of passengers and the need for terminal efficiency.[191] The fact that the general public are recognized as customers of airports by ICAO policy leaves room to attribute to the wisdom of the policy statement the acknowledgment that airports do not only cater to airline passengers and their visitors, but also to shoppers who may wish to pick up a bargain at the airport.

The ICAO Council Statements leave it wide open for airports to optimize their revenue to exceed all direct and indirect operating costs, including general administration and so on, and so provide for a reasonable return on assets (before tax and cost of capital) to contribute towards necessary capital improvements.[192]

This policy statement encourages commercial autonomy of airports and the practice of deviating from being instrumentalities of the state. *A fortiori*, it urges airports to optimize revenues in order to boost capital investment towards improvement, which would not necessarily mean such revenues should subsidize airport and air navigation service charges. The *Airport Economics Manual* of ICAO states:

> It should be noted that revenues from non-aeronautical activities are in fact the principal means by which a growing number of airports are able to recover their total costs because their profits from these activities more than cover the losses most of them incur on their air side operations[193] ... and in so far as ICAO cost recovery policies are concerned, not subject to the same limitations that it is recommended apply to charges on air traffic.[194]

It is arguable in the context of the above-mentioned policy that, if two different criteria are applied, one strictly on the basis of recovery of costs of services provided which would essentially be a non-profit operation, as in the case of charges levied for the provision of airport and air navigation services, and another strictly on a profit-making business basis, whether the latter, applicable to non-aeronautical revenues, is mutually exclusive from the former. If this argument were to prevail, one could maintain that charges for airport and air navigation services need not as of necessity be minimized as a result of capital injection towards facilities providing such services if such capital were to be derived from the non-aeronautical activities of the airport. Of course, this does not mean that an airport which wishes to inject some capital derived from one source to another should be precluded from doing so in the best interests of aviation.

Airports, like any other business enterprises, are compelled to compete with each other to attract air traffic and business flowing therefrom and from the general public. To this end, many airports are now privatized and operate as autonomous entities. Privatization brings not only fiscal benefits, but also legal liability (as the discussion below will show) which is a possible cost factor that should be taken into account. More importantly, privatization connotes a businesslike approach that requires a certain involvement with market forces and competition that would necessitate reinvestment in the airport business for the commercial sustainability of the airport.

All the above factors go to show that the 'single till' is not an incontrovertible application *per force* in airport economics. If airports are to be privatized as recommended, they should be viewed in the same manner as other profit-making businesses are, in terms of equity requirements, capital injection and liability issues. Merely 'taking from Tom to support Jack' is not advisable from a market perspective, as it would seriously hinder progress and development of an airport as a business enterprise. A blanket application of the 'single till' concept would make airport privatization a toothless tiger and could even be counterproductive and anti-competitive. On the other hand, one should not summarily dismiss the importance of civil aviation to the very being of airports. Of high concern should remain the viability of air transport and the costs incurred in providing airport and air navigation services. The more practical approach in this context should be a balanced one, varying from airport to airport, where a certain capital injection to develop facilities needed for air transport services could be made, while maintaining the competitive edge of the airport concerned. The 'single till' would essentially remain a tightrope walk for all concerned, given the increasing competition in the airport industry.

Marginal cost pricing

The suggestion that marginal cost pricing be considered in setting charges, was rejected at an earlier ICAO Conference held in 1991.[195] Subsequently, the Air Navigation Services Economics Panel (ANSEP) of ICAO addressed the possibility but rejected it on the grounds that such a practice would not be consistent with the equity principles enunciated by article 15 of the Chicago Convention. Current policy on cost pricing of airports and air navigation services can be found in the ICAO *Manual on Air Navigation Services Economics*[196] which, under paragraph 5.11, provides that unit cost is determined by dividing the cost base by the estimated charging units, making the charges structure accomplish the averaging out of costs among the various users, irrespective of the costs that individual users impose. In practice, the implementation of ICAO's pricing strategy of the recovery of cost through a process of non-discrimination has led to cost pricing combined with factors determining the user's ability to pay based essentially on the weight of the aircraft for which services are rendered.

The theory of marginal cost pricing admits of fixing a price equivalent to the cost of producing one additional unit.[197] Translated to the context of airports and air navigation services, it would mean that marginal cost is that cost incurred in providing an additional unit of output. Although an efficient allocation of resources can be optimally achieved by a pricing policy when the price of goods or services is set equal to the marginal cost of providing such goods or services, the economic rationale of marginal pricing is essentially based on the principle that only users who would value a service as much as its cost of provision will be prepared to pay for using the service.

In order to study the applicability of marginal cost pricing to the provision of airports and air navigation services, ICAO appointed in 1999 a Secretariat Study Group composed of members from six contracting states. The Study Group concluded that the application of economic principles within the parameters of the equity and non-discrimination principles of article 15 was permissible, noting the inherent difficulties that would be posed by the application of principles of marginal cost pricing, owing to the complex calculations involved. The group suggested that such an application should remain optional, perhaps to be used only in instances where airports and air navigation services were provided under congestion and space constraints. The group's conclusion was that marginal cost pricing, owing to its complex nature, should be applied with caution.

The recommendation of the ICAO Secretariat Study Group, that principles of marginal cost pricing be applied with caution, should be given serious consideration in the context of civil aviation, particularly in applying the attributes of marginal cost pricing to aviation. Simply put, if a service provider incurs a certain cost in providing services for regular-flow traffic, any additional traffic that may flow requiring the services of that provider would incur additional marginal costs which such additional traffic may have to bear. In other words, if total costs for the provision of regular services at a fixed cost basis were to be represented by p and the regular flow of aircraft were to be represented by q, each user would pay p / q as a cost-based price varying of course with the weight of each aircraft. If an additional flow, represented by r were to cost an additional price of s, the user causing s would have to pay $(p / q) + (r / s)$.

Since $(p / q) < (p / q) + (r / s)$, the average marginal costs borne by the additional flow would be greater than the cost borne by the regular flow. This would prove particularly iniquitous if an aircraft of lesser weight were to pay more than an aircraft of higher weight. Although, as the Secretariat pointed out to ANSConf 2000,[198] such pricing policy may achieve the objective of encouraging air traffic to move from congested peaking hours to periods of less peaking or no congestion, the International Air Transport Association (IATA) pointed out that marginal cost pricing is concerned with current and future costs and not with past sunk costs which do not apply to an additional user.[199] IATA also referred to the distinction between short-run and long-run marginal cost pricing, cautioning that long-run marginal cost pricing will pose difficulties with regard to amorphous long-term infrastructural costs (such as are incurred for the construction of terminals and runways over a period of time).

Being mindful of these difficulties, but at the same time considering the need for and value of additional work on this area to cover all grounds, the Secretariat has suggested to ANSConf that ICAO policy be reworded in the Council Statements to read as follows:

> The costs should be determined on the basis of sound accounting principles and may reflect as required *other economic principles* (my emphasis) provided these are in conformity with Article 15 of the *Convention on International Civil Aviation* and other principles in the present document.

The ICAO Secretariat also advised ANSConf 2000 of text inserted in the *Manual on Air Navigation Services Economics* (Doc. 9161/3) in paragraph 5.7 to the effect that the application of economic principles to setting charges should emphasize the need to recover costs in an equitable manner from the use of air navigation services. The two governing criteria are the cost of providing air navigation services and the effectiveness of services rendered. Paragraph 5.8 stipulates that the aim of an economic approach to setting charges is to bring the demand for and the offer of air navigation capacity into equilibrium so that the provision of additional capacity is encouraged. The level of charges should be considered in performing the required investment appraisal (including cost/benefit analysis). An example of an appropriate economic approach would be to apply a two-part tariff with a fixed rate for 'entry' into the system and a variable element to reflect the extent of the service rendered. It was also contended that, in order to apply economic principles to setting charges, it would be necessary to identify costs associated with the air navigation services components being charged for.

The Secretariat subsumed ICAO philosophy by quoting a text inserted in paragraph 5.6 of the *Airport Economics Manual* (Doc. 9562) that the application of economic principles to setting charges which are consistent with the Council Statements in Doc. 9082/5 should emphasize the need to recover costs in an equitable manner from the users of airport services.[200]

ANSConf 2000 consensually agreed that states should not be restricted to resorting to a single principle in setting their airport and air navigation charges. An approach best suited to states, in terms of their own local circumstances, was acceptable, according to the conference, provided such an approach met internationally accepted standards and principles. Consideration was given to the significance of demand factors and the deleterious effect of abuse of market power if advanced economic principles on pricing were to be set arbitrarily and contrary to the principles of equity and non-discrimination as enunciated in article 15 of the Chicago Convention. Accordingly, the conference made two recommendations, the first being that a suitable amendment be made to the Council Statements in Doc. 9082 to the effect that charges should be determined on the basis of sound accounting principles and may reflect, as required, other economic principles, provided that these are in conformity with article 15 of the Chicago Convention and other relevant principles in Doc. 9082.[201]

The second recommendation of the Conference called upon states to urge their service providers that adopt economic pricing principles to report details on both the level and allocation of fixed and variable costs, and to consult with users on how marginal costs are estimated and used in setting charges. In this regard, ICAO is requested to introduce supplementary guidance aimed at ensuring that the use of economic pricing for capacity management does not result in over-recovery of costs while at the same time providing for a reasonable return on investment. ICAO is also charged with the task of examining whether the traditional approach to measuring discrimination and cross-subsidization needs to be revised, given the increased interest in applying economic principles in setting charges.[202] These recommendations were made on the basis of suggestions of the ICAO Secretariat[203] and Airports Council International.[204]

Although economic aspects of marginal cost pricing of airports and air navigation services are undeniably complex, they bring to bear a compelling need to balance economic growth and social justice in order to accord with the phenomenal growth of the air transport industry and the demands that the industry may place on service providers in the years to come. The most important factor in marginal pricing therefore becomes the extent of moral justification in applying such complex economic issues to an area which rigidly adheres to the principles of equity and non-discrimination.

The concept of marginal cost itself is a fairly simple one, as explained earlier in this section. However, the process of providing airports and air navigation services is a complex one. Accordingly, the structure of marginal costs related to these services is also somewhat complicated. Inevitably, pricing units must be modified and simplified from actual marginal costs if they are to be identified as price signals. There must also be an effort on the part of the service provider to reflect the essential characteristics of marginal cost structure in pricing units.

Marginal pricing is the benchmark for efficient pricing in the regulated commercial sector. The principal feature affecting the basic structure of marginal costs is peaking of traffic at an airport. The extent and scope of services available at peak traffic hours and the excess of services available during non-peak hours would be a distinct determinant of marginal cost pricing. Time therefore becomes an influential determinant of the cost factor involved.

Equity, in the context of article 15 of the Chicago Convention, is used in the sense of consideration of fairness, reasonableness and policy often necessary for the sensible application of the more settled rules of law. Non-discrimination, in the same context, could be legally interpreted as the quality of treating equals equally. In other words, if equals are treated unequally, such becomes discrimination. These legal principles, when applied to the fundamental postulate of article 15, which merely provides that states should not permit service providers to charge foreign airlines more than their own airlines are charged for identical services provided, do not admit any difficulty of application. The marginal pricing theory, in its normative sense, or in presenting various modalities, would not derogate the equity or non-discrimination philosophies in that the theory will apply to all aircraft in a particular situation equally, while effectively precluding overcharging of smaller aircraft by factoring in a formula of pricing based on weight. To this end, marginal cost pricing, when applied to airports and air navigation services, should be devoid of peaks and valleys which vacillate with different circumstances or aircraft which come within marginal pricing on selected criteria. Therefore the application of marginal cost pricing to these services would be justifiable within the parameters envisioned, provided the complex economic principles involved could first be identified in the particular instance of international civil aviation.

3 THE 'SINGLE TILL' AND AIRPORT PRIVATIZATION

Legal issues

The fundamental postulate which establishes a global legal basis for the provision of airports is contained in article 28 of the Convention or International Civil Aviation,[205] which provides that each contracting state undertakes, as far as practicable, to provide in its territory airports, radio services, meteorological services and other air navigational facilities to facilitate international air navigation in accordance with the standards and practices recommended or established from time to time, pursuant to the convention. In addition, the Chicago Convention also stipulates, *inter alia*, that every aircraft which enters the territory of a state shall, if the regulations of that state so dictate, land at an airport designated by that state for purposes of customs and other examination.[206] Each contracting state to the Chicago Convention could also, subject to the provisions of the convention, designate an aircraft which passes through the airspace over the territory of the state and another state to the route it may follow within the territory of the state concerned and the airports it may use within the territory of the state.[207]

Privatization

Privatization of airports is yet another commercial tool which is sweeping the globe clear of modern challenges faced by the aviation industry. The almost uncontrollable growth in demand for air transport services has prompted countries across the world, from Australia to Zimbabwe, to consider seriously the selling of their airports to private entrepreneurs. It is distinctly possible that, in keeping with this trend, hundreds of airports may be sold over the next few years in order that airport infrastructures be broad-based so as to accommodate the overall passenger growth of 5.7 per cent between 1999 and 2000,[208] and of 6 per cent thereafter, until the year 2005.[209]

Another reason which impels airports to go in for privatization and optimize their services is the impact of airline alliances on airport facilities. A good example is Miami International Airport, which has made changes to a capital improvement programme, adding $500 million to an already buffered $5.4 billion programme in order to accommodate the alignment of airlines under Oneworld, Star and North West–Continental alliances.[210]

Privatization involves a whole spectrum of economic activities which affect infrastructural services and could extend to such facilities as power generation and clearing services. Two of the main advantages of privatization, of course, are maximizing profit and improving efficiency of the services at airports.[211] Public enterprises, in sharp contrast, tend to focus on job creation, supporting national identity and pride and stimulating tourism, all of which could have a stultifying effect on profit making and efficiency. Be that as it may, public enterprise has largely lost its appeal, not only because of the cumbersome bureaucracy involved but also because of the evolution of globalization which has changed economic reality and made enterprises move towards markets and efficiency from being mere non-profit-making services and facilities.

The liberalization and globalization of markets were a necessary corollary to the shift in perception of world leaders from the evils of monopoly to the advantages and virtues of competition. This change in attitude was mainly due to the realization that with liberalization come more entrepreneurs and companies who, in turn, with their market entry, make larger markets potentially available. Furthermore, with liberalization and globalization come better opportunities for entrepreneurs to enter markets, thus intensifying competition. The result is of course more quality service at more competitive prices. In the case of airports this effect can immediately be seen in the typical reduction of consumer goods in some airport shops immediately after they are privatized.

In 1994, the World Bank reported that privatization provides countless examples of dramatic improvements in efficiency as a result of the alleged superiority of the private enterprise system and pointed out that, in developing countries in which utilities were largely run by instrumentalities of state, 40 per cent of power-generating capacity was out of commission.[212] Harry P. Hatry contradicts the World Bank's thesis by stating:

> the major advantage of the privatization movement is not that the private sector can reduce costs or improve service to a great extent, but that consideration of privatization encourages public officials and public employees to innovate and to break down obstacles to improving public employee efficiency.[213]

Hatry continues with the argument – that privatization would not necessarily lower costs – by showing the inherent disadvantages of privatization as encouraging corruption, reducing quality of service and reducing access to service by disadvantaged citizens.[214] Concern has also been raised elsewhere with regard to disadvantages which may accompany privatization of airports, with the possibility of private airport owners taking on projects or opening new businesses within the umbrella of airport activity which are not related to the core airport business.[215] There is also the apprehension that the sale of equity shares may lead new owners of airports to hasten towards quick profit making and a short-term mentality that would effectively preclude the essential act of reinvesting of profits for infrastructure development.[216] Another negative throwback of airport privatization could well be related to public accountability or lack thereof where privatization may lead to cutbacks in expansion programmes and a reluctance to invest in infrastructure expansion.

On balance, however, it could be argued *a fortiori* that the advantages of airport privatization outweigh the disadvantages. For instance, privatization usually results in improved operational efficiency and aggressive market-related business practice such as opening up new, non-traditional capital sources calculated to contribute towards financing airport infrastructure and service development. Privatization remains a part of an overall strategy to replace the public sector culture with a private sector culture by more efficient use of resources and modernization of the economy concerned.[217]

Perhaps the most important feature of privatization is that it is essentially a political process involving a change in the role of the state with the sale of state or publicly owned property, or with transfer of management from state to private sources. This inevitably leads to issues of responsibility and legal liability. For instance, an airport which is publicly owned may not be under the same rules of legal liability as it would once privatized.

The United Nations General Assembly, at its 93rd Plenary Session in December 1992 endorsed privatization in the context of economic restructuring, economic growth and sustainable development. By Assembly Resolution A 47/171 the General Assembly, while noting, *inter alia*, that many countries were attaching growing importance, in the context of their economic restructuring policies, to the privatization of enterprises, urged member states to support when requested the national efforts of states in implementing privatization. In 1993, the General Assembly followed up its stance on privatization by adopting Resolution A 48/180 which, *inter alia*, requested the secretary general to strengthen the activities of the United Nations system related to the promotion of entrepreneurship and to the implementation of privatization programmes.

On the specific issue of airport privatization, the Latin American Civil Aviation Commission (LACAC), at its Thirteenth Ordinary Assembly held in Chile in July 1998, adopted Recommendation A 13-4 which recognized, *inter alia*, that airport privatization was becoming more prevalent in the Latin American Region and that the process of privatization involves a detailed analysis of different factors. Accordingly, the assembly recommended that the LACAC member states consider the following issues in order to obtain the best results from the privatization process.

a Define the role of the state and the responsibilities it must fulfil in order to guarantee the rights of users, as well as airport security and operational safety, in accordance with international standards in force.
b Consider the convenience of maintaining public ownership of airports, granting concessions for suitable periods of time in keeping with investments made.
c Clearly establish the required infrastructure, whose costs the state and/or the users will be willing to recognize, avoiding surpluses or deficiencies which may be detrimental to them.
d Determine the services to be transferred to the private sector and those which will remain in the hands of the state, describing the standards to be used in defining the quality of the services provided.

e As much as possible, aim at establishing a competitive environment for providers of the various services, seeking mechanisms such as public tenders. Maximum allowable rates should be established for monopolistic services.

f Define the financing of the air transport sector, deciding whether higher-income airports should support economically the less profitable ones or those working at a loss, in order to maintain a self-financed airport network compatible with national civil aviation needs.

g The contract between the state and private airport service operators must be the result of an open public tender where the required conditions, evaluation formulae and criteria to be used to award the contract must be clearly established and made known to all interested parties, in an absolutely transparent way.

h Reserve the right to implement the relevant measures to follow up, and maintain operational control over the concession contract.

i Pay special attention to the contract termination clause for its timely enforcement in case of non-compliance and recovery of the relevant value.

j The civil aviation administrations should actively participate in all privatization processes.

The privatization process would usually involve a sustained consultation period between the parties, particularly involving the fundamental issue of the exact mode of privatization involved. Some of the options which may be considered are the creation of a new corporation whereby existing assets could be vested in the new entity and be floated publicly. Privatization could also be partial, involving just some assets of the enterprise. There might also be a full public share flotation of the enterprise or a management buy-out structure where a company could provide backing finance in order to take the airport concerned into the private sector. There could also be a joint venture arrangement in airport privatization where private sector and government could share their equity involvements.

At the implementation stage of the privatization process, a tremendous amount of information is usually exchanged, particularly from the owners of the enterprise to the investors. Such information should demonstrate the legal rights of the parties and stipulate the rights and liabilities that would remain as residual rights and obligations of the state. A privatization process, whether it be by concession or trade sale would also entail a complex series of negotiation and contractual wrangling. Competing companies would bid against each other for the enterprise being offered for privatization.

Liability of the state

It is incontrovertible that the responsibility of the state is not extinguished merely because an airport is made subject to private ownership or private management control. In international air transport, the mere fact that the state has to provide airport services under article 28 of the Chicago Convention and indeed designate airports within its territory for landing purposes as per articles 10 and 68 imposes legal responsibility upon the state to be accountable at public international law for any liability incurred as a result of action on the part of airports within its territory.

The provisions of the Chicago Convention, which is an international treaty, are binding on contracting states to the convention and therefore are principles of public international law. The International Court of Justice (ICJ), in the *North Sea Continental Shelf Case*,[218] held that legal principles that are incorporated in treaties become customary international law by virtue of article 38 of the 1969 Vienna Convention on the Law of Treaties.[219] Article 38 recognizes that a rule set forth in a treaty will become binding upon a third state as a customary rule of international law if it is generally recognized by the states concerned as such. Article 28 of the Chicago Convention which requires states to provide airports for purposes of air transport operations therefore becomes a principle of customary international law, or *jus cogens*. Obligations arising from *jus cogens* are considered applicable *erga omnes*, which would mean that states using space technology owe a duty of care to the world at large in the provision of such technology. In the *Barcelona Traction Case*, the ICJ held:

> an essential distinction should be drawn between the obligations of a State towards the international community as a whole, and those arising *vis à vis* another State in the field of diplomatic protection. By their very nature, the former are the concerns of all States. In view of the importance of the rights involved, all States can be held to have a legal interest in their protection; they are obligations *erga omnes*.[220]

The International Law Commission has observed of the ICJ decision: 'in the Court's view, there are in fact a number, albeit limited, of international obligations which, by reason of their importance to the international community as a whole, are – unlike others – obligations in respect of which all States have legal interest'.[221]

The views of the ICJ and the International Law Commission, which has supported the approach taken by the ICJ, give rise to two possible conclusions relating to *jus cogens* and its resultant obligations *erga omnes*: (a) obligations *erga omnes* affect all states and thus cannot be made inapplicable to a state or group of states by an exclusive clause in a treaty or other document reflecting legal obligations without the consent of the international community as a whole; and (b) obligations *erga omnes* pre-empt other obligations which may be incompatible with them.

Some examples of obligations *erga omnes* cited by the ICJ are prohibition of acts of aggression, genocide, slavery and discrimination.[222] It is indeed worthy of note that all these obligations are derivatives of norms which are *jus cogens* at international law.

International responsibility relates both to breaches of treaty provisions and other breaches of legal duty. In the *Spanish Zone of Morocco Claims* case, Justice Huber observed: 'responsibility is the necessary corollary of a right. All rights of an international character involve international responsibility. If the obligation in question is not met, responsibility entails the duty to make reparation'.[223] It is also now recognized as a principle of international law that the breach of a duty involves an obligation to make reparation appropriately and adequately. This reparation is regarded as the indispensable complement of a failure to apply a convention and is applied as an inarticulate premise that need not be stated in the breached convention itself.[224] The ICJ affirmed this principle in 1949 in the *Corfu Channel* case,[225] by holding that Albania was responsible under international law to pay compensation to the United Kingdom for not warning that Albania had laid mines in Albanian waters which caused explosions, damaging ships belonging to the United Kingdom. Since the treaty law provisions of liability and the general principles of international law as discussed complement each other in endorsing the liability of states to compensate for damage caused by space objects, there is no contention as to whether in the use of nuclear power sources in outer space, damage caused by the uses of space objects or use thereof would not go uncompensated. The rationale for the award of compensation is explicitly included in article XII of the Liability Convention, which requires that the person aggrieved or injured should be restored (by the award of compensation to him) to the condition in which he would have been if the damage had not occurred. Furthermore, under the principles of international law, moral damages based on pain, suffering and humiliation, as well as on other considerations, are considered recoverable.[226]

The sense of international responsibility that the United Nations ascribed to itself had reached a heady stage at this point, where the role of international law in international human conduct was perceived to be primary and above the authority of states. In its Report to the General Assembly, the International Law Commission recommended a draft provision which required: 'Every State has the duty to conduct its relations with *other* States in accordance with international law and with the principle that the sovereignty of each State is subject to the supremacy of international law.'[227] This principle, which forms a cornerstone of international conduct by states, provides the basis for strengthening international comity and regulating the conduct of states both internally – within their territories – and externally, towards other states. States are effectively precluded by this principle from pursuing their own interests untrammelled and with disregard to principles established by international law.

Liability of the state at common law is best exemplified by the legal process of the United Kingdom. At private law involving issues of state liability and responsibility, the perennial adage that 'the king can do no wrong' extended from immunity of the sovereign to cover actions of the central government and its servants when acting within the scope of their employment. This immunity was more focused on exemption from tortious liability rather than on contractual liability and obviated the state's exposure to compensatory damages arising out of injury. There was, however, no bar to imposing personal liability of civil servants and, in 1765, the British government agreed to pay *ex gratia* damages awarded against one of its servants.[228] In the 1946 case of *Adams* v. *Naylor*,[229] the principle of *ex gratia* payment was rejected, giving way to the enactment in Britain of the Crown Proceedings Act of 1947 which allowed a plaintiff the right to take up a matter involving Crown liability directly in the courts of law. The Act did not apply to members of the armed forces, which essentially meant that, if an airport were to be manned by the armed forces, there would be no Crown liability for acts committed officially by the airport management concerned.

Private liability

Liability towards users Irrespective of the responsibility of a state with regard to airports within its territories, which is founded both at customary international law and at private law for liability incurred by airports, a privately run airport may incur tortious liability on a private basis, as the occupier of the premises. Legal liability of airports run by private entities would be liable to the various users of airports, including air carriers, and to non-users who may be outside the premises of the airport but be injured by the activities of the airport. A good example of the latter is damage caused by environmental pollution through noise within the vicinity of the airport.

In the instance of a privately managed airport where the entity charged with managing airport services is located within the airport premises, such an entity would be considered as a legal occupier for purposes of liability. The leading case which expands the definition of 'occupier' is the House of Lords' decision in *Wheat* v. *E. Lacon & Co. Ltd*,[230] where the defendants owned a public house of which R was their manager. R and his wife were allowed by agreement to live in the upper floor, access to which was by a door separate from the licensed premises. Mrs R was allowed to take paying guests on the upper floor. An accident was sustained by a paying guest on the staircase leading to the upper floor. It was held that the defendants were occupiers of the upper floor. Mr R was only a licensee of that part, and the defendants had enough residuary control to be treated as occupiers. In fact the defendants, Mr R and Mrs R were all occupiers.

The case recognizes three principles: that there may be two or more occupiers at one time,[231] that exclusive occupation is not required, and that the test is whether a person has some degree of control associated with and arising from his presence in and use of or activity in the premises. The following principles, enunciated by earlier decisions, that a concessionaire without a lease in a fairground is an occupier,[232] a contractor converting a ship into a troopship in dry dock occupies the ship,[233] and a local authority which has requisitioned a house[234] is an occupier (even in respect of those parts of the house in which it is allowing homeless persons to live)[235] are also valid.

Although the *Wheat* case contains a decision on the meaning of 'occupier' for the purposes of the Occupiers' Liability Act 1957 of the United Kingdom, the judgments following the case show that it applies to all cases, whether at common law or under that Act, or the Occupiers' Liability Act 1984 which now regulates occupiers' duties to trespassers, where it is necessary to determine the duty of care owed by occupiers to entrants.

The Occupiers' Liability Act 1957 was enacted to give effect to the recommendations of the Law Reform Committee[236] and to eliminate the confusion that had clouded the common law rules on liability to entrants on premises. The rules enacted by sections 2 and 3 of the Act 'have effect, in place of the rules of the common law, to regulate the duty which an occupier of premises owes to his visitors in respect of dangers due to the state of the premises or to things done or omitted to be done on them'.[237]

At common law it was necessary to distinguish between invitees, licensees and other entrants on premises. The approximate distinction was that an invitee was requested to enter the premises in the interest of the occupier, whereas a licensee was merely permitted to enter. 'Visitors' for the purposes of the Act are those persons who were invitees or licensees at common law:

> The common duty of care of an occupier is a duty to take such care as in all the circumstances of the case is reasonable to see that the visitor will be reasonably safe in using the premises for the purposes for which he is invited or permitted by the occupier to be there.[238]

If the entrant does not use the premises for that purpose which entitles him to be there, no duty is owed to him under the 1957 Act and any remedy which he might have would be regulated by the 1984 Act on the duty owed to trespassers.

Those entering as of right are not 'invited or permitted' by the occupier for any purpose. Section 2(6) of the Act nonetheless makes the common law duty extend to them by providing that 'persons who enter premises for any purpose in the exercise of a right conferred by law are to be treated as permitted by the occupier to be there for that purpose, whether they in fact have his permission or not'. Section 2(6) does not extend the category of visitors beyond the common law definition – it merely extends the circumstances when a visitor will be owed the common law duty of care by providing that visitors who enter for any purpose in the exercise of a right conferred by law are to be treated as permitted by the occupier to be there for that purpose.[239]

Whether the standard required by the common duty of care has been attained in a case involving liability of an airport authority is a question of fact and the important issues will be resolved by inference rather than on primary facts. The relevant circumstances would include the degree of care, and want of care, which would ordinarily be looked for in a visitor, on the following basis: an occupier must expect children to be less careful than adults; and an occupier may expect that a person, in the exercise of his calling, will appreciate and guard against any special risks ordinarily incident to it, so far as the occupier leaves him free to do so.[240]

The above principles reiterate existing rules of common law, and therefore support the view that, in deciding the countless issues of fact which will arise in applying the 'common duty of care', it will be proper to consider cases decided before the Act as guides (but certainly no more than guides) in interpreting the duty where no unambiguous rule is laid down in the Act itself.

One of the most significant principles at common law on occupier's liability is the consideration of the child visitor. In deciding whether there is a danger, an occupier, such as an airport authority, must especially consider the physical and mental powers of a child visitor on the basis that what is not a danger to an adult may be a danger to a child.[241] And this may be so because of the allurement or property of temptation, to a child, of some condition on the land.[242] In determining the standard of care owed to a child who is not accompanied by a guardian, it will be material to inquire whether, in the circumstances, the occupier could reasonably have expected the presence of the infant unaccompanied.[243]

At common law an occupier discharges his duty to a visitor by a warning sufficient to convey to the visitor full knowledge of the nature and extent of the danger. That rule is changed by section 2(4)(*a*) of the Act[244] which provides that, where damage is caused to a visitor by a danger[245] of which he had been warned by the occupier, the warning is not to be treated without more as absolving the occupier from liability, unless in all the circumstances it was enough to enable the visitor to be reasonably safe.

For example, the farmer who warns the veterinary surgeon whom he has summoned to the farm at night to attend a sick cow by saying 'be careful how you go down the yard or you may fall into a tank', or the railway company which warns of the dangerous roof over what is the sole approach to the ticket office can no longer absolve themselves from liability by that warning alone. On the other hand, where a customer does not heed the warning of a shopkeeper not to go to the far end of the shop because there is a dangerous hole, it might presumably be held in all the circumstances that the common duty of care owed to him under the Act has been discharged. If the defendant does not know of the danger he cannot rely on section 2(4)(*a*), although he may still have a defence under section 2(1).[246]

Assumption of risk The common duty of care does not impose on an occupier any obligation to a visitor in respect of risks willingly accepted as his by the visitor (the question whether a risk is so accepted should be decided on the same principles as in other cases in which one person owes a duty of care to another).[247] According to the ordinary principles of negligence, a defendant breaches no duty of care towards a plaintiff who has voluntarily assumed the risk.

At common law no duty of care was owed to a visitor who had full knowledge of the nature and extent of the danger.[248] Knowledge is not specifically mentioned as a relevant circumstance in determining whether the common duty of care has been discharged. But since the Act expressly provides that voluntary assumption of a risk discharges the duty of care, its silence about the effect of mere knowledge of the risk makes it clear that knowledge on the part of the visitor in itself no longer serves to discharge the duty of care. Yet the visitor's knowledge of the danger remains relevant in deciding whether in all the circumstances it was enough to enable him to be reasonably safe.[249]

Liability towards neighbours The risk created by dangers caused by the defective state of premises is not confined to entrants to those premises. Slates falling from roofs, crumbling walls and dangerous activities carried out on premises are just a few examples of risks as likely to endanger passers-by on the highway, or persons on adjoining premises, as to injure persons actually on the occupier's premises. The circumstances in which a duty of care is owed to such persons by the occupier of premises therefore warrant brief consideration.

An action in nuisance, derived from public nuisance, often lies at the instance of those injured on a highway as a result of harmful conditions on adjoining land. Because of this historical anomaly, in a large number of situations a plaintiff may now sue either in negligence or in nuisance (or, as often happens, in both) for personal injuries; and yet the law is the same whichever tort is relied on. In several House of Lords cases, it has been a matter of indifference whether the case was decided in negligence or in nuisance, both of which were pleaded.[250] Often, it seems quite fortuitous which tort is relied on: if, for instance, some act of negligent omission stands out, the claim will often be negligence. The 1948 decision in *Holling* v. *Yorkshire Traction Co. Ltd.* is a typical example of this ambivalence.

> The defendants emitted so much steam and smoke on to the highway from their adjoining factory that the view was obscured and two vehicles collided, killing the plaintiff, who was on the highway. It was held to be negligence on the part of the defendant to fail to post a man at each end of the affected area. They were also held liable in nuisance.[251]

Accordingly, there is no room for doubt that the ordinary principles of negligence can be applied where highway users are injured because of harmful operations being carried out there.[252]

Occupiers are also under a general duty to take reasonable care to prevent dangers existing on their premises from damaging persons or property on adjoining premises.[253] This is so whether the danger arises from disrepair on the premises or from some natural or man-made hazard, for example fire caused by lightning striking a tree.[254] It has been held that, where adjoining properties have mutual rights of support, an occupier who negligently allows a property to fall into dereliction so as to damage the adjoining premises is liable in negligence as well as in nuisance.[255] There are two issues of particular difficulty affecting the duties of care owed *inter se* by occupiers of adjoining premises.

Where a plaintiff tenant sues his landlord for damage resulting from the defective state of repair of premises retained by the landlord the case law is somewhat ambivalent. The facts in *Cunard* v. *Antifyre Ltd.*[256] were that some defective roofing and guttering, which formed part of the premises retained by the defendant landlord, fell into a part of the premises let by him to the plaintiff tenant. As a result, his wife was injured and his goods were damaged. Damages in general negligence were awarded to both the tenant and his wife.

However, in *Cheater* v. *Cater*,[257] the Court of Appeal had held earlier that a landlord, who had let a field to a tenant at a time when there was a yew tree on the adjoining premises retained by the landlord, was not liable in negligence when the tenant's horse died through eating leaves from that tree which was then in the same state as at the date of the lease. The Court of Appeal in *Shirvell* v. *Hackwood Estates Co. Ltd.*,[258] a later case, questioned *Cunard* v. *Antifyre Ltd.* and held that a workman of a tenant could not recover in negligence from the landlord whose tree on adjoining land fell on him. In *Taylor* v. *Liverpool Corpn* the plaintiff, the daughter of a tenant of one of the defendant landlords' flats, was injured by the fall of a chimney stack belonging to these flats into the yard adjoining the premises. The landlords had negligently maintained this chimney, which formed part of the building retained by them.[259]

Stable J found for the plaintiff in negligence, following *Cunard* v. *Antifyre Ltd.*, and distinguishing *Cheater* v. *Cater* on the ground that the tenant had there impliedly agreed to take the risk in respect of danger existing on the premises at that time. His lordship treated the observations in *Shirvell*'s case as *obiter* on the ground that no negligence had in any event occurred. The above notwithstanding, the principle in the *Cunard* case is more plausible than one which gives the landlord blanket immunity.

Comments

An airport should generally improve its efficiency levels upon privatization. This could only be optimized if the airport concerned received a fresh start, preferably with a debt write-off and a clean slate for a balance sheet. There should also be potential for new capital injection and effective measures should be taken to offset the loss of government support which the airport would have had while under public control.

It is important to bear in mind that it can take a long time to make profits out of infrastructural improvements carried out as a result of airport privatization. This may discourage foreign investment in the privatization process of an airport. However, airports are essentially monopolies in their geographic regions and therefore could recover profits easily. Legally, as was discussed, neither the state nor the airport can avoid liability on account of privatization. The state entails liability primarily at public international law and also at public law in general, and the airport incurs liability on a private basis in a private action that may be brought, under tort law principles or under contract law, as the case may be.

4 FUNDING AN INTERNATIONAL FINANCIAL FACILITY FOR AVIATION SAFETY

Introduction

The perceived incoherence of current aviation policies in the face of socioeconomic indicators which reflect that world populations will largely be migratory in the new millennium and therefore air travel will increase significantly has spawned a dichotomy between the provision of air transport services *per se* and the availability of infrastructure. For instance, while market access has been largely liberalized, markets, largely deregulated and airlines have been privatized for purposes of optimal competitive utilization, airport and air navigation services infrastructure providers by and large have remained within governmental control and are constrained in their efforts to respond to market forces.

Travel and tourism represent a gross economic output of USD$3500 billion (nearly 12 per cent of the world economic output). The lack of economic consistency between the capacity of providers in offering airport and air navigation services to such a large air transport industry and the enormous demands growing at 5 per cent per annum for such services not only reflects that air transport is one of the largest industries in the world today, but also brings to bear the most serious concern of modern air transport – safety. Aviation safety could be seriously compromised if airport and air navigation services do not meet the rigorous demands placed on them by the air transport industry.

Safety is the primary concern of the world aviation community at the present time. It is not only because the fundamental postulates of the Chicago Convention of 1944[260] call for the safe and orderly development of international civil aviation[261] and mandate ICAO to ensure the safe and orderly growth of international civil aviation throughout the world,[262] but also because the aviation world faces a critical era where, in the words of Dr Assad Kotaite, President of the ICAO Council: 'the international aviation community cannot afford to relax its vigilance ... ICAO would continue to take timely action to ensure safety and security standards are in effect, and that deficiencies are properly and efficiently addressed'.[263]

There is a compelling need to align the service providers and their services with the wave of commercialization and privatization which is sweeping the airline industry, in order to meet the increasing demands by the airlines for these services. The establishment of autonomous entities by the creation of independent, publicly owned corporations and funding them adequately is one option to achieve this objective. Privatization of airports and air navigation services is another option. Financing, through an investment banking mechanism, is the third option. The fourth option is pre-funding the needed resources through a charges system levied on airline passengers. Some of these options will be discussed below.

The investment banking mechanism as a funding source

Airport-related risks, in the eyes of the investment banker, will be bifurcated into (a) risks that pertain to the operation of services or projects relating to such operations by the private sector; and (b) risks that emerge from actions of a sovereign in control of services provided which may bring to bear an influence on airport and air navigation services economics or non-project-related risks.

In developing economies, a popular practice for financing would be through a process of privatization with build–operate–transfer (BOT) schemes that are founded on concessionary contracts with written-in investment requirements for expansion, upgrading or building airport and air navigational facilities. In developed countries, within a state regulatory structure, the model would look to establishing financially autonomous entities of a private sector nature, under state ownership. In the former case, the funding source will be cautious of political risk as well as risks entailed in the normal process of contractual obligation between parties. Emphasis will be laid, for purposes of borrowing by the airport or other service concerned, of the applicable fee structure and charging policy, together with the potential of equity inflow. The greatest challenge to this process would be in determining the most appropriate regulatory structure and mechanism for funding and recovery, enforcement mechanisms and the dispute resolution structure.

In order to attract investment bankers to fund projects for aviation safety, such as in providing state-of-the art air navigation services, states should project a certain profile towards absorbing globalization through competitive privatization. National competitiveness has become one of the central preoccupations of government and industry in every nation. Yet, for all the discussion, debate and writing on the topic, there is still no persuasive theory to explain national competitiveness. What is more, there is not even an accepted definition of the term 'competitiveness' as applied to a nation.

The only meaningful concept of competitiveness at the national level is *productivity*. The principal goal of a nation is to produce a high and rising standard of living for its citizens. The ability to do so depends on the productivity with which a nation's labour and capital are employed. Productivity is the value of the output produced by a unit of labour or capital. Productivity depends on both the quality and the features of products (which determine the prices that they can command) and the efficiency with which they are produced. Productivity is the prime determinant of a nation's long-run standard of living; it is the root cause of national per capita income. The productivity of human resources determines employee wages; the productivity with which capital is employed determines the return it earns for its holders.

A nation's standard of living depends on the capacity of its companies to achieve high levels of productivity – and to increase productivity over time. Sustained productivity growth requires that an economy continually *upgrade itself*. A bank seeking to fund projects within a state would expect a nation's companies to improve productivity relentlessly in existing industries by raising product quality, adding desirable features, improving product technology or boosting production efficiency. They must develop the necessary capabilities to compete in more and more sophisticated industry segments, where productivity is generally high. They must, finally, develop the capability to compete in entirely new, sophisticated industries.

In order to attract an investment banker, a nation and an enterprise within, such as an airport or air navigation service provider, must initially subscribe to the classical theory which explains the success of nations in particular industries based on so-called 'factors of production' such as land, labour and natural resources where nations gain factor-based comparative advantage in industries that make intensive use of the factors they possess in abundance. Classical theory, however, has been overshadowed in advanced industries and economies by the globalization of competition and the power of technology.

A new approach must recognize that, in modern international competition, companies compete with global strategies involving not only trade but also foreign investment. What a new theory must explain is why a nation provides a favourable home base for companies that compete internationally. The home base is the nation in which the essential competitive advantages of the enterprise are created and sustained. It is where a company's strategy is set, where the core product and process technology is created and maintained, and where the most productive jobs and most advanced skills are located. The presence of the home base in a nation has the greatest positive influence on other linked domestic industries and leads to other benefits in the nation's economy. While the ownership of the company is often concentrated at the home base, the nationality of shareholders is secondary.

The new approach must move beyond comparative advantage to the competitive advantage of a nation, giving airport and air navigation services of that country a profile of competitiveness. It must reflect a rich conception of competition that includes segmented markets, differentiated products, technology differences and economies of scale. A new theory must go beyond cost and explain why companies from some nations are better than others at creating advantages based on quality, features and new product innovation. A new theory must begin from the premise that competition is dynamic and evolving; it must answer questions. Why do some companies based in some nations innovate more than others? Why do some nations provide an environment that enables companies to improve and innovate faster than foreign rivals?

An international aeronautical fund

During the 31st Session of the ICAO Assembly in September 1995, eight members of the Latin American Civil Aviation Commission (LACAC)[264] presented their proposals for the setting up of an aeronautical monetary fund for the benefit of the aviation community. Citing the reason for the proposal as the difficulties faced by governments and airlines to obtain financing at reasonable costs for the modernization of airlines, airport infrastructure, air traffic services and navigation aids, LACAC introduced the proposal as a means to contribute to the balanced development of international air transport.[265]

The proposed international aeronautical monetary fund has its origin in LACAC which, at its Panel Meeting on 13–14 June 1994, held in Salvador, Brazil, proposed the inauguration of the fund to finance air navigation services provided by the satellite based Communications, Navigation, Surveillance/Air Traffic Management (CNS/ATM) system. It was the consensus in LACAC that the fund should be created by international agreement, and that the entity which would receive and administer the financing of the CNS/ATM system under the fund should be an international bank established for that purpose. The overriding principle of the aeronautical monetary fund remained, however, that its administration should be supervised by ICAO.

The LACAC initiative was in response to the introduction of satellite technology to future air navigation systems which ICAO has been energetically involved in since 1993. These new air navigation systems would be operated through a satellite network dedicated to the air transport industry. In order to ensure such an exclusive dedication to air transport users of a satellite system, the costs that have to be incurred would also be substantial. These costs that would enable the transition of air navigation from currently used navigation systems to satellite technology would have to be absorbed by a funding source in order that an efficient and effective CNS/ATM system be implemented globally.

The objective of the fund, according to LACAC, was to provide the financial resources necessary to meet the most pressing needs of LACAC member states for the construction and modernization of airport infrastructure, air traffic services and navigation aids. Also included in the list of beneficiaries were airline fleets which needed expansion and modernization.

LACAC proposed that the fund be created through an international convention open to ICAO contracting states. The convention would necessitate adherence by states if their airlines, airports and other initiatives were to benefit from the fund. The fund would be totally autonomous and politically independent from the control of individual or collective governments. The money that formed the fund would come from the user – the airline – and any other interested financial institution and would be collected semi-annually in accordance with a procedure agreed upon between the parties to the convention.

It was also proposed that the fund be administered by a board of governors (one appointed by each member government), five executive directors elected by the board and a managing director who should ideally be a senior member of the international banking community and elected by the executive directors. The administration of the fund included audit of accounts to be carried out annually by a specialized international firm of accountants. Inherent in the audit principles was a proposal for absolute transparency devoid of diplomatic immunity and commercial confidentiality.

The advantage of the fund was identified by LACAC primarily as self-sufficiency. Other advantages were the improvement of air navigation facilities worldwide by both the developed and developing world, and the possibility of making available credit facilities through the fund to civil aviation bodies and the air transport industry. The most significant feature of the LACAC proposal is that the aeronautical monetary fund would act as a tool which would promote the implementation of ICAO's Strategic Action Plan.

Implied in the proposal is the incontrovertible fact that the Strategic Action Plan (SAP) cannot be implemented unilaterally by ICAO without the cooperation of its member states. Fundamentally, and from a legal standpoint, the position of ICAO in the international aviation community is not one that is compatible with being absolutely legislative in capacity. ICAO sets guidelines on civil aviation and facilitates the adoption of treaties and regulations, with the approval of its member states. It is then up to the member states themselves to implement them. The SAP is therefore essentially a two-sided issue and may be adequately subsumed by the adage 'one cannot clap with one hand'. The obligations of ICAO member states are paramount in giving teeth to ICAO's Standards and Recommended Practices and other guidelines, as much as in satisfying or otherwise accepting treaties of air law that they themselves have adopted under ICAO auspices.

The LACAC proposal therefore suggests that it is essential for ICAO contracting states to recognize the compelling need to address the issue of the establishment of the aeronautical monetary fund in the context of its supportive role in financing on a global scale the key elements of the Strategic Action Plan.

In the context of the above observations on the relevance of the fund to the implementation of the ICAO Strategic Action Plan, it is significant that the LACAC proposal called upon the ICAO Assembly to request the council to establish a working group to study the need, appropriateness and usefulness of establishing an international aeronautical monetary fund for the above-mentioned purposes. The ICAO SAP, which was adopted by the ICAO Council on 7 February 1997, is primarily aimed at promoting the principles enshrined in the Chicago Convention[266] in the most efficient manner so that the challenges posed by modern exigencies of civil aviation are met. The SAP would accomplish the following:

- ensure that ICAO maintains its position as the main standard-setting body for international civil aviation;
- encourage national ratification of instruments of international air law and implementation of ICAO Standards and Recommended Practices to the greatest extent possible so as to maintain a common aviation system worldwide;
- ensure that ICAO continues to focus on the exploration and development of aviation issues of a multilateral nature in the fields of legal, economic and technical regulation, and thereby remains a world forum for these issues;

- identify priorities for ICAO and seek to ensure that sufficient resources are made available to respond to the major challenges concerned; and
- develop a continued efficient and cost-effective mechanism in ICAO for the management of technical cooperation activities.[267]

The issues that are identified by ICAO as requiring the above action are:

- communications, navigation and surveillance/air traffic management (CNS/ATM),
- airport and airspace congestion,
- commercial developments and economic regulation,
- financial resources,
- unlawful interference,
- human factors in flight safety,
- environmental protection,
- human resources,
- enhancement of ICAO standards: safety oversight.

The legal aspects of these issues form separate studies by themselves and have largely been addressed elsewhere.[268] However, for the purposes of identifying a link between the aeronautical monetary fund and the primary areas of importance for civil aviation as identified by the Strategic Action Plan, it is evident that CNS/ATM, airport and airspace congestion alleviation and safety take a pre-eminent place in requiring financial resources for global implementation. Of primary relevance, therefore, are the legal issues that underline the justification of creating the fund and an overall legal analysis which would inquire whether the application of finances from an established aeronautical monetary fund to the above areas would be consistent with established ICAO policy.

At the 31st Session of the ICAO Assembly, held in 1995, contracting states adopted Assembly Resolution A31-2 (increasing the effectiveness of ICAO) which calls for the SAP to be 'updated and rolled forward' at least triennially. Following a comprehensive overview by the ICAO Secretariat, the council on 12 June 2000 adopted a revised text for the plan which, *inter alia*, updated the original plan to address long-term strategic objectives, including the introduction of the Universal Safety Oversight Audit Programme of ICAO and consideration of its development with a view to its expansion to cover all safety-related annexes to the Chicago Convention.

Although the Executive Commission of the 31st ICAO Assembly, which considered the LACAC proposal, had great sympathy for the objectives of the proposal, it was generally noted that the establishment of an international convention was both a complex and a time-consuming undertaking needing careful thought and detailed consideration of the issues involved before it attains fruition. While some members of the commission recommended the consideration of more innovative financial instruments to realize funding for CNS/ATM, others, such as the observer for IATA, strongly opposed the proposal on the grounds that it was inconsistent with ICAO policies to create a fund which was financed by users of civil aviation.[269]

The commission concluded that the proposal for the creation of an international aeronautical monetary fund was laudable, and indeed, a valuable one, but thought it fit to leave it to the ICAO Council to decide how best the proposal should be pursued further. The ICAO Council, following the position taken by the ICAO Assembly at its 31st Session, commissioned the secretariat to study the proposal further. Consequently, a preliminary study was conducted by the secretariat and considered by the 32nd Session of the ICAO Assembly in 1998. Flowing from the request of the assembly at this session, for a more detailed study of the subject by the secretariat, a study has been prepared, and was before the ICAO Council at the time of writing.

Institutional issues

The main thrust of the proposal for the establishment of the aeronautical monetary fund is in the levy of an additional one US dollar per passenger ticket sold. Using this concept in the context of 1996, where the airlines of the 185 ICAO contracting states carried 1 380 million passengers,[270] it is reasonable to assume that the fund would have generated at least 1 380 million US dollars in the first year of its operations if it were established in 1996. The ICAO forecast that airline passenger traffic will grow at an average rate of 5 per cent annually until 2003[271] will only make the fund grow larger by 5 per cent annually in the foreseeable future.

The concept of the international aeronautical monetary fund had been recommended in 1993 by a commentator who had acknowledged the practical and political possibility of establishing an aeronautical monetary fund for the financing of the CNS/ATM system's implementation worldwide. The Hon. Saeed A. Al-Ghamdi, Representative of Saudi Arabia on the Council of ICAO, observed in 1993:

> The precedents set by the joint financing agreements between Denmark and Iceland for the provision of air navigation services over the North Atlantic, and the existence of intergovernmental organizations such as the International Maritime Satellite Organization (Inmarsat), are examples of what international cooperation can accomplish when the political will exists. Similar cooperation is possible in the implementation of the CNS/ATM systems despite the massive size of the financial requirement.[272]

Mr. Al-Ghamdi lists numerous advantages of the proposed levy, some of which are the provision of unified satellite-based CNS coverage for air traffic movements in every region of the world based on ICAO's Standards and Recommended Practices;

global adherence to safety criteria and regulatory parameters through worldwide implementation of CNS/ATM systems; limitation of the financial burden imposed on users (airlines) owing to the lack of adequate services around the world; meeting the rate of growth predicted for the air transport industry in the 21st century; and guaranteeing the implementation of the principles of the Chicago Convention and the promotion of harmonized global planning and implementation of the future air navigation systems.[273]

The seminal principle which mandates ICAO as the organization responsible for the international regulation of civil aviation is found in article 44(*a*) of the Chicago Convention which requires the organization to ensure the safe and orderly growth of international civil aviation throughout the world. The word 'ensure' devolves upon ICAO the responsibility to make absolutely certain that international civil aviation grows safely and in an orderly manner. ICAO is also required, by article 44(*d*), to meet the needs of the peoples of the world for safe, regular, efficient and economical air transport. Therefore there is no room for doubt that the contracting states of ICAO, by the Chicago Convention itself, will hold ICAO accountable for ensuring safety and efficiency in air transport. In this context, even though ICAO has performed an admirable task in introducing a safety oversight programme and a highly adequate CNS/ATM system for air navigation, it still has to make certain that this programme and system are implemented globally. Article 54(*i*) of the Chicago Convention authorizes the council to request, collect, examine and publish information relating to the advancement of air navigation and the operation of international air services, including information about the costs of operation and particulars of subsidies paid to airlines from public funds. This provision enables the ICAO Council to make an exhaustive study of the financial outlay needed for the 185 contracting states of ICAO to implement not only the CNS/ATM system but also related programmes such as safety oversight, which is often dependent on the availability of proper air navigation facilities and training in the states concerned.

The ICAO Council can also, by virtue of article 69 of the Chicago Convention, intervene in instances where the council believes that a state does not have adequate air navigation facilities, and make recommendations for remedying the situation. Following this, a contracting state may conclude an arrangement with the council for giving effect to such recommendations, as provided for by article 70. More importantly, article 71 of the Chicago Convention empowers the ICAO Council, at the request of a state, to provide, man, maintain and administer the state's air navigation facilities and airports for the safe, regular, efficient and economical operation of air services of the other contracting states. Article 71 also empowers the council to specify just and reasonable charges for the use of the facilities provided.

Article 77 of the Chicago Convention enables all the 187 contracting states of ICAO to form a joint air transport operating organization to pool their services on any routes or regions. The provision does not exclude the possibility of states pooling parts of revenue obtained from their air carriers' services, such as an additional levy to be charged from each passenger of the pooled services, to be remitted to the joint air transport operating organization.

It is therefore clear that the Chicago Convention provides for the administration of air navigation services by the ICAO Council on a global scale, consequent to a detailed study of the cost implications of such administration. The convention also provides for the pooling of air services for purposes of collecting revenue, which could be deposited in an international organization formed for that purpose.

The joint financing mechanism

A regional analogy of financing of air navigation services which is administered by ICAO already exists in the nature of the joint financing agreements. The operation of joint financing in civil aviation became necessary in the context of non-stop transatlantic flights north of the 45th parallel, which is covered by the Flight Information Region (FIR) of Iceland. Air navigational facilities offered by Iceland are indispensable for aircraft flying within this region. Since major storm tracks converge very near Iceland and that area of the Atlantic around Iceland is favourable to the redevelopment of certain types of storms and to the formation of secondary depressions, it is generally during unfavourable meteorological conditions that the greatest number of aircraft operate in the vicinity of Iceland and traffic becomes congested, requiring full utilization of the air traffic control and flight information services offered by Iceland. Such services were required to be given for the safe operation of international air services in the North Atlantic. At the North Atlantic Route Service Conference, held in Dublin in March 1946, a recommendation was made, *inter alia*, that Iceland should provide an Area Control Centre in Reykjavik and certain telecommunications and meteorological services for the North Atlantic Region. These recommendations were approved subsequently by the PICAO[274] Council on 17 April 1946 and 9 May 1946.[275] During the conference, the delegation from Iceland made a statement to the effect that Iceland would not be able to provide the services recommended by the conference, owing to the magnitude of aircraft crossings that required services. On 16 May 1947, as a follow-up to its statement, Iceland submitted to ICAO a request for financial and technical aid in regard to the air traffic control, communications and meteorological services in Iceland in accordance with Chapter XV of the Chicago Convention. The ICAO Council, on 25 June 1947, concluded that the request of Iceland constituted *prima facie* grounds for aid to be rendered in the manner sought.[276]

Article 68 in Chapter XV of the convention brings the joint financing concept into immediate focus, and impliedly extends the concept of sovereignty as enunciated in article 1 by providing that each contracting state may designate the air route(s) to be followed within its territory by any international air service. If states have control over the designation of air routes over their own territories, it automatically follows that ICAO, which is charged by the convention to develop the principles and techniques of air navigation[277] and foster the planning and development of international air transport by, *inter alia*, encouraging the development of airways, airports and air navigation facilities for international civil aviation,[278] should adopt measures to improve air navigation facilities worldwide. The concept of joint financing is therefore a measure to improve air navigation facilities and airports throughout the world. As discussed earlier, the seminal provision that reflects the philosophy of the concept is seen in article 70 of the convention, which provides that a contracting state may arrange with the ICAO Council to implement the council's recommendations relating to the improvement of air navigation facilities[279] either by bearing all costs involved or by jointly financing such implementation process with the council. A joint financing agreement between a contracting state and the ICAO Council is calculated to facilitate the use of land by the council at reasonable terms,[280] provide technical assistance by the council[281] and funding by the Council – all in pursuance of the objective of improving or developing air navigation facilities. Funding for a joint financing project is provided by the states whose airlines use the routes in question.[282]

Another provision which is relevant to the establishment of the monetary fund is article 75, which provides for the discharge of obligations by a contracting state under the joint financing agreement by taking over from the council its airports and other facilities that were handed over to the council in pursuance of a joint financing agreement. The state may then pay the council whatever monies had been incurred in the development of air navigation in the territory of that state. The council should then return the funds to the states who paid them. This reimbursement is done on guidelines already set by the convention.[283]

States' obligations to provide air navigation services to the international community stem from article 28 of the convention, which provides that each contracting state undertakes to provide, in its territory, such facilities as airports, radio and meteorological services and other air navigational facilities while adopting standards of communication and collaborating with a unified communications methodology.

The ICAO Assembly, by Assembly Resolution A1-65, established the general policy of ICAO relating to the joint support of air navigation services. The ensuing Joint Financing Agreement of 1948 has since been replaced by the agreement of 1956,[284] which has been amended by the Montreal Protocol of 1982.[285] This agreement requires Iceland to operate and maintain air navigation services without interruption[286] and provided for reimbursement of 95 per cent of the costs to be made to Iceland by contracting states to the agreement.[287]

Assembly Resolution A14-37 made further provision in 1962 for increased participation by 'user states' in joint financing agreements that were contemplated between the council and the states involved. At its 16th Assembly in 1968, the ICAO issued guidelines for the implementation of economic aspects of joint financing agreements.[288] Since its inception, ICAO has held several conferences on joint financing: in Geneva, 8–26 June 1948 on the subject of Iceland; in London, 20 April–12 May 1949 on Greenland and the Faroes; and in Geneva, 6–24 September 1956 for the revision of the Danish and Icelandic arrangements.

There are now 23 contracting states to the Icelandic Agreement and they reimburse 95 per cent of the total costs of air navigation services under the agreement, which amounts to approximately $21 million. Of this sum, user charges levied on airlines account for 90 per cent of the total cost. ICAO's involvement in the Joint Financing Agreement has been succinctly described by Gerald Fitzgerald:

> Through its participation in joint financing schemes, contemplated by Chapter XV of the Chicago Convention, ICAO has made an important pioneering contribution by developing legal, consultative and administrative techniques to be used in the management of such schemes ...The ICAO programme ... was a great success in the North Atlantic area ... through the use of innovative administrative and legal techniques, ICAO has demonstrated that it is possible to use the services of a neutral, inter-governmental organization for the administration of a complicated system of air navigation services required by the international community.[289]

The joint financing agreements, and their successful implementation under ICAO's administration over the years, have amply demonstrated that, given the political will of states, it is conceptually possible to establish and administer a fund which implements the ICAO SARPS on safety and efficiency in air navigation through the implementation of global safety standards, a CNS/ATM system and other related mechanisms of current importance to civil aviation.

The practicality of implementing an aeronautical fund for safety by using the joint financing analogy brings to bear the need to analyse the two concepts for consistency and comparison. The following facts are relevant for such an analysis:

- the Danish and Icelandic joint financing funds were created after World War II to ensure the availability of air navigation services needed for the safety of civil aviation over the North Atlantic;
- installations in Greenland, Iceland and the Faroe Islands put into place and used during the war were retained to service civil flights after the war;
- since Denmark and Iceland were only modest users of the services, it would not have been fair to ask them to bear the full costs of the services benefiting all users operating flights over the North Atlantic;
- in the early years of the joint financing agreements there were no user charges; the costs of the services were financed by the states parties to the joint financing agreements on the ratio of the crossings by airlines of their states to crossings by airlines of all the states parties to the agreements;
- in the 1970s, a user charge mechanism was introduced to provide for the recovery of the costs allocatable to international civil aviation;
- the joint financing agreements ensure that funds are available on a timely basis to provide the stipulated services and that the governments of Denmark and Iceland do not have to bear the costs of services for which they are only modest users;
- the joint financing agreements are administered by the ICAO Secretariat

under the direction of the ICAO Council and the council's Joint Support Committee; and

- the role of the Joint Support Committee includes mainly the approval of cost estimates, actual costs, audit reports, assessments on contracting governments, user charges, adjustments and payments to the provider states. It also considers proposals for new projects and new capital expenditures for the services provided by Denmark and Iceland under the joint financing agreements.

On the basis of the above facts, the following fundamental differences between the proposed aeronautical monetary fund and the joint financing mechanism may be noted.

- The joint financing funds and the international aeronautical monetary fund serve two different purposes. The joint financing funds were created in order to finance services essential to international civil aviation. These services needed to be operated by Denmark and Iceland because of the geographical location of Greenland, Iceland and the Faroe Islands in the North Atlantic. The services had to be financed by the various states whose airlines were major users of those services in due fairness to Denmark and Iceland which were and still are only modest users of the services. In the case of the international aeronautical monetary fund, this fund is destined to finance services required by specific states in great part for their own purposes in ensuring safety and efficiency in their territories. Therefore the international aeronautical monetary fund has a commercial value to the states requesting assistance, being considered as an absolute grant or as a loan which acts to the benefit of the beneficiary state. The joint financing mechanism, on the other hand, effects the reimbursement of expenses incurred for the benefit of the international aviation community.
- The two joint financing funds provide services which are similar and recur every year. It is possible to administer these funds with a minimum of staff and a few meetings of the joint support committee every year. There are also proposals for new projects and new capital expenditures, but these are linked to the services to be provided under the joint financing agreements. In the case of the international aeronautical monetary fund, there would be as many different projects as there are requests. It may require great effort by the staff concerned in evaluating each of the proposed projects which may invariably be very different from each other. Furthermore, it may require significant resources to administer the numerous projects retained and to follow up each of the approved projects. The administrative workload involved could be very heavy and may require more than a Section staffed at minimum. The same problem could confront the special panel, task force or board, as the case may be, which may be required to decide upon the validity or necessity of numerous non-recurring projects. As opposed to this scenario, the Joint

Support Committee, which is mandated to oversee the joint financing mechanism, can follow up more easily the provision of the services under the joint financing agreements owing to the recurring aspects of most of the activities provided by Denmark and Iceland.

- The Danish and Icelandic joint financing agreements have no political implications since the services financed are necessary for the international aviation community. The international aeronautical monetary fund, on the other hand, is established to consider the request for assistance by each state on a piecemeal basis.
- The joint financing funds are now financed mostly by users through a user charge imposed on flights crossing the area determined in the agreements. The contracting states still contribute a small portion of the costs which cannot be attributed to international civil aviation. There is an adjusting mechanism of the user charges and the assessments to contracting governments through which they may be no more and no less than the audited actual costs of the services. The international aeronautical monetary fund would have no such mechanism in operation.

Collection of funds

Although the collection of funds would be relatively easy once an appropriate mechanism was decided upon, the equitable disbursement of funds would be a more onerous prospect, given that such criteria as merit, and incremental financial benefit on costs incurred, which is brought upon by funds allocated, have to be determined under an equitable and transparent mechanism. However, the difficulties that would emerge in collection cannot be underestimated in the face of the proliferation of charges and taxes being levied at present. For example, in 1992, IATA catalogued a little under 700 different taxes and charges: IATA claims that the total now exceeds 1000.[290] In order to alleviate this situation, the proposed aeronautical monetary fund could avoid any 'tax' or 'charge' connotations by being considered as a supplemental fund which would finance such elements as installation and maintenance of the CNS/ATM systems, and projects needed for general development of international civil aviation such as the maintenance of safety and provision of training where necessary, in states which do not have adequate infrastructure and facilities. It would, of course, be established and used for a limited time, until the systems so funded could be maintained independently by states on a global scale.

The aeronautical monetary fund should be independent and mutually exclusive of charges levied by states for the provision of air navigation services. The basic principle underlying the philosophy of the additional levy should be consistent with the policy followed by ICAO as recommended by the Conference on Airport and Route Facility Management (Montreal, 29 October–9 November 1991) that states should refrain from imposing charges for services and functions which are not associated with international civil aviation.[291]

Considering the fact that safety in international civil aviation is indivisible, and in order to ensure that the fund is made up of levies imposed equitably, the ideal scenario for the accumulation of substance to the fund would be for users whose states do not need financial assistance for the implementation of ICAO SARPS on safety or the CNS/ATM system also to be charged the additional levy on their passenger tickets so that all airline passengers would contribute to the fund. In this context, ICAO Council policy is clear. It states that providers of a service may require users to pay their share of the costs incurred on the basis that an equitable cost recovery system should take into account total air navigation costs incurred on behalf of aeronautical users and allocate such costs to categories of users.[292]

If the above policy were to guide the functioning of the aeronautical monetary fund, in practical application, it would mean that the additional levy for the aeronautical monetary fund should be charged on passengers who use the services provided on the basis that the costs incurred by the state concerned in providing the service has to be recovered. To ensure that the allocation of air navigation services costs among aeronautical users should be carried out in a manner equitable to all users, the ICAO Council would, under powers vested by article 54(*i*) of the Chicago Convention, acquire through states basic utilization data in respect of air navigation services, thus ensuring the equitable subscription of funds by a system of professional accounting.

The difficulty with the above methodology of levy is that airline passengers would be paying a sum of money (in addition to the usual user charges levied for air navigation services) beforehand, to fund a service *in futuro*, thus causing 'pre-funding'. This impinges on the basic 'cost recovery' principle attached to ICAO policy on charges: that charges could only be levied to defray costs actually incurred, and would require a modality which could justify such a levy, on the basis of a definite identification of the benefits accrued to international civil aviation by the aeronautical monetary fund.

In order to circumvent the argument that the proposed aeronautical monetary fund, if funded purely for air navigation services rendered, would be inconsistent with existing ICAO policy, the funding mechanism may be constructed on a general basis devoid of the connotation of charges for services rendered. If the levy on each passenger ticket could be implemented on the basis of creating a monetary fund which could be available to any applicant purely on the principle that monies of such a fund would be available for states to implement aviation policy in keeping with the SARPS of ICAO, the obstacle posed by the possible argument that the fund would be based on 'pre-funding' for services *in futuro* could be obviated. With stronger reason, there is a compelling need at the present time to ensure aviation safety and an additional levy could easily be justified on that basis.

There are several provisions in Appendix 5 of the *Manual on Air Navigation Services Economics* (Doc. 9161) which address the subject of the provision of multinational facilities and services and which lend themselves to a way out of the 'pre-funding' dilemma. The first instance can be found in paragraph 2.6, which provides that changes in regional air navigation plans are organized within a coherent development framework, that is, at the level of the plan for the whole region. Therefore a review of part of the plan is conducted as a fully integrated operation on a system planning basis. Consequently, it is possible that facilities or services could be planned and not yet physically implemented (at least at the beginning of the period) for some parts of the plan, but nevertheless could be included in the plan, and then financed together with other parts already implemented. According to this paragraph, the distinction between the different components may not be all that relevant.

Paragraph 2.6 brings to bear the fact that, since a regional plan is a general framework, it usually includes several phases; and the whole plan involves an overall cost. Recovery charges are based on this overall cost, which includes both parts of the plan that are already implemented and parts that are not.

Another helpful paragraph of the *Manual* is paragraph 3.2(*b*), which states that total costs cover 'research and development, implementation, operation and maintenance, administration and capital costs'. It also opens up the possibility for a special provision to be included on how 'all costs incurred prior to the operational phase will be financed'.

Paragraph 4.5 reflects the possibility of incorporating 'pre-financing, to be undertaken by those States that accept the responsibility for bringing the facility/service up to operational status', while paragraph 4.20, in section *H*(*a*), is even more specific as to how to proceed, stating:

> bringing the facility/service up to implementation status can involve the costs of implementation being financed by one or more of the participating States. However, once the facility/service has been implemented, these costs would be capitalized and then included as depreciation (together with accumulated interests) in the overall cost base to be shared among the States participating in the provision of the facility/service concerned.

Paragraph 4.29 can also be cited in this context. It provides that 'as a rule, a multinational facility/service would have to be "multinationally" financed or pre-financed by a State, group of States or by an agency as established under the authority of an agreement by States'.

The Conference on the Economics of Airports and Air Navigation Services (ANSConf 2000), held by ICAO on 19–28 June 2000, addressed the problems faced by some states in obtaining financing for infrastructure development, and concern was expressed at these problems. Accordingly, the conference adopted Recommendation 3/1 which aims at a revision and updating as required to the guidance on infrastructure financing contained in the *Airport Economics Manual* and the *Manual on Air Navigation Services Economics*.

The conference also adopted Recommendation 4/1, whereby ICAO is requested to include in the Council Statements in Doc. 9082 advice to the effect that, where an autonomous body or entity is created, whether by government or by private interests, to operate an airport or airports and/or air navigation services, the state should stipulate as a condition for its approval of the new body or entity that it observe all relevant obligations of the state specified in the Chicago Convention. This recommendation makes the observance by autonomous bodies or entities of other ICAO policies and practices, such as those contained in ICAO documentation mentioned above, a necessary practice.

The philosophy applicable to the disbursement of funds from the monetary fund could be based on the postulate on which ICAO is run: that although states' contributions to the sustenance of ICAO vary, the service provided by ICAO to all its member states is equal. As stated earlier, the aeronautical monetary fund could exist only until needed, after which it could be disbursed on an equitable basis to be worked out by ICAO member states. The independence of the aeronautical monetary fund from any given objective such as the funding of CNS/ATM systems implementation or the implementation of safety oversight could even give the fund sufficient flexibility to supplement ICAO's budget in the implementation of ICAO's work programme, when the need arises.

Any participating state may have access to financial support from the aeronautical monetary fund on a loan basis with an interest-free, predetermined and common payment method. The ICAO Council may appoint a special panel or other group of persons as it deems fit to be administrator of the fund, and which could decide on the merits of each application for assistance. The collection of monies under the fund may be handled by a professional collector such as the IATA Clearing House, or administered by ICAO, such as in the joint financing mechanism, or by another entity.

Comments

The international aeronautical monetary fund is now called the International Financial Facility for Aviation Safety (IFFAS). The IFFAS concept was endorsed by the ICAO Assembly at its 33rd session held in September/October 2001, where, by Resolution A33–10, the Assembly requested the ICAO Council to pursue the establishment of the IFFAS early in the 2002–2004 triennium.

The mainstay of a funding programme and its sustenance depend largely on the element of state regulation and state involvement in an autonomous venture. Therefore external resources, whether a charge levied on passengers or financing by investment banks, depend upon a nation's potential to achieving prosperity. National prosperity is created, not inherited. So is national competitiveness. Although national resources are a state's assets, the prosperity of a nation does not necessarily emerge solely from the natural endowments of the state concerned, or from its labour resources, but rather from a certain localized process which engulfs economic structures, natural values culture, and institutions. The essential catalyst to trade is national competitiveness.

National competitiveness has become one of the central preoccupations of government and industry in every nation. Yet, for all the discussion, debate and writing on the topic, there is still no persuasive theory to explain national competitiveness. What is more, there is not even an accepted definition of the term 'competitiveness' as applied to a nation. While the notion of a competitive company is clear, the notion of a competitive nation is not.

Some see national competitiveness as a macroeconomic phenomenon, driven by variables such as exchange rates, interest rates and government deficits. But Japan, Italy and South Korea have all enjoyed rapidly rising living standards despite budget deficits, Germany and Switzerland despite appreciating currencies, and Italy and South Korea despite high interest rates. Others argue that competitiveness is a function of cheap and abundant labour. But Germany, Switzerland and Sweden have all prospered even with high wages and labour shortages. Besides, should not a nation seek higher wages for its workers as a goal of competitiveness? Another view connects competitiveness with bountiful natural resources. But how, then, can one explain the success of Germany, Japan, Switzerland, Italy and South Korea – countries with limited natural resources?

More recently, the argument has gained favour that competitiveness is driven by government policy: targeting markets, protection, import promotion and subsidies have propelled Japanese and South Korean motor, steel, shipbuilding and semiconductor industries into global pre-eminence. But a closer look reveals a spotty record. In Italy, government intervention has been ineffectual – but Italy has experienced a boom in world export share second only to Japan. In Germany, direct government intervention in exporting industries is rare. And even in Japan and South Korea, the government's role in such important industries as facsimile machines, copiers, robotics and advanced materials has been modest; some of the most frequently cited examples, such as sewing machines, steel and shipbuilding are now quite dated.

A final popular explanation for national competitiveness is differences in management practices, including management–labour relations. Different industries require different approaches to management practices governing small, private and loosely organized companies. Despite the commonly held view that powerful unions undermine competitive advantage, unions are strong in Germany and Sweden – and both countries boast internationally pre-eminent companies.

Clearly, none of these explanations is fully satisfactory; none is sufficient by itself to rationalize the competitive position of industries within a national border. Each contains some truth; but a broader, more complex set of forces seems to be at work. The lack of a clear explanation signals an even more fundamental question. What is a 'competitive' nation in the first place? Is a 'competitive' nation one where every company or industry is competitive? No nation meets this test. Even Japan has large sectors of its economy that fall far behind the world's best competitors.

Is a 'competitive' nation one whose exchange rate makes its goods price competitive in international markets? Both Germany and Japan have enjoyed remarkable gains in their standards of living – and experienced sustained periods of strong currency and rising prices. Is a 'competitive' nation one with a large positive balance of trade? Switzerland has roughly balanced trade; Italy has a chronic trade deficit – both nations enjoy strongly rising national income. Is a 'competitive' nation one with low labour costs? India and Mexico both have low wages and low labour costs, but neither seems an attractive industrial model.

International trade and foreign investment can both improve a nation's productivity as well as threaten it. They support rising national productivity by allowing a nation to specialize in those industries and segments of industries where its companies are more productive and to import where its companies are less productive. No nation can be competitive in everything. The ideal is to deploy the nation's limited pool of human and other resources into the most productive uses. Even those nations with the highest standards of living have many industries in which local companies are uncompetitive.

International trade and foreign investment can also threaten productivity growth. They expose a nation's industries to the test of international standards of productivity. An industry will lose if its productivity is not sufficiently higher than foreign rivals' to offset any advantages in local wage rates. If a nation loses the ability to compete in a range of high-productivity/high-wage industries, its standard of living is threatened.

Defining national competitiveness as achieving a trade surplus or balanced trade *per se* is inappropriate. The expansion of exports because of low wages and a weak currency, at the same time that the nation imports sophisticated goods that its companies cannot produce competitively, may bring trade into balance or surplus but lowers the nation's standard of living. Nor does competitiveness mean jobs. It is the *type* of jobs, not just the ability to employ citizens at low wages, that is decisive for economic prosperity.

Seeking to explain 'competitiveness' at the national level, then, is to answer the wrong question. What we must understand instead is the determinants of productivity and the rate of productivity growth. To find answers, we must focus, not on the economy as a whole, but on *specific industries and industry segments*. We must understand how and why commercially viable skills and technology are created, which can only be fully understood at the level of particular industries. It is the outcome of the thousands of struggles for competitive advantage against foreign rivals in particular segments and industries, in which products and processes are created and improved, that underpins the process of upgrading national productivity.

When one looks closely at any national economy, there are striking differences among industries in competitive success. International advantage is often concentrated in particular industry segments. German exports of cars are heavily skewed towards high-performance cars, while Korean exports are all economy models. In many industries and segments of industries, the competitors with true international competitive advantage are *based in only a few nations*. Our search, then, is for the decisive characteristic of a nation that allows its companies to create and sustain competitive advantage in particular fields: the search is for the competitive advantage of nations. We are particularly concerned with the determinants of international success in technology and skill-intensive segments and industries, which underpin high and rising productivity.

In the continuing debate over the financing of asset based entities, such as airports and air navigation service providers, no topic engenders more argument or creates less understanding than the role of the government. Many see government as an essential helper or supporter of industry, employing a host of policies to contribute directly to the competitive performance of strategic or target industries. Others accept the 'free market' view that the operation of the economy should be left to the workings of the invisible hand.

Both views are incorrect: either, followed to its logical outcome, would lead to the permanent erosion of a country's competitive capabilities. On the one hand, advocates of government help for industry frequently propose policies that would actually hurt companies in the long run and only create the demand for more help. On the other hand, advocates of a diminished government presence ignore the legitimate role that government plays in shaping the context and institutional structure surrounding companies and in creating an environment that stimulates companies to gain competitive advantage.

Government's proper role is as a catalyst and challenger; it is to encourage – or even push – companies to raise their aspirations and move to higher levels of competitive performance, even though this process may be inherently unpleasant and difficult. Government cannot create competitive industries; only companies can do that. Government plays a role that is inherently partial, that succeeds only when working in tandem with favourable underlying conditions in the factors governing competition. Still, government's role of transmitting and amplifying these forces is a powerful one. Government policies that succeed are those that create an environment in which companies can gain competitive advantage rather than those that involve government directly in the process, except in nations early in the development process. It is an indirect, rather than a direct, role.

Funding a financial facility for aviation safety projects, whether through the establishment of a private entity or through a governmental entity, must essentially retain the element of regulation. The regulator would be invaluable in ensuring some degree of state control over the provision of services and charges connected thereto. If there were to be a drop in standards of services provided, the state might have to intervene. Finally, airlines and airports could abandon their current approach of isolationism and embark upon joint planning of airport and air navigation services infrastructure.

5 SMUGGLING OF ILLEGAL MIGRANTS BY AIR

Introduction

Illegality or irregularity in migratory movements, although generally viewed from the perspective of the destination country, may occur in either one of the countries of origin, transit or destination, or all of them. The country of origin becomes involved when a person leaves that country without a valid passport or an equivalent document of identity as required by national legislation. As regards the country through which an illegal migrant travels (or the transit country), its laws may be infringed upon if the person being smuggled did not have a transit visa to travel through that country. From the perspective of the country of destination, the main characteristics of illegal or irregular migration are more readily discernible. They are the arrival by a person in a country and an attempt thereafter to enter without compliance with required formalities or without authorization required by law for admission or stay in that country; or the cessation by a person of meeting conditions to which that person's stay or activity is subject.[293]

Human migration is a compelling social indicator of the future and is driven by economic and social factors. Economically motivated migration characteristically takes place between countries which show a marked disparity in labour market situations (typically when one country shows shortage of labour and the other shows a surplus of labour) and sharply different levels of income. The magnitude of the problem naturally spawns opportunities for profit making which in turn have given rise to the multi-billion dollar human smuggling industry. In 1995, the *Economist* recorded:

> Around the world, smuggling organizations ranging in size and degree of sophistication are smuggling tens of thousands of people from poorer to richer countries. In the process, they are earning at least $7 billion per year, with the potential for even greater future profits.[294]

The risk element involved in the smuggling of humans is far less than in the smuggling of narcotics and therefore some gangs of notoriety have reportedly abandoned the drug trade in favour of smuggling humans.[295] Human smuggling, to be defined as such, has to be composed of two different kinds of activity: the exchange of money or other form of payment between the would-be illegal migrant and smuggler; and the arrangement by a 'facilitator' of passage across an international border. The movement has to be voluntary and the passage from one border to another should be illegal.

Smuggling is a popular recourse and an easy 'way out' to the illegal immigrant who faces huge distances to travel, difficulties imposed by states' anti-immigrant restrictions, and difficulties adjusting to life in the host country. Ironically, the last – difficulty in adjusting to life in the host country – works to the advantage of the smuggler. The process of payment, which is the essential part of the transaction of smuggling, is not always concluded with the act of smuggling. It may extend well beyond that point. The form and method of payment often reach insidious proportions of exploitation where the smuggler may discourage payment at the outset, making the illegal migrant an easy victim to exploitation and abuse. In many cases, the person seeking to be smuggled into a country illegally welcomes such deferral of payment, making the smuggler's business flourish through easier recruitment of candidates for illegal migration. This situation also strengthens the position of the smuggler to tighten his grip on the migrants and use their virtually indentured services for unlawful and criminal activities.

A 1995 study on smuggled women carried out in Belgium suggests that, although most women were not required to pay the smuggler in advance, a high proportion of them had found themselves on arrival to be required to perform various services for the smuggling network.[296] The Vienna-based International Centre for Migration Policy Development (ICMPD) has revealed that 15–30 per cent of those who went illegally into Western Europe for purposes of employment or residence, estimated in 1993 at 250 000 to 300 000 persons, used the services of smugglers.[297]

United Nations' initiatives

Concerned that the activities of criminal organizations that profit illicitly by smuggling human beings were becoming a threat to the world community and recognizing that international criminal groups often convince individuals to migrate illegally by various means for enormous profit, the United Nations, at its 48th General Assembly in December 1993, adopted Resolution 48/102 on the prevention of smuggling aliens. This resolution makes mention of smuggling of illegal migrants as an activity that endangers the lives of those smuggled and imposes severe costs on the international community. The United Nations noted that smuggling of aliens can involve criminal elements in many states and condemned the practice of smuggling aliens in violation of national and international law. Resolution 48/102, while urging states to adopt measures to frustrate the objectives and activities of smugglers of illegal migrants, identifies the International Civil Aviation Organization (ICAO) as one of the specialized agencies of the United Nations that could consider ways and means to enhance international cooperation to combat the smuggling of aliens. At the same meeting, the General Assembly of the United Nations adopted Resolution 48/103 on crime prevention and international justice, which reaffirmed the importance of the United Nations crime prevention and criminal justice programme and the crucial role the ICAO has to play in promoting international cooperation in crime prevention and criminal justice. Resolution 48/103, *inter alia*, invites governments to lend their full support to the United Nations crime prevention and criminal justice programme.

In a subsequent 1997 resolution,[298] the United Nations General Assembly, at its 51st session, *inter alia*, recognized that international criminal groups often convinced individuals to migrate illegally by various means for enormous profits and that socioeconomic factors influenced the problem of the smuggling of aliens and also contributed to the complexity of current international migration. The assembly requested states to cooperate bilaterally and on a multilateral basis to prevent the use of fraudulent documents and reaffirmed the need to fully observe international and national law in dealing with the smuggling of aliens, including the provision of humane treatment and strict observance of all human rights of migrants.

Following up its early initiatives, the United Nations General Assembly, at its 53rd Session, held in December 1998, adopted Resolution 53/111 establishing an open-ended intergovernmental *ad hoc* committee for the purpose of elaborating a comprehensive international convention against transnational organized crime. This resolution gave rise to the United Nations Convention against Transnational Organized Crime.[299] The purpose of the convention is to promote cooperation to prevent and combat transnational organized crime more effectively.

The convention, by article 3, requires contracting states to establish as criminal offences, when committed internationally, the act of agreeing with one or more persons to commit a serious crime for any purpose relating directly or indirectly to the obtaining of financial or other material benefit and conducted by a person with knowledge tantamount to participation in criminal activities of an organized criminal group.

The convention also considers organizing, aiding, abetting, facilitating or counselling the commission of serious crime involving an organized criminal group to be a criminal offence.[300] The convention attributes to any person who aids and abets a crime, knowledge, intent, aim and purpose to commit such crime as provided for in article 3, which makes the conduct by a person who knowingly aids and abets a criminal or criminal organizations a crime. The provision does not impute liability to any person who aids and abets a crime if that person ought to have known that his conduct would aid and abet a crime. In other words, any person who commits a crime under the convention should essentially have the knowledge that his conduct would facilitate, aid or abet a crime.

The protocol[301] which supplements the convention specifically addresses the smuggling of migrants by land, air and sea and records, *in limine*, the concern of the states parties to the protocol that the smuggling of migrants may lead to the misuse of established procedures for immigration, including those for seeking asylum. The protocol defines the smuggling of migrants as follows '"Smuggling of migrants" shall mean the procurement of the illegal entry into or illegal residence of a person in [a] [any] State Party of which the person is not a national or a permanent resident in order to obtain, directly or indirectly, a financial or other benefit.'[302] The protocol defines illegal entry as crossing of borders without complying with the necessary requirements for legal entry into the receiving state.

The purposes of the protocol are to prevent, investigate and prosecute the smuggling of migrants, when involving an organized criminal group, as defined in the convention and to promote international cooperation to meet these objectives.[303] The protocol excludes the prosecution of persons who are smuggled, thus exclusively applying only to those responsible, directly or indirectly, in carrying out the act of smuggling.[304]

Article 4 of the protocol requires states parties to enact domestic legislation that would criminalize, *inter alia*, the act of producing a fraudulent travel or identity document. This would also mean that a person who aids and abets such an act would be deemed criminally liable under the convention. Article 12 of the protocol provides that state parties shall adopt such measures as may be necessary, in accordance with available means, to ensure that travel or identity documents issued by them are of such quality that they cannot easily be misused and cannot readily be unlawfully altered, replicated, falsified or issued. The provision also calls for states parties to ensure the integrity and security of travel or identity documents issued by or on behalf of the states parties and to prevent their unlawful creation, issuance and use.

ICAO initiatives

ICAO initiatives on the development of secure identity documents, which has gained rapid momentum over the past decade, goes back over three decades. The 7th session of the ICAO Facilitation Division in 1968 recommended that a small panel of qualified experts, including representatives of the passports and/or other border control authorities, be established to determine the following:

a the establishment of an appropriate document such as a passport card, a normal passport or an identity document with electronically or mechanically readable inscriptions that meet the requirements of document control;
b the best type of procedures, systems (electronic or mechanical) and equipment for use with the above documents that are within the resources and ability of member states; and
c the feasibility of standardizing the requisite control information and methods of providing this information through automated processes, provided that these processes will meet the requirements of security, speed of handling and economy of operation.[305]

The FAL/7 Division also recommended that contracting states should simplify the documentary requirements and other formalities for the issue of entrance visas for temporary visitors and should ensure that such visas are issued as quickly as possible after receipt of the application.[306] Thus was born the passport card[307] – the ancestor of the machine-readable passport.

In its early stages, the Passport Card Panel acted on the basis that a document with electronically or mechanically readable inscriptions could be accomplished only through the creation of a passport which took the form of a card. As there was no possibility at that time for available technology to admit of the development of a machine-readable document in conventional passport form, the panel concentrated solely on developing a machine-readable passport card, at least for the duration of its first three meetings. The panel also came to the conclusion that a universal process of change from the conventional passport to a more simplified machine-readable card would only be possible through a cautious process of evolution. The main advantage of the passport card was considered to lie in the fact that, since visas obviously cannot be endorsed on a card by traditional methods as on pages of a conventional passport, contracting states would be compelled to eliminate visa requirements when the card was being used. The concept of the machine-readable passport card, however, was later not considered an immediately viable proposition and the panel agreed that a viable interim measure might be an improved conventional passport with machine-readable characteristics,[308] thus giving rise to the birth of the currently used machine-readable passport (MRP). This reversal of priorities, from the machine-readable passport card to the machine-readable passport, is interesting, since the progenitor – the passport card – had now become the progeny and the ultimate aim in the scheme of evolution of machine-readable travel documents.

The machine-readable passport

The machine-readable passport (MRP) is a passport that has both a machine-readable zone and a visual zone in the page that has descriptive details of the owner. The machine-readable zone enables rapid machine clearance, quick verification and instantaneous recording of personal data. Besides these advantages, the MRP also has decided security benefits, such as the possibility of matching very quickly the identity of the MRP owner against the identities of undesirable persons, while at the same time offering strong safeguards against alteration, counterfeit or forgery. Another advantage of the MRP is the fact that the document obviates the need for passengers to lodge embarkation or disembarkation cards, on the assumption that countries installing automatic reader equipment would accept the data on the passport as sufficient for their clearance purposes. Of course, the MRP had to offer safeguards equal to or better than those of conventional passports and satisfy those control requirements already set by conventional passports and other travel documents in use throughout the world. Also, since it was only natural that a certain number of states would not have wished to issue the MRP or adopt new procedures related thereto, it was expected that a machine-readable system and conventional passport procedures would operate side-by-side for some time.

Although the MRP may be produced and used as a single and separate card, it has to take booklet form since most states still insist on entrance visas, which have to be accommodated in the passport. The MRP's dimensions are smaller than those of most traditional passports, its overall dimensions being 88.75mm by 125.75mm.

The page has the visual inspection zone on top of the page as the first area, and the machine-readable zone at the bottom, as the second area. The visual inspection zone contains the photograph and personal data of the owner. At the bottom – in the machine-readable zone – are prescribed data elements printed in machine-readable form in a prescribed sequence and position. When being used, the MRP is opened at the page containing the visual inspection and machine-readable zones and placed face down on a glass surface in the reading machine, thus activating an electro optical scanning mechanism. The mechanism illustrates the two machine-readable lines and surrounding background using a light source. The whole process operates on a principle of 'light absorption' where the mechanism in the reader uses an optical sensor to measure the presence or absence of light reflecting off the page. The cumulative efforts of this 'imagery' process and a computer installed in the reader then produces on the screen of the reader all the information that the inspecting officer requires, such as the passport number, date of expiry of the passport, name of the issuing state, passport owner's name, nationality, sex, date of birth and, optionally, national ID number. The computer also interrogates simultaneously a data base containing a list of persons considered undesirable by the state of entry and the results thereof are displayed on the screen momentarily, enabling the inspecting officer to decide whether the bearer of the passport can be admitted to the country. This process takes a mere ten seconds,[309] and adds a tremendous impetus to the facilitation efforts of ICAO.

ICAO recommends the use of the MRP by all states, even if meagre traffic flows may not justify the use of reading equipment.[310] The first MRP was issued in the United States of America in 1981 and, since then, well over 35 million MRPs have been issued worldwide, while millions more are being issued every year in countries such as Canada, Australia and Germany.[311] Technical specifications for MRPs were first published by ICAO in the first edition of Doc. 9303 in 1980, based on Standard 7501 of the International Organization for Standardization (ISO). Developments in technology and modern exigencies of prolific air travel, however, dictated that the specifications contained in Doc. 9303 be improved. As the ICAO Panel on Passport Cards had become extinct with the publication of its Fifth Report in 1978, the ISO took it upon itself to establish a working group to update the provisions of Doc. 9303 so that the outcome of their deliberations would be published as a new ISO standard. The care taken by the ISO working group led to considerable time being spent, compelling ICAO to establish a new group to succeed its Panel on Passport Cards, namely the Technical Advisory Group on Machine-Readable Passports (TAG/MRP) which met for the first time in 1986.[312] ICAO thus regained its lead in developing MRP specifications and coordinating with other organizations the task of developing a single set of specifications for machine-readable travel documents. On the strength of ICAO's new leading role, the Air Transport Committee of ICAO widened the scope of the terms of reference of ICAO to include the development of specifications for machine-readable visas and to provide for the group's membership to include participation by the authorities responsible for visas. Accordingly, the ISO Technical Committee, in the light of ICAO's new role in updating specifications in Doc. 9303, adopted a proposal to withdraw ISO Standard 7501, so that there would not be confusion resulting from the introduction of double standards or 'overlapping' of specifications of ICAO and ISO.

ICAO's terms of reference in the development of specifications for MRPs stem from the Chicago Convention itself which provides for ICAO's adoption of international standards and recommended practices dealing, *inter alia*, with customs and immigration procedures.[313] It is interesting that passports apply to other modes of international travel as well, and the fact that ICAO has been singly designated to adopt specifications speaks for the uniqueness of its facilitation programme.[314]

The machine-readable visa

With the terms of reference of ICAO having been expanded to cover the development of machine-readable visas (MRV), the Technical Advisory Group changed its name to the Technical Advisory Group on Machine-Readable Travel Documents (TAG/MRTD), and in 1992 released specifications relating to a machine-readable visa.[315] Since the visa is inextricably linked to the passport, the MRP and the MRV go side-by-side, and are not considered in isolation. As long as visas were required and needed to be attached to the passport, it was difficult to envisage the development of a passport card, and a booklet-type passport was required for visual inspection. The MRV, therefore, is the main reason for the retention of the MRP concept in its present form. Since MRVs can be accommodated in any type of passport (whether machine-readable or conventional) the placement of an MRV in a conventional, non-machine-readable passport would make that passport machine readable worldwide.

Official travel documents

The Technical Advisory Group on Machine-Readable Travel Documents has also developed the Size 1 and Size 2 Official Travel Documents[316] (TD-1), which are cards conforming to Specification 7810 of the International Standards Organization (ISO) and are designed to be read by machine, similarly to the machine-readable passport and visa. The specifications stipulate standards for official documents of identity which can be used for travel purposes in terms of acceptance of a person by a receiving state. In the same year during which the official travel document specifications were released by ICAO (1996) the organization released specifications for machine readability of the crew member certificate.[317]

At its eleventh meeting, held in September 1999, the Technical Advisory Group on Machine-Readable Travel Documents reiterated its support for continued work to develop a set of indicative, probably short-term, test methods that could emulate failure modes commonly found in travel documents.[318] The group also approved in principle that the future direction of the group's work should include, *inter alia*, the development of specifications for an electronic visa; an integrated automated border clearance system; a survey of user requirements and current applicability of machine-readable travel documents; and specifications for a logical record format for use with optional capacity expansion technologies.[319]

Annex 9 provisions and related issues

The 10th session of the Facilitation Division of ICAO, held in September 1988, considering that several states were issuing MRPs and that a standard document would greatly assist the clearance of persons through airport controls, recommended that contracting states should issue machine-readable passports in the layout as set out in Doc. 9303.[320] This recommendation was adopted by the FAL/10 Division[321] and incorporated in Annex 9 (9th edn) to the Chicago Convention.[322] In so far as visas were concerned, the FAL Tenth Division recommended that, in cases where contracting states continued to require entry clearances or visas, these should be issued in machine-readable form compatible with the layout specified in ICAO Doc. 9303 even if the travel document in which they are placed is not established in machine-readable format.[323] This recommendation was later incorporated in its Report, and adopted as a Recommended Practice in Annex 9 (9th edn).[324]

At the 11th session of the ICAO Facilitation Division, which was held in April 1995, the division recommended that, in cases where states cannot yet issue machine-readable passports, they shall issue passports which conform to the format set forth in Doc. 9303, Part 1, leaving the machine-readable zone blank. This recommendation was later included as a standard in Annex 9.[325]

At its 32nd session, held in Montreal between 22 September and 2 October 1998, the ICAO Assembly adopted a resolution which requests the Council of ICAO to study specific actions and measures for enhancing the effectiveness of controls on passport fraud, including the possible preparation of necessary standards and recommended practices (SARPS) and guidance material, to be implemented by contracting states in the interests of maintaining the integrity and security of passports and other travel documents. The resolution also calls upon all contracting states to intensify their efforts to safeguard the security and integrity of their passports, to protect their passports against passport fraud and to assist one another in these matters.[326]

Liability of the air carrier

The primary consideration when examining an air carrier's liability for transnational crime is that it would be unrealistic to envisage a carrier colluding with organized criminal elements or initiating the smuggling of persons across borders for financial or other gain. The only implication for carriers would be for aiding and abetting organized crime, and the Convention Against Transnational Organized Crime explicitly provides that such aiding and abetting should be accompanied by knowledge. Thus, if a carrier unknowingly facilitates organized transnational crime, it could not be directly held liable under the convention. The only difficulty that a carrier may face is on the question of whether liability could be imputed to a carrier in circumstances where it ought to have known that a crime under the convention would be facilitated by the carrier's actions or absence thereof.

The Chicago Convention of 1944,[327] in its article 13, provides that the laws and regulations of a contracting state with regard to the admission to or departure from such state of passengers, crew or cargo of aircraft, in relation to their entry, clearance, immigration, passports, customs and quarantine, should be complied with by or on behalf of such passengers, crew or cargo, upon entrance into or departure from, or while within the territory of that state. This provision *prima facie* imposes a legal duty on the airline passenger concerned to comply with the legislation of the country he is attempting to enter, presumably by ensuring, *inter alia*, that he carries all necessary legal documentation to enter that country. The provision also carries the implied requirement that, if the passenger fails to comply with such laws, they should be complied with on behalf of the passenger. By this, article 13 of the Chicago Convention, without explicitly stating that it is the airline's responsibility to ensure, on behalf of the passenger, compliance with laws of the country of arrival, imputes to the airline that responsibility. Of course, one can argue that, in the absence of explicit mention in the provision, the airline is not responsible for ensuring that a passenger is admissible in the country to which it carries that passenger, particularly since the Chicago Convention is a treaty establishing the obligation of states towards each other. Therefore, logically, it may be arguable that, when article 13 uses the words 'on behalf of', it may well be applicable to the duty devolving upon the authorities of the state in which the person embarked on his flight.

Annex 9 to the Chicago Convention (on facilitation of air transport) dedicates section E of its Chapter 3 to inadmissible persons carried by air. An inadmissible person is defined at air law as 'a person who is or will be refused admission to a state by its authorities'. The annex provides that the operator (airline) which carries a passenger to a country shall be responsible for the custody and care of passengers and crew until they are accepted for examination for the purposes of immigration[328] which that country is obligated to do without unreasonable delay.[329] The authorities take responsibility for such passengers and crew once they are so accepted for examination, until a determination is made whether they are admissible to the country or not.[330]

A person found inadmissible is required to be handed over by the authorities who find him so inadmissible to the operator (airline) who brought him in.[331] The airline is then responsible for taking the person back to his country of origin (where he commenced his flight) or to any other place which accepts him.[332]

The annex casts a burden on a state in which a person has stayed for a period of time (not merely in transit) prior to his landing in another state, which finds him inadmissible, to accept such person for examination, subject to the fact that, by doing so, the state which accepts the person for examination does not jeopardize his life or freedom.[333] Perhaps the most relevant provision of Annex 9 to the question at issue is Standard 3.40.1 which stipulates:

> Contracting States shall not fine operators in the event that passengers are found inadmissible unless there is evidence to suggest that the carrier was negligent in taking precautions to the end that passengers complied with the documentary requirements for entry into the receiving State.

There is also the provision that contracting states and operators shall cooperate, where practicable, in establishing the validity and authenticity of passports and visas,[334] with a recommendation that, where operators cooperate with the control authorities to the satisfaction of those authorities, contracting states should mitigate fines and penalties that might otherwise be applicable to the operators for inadmissible passengers carried to those states.[335]

A strict interpretation of regulatory provisions on air carrier liability for the carriage of inadmissible persons seems to suggest that there is no *prima facie* presumption of guilt on the airline. On the contrary, article 13 of the Chicago Convention, which is strictly an international treaty containing provisions setting out legal obligations between states, provides that applicable laws have to be 'complied with by the passenger, *or on behalf of the passenger*' (my emphasis), which may be interpreted as indicating that state authorities, such as customs and immigration or consular authorities, would have a greater burden of ensuring compliance with article 13 than the airlines.

A fortiori, Annex 9, by Standard 3.40.1 explicitly requires that, in the absence of evidence of the carrier's negligence, the carrier shall not be fined. Although the linkage between the convention and the annex is at times doubted in view of the statement in article 54(1) in the convention that the annexes to the convention are so named for convenience, nonetheless it is an incontrovertible fact that Annex 9 derives its authority from the convention and therefore is an integral part of it. Standard 3.40.1, which has been developed by the Council of ICAO with the approval of ICAO member states, is therefore international in scope and not diminished in its legal authority, but rather acts as an explanatory note to article 13 of the Convention.[336]

The security and integrity of the passport,[337] which is usually recognized as the fundamental legal document of travel between countries, becomes a critical issue in the determination of liability. The passport carries details of a person's identity, country of citizenship and entitlement to travel privileges. Above all, and in the context of inadmissible passengers, the passport would serve as assurance to the country in which a person is found inadmissible that he can return to the country which issued the passport.

Unless otherwise specified, a passport remains the property of the state of issue, and therefore misuse or destruction of a passport becomes an infringement of law against that state. Conversely, a grave responsibility devolves upon states to ensure that their property is secure from such misuse or fraud – particularly the commonest known abuse or fraud in the nature of forgery. The use of forged or counterfeit passports, the use of valid passports by imposters, and the misuse of valid passports by their rightful owners in the perpetration of an offence are some of the common ways in which passport fraud is perpetrated today.[338]

If an air carrier were to be found guilty of aiding and abetting a crime of transnational smuggling of persons, it would have to be proved that the carrier would at least have had reasonable knowledge that its actions or inaction would assist in the offence. Mere carriage of the person by the carrier concerned would not be sufficient grounds. Although the distinction between aiding and abetting is not easily distinguishable, it is reasonably clear that the act of aiding is giving some assistance in the commission of a crime while abetting is being present at the scene of the crime and encouraging or procuring the commission of a crime. A person who distracts a security guard while his friends shoplifts may be aiding the offence, while a sales clerk who encourages or stands by while a person shoplifts may abet in the offence. The element of positive intention is critical to determining the offences of aiding and abetting. Be that as it may, one could well ask the question, 'what if a carrier, knowing full well that a grave risk of allowing the smuggling of illegal migrants on its flights would exist if proper security measures are not adopted, does not adopt such measures and as a consequence has persons smuggled in its aircraft?' Is this tantamount to aiding and abetting the smuggler under the convention? Is the carrier encouraging the smuggler to pursue his criminal activity?

Of course, much would depend on the circumstances of each case. Although there is a traditional reluctance in criminal law to penalize omissions, courts have distinctly recognized exceptions to this principle in cases where a person who stands by is under a specific legal duty to act. A driver of a car who tacitly acquiesces by doing nothing on the road while the person next to him is engaging in dangerous driving has been held to have abetted the dangerous driving because he did not exercise his power to control the use of his vehicle.[339] In a 1990 Canadian case,[340] a senior officer of a police lock-up was found to have aided and abetted an assault on a prisoner on the ground that he failed to exercise his statutory authority to protect the prisoner. If this principle were to be applied in analogy to a carrier who stands by without adequate checking of travel documents of persons boarding its flights or does not employ adequate security measures that would discourage potential transnational smuggling of persons, one could certainly expect a common law court to consider such a carrier within the parameters of national legislation adopted in accordance with the Convention Against Transnational Organized Crime as having aided and abetted a crime, although such carrier may not have had the necessary intent as required, and notwithstanding the fact that, as discussed above, the Chicago Convention and Annex 9 do not impose liability on the carrier with regard to fraudulent travel documentation. The 1994 American case of *Argenbright Security* v. *Ceskoslovenske Aeroline*[341] is a good analogy where, in determining the liability of an airline's omission to detect stowaways, whose presence in an aircraft would impute to the carrier knowledge of such presence on the basis of negligence to discover such passengers and eject them from the flight prior to take-off, the court upheld a fine imposed on the carrier by the Immigration and Naturalization Services (INS). In such an instance, where the airline ought to have known of the stowaway, a penalty is imposed by INS, as a penal sanction rather than as coverage for administration costs involved in the application for asylum made by the stowaway. The court held:

> This penalty is clearly designed as a sanction for carriers who fail to detail or deport a stowaway and has nothing to do with the cost of detention of stowaways who are properly detained pending a hearing … As a result, the availability of this fine does not relieve the airline of its statutory responsibility … to bear the full maintenance costs associated with the detention of excluded stowaways.[342]

This decision demonstrates that air carriers are required to exercise due diligence in carrying persons on board their aircraft and to prevent the unauthorized carriage of persons.

Comments

It is clear that, on the issue of the determination of air carrier liability for the carriage of illegal migrants, what is seemingly a straightforward regime concerning criminality that requires knowledge and intent could now be stretched to accommodate subjective interpretations of aiding and abetting. The reason for this is the rapid development of information technology which has placed in the hands of states such sophisticated security tools as the machine-readable travel document. Although all readings of existing regulatory instruments such as those promulgated by ICAO and the Convention Against Transnational Organized Crime do not admit of air carrier liability (unless the elements of knowledge and intent are present as stipulated in the convention), the fact that a person cannot just stand by when he has a specific duty to act is a strong factor that would militate against the provision requiring knowledge and intent. Air carriers must, as a necessity, strengthen their security and take all necessary measures to prevent crime within their business operations.

A fortiori, airlines will be required to exercise more vigilance in the future, particularly with the introduction of the excellent initiative of the International Air Transport Association (IATA) for Simplified Passenger Travel (SPT) which has now gained momentum. The SPT concept, which is calculated to be essentially a tool for facilitating air travel, uses a smart card which confirms a traveller's identity through trip-related information and biometric data which are encoded.[343] The check-in takes less than a minute with the SPT card. Reportedly, a number of airlines are already well into the process of developing smart card technology. This could only mean that such a process, when developed by some, would have a coercive effect on other airlines which are able to follow suit. Failure to follow such industry practices may have negative implications for an air carrier's security record and may result in uncalled-for legal liability.

6 THE ECONOMY CLASS SYNDROME

Introduction

There is a sustained record of medical research that brings to light a disturbing fact in long distance travel, that air travel in particular may cause venous thromboembolism, or deep vein thrombosis – commonly called the 'economy class syndrome'. Thrombosis, which is the medical term used for the formation of a blood clot in the heart or in a blood vessel,[344] can be triggered, according to medical studies, by long periods of confinement in bed or cramped airline seats, which reduce circulation, causing blood to pool and clot.

Normally, the formed elements of the blood – the red and white blood cells and platelets – move along in the centre of the stream in a blood vessel. If there is alteration to normal flow, which may be caused, *inter alia*, by inactivity of a person's limbs for long periods of time, the platelets and blood cells may scrape along the blood vessel lining. Abnormally large numbers of platelets so assembled may cause an increased tendency of the blood to coagulate.[345] There are of course other symptoms shown as a result of long confinement to small spaces, such as leg swelling, pulmonary embolism, strokes and even death.[346]

In 1856, scientist Rudolf Virchow conducted detailed autopsies on 76 patients, eleven of whom had died from massive thrombi in the pulmonary arteries. He identified through scientific methodolgy that ten of the 11 patients' thrombi in the pulmonary arteries had started in the legs and concluded that arterial thrombosis had emanated from the leg veins. This led to the development of the famous 'Virchow's Triad' of causation of thromboembolism: trauma to the vein wall; decreased velocity of venous blood flow; and increased blood coagulability.[347] The syndrome was first identified and described in 1940, as a result of a finding that, during the war, cramped seating in air raid shelters for prolonged periods during the London 'blitz' had frequently resulted in pulmonary embolisms in many instances.[348] However, embolisms related to air travel were first described in 1946 after a 54-year-old man had developed thrombophlebitis after sitting for 14 hours during a flight from Boston to Venezuela.[349] There have been several subsequent cases of thrombophlebitis reported as a consequence of air travel.[350] It is reported that at least 20 of the cases reported in the research have been definitely linked to air travel.[351]

It is an incontrovertible fact that air travel at high altitudes and of long durations may involve stagnant recycled air, fluctuations in cabin pressure and jet lag. The passenger may end up at his destination dehydrated and disoriented. Additionally, smaller seat pitch, particularly in economy class, may seriously affect the circulatory process, causing thromboembolism. It is reported that the *Aerospace Medical Association Journal* in 1988 concluded that the risk of fatal pulmonary embolism was at least ten times greater after travel than before, linking the risk to long periods of sitting and cramped seating.[352]

A case study

In 1998, a study was conducted at Tripler Army Medical Center, Honolulu, Hawaii, which reviewed hospital records of patients discharged over a four-year period with a final diagnosis of venous thromboembolism.[353] The term 'venous thromboembolism' was broadly used in the study to describe a continuum of diseases including deep vein thrombosis, pulmonary embolism or both. Inpatient medical records of 207 patients with a discharge diagnosis of venous thromboembolism were available for analysis and review. Of the patients reviewed, 134 met the case criteria for venous thromboembolism and, of those, 66 patient records reflected some information evidencing presence or absence of travel. Of these 66, 33 patients had travelled one month prior to the onset of the thromboembolism and eight patients had travelled within a six-month period. All 33 patients (none of whom was an aircraft crew member) had travelled at least four hours non-stop. Their profiles showed that eight had onset of thromboembolism on the first day of travel, four had onset during the journey and 27 had onset symptoms on or before travel day.[354] The study also took into consideration a study which had revealed that, at London's Heathrow Airport, of the 104 natural deaths reported to the coroner from 1979 to 1982, 12 had been attributed to pulmonary embolism.[355] An earlier 1992 study,[356] which had reviewed 25 patients with travel-associated venous thromboembolism, had noted that in seven patients (six of whom travelled by air) the onset of symptoms had occurred during travel or on disembarkation, and the onset of symptoms had occurred within 96 hours in 23 patients. Another two patients had experienced onset of symptoms within ten to twelve days of travelling. All had travelled non-stop for at least three hours.

The 1992 study concluded that air travel appeared to be a significant risk factor for venous thromboembolism. However, it is important to bear in mind that the study was a retrospective one which had no way of determining the true number of travellers among the various thromboembolism patients. There is also the danger that the patients considered by the study may have been under-diagnosed. Perhaps the most serious flaw in the study was that it was unable to document such important, key factors as the class of travel, seat pitch, type of airline service offered in flight, leg room, body habitus or intravascular volume during flight. Thus the question arises as to whether it is even justifiable to call symptoms of venous thromboembolism consequent to flight 'the economy class syndrome'.[357]

The study is by no means conclusive medical evidence that prolonged air travel inevitably causes venous thromboembolism. At best, it concludes that long periods in the air within confined spaces, without the movement of limbs may be a risk factor towards causing deep vein thrombosis. More prospective, controlled studies are needed to determine the true incidence of venous thromboembolism among air travellers and its link with air travel *per se.* A study of airline pilots and the incidence of disease among them would be particularly valuable, since arguably the airline pilot is the most prolific individual air traveller.

Although studies on the subject are still somewhat inconclusive from a medical perspective, the issue of venous thromboembolism brings to bear important legal issues pertaining to the liability of the air carrier who knows or ought to know of this particular risk factor. Inasmuch as the carrier is required to take all possible measures to ensure clean air in the cabin, consistent cabin pressure and the ultimate safety of the flight, all of which portend risk factors if not attended to, a restricted seat pitch may be a potential hazard to the health of the passenger, as the foregoing study reveals. Furthermore, the question also arises as to whether the carrier's failure to advise the passenger of the ill effects of being cramped in a seat without moving would give rise to the carrier's liability.

Legal liability of the carrier

As the discussion below will reflect, the most fundamental postulate of air carrier liability for death or injury caused to a passenger should involve an accident if liability were to be decided under applicable treaty law.[358] As to whether the term 'accident' means an unexpected or unusual event or happening,[359] in which case it may be arguable that, if injury were to ensue as a result of the passenger's own internal reaction to the usual, normal and expected operation of the aircraft, where, as a matter of course, the passenger has to be seated in cramped space for long periods of time, the carrier may not be liable. However, if it can be argued that the act of the carrier in providing seats known to be too small or crowded together and not warning the passenger of the hazards of travelling in confined spaces for long periods of time, brings about results to the average passenger who has no knowledge of the risk involved, it would not be surprising to find a court awarding damages against a proven incidence of venous thromboembolism which results after flight.

A somewhat delicate balance is called for in determining whether, in the absence of cogent evidence that a restricted seat pitch in the economy class of an aircraft would inevitably cause venous thromboembolism in passengers, an exigency involving the affliction of a passenger would be considered 'unexpected' and therefore an accident, or whether the carrier knows or ought to know of the risk and takes necessary measures to avoid the danger or risk, in which case absence of such measures would impute to the carrier a certain intent, proving his wilful misconduct. An accident is purely an 'inappropriate and unexpected happenstance'[360] which does not happen as a matter of course. Sudden turbulence, or the sounding of a smoke alarm in the cabin which is unexpected, are typical profiles of an accident. If such were to be the case, would it be reasonable to consider the infliction on a passenger of venous thromboembolism an accident?

A probable approach that a common law court may adopt is to treat a proven instance linked to air travel as an accident in the same way as in instances of turbulence. Of course, in similar vein, the carrier may be expected to issue prior warning and advice as to how to cope with the risk. In such circumstances the analogy of an accident and possible negligence that would take the issue beyond a mere accident would be a distinctly logical sequence.

The Montreal Convention of 1999,[361] in article 17, provides that the carrier is liable for damage sustained in the case of death or bodily injury of a passenger upon condition only that the accident which caused the death or injury took place on board the aircraft or in the course of the operations of embarking or disembarking. Liability of the carrier is limited on the basis of strict liability at 100 000 special drawing rights (SDR). Furthermore, this limit cannot be exceeded if the carrier proves that he and his servants or agents were not negligent or did not commit a wrongful act or omission in connection with the injury, or such damage was solely caused by the negligence or wrongful act or omission of a third party.[362] The Montreal Convention, which is yet to come into force, seemingly makes provision to recognize carrier negligence both in terms of the provision of abnormally small seat pitches in his aircraft and in regard to his neglect in warning passengers of potential hazard of prolonged air travel in restricted areas and not advising passengers of ways and means to mitigate possible risk of venous thromboembolism.

The currently operative legal regime in this area is governed by the Warsaw Convention of 1929,[363] which provides that the carrier is liable for damage sustained in the event of death or wounding of a passenger or any other bodily injury suffered by a passenger, if the accident which caused the damage so sustained took place on board the aircraft or in the course of any of the operations of embarking or disembarking. Of course, on the face of the provision, the words 'wounding' and 'bodily injury' do not necessarily lend themselves to being associated with infection. *A fortiori*, according to the Warsaw Convention, the wounding or injury must be caused by 'accident', which is not typically a synonym for 'infection'. However, the recent decision in *El Al Israel Airlines Limited* v. *Tseng*[364] introduced a new dimension to the word 'accident' under the Warsaw Convention by giving it pervasive scope to include such acts as security body searches performed by the airlines. In this context, the word 'accident' loses its fortuity and it becomes applicable to an expected or calculated act. Thus, if an airline knows or ought to have known that an infected passenger was on board its flight, causing others on board to be infected, it may well mean that the act of the airline would be construed by the courts as an accident within the purview of the Warsaw Convention.

Liability under the Warsaw Convention

It is an incontrovertible principle of tort law that tortious liability exists primarily to compensate the victim by compelling the wrongdoer to pay for the damage he has done.[365] The second international conference on Private International Law,[366] which led to the introduction of the Warsaw Convention,[367] obviously followed this basic principle but deviated to align the provisions of the Warsaw Convention with existing exigencies of civil aviation. The conference based its approach towards air carrier liability on the fault theory of tort, which has its genesis in the Industrial Revolution where common law adopted the principle that a wrongdoer or tortfeasor must be at fault for him to be compelled to compensate the injured. The fault theory was introduced as a solution to the problems caused by injury to persons by the proliferation of machinery during the Industrial Revolution and on the basis that those responsible for introducing faulty machinery should pay those who are injured by it.

One of the fundamental deviations from the fault liability principle in the context of the Warsaw Conference was that, instead of retaining the basic premise that the person who alleges injury must prove that the injury was caused by the alleged wrongdoer, the conference recognized the obligation of the carrier to assume the burden of proof. This was done seemingly to obviate the inherent difficulties which are posed in situations of air carriage where it would be difficult, if not impossible, to determine fault from evidence which is reduced to debris and wreckage after an aircraft accident.

The conference succinctly summed up its views on liability through the words of its Rapporteur:

> These rules sprang from the fault theory of the liability of the carrier toward passengers and goods, and from the obligation of the carrier to assume the burden of proof. The presumption of fault on the shoulders of the carrier was, however, limited by the nature itself of the carriage in question, carriage whose risks are known by the passenger and consignor. The Conference had agreed that the carrier would be absolved from all liability when he had taken reasonable and ordinary measures to avoid the damage ... one restriction on this liability had been agreed upon. If for commercial transactions one could concede the liability of the carrier, it did not seem logical to maintain this liability for the navigational errors of his servants, if he proves that he himself took proper measures to avoid a damage.[368]

The conference went on to suggest that, if the damage arises out of an 'intentional illicit act' for which the carrier was liable, he should not have the right to avail himself of the provisions of the convention.[369] The words 'intentional illicit act' were later changed to 'wilful misconduct' by the conference at the request of the British delegate, Sir Alfred Dennis, and the Greek delegate, Mr Youpis.[370]

Deeming that it was not equitable to impose absolute liability upon the carrier, the conference admitted that the carrier's responsibility would be limited to liability limits of monetary value and, furthermore, he could be freed of all liability when he had taken the reasonable and normal measures to avoid the damage.[371]

The conference obviously based the Warsaw Convention on tort law principles of liability, where tort duties are primarily fixed by law in contrast to contractual obligations which can arise only from voluntary agreement.[372] Sixty-six years after the Warsaw Convention was introduced, however, there was a palpable shift towards introducing a contractual element by the 1995 IATA Inter-carrier Agreement which, although not having the legal status of a convention but remaining an agreement among air carriers, retains the basic presumption of air carrier liability of the convention but rejects the liability limitations of the convention and its protocols by recognizing that the compensatory amount that a carrier should pay for personal injury or death may be contractually agreed upon by the carrier and claimant according to the law of the domicile of the claimant.

Admittedly, this is not what the conference envisaged. However, it must be borne in mind that the conference recognized that the Warsaw Convention applied only to the unification of 'certain' rules, as proposed by the delegate of Czechoslovakia. Also the underlying purpose of the IATA initiative – which is to allow for greater flexibility for insurance underwriters on the one hand, and more leverage for airlines in their risk management, on the other – is fundamentally consistent with the views of the Warsaw Convention. At the same time, the convention does not preclude the right of a carrier to enter into agreement with a claimant on the issue of compensation. The Warsaw Convention itself recognized that:

> in reality, this Convention creates against the air carrier an exceptional system, because in the majority of the countries of the world, contracts of carriage are concluded under a system of free contract. The carrier is free to insert in the contract clauses which exclude or reduce his liability, as much as for goods as for travellers.[373]

The Inter-carrier Agreement, which was approved by IATA carriers at their Annual General Meeting in Kuala Lumpur in October 1995, claims to preserve the Warsaw Convention but carriers agree to take action to waive the limitation of liability on recoverable compensatory damages in claims for death, wounding or other bodily injury so that recoverable compensatory damages may be determined and awarded by reference to the law of the domicile of the passenger. This provision in effect introduces a contractual element to an otherwise pure tortious liability regime. The agreement attacks the monetary limits of liability of the convention and retains all other provisions of liability, which are essentially the presumption of liability of the carrier and his defences against such a presumption.

With the rejection of the liability limits, the provision relating to breaking such limits in instances where the carrier is guilty of wilful misconduct has also been rejected. Therefore, effectively, certain elements of tortious liability that the convention had have been expunged. In the final analysis, the principle of fault which the architects of the Warsaw Convention entrenched in the convention has been rejected by the IATA agreement. Lee Kreindler observes:

> The fault system is extremely important to the public. It is a public protection. It has improved aviation safety and security. While I don't profess to understand what the international airlines are now up to, it is clear to me that one of their purposes is to put an end to the tort system, in international airline transportation, at least as between the passenger and the airline, and that I oppose.[374]

Kreindler points out the ambivalence of the IATA agreement in designating the law of the domicile of the passenger as being applicable for the award of compensatory damages, while it retains the provision of the Warsaw Convention which designates jurisdictions.[375] Sean Gates picks up the issue of 'domicile' and observes that the IATA agreement refers to article 28 of the Warsaw Convention which it claims relates to 'domicile' but in actual fact does not. In fact, Gates questions whether 'domicile' would cover personal or corporate domicile and holds that this is another area where the IATA agreement has not shown clarity.[376]

General principles

Generally in law an accusation has to be proved by the person who makes it. Therefore a presumption of innocence applies to an accused person until he is proven guilty. However, in the instance of carriage by air of passengers, the airline is presumed liable if a passenger alleges personal injury or if his dependants allege that his death has been caused by the airline.[377] Of course, the airline can show in its defence that it had taken all necessary measures to avoid the damage,[378] or that there was contributory negligence,[379] and obviate or vitiate its liability. This curious anomaly of the law imposing on the airline a presumption of liability is contained in the Warsaw Convention, article 17 of which states:

> The carrier shall be liable for damage sustained in the event of the death or wounding of a passenger, if the accident which caused the damage so sustained took place on board the aircraft or in the course of any of the operations of embarking or disembarking.

To control the floodgates of litigation and discourage spurious claimants, the convention admits of certain defences the airline may invoke and above all limits the liability of the airline to passengers and dependants of deceased passengers in monetary terms. The Warsaw system therefore presents to the lawyer an interesting and different area of the law which is worthy of discussion.

Article 17 of the Warsaw Convention needs analysis in some detail in order that the circumstances in which a claim may be sustained against an airline for passenger injury or death may be clearly identified. Further, the defences available to the airline and the monetary limits of liability also need to be discussed.

'Accident' in air law In commercial aviation, the word 'accident' is sometimes given as broad a definition as those just considered. The Chicago Convention of 1944 defines accident as 'occurrence associated with the operation of an aircraft'.[380] The Warsaw Convention in article 17 speaks of the 'the accident which caused the damage' reducing the accident to the cause rather than to the death or injury.[381] The United States Supreme Court has held that *in limine* an accident must be unexpected and external to the passenger.[382] It is not sufficient that the plaintiff suffers injury as a result of his own internal reaction to the usual, normal and expected operation of the aircraft.[383] Such incidents as hijackings, terrorist attacks and bomb threats have been considered to be accidents, together with aircraft crashes.[384] An accident could even involve such lesser incidents as tyre failure on take-off[385] and the supply of infected food causing food poisoning of passengers.[386]

In 1982, a passenger travelling from New York to Manila suffered a massive coronary seizure in flight. The allegation against the airline was that, as a result of the failure of the employees of the airline to render medical assistance, the patient's condition suffered irreparable deterioration resulting in death. Responsibility devolved upon the court to fit this incident to that of an 'accident' within the meaning of the Warsaw Convention. The court readily did this by deeming that the word 'accident' in air law in this instance was not the heart attack itself but the failure on the part of the airline to render medical assistance in flight. The court said 'After all, it is no different from an airline's liability in a hijacking incident where the accident is not the acts of the hijackers but the alleged failure on the part of the carrier to provide adequate security.'[387] The airline was accordingly found liable for damage so sustained by the deceased passenger.

In a contemporaneous case, a passenger brought an action in the US District Court of Puerto Rico for a hernia sustained by the lifting of a heavy suitcase from the conveyor belt. A baggage handler of the defendant airline had refused to carry the suitcase and the plaintiff had solicited aid from her relatives who were not allowed to enter the baggage area by a guard on duty. The action against the airline was dismissed by the court primarily on the grounds that the plaintiff did not suffer an unexpected injury as she had previously undergone a gall bladder operation and would have known her condition to be delicate.[388]

In 1983, a medical practitioner suffering from a head cold and respiratory infection boarded an aircraft. He disembarked completely deaf. The plaintiff averred that he suffered discomfort in his ears at descent probably due to sudden pressure changes that may have occurred. He alleged that the airline knew or ought to have known that passengers suffering from head colds would risk losing their hearing. In addition, it was alleged that the airline owed a duty to warn the passenger that it was dangerous to travel with a head cold. The airline denied the existence of such a duty. The US District Court for the Southern District of New York reasoned that it would be incongruous to impose a duty on an airline to envisage all possible human afflictions and assess their effect on air travel and warn passengers accordingly. In any event, the airline was in this instance not aware that the passenger was suffering from a head cold. In this decision the court clearly indicated that the presumption of liability imposed by the Warsaw Convention on airlines and the highest-degree-of-care doctrine applicable thereto should not be taken advantage of by plaintiffs.[389] Similarly, there would be no cause of action against an airline where a passenger's ill-health is aggravated owing to acceleration at take-off or deceleration at landing.[390]

In April 1984, an intermediate Appellate Court in New York was faced with the task of deciding whether an airline can be held liable for the death of a passenger who chokes to death owing to his own intoxication. The decision was in the affirmative and the court in enforcing judgment against the airline drew the analogy between a dispensing druggist and an airline. The airline serves its passengers with drink and thus undertakes the responsibility not to serve in excess and to exercise reasonable care for the safety of passengers. In addition, in the event of excessive intoxication of a passenger, the airline is under a legal duty to render such medical assistance as is necessary to revive the passenger or in any event to keep him out of danger. In the light of this principle, the airline has a further duty to protect others from a drunken passenger who gets out of control.[391]

In *Air France* v. *Saks*,[392] the United States Supreme Court interpreted the word 'accident' in the context of the Warsaw Convention to mean an occurrence whereby a passenger is injured owing to an unexpected or unusual event or happening that is external to the passenger,[393] and that, where the injury results from the passenger's own internal reaction to the normal exigencies of air travel, such injury would not be construed as having resulted from an accident. In this case, the plaintiff was a passenger on an Air France flight from Paris to Los Angeles. During the descent the plaintiff suffered severe pain in her left ear which was aggravated thereafter. The plaintiff, who consulted a doctor after the plane landed, was informed that she was rendered completely deaf in her left ear. The plaintiff brought an action in a California State court on the grounds that her hearing loss was due to the negligent maintenance by the airline of the pressurization system of the aircraft which transported her. Air France moved that the allegation of the plaintiff cannot be sustained within the meaning of the word 'accident' of article 17 of the Warsaw Convention, which was meant to be an unusual and unexpected happening. Further, the airline alleged that at all times the pressurization system of the aircraft had been normal. The District Court granted summary judgment to the plaintiff on the basis that 'accident' in article 17 was meant to be an unusual and unexpected happening. The Supreme Court rejected the rationale adopted by the lower court on the ground that article 17 refers to an accident which causes an injury and therefore it is the cause and not the effect that is the determinant. Accordingly, the Supreme Court held that air carriers would be liable only if an accident caused the passenger injury. Thus an injury that was in itself an accident was insufficient to satisfy the requirements of article 17 of the Warsaw Convention.

There will be no accident if in a normal flight free of turbulence a passenger suffers discomfort from a condition he suffers from, such as a hiatus hernia[394] or thrombophlebitis.[395] In *Abramson* v. *Japan Airlines*, an airline passenger suffered an aggravation of a pre-existing hiatal hernia shortly after take-off from Anchorage on a flight to Tokyo. The passenger, who was under medication for his condition for six years, had not informed the carrier prior to boarding. The passenger, however, claimed that, had he been given occupation of a few empty seats, he could have massaged his stomach to normality. The airline had claimed that there were no empty seats in flight, contrary to the passenger's claim that there were in fact nine empty seats in flight in the first class section of the aircraft. The passenger claimed that his hernia attack constituted an 'accident' within the provisions of article 17 of the convention. The court rejected this claim and held that the plaintiff's difficulty was not in any way related to his transportation by air and, accordingly, there was no accident under article 17.

It would have been interesting if the court applied the principle of *Seguritan's* case,[396] where failure to render medical assistance by the airline was construed as falling within the purview of the word 'accident'. After all, the airline did not make any attempt at rendering assistance to the passenger in *Abramson*'s case. The court's reasoning in the latter case contradicts the earlier decision and leads to a logical absurdity. The intention of the convention was seemingly to provide a uniform system of compensation for passengers bringing claims against airlines operating international air services. To suggest that the failure of an airline to render required assistance is excusable under the convention is completely at odds with earlier decisions and also, arguably, with the intention and purpose of the convention itself.

In so far as the word 'wounding' of a passenger in article 17 is concerned, courts have initially held that such would only be in instances of 'bodily injury' and consequently would be palpably conspicuous physical injury.[397] This excluded mental injury. However, a later decision[398] held that types of injuries enumerated should be construed expansively to encompass as many types of injury as are colourably within the ambit of the enumerated types including mental and psychosomatic injuries. This decision has been followed consistently in a strong line of cases.[399] In the United States mental injury is now entrenched in most jurisdictions as an independently compensable head of damages.[400] As, indeed, Burnett CJ said in *Medlin* v. *Allied Investment Co*:[401]

> Memory and empathy tells us that 'hurt' perceived through sensory media other than that of touch may be just as painful if not more than the hurt perceived by the tactile sense. Moreover, physicians tell us that the consequences of invasion of the person accomplished through the perceptory media of sight and sound may be also as damaging if not more damaging than invasions of the persons accomplished through the sense of touch.[402]

Indeed, mental anguish or injury would now be recognized by most jurisdictions as falling within the purview of 'wounding' of a passenger under article 17 of the Warsaw Convention.

It is apparent from the *cursus curiae* that a stringent standard of proof of the nature of the occurrence is insisted upon by the courts if liability of the carrier is to be established under article 17 of the Warsaw Convention. In *Salce* v. *Aer Lingus Airlines*[403] the District Court for the Southern District of New York required of the plaintiff to show that the landing of the aircraft in which the plaintiff travelled was anything other than a normal landing. The plaintiff averred that he had received personal injuries due to the hard landing of the aircraft. In the absence of clear evidence of a hard landing, the court would presume that the landing performed by the aircraft in this instance was not an unexpected or unusual event that would satisfy the requirements of an 'accident' under the Warsaw Convention.

However, when facts are self-evident, as in the case of *Salerno* v. *Pan American World Airways*,[404] the courts would not hesitate to award damages to a plaintiff passenger. In this case, the District Court for the Southern District of New York held that knowledge of a bomb threat which subsequently caused a miscarriage to a passenger came within the meaning of scope of the word 'accident'. The plaintiff and her two children were passengers aboard a PAN AM flight from Miami to Uruguay. The cockpit crew, after take-off, instructed the cabin crew to look for a bomb which the former had been informed by air traffic control to be on board. The crew notified the passengers, including the plaintiff. She suffered a miscarriage 24 hours after having been informed of the alleged bomb on board and having watched the cabin crew looking for the object. The court held that an 'accident' within the meaning of the Warsaw Convention caused the plaintiff's injuries because a bomb threat is 'external to the passenger' and is an unexpected and unusual event outside the usual, normal and expected operation of the aircraft.[405]

The above discussion brings to the surface the salutary principle that the word 'accident' is considered far more liberally in modern air law than is done under other areas of common law. It also underscores the fact that courts would be more inclined to treat acts of omission on the part of airlines as an 'accident', as was shown in *Seguritan's* case.[406] The airline is presumed liable for an 'accident' where a drunken passenger assaults another, or where a passenger suffers a heart attack and is not given the necessary medical attention in flight, as is possible, just to name two instances. Of course, the claimant has to adduce clear evidence of the event and the ensuing injury.

Although Professor Bin Cheng holds the view that the Montreal Protocols are heavily weighted towards the carrier, the limits therein are inadequate, and that the unbreakability of the limit of the SDR value is undesirable,[407] the view that strict liability should be embraced seems more sensible, in view of the inconceivable number of passengers carried every year by air, the possible eradication of legal contingency fees and, above all, giving teeth to the meaning and purpose of law: that it should be an instrument of solace, not an opportunity for debate.

In an evaluation of the Warsaw system,[408] it was said in 1979 that, during the first 25 years of the existence of the Warsaw Convention, it had served the aviation community satisfactorily.[409] Peter Martin bases this observation on the argument that, when the Hague Protocol was being drafted in 1955, it was recorded that only 55 Warsaw cases had been adjudicated, and that is a very small number of cases for an instrument of the stature of the Warsaw Convention.[410] The unifying process of the liability of an air carrier, started by the Warsaw Convention, dealt with liability concepts, quantum of compensation, exceptions on liability, jurisdictional issues and prescription of action. It is sad, however, that, together with the original Warsaw Convention, there are now seven other international agreements, few of which have ever seen the light of day. This means that the unification process started by the Warsaw Convention had been criticized and found wanting at various stages of its chequered history. The original document has been excoriated many times, prompting Professor Cheng to call it the 'Warsaw shambles',[411] although it remained, when these comments were made of it, the most widely implemented private international law convention.[412]

Ex facie, from a strictly practical standpoint, it would appear that many facets of unification of the Warsaw Convention have come under interpretation by different philosophies, presumably because of the lack of specificity of the principles of unification and, *a fortiori*, the language used. For instance, the delivery of the passenger ticket and the attendant carrier liability came under a series of confounding judicial thought processes, where in two cases[413] the courts decided that the ticket had to be delivered in such a manner as to afford the passenger a reasonable opportunity to take measures to protect against liability insurance, only to decide in *Chan* v. *Korean Airlines*[414] that the only requirement of article 3 of the convention was that a ticket be delivered. *Goldman* v. *Thai Airways International Limited*[415] was another case where two confusing issues were decided upon. The first involved the question whether the concept of 'wilful misconduct' as reflected in article 25 of the convention was to be interpreted objectively or subjectively. The second issue concerned compensatory limits which were so confusing to both the courts and the parties to litigation that an outside settlement was effected on a mutually acceptable basis.[416] The issue regarding compensatory limits for death or personal injury has had a consistent evolution, starting from the Warsaw Convention at approximately 8300 US dollars, increased twofold by the Hague Protocol of 1955, increased again by the Guatemala City Protocol to 100 000 special drawing rights (SDR) (about 130 000 US dollars) and with the Montreal Protocols going even higher. The currency conversion to gold value has been another source of contention of many parties to litigation and the case of *Franklin Mint* v. *TWA*[417] left the situation in fiscal anarchy by deciding that, in the United States, the Poincaré gold franc has to be converted to the last official price of gold before the USA left the gold market, and not the free market price of gold. This not only made the overall American attitude towards seeking enhanced compensation turn 360 degrees, but also awarded unrealistically low compensation to the plaintiff. Further, a case in Australia has given a new interpretation to the notion of carrier negligence in the carriage of cargo[418] and a New Zealand case has decided that any interested party can now claim compensation under a cargo claim.[419]

The Montreal Agreement of 1966, a private agreement between carriers plying the United States, was also the result of failure by contracting states to reach an international solution to the problem of unifying principles of liability, particularly in so far as the quantum of damages was concerned. The Montreal Agreement amply demonstrates, as an ICAO document[420] points out, that a private agreement between air carriers, sponsored by IATA, can unhinge and question the credibility of a multilateral international treaty between sovereign states. Mankiewicz attributes this chaotic state of disagreement to the stand taken by the United States, when he states:

> Indeed, there is real irony in the history of the Warsaw Convention. For more than thirty years, the United States of America have steadily and successfully fought for, and obtained and signed six protocols to amend the Warsaw Convention as well as a 'Convention Supplementary to the Warsaw Convention'. But they have ratified not one of these Warsaw instruments. In spite of the huge amounts of time and money spent all these years by ICAO and its member States, the US judiciary is still saddled with the awkward task of applying, construing constructively or destructively, misinterpreting and circumventing a convention which is now 60 years old.[421]

There is only one viable alternative towards rectifying this anomaly and preserving the unification efforts of the Warsaw Convention, and that comes in the nature of ratifying the Montreal Protocols 3 and 4. As Professor Michael Milde states:

> There is hardly any viable alternative to a determined effort to bring the Montreal Protocols Nos 3 and 4 into force. If that aim is not accomplished in the very near future, we may witness a trend to denunciation of the Warsaw System by several States with the ensuing chaotic conflicts of laws, conflicts of jurisdiction, unpredictably high compensation claims and skyrocketing increase in insurance premiums.[422]

The civil liability of an airline for the causing of death or injury to passengers has been established by international treaty and entrenched in law by judicial interpretation. The courts have attempted to balance the interest of both the airline and the passenger, as indeed has been the perceived intention of the Warsaw Convention. The predominant feature of this area of civil liability is that air transport in terms of the commercial transportation of passengers is incontrovertibly the mode of transport that involves the highest levels of technology. Therefore courts may find difficulty in ascertaining negligence, wilful misconduct and the overall liability of the airline in the face of complex technical arguments and defence. However, this reason alone should not justify obviating the tortious element that has so carefully been entrenched in the Warsaw Convention by its founders and used by courts since 1929. As the foregoing discussions reflect, liability issues under the Warsaw Convention have been consistently addressed by the courts on the basis of their interpretation of negligence, wilful misconduct and contributory negligence, all of which are exclusively issues involving principles of tort law.

Relevance of 'accident' to the economy class syndrome It is clear that the conventional interpretation of the term 'accident' in tort liability has been extended in aviation cases under article 17 of the Warsaw Convention where the courts have imputed intention to the carrier in certain instances. To this extent, the *Seguritan*[423] case, which addressed the issue of the carrier's liability in not being able to provide regular medical assistance when necessary, and the *O'Leary* case,[424] where a passenger had more liquor than he could consume in flight, perforce prove that the courts have interpreted the Warsaw Convention to enforce liability of the carrier on the principles of intention. Wilful misconduct, therefore, has played an important role in establishing that, in certain circumstances at least, one would be justified in considering that the extent of the carrier's fault is a valid consideration in the award of damages.

Fault liability as enforced by the Warsaw Convention may also be adequately reflected in intentional negligence, where the carrier intentionally breaches the duty of care he owes the passenger. Determination of a breach of a duty of care as a distinct evidentiary tool by the courts would act towards accident prevention in that instances of carrier liability which emerge from accident investigations could then be used as admissible evidence.

The new trend introduced by the Montreal Convention of 1999 in doing away with fault liability and introducing a system of liability that may apply irrespective of fault, but aligned to monetary compensation based upon subjective assessments of jurisdictional liability, has its genesis in the decade between 1960 and 1970. During this period civil law liability in tort entered a new phase, effectively superannuating the existing system of liability and replacing it with a system of liability insurance. Tortious liability was no longer considered cost-effective, and was no match for less expensive insurance. Jurists thought it more equitable and, above all, practical to embrace a legal system that espoused loss distribution, which acted as the national precursor to liability insurance. This system of liability was assisted along the way by three reasons which militated against fault liability and acted as catalysts for the successful launch of liability insurance. Firstly, a tort system based upon fault was expensive to administer, when compared with any system of insurance; secondly, litigation was fraught with delay, which a plaintiff could often ill afford; thirdly, the unpredictability of the result of cases based upon fault liability often put plaintiffs under pressure to settle their claims for amounts less than they would receive if their claims went successfully to trial.

Wilful misconduct of the carrier Of the two instances in which the Warsaw Convention provides that the carrier's liability is unlimited, one relates to the absence of documentation (absence of the passenger ticket and baggage check or air waybill) on the grounds that the document of carriage evidences the special regime of limited liability as prescribed in the Warsaw Convention. The other, which has turned out to be contentious, deals with instances where the damage is caused by the carrier's wilful misconduct, or such default on his part as, in accordance with the law of the court which exercises jurisdiction in the case, is considered to be the equivalent of wilful misconduct. Article 25 of the Warsaw Convention provides:

> The carrier shall not be entitled to avail himself of the provisions of this Convention or exclude or limit his liability, if the damage is caused by his wilful misconduct or by such default on his part as, in accordance with the law of the Court seized of the case, is considered to be equivalent to wilful misconduct.[425]

The provision further stipulates that the carrier shall not be entitled to avail himself of the above provisions if the damage is caused as aforesaid by any agent of the carrier acting within the scope of his employment.[426]

The primary significance of article 25 is that it addresses both wilful misconduct and the 'equivalent' of wilful misconduct. The authentic and original text of the Warsaw Convention, which is in the French language, uses the words 'dol' and 'faute … equivalente au dol'. There is a palpable inconsistency between English translation of the original text and the original text itself, in that the French word 'dol' personifies the intention to inflict an injury on a person, whereas the English words 'wilful misconduct' requires the defendant carrier to be aware of both his conduct and the reasonable and probable consequences of his conduct, in the nature of the damage which may ensue from the carrier's act. Wilful misconduct, therefore, may not necessarily involve the intention of the carrier, his servants or agents and remains wider in scope as a ground of liability.

Most civil law jurisdictions have equiperated 'dol' with 'gross negligence'. Drion[427] dismisses the element of intention by citing examples such as the theft or pilferage of goods or baggage (which are more frequent in occurrence than aircraft accidents) which may not necessarily always occur with the concurrence or knowledge of the carrier, and cites a list of possible instances where gross negligence would form more justification for the invocation of article 25. Notable examples are assault or indecent behaviour by personnel of carrier; accidents caused by conduct of personnel; serving bad food; bumpy rides causing passenger injury; and failure to instruct passengers of rough weather and so on.[428] Drion also makes the valid point of citing delay in carriage as having many dimensions which may be accommodated within the purview of article 25 without warranting the consideration of intention.[429]

Common law jurisdictions, on the other hand, have separated 'wilful misconduct' from 'negligence' and insisted that the conduct of the carrier has to be 'wilful' or intentional for a successful case to be grounded on article 25 of the Warsaw Convention. This approach is consistent with the original contention of the British delegate to the Warsaw Conference, who claimed that wilful misconduct should pertain to 'acts committed deliberately or acts of carelessness without any regard for the consequences'.[430] In the 1952 British case of *Horabin* v. *British Overseas Airways Corporation*, the court held:

> To be guilty of wilful misconduct the person concerned must appreciate that he is acting wrongfully, or is wrongfully omitting to act and yet persists in so acting or omitting to act regardless of the consequences, or acts or omits to act with reckless indifference as to what the result may be.[431]

In the same year, in the United States, the New York Supreme Court Appellate Division held that wilful misconduct was

> dependent upon the facts of a particular case, but in order that acts may be characterized as wilful there must be on the part of the person or persons sought to be charged, a conscious intent to do or to omit doing the act from which harm results to another, or an intentional omission of a manifest duty. There must be a realization of the probability of injury from the conduct and a disregard of the probable consequences of such conduct.[432]

The above approach has been followed by subsequent American decisions which have classified wilful misconduct as requiring 'conscious intent to do or omit doing an act from which harm results to another'[433] and 'wilful performance of an act that is likely to result in damage or wilful action with a reckless disregard of the probable consequences'.[434]

As to the second limb of article 25.1, which provides that the equivalent of wilful misconduct would suffice to impose liability, the convention leaves the scope of the provision wide open to include an instance of the carrier knowingly providing small seats and not advising the passenger of the inherent dangers related thereto.

Judicial decisions on wilful misconduct

Arguably, the watershed decision on the notion of wilful misconduct in recent times was contained in the case *In re Korean Airlines Disaster of September 1, 1983*,[435] where the trial court considered wilful misconduct to be 'The performance of an act with knowledge that the act will probably result in an injury or damage, or in some manner as to imply reckless disregard for the consequences of its performance'. The above pronouncement was used by the American courts, in the 1994 decision of *Pasinato* v. *American Airlines Inc.*,[436] who concluded that the act in question of a flight attendant did not constitute wilful misconduct within the purview of article 25.2 of the Warsaw Convention. In the *Pasinato* case, a passenger of an American Airlines flight which was bound for Chicago from Italy was struck on the head when a heavy bag fell from an overhead bin in the cabin. The incident was the outcome of an initial request by the passenger for a pillow immediately after take-off, where the flight attendant, in a bid to open the overhead bin above the passenger to retrieve the pillow, was unable to prevent a bag falling from the bin onto the passenger's head. The passenger and her husband sued American Airlines under article 25 on the grounds of wilful misconduct. The trial court was of the view that

> there is no dispute that the flight attendant opened the overhead bin to get a pillow for another passenger. The flight attendant's disposition indicates that she opened the bin with one hand, in her customary manner, with the other hand placed defensively above her head near the bin to prevent an object from falling upon her or a passenger sitting below. Further, the flight attendant stated that she tried to catch the totebag that fell from the bin (and may have touched it as it fell), but that it fell too quickly.[437]

The court took cognizance of the contention of American Airlines that the technical and cabin crews give repeated warnings to passengers of the dangers of opening overhead bins, both over the public address system of the aircraft and by personal messages. The evidence of the flight attendant, that incidents of objects falling from overhead bins were infrequent and generally harmless, based on her experience, was also considered relevant. The court found difficulty in applying the criterion of the *Korean Airlines Disaster* case,[438] in that it was difficult for the court, if not impossible, to envision how the flight attendant's actions could amount to wilful misconduct. It was of the view that the pivotal criterion for determining the existence of wilful misconduct – knowledge that the act would probably result in an injury or damage – was absent. *A fortiori*, the court observed that the other criterion established in the *Korean Airlines* case (that of an act which is performed in a manner indicating reckless disregard for the consequences) was also missing in the *Pasinato* case.

In the 1994 case of *Baba* v. *Compagnie Nationale Air France*,[439] involving damage to cargo, a Federal trial court in Washington found for the plaintiff and awarded damages against the act of the defendant carrier for improperly packing and storing hand-woven Persian carpets, as a result of which some of the carpets were damaged owing to the seepage of rainwater when the carpets were kept outside by the carrier pending their loading onto the aircraft. The court in this instance followed the bench in *Pasinato* by reiterating the criteria for the proof of wilful misconduct as established by the *Korean Air* litigation. A compelling piece of evidence which enabled the court to arrive at its conclusion in the *Baba* case was the fact that the air carrier had disregarded its own cargo handling regulations in storing the carpets outdoors, in the rain. In its findings the court held: 'In short, through a series of acts, the performance of which were intentional, the carrier has demonstrated a reckless disregard of the consequences of its performance. This disregard is emphasized by the fact that no damage report was ever produced.'[440]

The court, while waiving the liability limits of the Warsaw Convention in the *Baba* case, noted that a combination of facts can, taken together, amount to wilful misconduct. It was sufficient, in the court's view, for an act to be intended, and not necessary for the resulting injury or wrongfulness of the act to reflect intention or knowledge. It was also significant that the court further observed that a finding of wilful misconduct was appropriate when the act or omission constituted a violation of a rule or regulation of the defendant carrier itself.

Courts in the United States have been cautious in determining the parameters of 'scope of employment' as envisaged in article 25.2 of the Warsaw Convention, which imputes liability to the carrier with regard to acts of its employers acting within the scope of their employment. In the 1995 case of *Uzochukwu* v. *Air Express International Ltd*,[441] where a New York Federal trial court had to decide on a case of theft by two airline employees of cargo of the two carriers, it was held that the fact that the employers had used forged documents to perpetrate the offence of theft was sufficient to conclude that the act was outside the scope of employment and that the carrier could not be held liable under article 25.2. It is arguable that the conclusion of the court was based on the fact that generally, in the United States, 'wilful misconduct' is regarded as the intentional performance of an act with knowledge that the performance of that act would probably result in injury or damage or the intentional performance of an act in such a manner as to imply reckless disregard of the probable consequences.

In *Robinson* v. *Northwest Airlines Inc.*,[442] a case decided in March 1996 and involving circumstances similar to the *Pasinato* case, the United States Court of Appeals dismissed the appeal of the plaintiff who had lost judgment in the trial court against the carrier. The trial court had allowed a motion of the carrier that the plaintiff's claim in relation to her being injured by a piece of hand luggage falling from an overhead bin while the plane was taxiing, and additional injuries caused to her by a passenger striking her on the head with the latter's baggage, were valid at law.

The Court of Appeals in affirming the dismissal of the action of the plaintiff noted that, while a common carrier (a carrier who opens itself to the world to conduct business in the carriage by air of passengers, baggage and goods) owes a high degree of care to its passengers, it cannot be considered an insurer of the passenger's safety. The court found that the plaintiff failed to raise an issue of fact regarding the carrier's breach of duty towards her. The court was of the following view:

> Short of physical constraint of each passenger until each is individually escorted off the plane, we fail to see what Northwest could have done to prevent this accident. At best, that is precisely what the plaintiff has established; the fact that an accident occurred. However, as noted above, common carriers are not insurers of their passenger safety.[443]

A similar approach can be seen in the contemporaneous case of *Bell* v. *Swiss Air Transport Co. Ltd*,[444] where an intermediate appellate Court in New York State refused to allow the plaintiff's claim that the loss of his laptop computer during a security check of the airline was due to the airline's wilful misconduct. In the court's view, the plaintiff had failed to prove that the airline intentionally mishandled his baggage with knowledge or reckless disregard for the probable consequences of its conduct. The court also noted that it was the local police, and not the airline, who had required the carrying out of the security check.

The case of *Singh* v. *Pan American World Airways*,[445] decided in May 1996, offers a helpful insight into the rationale for determination of wilful misconduct. In wrongful death and personal injury actions arising out of the 1995 hijacking of a PAN AM flight between Bombay and New York, the jury concluded that the carrier had been guilty of wilful misconduct on the reasoning that the management of the carrier knew, or ought to have known, of serious lapses in its security programme. In fact, there had been representations made by the carrier's staff to the management on several occasions prior to the hijacking. Furthermore, the jury was influenced in its conclusion by the fact that the carrier was aware of terrorist activity at European, Middle Eastern and Asian high-risk airports and that very little had been done by the carrier to provide enhanced security at these airports.

In the case of the crash of *Thai Airways Flight TG-311 near Katmandu, Nepal in July 1992*,[446] the question at issue was whether the air crew had been guilty of wilful misconduct in flying into terrain. The fatal crash occurred during approach to Kathmandu airport, an airport known to be one of the most difficult in the world in which to land.[447] Evidence had revealed that the captain had given the bearings of the aircraft to the control tower shortly before the crash, and that such were inconsistent with instruction previously given by the tower to the crew in the cockpit of the aircraft. The court concluded that the plane had veered towards terrain surrounding the airport because of the crew's conscious failure to monitor their navigational instruments. The court held:

> the captain and the first officer knew or should have known that failing to perform their duty to continuously monitor the aircraft's navigational instruments would create a grave danger under the circumstances … both the captain and the first officer were well aware that their duty to consciously monitor navigational instruments was an act *necessary for safety* … their duty to perform this crucial act was so obvious under the circumstances that failing to perform it was *reckless in the extreme*.[448]

The Thai Airways case therefore marks an instance where the elements of wilful misconduct were imputed to the crew on the basis that, owing to their expertise, they knew or ought to have known the reasonable and probable consequences of their act.

A further dimension to the notion of wilful misconduct was added in the *Northwest Airlines Air Crash Case*[449] of August 1996, where the Court of Appeals of the Sixth Circuit added that a finding of wilful misconduct may be based upon consideration of a series of actions or inactions. The court was of the view that, since many complex safety systems interact during an aircraft's flight, an air disaster would usually require multiple acts. In other words, the court held that it was permissible for a jury to consider an airline's individual errors or a series of errors and not restrict itself to the only act which seemingly caused an accident.

If one were to analyse the rationale of wilful misconduct in the light of the *cursus curiae* so far discussed, one would conclude that wilful misconduct hinges itself on knowledge of the perpetrator that damage would result or reckless disregard for consequences of an act on the part of the perpetrator. The question which then arises is whether an instance of the carrier knowingly providing small seats and not advising the passengers of the dangers of prolonged air travel in confined spaces, would subscribe to the notion of wilful misconduct as it is perceived at the present time.

Comments

Admittedly, it would be extremely difficult for an airline to determine the proclivity of their passengers to latent illnesses such as venous thromboembolism. Therefore instances of negligence pertaining to an airline accepting for travel a person who could possibly be afflicted with the disease may arguably be difficult to determine. However, it would not be uncommon to evaluate critically the conduct of an airline which, knowing full well that the seat pitch in the aircraft would cramp an average-size passenger and being cognizant of the medical evidence which identifies prolonged air travel in confined spaces as a risk factor for deep vein thrombosis, does not take any precautions towards the prevention of the occurrence. The cases of *Seguritan, Horabin, Thai Airways* and the *Korean Airlines Disaster* strongly suggest the need for vigilance on the part of airlines to follow scientific and medical developments related to air transport and passenger safety.

It must be emphasized that, in selling an airline ticket for travel by air, an airline offers a composite service, not only to carry a passenger from point A to B, but also to ensure that transportation is accomplished in a safe and sanitary manner. Therefore the services offered by the airline in the area of ergonomics and professional advice as to the risks entailed in air travel become extremely relevant and critical to the issue.

As for issues of liability under the Warsaw Convention, although the *Tseng* case[450] widened the scope of the word 'accident', the case itself addressed a personal security check on a passenger and it remains to be seen whether courts would interpret negligence on the part of the airline to warn the passenger of inherent dangers and advise him of the appropriate precautions as wilful misconduct under the Warsaw Convention. It certainly could be argued that, in the light of the varied interpretations emerging from the *cursus curiae*, an accident under the convention, although not explicitly defined in any past instance, could be considered as 'any incident unexpected and external to the passenger which is avoidable by the airline and which causes death, wounding or injury to a passenger'. Therefore, although no conclusive medical evidence has been released distinctly and conclusively linking venous thromboembolisms to the so-called 'Economy Class Syndrome', since there is strong evidence to suggest a risk factor in air travel, the airline could be expected to take or be seen to take some precautions against the danger.

Airlines would be well advised to apprise passengers that, in order to minimize risk of venous thromboembolism, some of the guidelines are that they should not place baggage in the space under the seat, as it may reduce the ability to move the legs; should exercise legs at regular intervals while seated, in order to improve blood flow; should change positions regularly; should take a stroll down the aisle every once in a while; should avoid sleeping in a cramped position; should avoid using alcohol, tobacco, narcotic drugs and hypnotic drugs; and should consume as much water and other fluids during the flight as possible.

7 THE AEROTOXIC SYNDROME

Introduction

The premise that contaminated cabins can spread disease has been aired several times within the aviation community. At the 17th Annual International Cabin Safety Symposium, held in Los Angeles, California in March 2000, participants addressed the issue squarely, on the basis that the cabin of a modern jetliner, with its mix of fresh and recirculated air, is a veritable incubator of potential disease.[451] At this symposium, it was reported that the floors in locker room showers might be cleaner than some of the cabin surfaces in an airliner, according to recent measurements of in-service aeroplanes. The reasons for this problem have been identified as being twofold: diseases spread in the aircraft such as hepatitis through blood and bodily fluid pathogens and sickness such as influenza and tuberculosis spread through airborne pathogens.[452]

According to researchers' findings at the symposium, while blood and bodily pathogens can be transmitted through touch, the spread of airborne diseases is facilitated by fungus, bacterial and yeast growth caused by condensation of the inside walls of ducting and filters through which ventilation is provided inside the aircraft cabin.[453]

In addition to the possible spread of disease in the cabin through disease vectors, researchers have separately identified another health hazard in the cockpit and cabin which they call the 'aerotoxic syndrome' that may affect aircrew and passengers as a result of exposure to airborne chemicals in aircraft. This condition is caused by exposure at high altitude to atmospheric contaminants from engine oil or other aircraft fluids resulting in short-term skin, gastrointestinal, respiratory and nervous system effects and long-term central nervous and immunological effects. According to research conducted so far, it is believed that materials used in the operation of aircraft may contain hazardous ingredients, some with significant toxicities. Aircraft material such as jet fuel, de-icing fluids, engine oil and hydraulic fluids contain a range of ingredients, some of which are toxic.[454] Engine oil, hydraulic fluids and other materials which have in common the chemical presence of toxic ingredients such as organophosphates are used as of necessity by the aviation industry. Although these chemicals are usually contained within the engines and equipment into which they have been added, they can sometimes find their way into cabin air where crew and passengers are located. Most common causes of leakages of this kind are engine oil leaks, fluid ingestion by the auxiliary power unit and engines, and failure of seals designed to preclude seepage and leakage through ventilation systems.

Reported effects from short-term exposure to aerotoxins, particularly from fuel and oil leakage, include blurred or tunnel vision, disorientation, memory impairment, shaking and tremors, nausea/vomiting, vertigo and loss of consciousness. Long-term exposure often results, in addition to the above, in lack of coordination, respiratory problems, chest pain, severe headaches and weakness and acute fatigue.[455]

One of the reasons given for the incidence of the aerotoxic syndrome is that, in order to save fuel and thereby increase profits, airlines are cutting back on fresh air intake and using more recycled air.[456] It is also alleged that pilots and high-flying passengers in the forward cabins get the most oxygen. Oxygen deprivation, it is claimed, can lead to either anoxia or hypoxia. Anoxia, or the lack of oxygen in the blood, is allegedly a cause of aggressive and combative behaviour in individuals and the hypothesis has been put forward that the aerotoxic syndrome may be the cause of so many incidents of air rage. Hypoxia results in too little blood reaching body tissues, making people apathetic or comatose. Hypoxia is identified by some as the reason why most economy class passengers fall asleep immediately after the meal service on long flights.[457]

The above notwithstanding, it must be categorically stated, at the outset, that all allegations made so far with regard to the aerotoxic syndrome are anecdotal and hypothetical. However, it has apparently raised sufficient concern in the aviation community to necessitate study on the subject. This discussion addresses issues of legal liability of an airline if such issues are considered to warrant attention at a global level.

It is reported that the United Kingdom government is to commission a comprehensive study of evidence submitted by flight crew of being incapacitated in flight.[458] The concern stems from initial worries about the health of the crew to the safety of the entire aircraft and passengers. One pilot has reported: 'Every time I flew a plane I got influenza-like symptoms, including being bunged up in the head for about half an hour of flight … I frequently found myself feeling so poorly that I couldn't tell my first officer how bad I felt.'[459]

Before aviation technology evolved towards pressurized cabins, aircraft manufacturers built aircraft to reach a maximum altitude of 8000 ft (2400 metres) for the reason that the oxygen saturation limit at that altitude is well tolerated by the average healthy individual. Unfortunately the words 'average' and 'healthy' do not reflect or represent every airline passenger and some may suffer from hypoxia at that altitude.[460] A study published in the United States in 1992 describes a sub-group of the passenger population that will show symptoms at moderate altitudes.[461] More stringent standards have been suggested, and the Report of the Special Committee of the Aerospace Medical Association on Cabin Air Quality has suggested that aircraft manufacturers and airline companies pay more attention to cabin crew and passenger comfort when preparing technical bulletins. The association has further recommended that the ventilation issue be re-evaluated.[462]

Laboratory tests conducted in 1992 in the University of British Columbia in Canada have revealed a need for a fleetwide cabin air quality programme. The findings indicate that jet lubricating oils, when exposed to elevated temperatures, are sources of carbon monoxide and carbon dioxide and the carbon monoxide produced could become a hazard to the flight crew when operating aircraft with leaking engine oil seals.[463]

A grave danger that compounds the deleterious effects of the aerotoxic syndrome is pilot fatigue. Already, flight safety experts are using scientific methods to study the controversial issue of pilot fatigue as a cause of incidents and accidents. It may well be necessary to examine additionally the effect of a combination of toxic contaminants and fatigue on the performance of a pilot in flight. Usually, fatigue among cockpit crew, brought about by sleep deprivation or loss, causes loss of concentration, slow reaction time, disorientation, misinterpretation of flight instrument information and visual illusions. Pilots suffering from fatigue have been known to lose interest in completing flight procedures and routine tasks and to not perform their supervisory and decision-making tasks adequately.[464]

The human body's vital functions are dependent on a 24-hour circadian rhythm – a clock in the brain – and haemostatic regulatory mode. These command the fundamental features of equilibrium of the body, such as body temperatures. The circadian rhythm corresponds to earth's rotation and therefore is affected by time zones which, when crossed, disturb a person's biological rhythm, weakening physical and mental performance. A Boeing study on 'alertness management', aimed at helping airlines to better manage and control alertness in cockpit crew, has concentrated on fundamental issues such as direction of travel, number of time zones crossed, departure and arrival times, dietary patterns and exercise regimens of pilots as key factors in affecting the performance of cockpit crew.[465] It would be futile to expect meaningful results from such a study if it is based on the premise that the cockpit environment is always clean.

Air carrier liability

Liability under common law

There are three primary considerations which are calculated to expose cockpit crew, cabin crew and passengers to the risk of exposure to contaminants. The first consideration is justification, where all exposures to contaminants must be justified. Where exposure has been justified, the second consideration is that such exposure must be as low as reasonably achievable. The third consideration is that there are usually dose limits set for individuals at risk of exposure in order that the setting of such limits may act as a safety valve in case all other considerations are ignored.

Bodily integrity of aircrew and passengers The main legal issue to be considered in this context, which is whether an airline would be liable for injuries or death suffered by aircrew and passengers or their progeny as a result of sustained exposure to contaminants, would originate from a person's right to 'bodily integrity'. In other words, a person has a legal right in almost any jurisdiction of the world to know of and determine risks which may adversely affect his body through a process introduced by another. Airlines may arguably have a duty (particularly in the light of compelling facts now emerging through several studies on exposure of aircrew and passengers to contaminants) to their crew and passengers to apprise them of the risk involved and obtain, in the instance of crew, their consent that such risk would be an acceptable factor in the course of their employment. In the instance of passengers, the airlines have a duty to ensure that all possible precautions are taken against exposure. It is arguable that an analogy to the situation of aircrew and passengers in this regard is the voluntary exposure of persons to contaminants for purposes of medical research.

The seminal principle of 'bodily integrity' as a concept of a person's legal right is reflected in the Nuremberg Code which was formulated by the Nuremberg Trials after World War II. The code was articulated in a court opinion judging 23 Nazi physicians guilty of 'crimes against humanity' for their experimentation on humans during the war. Although, admittedly, the Nuremberg situation, which involved medical experimentation on individuals, is different from the situation of aircrew and passengers who are exposed to contaminants in the course of their air travel, it is logical to consider that the underlying principle of 'bodily integrity' applies in both situations, where, fundamentally, a person's knowledge and consent become necessary prior to exposure to risk. The first provision in the Nuremberg Code stipulates:

> The voluntary consent of the human subject is absolutely essential. This means that the person involved should have legal capacity to give consent; should be situated as to be able to exercise free power of choice, without the intervention of any element of force, fraud, deceit, duress, over-reaching or other ulterior form of constraint or coercion; and should have sufficient knowledge and comprehension of the elements of the subject matter involved as to enable him to make an understanding and enlightened decision.

The United States Supreme Court recognized the above provision as a cognizable factor in determining liability for contaminants exposure in the 1994 case *In Re Cincinnati Radiation Litigation*,[466] citing as persuasive authority the dissenting judgment of Judge O'Connor in *United States* v. *Stanley*,[467] where her honour underscored the fact that the United States Constitution ensured an individual's right to receive the protection of the Nuremberg Code. Justice O'Connor refused to accept the majority decision in the *Stanley* case that injuries arising out of the injection of drugs during the course of a person's employment were not compensable. It would seem therefore that the *Cincinnati Radiation Litigation* case has established that, in the United States, exposure to contaminants and injury therefrom which can be related to a person's employment can be compensable.

The *Cincinnati Radiation* case, which involved contaminants treatment on an experimental basis on several patients who were diagnosed with terminal cancer at the Cincinnati General Hospital from 1960 to 1971, left the courts to consider the liability of the hospital, particularly in the circumstances where the patients had not been informed of the risk of death from the contaminants experiments. In its analysis of applicable law the court anchored itself on the case of *Washington* v. *Harper*,[468] where the Supreme Court had held that state prison officials could administer antipsychotic drugs to a prisoner against his will or without his knowledge and consent only if the prisoner was dangerous, the treatments were justified in the medical interest and the prisoner received adequate protection and procedural safeguards.

Those three criteria can be analogically applied to the instance of aircrew members being exposed to scientifically known levels of contaminants at high altitudes without their knowledge or consent. The last criterion, that of ensuring protective safeguards, would act as an essential supplement to obtaining the consent of the aircrew for exposure to the risk, since it is an essential prerequisite for an employer to take adequate precautions against a danger in the workplace, whether or not the consent of the employee is obtained.

Safeguards and precautions to be taken by the carrier Whatever the technological measures are which may help alleviate the adverse effects of exposure to contaminants, the air carrier's liability for not taking precautionary measures is based on the fundamental tort law principle that the carrier owes a duty of care not to cause harm or injury to others who use the carrier's services, whether for purposes of employment or otherwise. If one were to consider cases regarding injury caused by tobacco smoking to passengers while in flight as an analogy, the 1980 decision of *Ravreby* v. *United Airlines Inc.*[469] would take a prominent place as persuasive authority. The Iowa Supreme Court in *Ravreby* implicitly recognized that air carriers owe a duty of care to non-smoking passengers and that care should be taken, to the extent possible, by the carrier not to expose non-smokers to tobacco smoke in the cabin. The court observed:

> The carrier's duty stops just short of insuring the safety of the passenger, and the common expressions of the law on this subject are that the carrier is bound to protect the passenger as far as human care and foresight will go, and that the carrier is liable for slight negligence.[470]

The significance of the *Ravreby* decision as an analogy to legal considerations with regard to exposure to contaminants in aircraft at high altitude also lies in the fact that the court balanced the interest of the passenger with the advantage of expedience inherent in air transport. It was the court's view that the carrier would be liable for damage caused by dangers which are reasonably and naturally anticipated and the required care on the part of the carrier must be such as not to prevent the practical performance of the carrier's duty to transport with expedition in accordance with the usual requirements of the business. Accordingly, a court adjudicating on a case which involves a claim of a person against exposure to contaminants while in flight may consider the justification for flight at high altitudes (to accomplish more speed and less fuel consumption) as a criterion which may mitigate a carrier's liability, without totally exculpating the carrier from liability. In any event, it is incontrovertible that the carrier has to take reasonable measures to protect its employees and passengers from injury, whatever the justification is.

Given the compelling nature of the scientific data available on the extent of injury which may be caused to a person by disease contracted in flight at high altitudes, a court may well consider the cause of such exposure as a tort – a private offence which is generally wrong at civil law and committed to the harm of a person's self or property by another person.[471] The exposure of aircrew and passengers by an air carrier to contaminants without the consent of those persons would therefore amount to the tort of battery, which has been defined as the intentional and direct application of force to another person[472] or unjustified intentional physical interference with a person.[473] To preclude such an inference by the courts, air carriers may have to show every evidence of there having been adequate measures taken to prevent or at least minimize the dangers of exposing their aircrew to contaminants.

In general common law terms, principles of liability of air carriers with respect to negligence in the spread of disease in their aircraft cabins caused by airborne vectors and aerotoxins are no different from liability principles pertaining to the spread of other diseases transmitted through food, such as salmonella poisoning, cholera and staphylococcal food poisoning.[474] In the case of the transmission of airborne vectors in the aircraft cabin, like the other diseases mentioned, the air carrier has a two-phased prospect for facing a claim for damages: prevention and contingency planning.

Prevention Any flow of aerotoxins is affected by the environment, particularly if such were to be an enclosed one, as in an aircraft cabin. The ventilation system plays a critical part in this regard and, therefore, it is crucial to an air carrier's conduct to determine the manner in which an air carrier decides on ventilation systems in its aircraft. For instance, early jet aircraft until the 1990s offered 100 per cent fresh air in the cabin. However, in the 1990s, ironically with more evolved technology, ventilation systems in aircraft were built in such a way as to recycle stale air, thus increasing the chances of survival of bacteria in the aircraft cabin. Even if such a practice were ineluctable, in that recycling is a universal practice which is calculated to conserve fuel, a prudent airline would take other measures, such as changing of air filters through which ventilation is provided.

Air in the cabin is usually dry and lacking in humidity, since the outside air at cruising altitudes has an extremely low water content. The humidity level in the air of an aircraft cabin at cruising level has been recognized as being of 10–20 per cent humidity, which is approximately the same as desert air.[475] The lack of humidity *per se* does not facilitate the transmission of bacteria, but makes breathing difficult, particularly for persons suffering from respiratory diseases, such as asthma. When dry air becomes stale through recycling, the chances of removing droplets of air, which is usually accomplished by fresh air, become remote. A suggested solution for a prudent airline to take in this regard is to reintroduce 100 per cent fresh air which is humidified.[476]

Contingency planning The other limb under which an airline could face a liability claim lies in the area of contingency planning through effective communications. Although it is incontrovertible that an airline cannot know beforehand whether one of its passengers carries disease-causing bacteria, it can, once advised of the fact, take effective measures to ensure fullest cooperation with the health authorities involved.

Although, usually, the health department is advised of an airline passenger who had travelled while infected, there may be instances where a passenger or his physician may contact an airline first. In such instances, the airline is obligated to advise the health authorities immediately of all details, not only of the patient concerned but of all passengers who were in the flight with the infected person.

An essential prerequisite of airline contingency planning is the establishment of a link between the medical centre of the airline and its central booking or reservations system whereby, when necessary, the reservations department of the airline can transmit full information to the medical centre to follow up instances of possible infections, particularly in the airline's home base. It is not sufficient for the airline to wash its hands of an infected flight by merely giving the passenger manifest to the health authorities. The airline's reservation system should be sufficiently well equipped to have all data relating to passengers' addresses, telephone numbers, and so on, which can be given to both the airline medical staff and the state health authorities.

A prudent airline would follow up diligently the list of infected passengers to ensure that they receive proper medical care and documentation necessary for the obtaining of whatever assistance is required. It is critical that the airline, at every moment, keeps its own medical staff involved in instances where its passengers have been or may have been infected, in order for the proper clinical determination of quarantine times and isolation to be professionally followed.

In the case of potential exposure of passengers to tuberculosis, airlines should have a mechanism in place that would advise the health authorities of the state concerned immediately. Airlines should give special training to its crews in using first aid for precautionary purposes. All necessary medical equipment should be stored in the aircraft. In case of possible infection, airlines should vigorously maintain all contact with those who may have been infected, offering them medical attention in addition to that which may be provided by the state authorities. In stations other than their own home stations, airlines should maintain their own medical contacts to assist infected persons from a flight.

Legal issues The pre-eminent legal provision which governs this issue is contained in the Convention on International Civil Aviation (Chicago Convention),[477] Article 14 of which states:

> Each contracting State agrees to take effective measures to prevent the spread by means of air navigation of cholera, typhus (epidemic), smallpox, yellow fever, plague, and such other communicable diseases as the contracting States shall from time to time decide to designate, and to that end contracting States will keep in close consultation with the agencies concerned with international regulations relating to sanitary measures applicable to aircraft. Such consultation shall be without prejudice to the application of any existing international convention on this subject to which the contracting States may be parties.

This provision explicitly devolves primary responsibility on states to take effective measures to prevent airborne diseases in aircraft that may be communicated and implicitly requires states to issue guidelines for airlines, by liaising with the international agencies concerned. *Non obstante,* airlines have to face certain legal issues themselves in terms of their conduct even in instances which involve non-communicable diseases such as those brought about by aerotoxins. Primarily, airlines are expected to conform to applicable international health regulations and the laws of the countries in which their aircraft land.[478] Furthermore, the airline owes its passengers a duty of care to exercise all caution in protecting their rights, so that a blatant instance of a person who looks sickly and coughs incessantly at the check-in counter cannot be ignored. Common law principles of tort law vigorously distinguish between negligence, recklessness and wilful blindness. Of these elements of liability, wilful blindness is particularly relevant since it brings to bear the need for an airline to be vigilant in observing passenger profiles in potentially dangerous or threatening situations. The Canadian Supreme Court has stated:

> Wilful blindness is distinct from recklessness because, while recklessness involves knowledge of a danger or a risk and persistence in a course of conduct which creates a risk that the prohibited result will occur, wilful blindness arises when a person who has become aware of the need for some inquiry declines to make the inquiry because he does not wish to know the truth. He would prefer to remain ignorant. The culpability in recklessness is justified by consciousness of the risk and by proceeding in the face of it, while in wilful blindness it is justified by the accused's fault in deliberately failing to inquire when he knows there is reason for inquiry.[479]

Civil wrongs which are exclusively breaches of trust or of some other merely equitable obligation are one of four classes of wrongs.[480] Therefore the tort of misfeasance (deliberate wrong), and nonfeasance (failure to take action to perform a duty of care owed) such as wilful blindness to a possible wrong that may be committed, both of which an imprudent and careless airline may be guilty of in the case of the spread of disease in the aircraft cabin, becomes 'a civil wrong for which the remedy is a common law action for unliquidated damages, and which is not exclusively the breach of a contract or the breach of a trust or other merely equitable obligation'.[481]

Therefore, in general terms, a tort arises from an act performed by the defendant whereby he/she has without just cause or excuse caused some harm to the plaintiff.[482] This rationale is grounded on the classical juridical maxim *sic utere tuo ut alienum non laedes*, which essentially means that no one can hurt another by word or deed. It follows naturally, therefore, that a person aggrieved as a result of a tort of another can claim pecuniary compensation in respect of damage suffered. A person who contracts tuberculosis, for example, while travelling in an aircraft which carried an infected person whose disease was transmitted to that person can, under this principle, expect compensation from the airline concerned if the airline is found to have breached its duty of care by either positively contributing to the damage (by knowingly allowing the infected person to travel or by knowingly installing a ventilator system in the aircraft which is not effective in preventing the spread of airborne disease) or by wilfully blinding itself to the potential danger of a sickly person entering the aircraft cabin without making further inquiry.

It is incontrovertible that proof of negligence of the airline, whether through wilful neglect or through wilful blindness, would be extremely difficult to establish in the case of the spread of an airborne disease such as tuberculosis, as against such diseases as cholera. The former cannot be linked to insanitary conditions in the cabin *per se*, whereas the latter can readily be determined through an *ex post facto* examination of the cabin. The only instance imaginable where an airline can be held reprehensible and consequently liable for pecuniary compensation is when an obviously sickly passenger is checked in by the airline without the latter making an inquiry; when the airline knows beforehand that a particular passenger is positively infected with the disease; or when the aircraft cabin is not properly equipped to prevent the spread of disease. Therefore air carrier liability for this particular tort would invariably be addressed after the fact: that is, after passengers have been infected with the disease, when action taken by the airline to assist both those infected and the health authorities concerned would become relevant.

In an instance where an airline is found liable, courts would be charged with quantifying the personal loss incurred by a person contracting the disease. In the 1964 case of *H. West & Son* v. *Shephard*,[483] decided in the House of Lords in Britain, Lord Morris of Borth-y-Gest rejected the argument that courts should decide whether a person, who was so debilitated by disease, was in a position to enjoy monies awarded in compensation. His lordship was of the view that the award of compensation was symbolic of reparation made, irrespective of its practical importance to the plaintiff:

> I consider that it is sufficient to say that a money award is given by way of compensation and that it must take into account the actual consequences which have resulted from the

> tort ... if damages are awarded to a plaintiff on a correct basis it seems to me that it can be of no concern to the court to consider any question as to the use that will thereafter be made of the money awarded.[484]

Lord Morris of Borth-y-Gest made the distinction between money given in the form of compensation as above in recognition of the damage caused, and compensation given to cover financial loss, such as payment for nursing and medical services and the cost of medicine, as two different elements of compensation. The overall point made by the *Shephard* decision is that compensation should be substantial and not merely a token, irrespective of whether the plaintiff was able to enjoy the money or not. In this sense, compensation is awarded for what is suffered by the plaintiff and is not based on an evaluation of a thing lost. In the Australian case of *Skelton* v. *Collins*,[485] Taylor J of the High Court of Australia observed: 'compensation cannot be based on evaluation of a thing lost. It must surely be based upon solace for a condition created, not upon payment for something taken away'.[486]

Taylor J's reasoning was further developed by the House of Lords three years later in the case of *Baker* v. *Willoughby*,[487] where Lord Reid said:

> A man is not compensated for the physical injury; he is compensated for the loss which he suffers as a result of that injury. His loss is not having a stiff leg; it is in his inability to lead a full life, his inability to enjoy those amenities which depend on freedom of movement and his inability to earn as much as he used to earn or could have earned.[488]

The issue of quantum of damages for personal injury has been addressed by courts on the basis that the damages awarded should be such that the ordinary rational man would not instinctively regard them as either mean or extravagant, but would consider them to be sensible and fair.[489] Indeed, as Lord Denning MR observed in 1966: 'the award of damages in personal injuries cases is basically a conventional figure derived from experience and from awards in comparable cases'.[490]

In addition to the compensation for damage caused, the plaintiff is also entitled to compensation with regard to pre-trial pecuniary loss as a result of expenses actually and reasonably incurred on account of the injury. Compensation under this heading may cover clothing and medical expenses[491] and nursing expenses.[492] As for future pecuniary loss, the usual consideration is towards loss of future income, although if the injured person dies, there could also be a claim for lost dependency.[493] Future pecuniary loss is usually calculated by the multiplier method, which is based on a calculation of the plaintiff's net annual loss multiplied by a figure chosen so as to produce an overall sum which is intended to provide, by withdrawals of both interest and capital, compensation for the lost income in the years ahead. The multiplier is not dependent upon the number of working years the plaintiff would have had ahead if not for the illness, since allowance is made in the calculation for contingencies such as illness which might have struck the plaintiff in any event. Therefore, in practice, the multiplier rarely exceeds eighteen, even in very young plaintiffs.

Of course, in the case of illness caused by the ingestion of aerotoxins, the court will also assess the period during which the incapacity will continue. Invariably, there will be consideration in this regard of whether there will be total incapacity for a particular period, followed by partial incapacity for a further period. The following four considerations would be critical to a court's assessment of future income loss:

1 for what period would income probably be lost;
2 what would the average loss of income be through that period;
3 what is the appropriate multiple to give the value of an annuity of that loss for the period concerned; and
4 what sum should be deducted from the multiple for contingencies?

In the case of a young child not yet in employment, and who is expected to be adversely affected by the disease contracted, the courts would have to determine whether the child could be permanently or temporarily disabled as a result of ill-effects of the disease. In addition, courts would have to hazard a conjecture as to the child's future progression had he/she not contracted the disease. In the 1975 case of *Taylor* v. *Bristol Omnibus Co. Ltd*,[494] The court assumed that the child's earning capacity would be similar to that of the father and assessed the loss at sixteen years' purchase, and reduced it by 50 per cent to give current value. In a later case,[495] where a child of five years was expected to live only up to the age of 27 years owing to a disease contracted, the court awarded a modest sum for that period concerned but refused to recognize that compensation should be awarded for 'lost years', which the court found to be nebulous and therefore valued at nil. In the 1981 case of *Croke* v. *Wiseman*,[496] which concerned a child aged two with brain damage who would live up to the age of 40, the court assumed that the child would earn the national average wage for 22 years and valued this figure at just under nine years' purchase, reducing the multiple to five to arrive at the current value.

Irrespective of the plaintiff's age, the rationale for determining future income loss was well laid down in the 1977 case of *Moeliker* v. *A. Reyrolle & Co. Ltd*,[497] where the court seized of the case gave the correct criteria for determining compensation. According to this decision, what has to be quantified is the present value of the risk of future financial loss. If there is no actual loss of earnings sooner or later, there should be no award. If, however, there is a significant risk, its value will depend on the magnitude of the risk and how far into the future. Based on this premise, another case[498] decided in the same year ended with the award of substantial compensation to a young man with an arm injury, on the basis that he was likely to suffer from osteoarthritis later in life, although this would be many years ahead.

Loss of a career, which a person injured or infected already enjoys, is another significant consideration. Of course, some occupations are more attractive than others, not necessarily in monetary terms but rather in the job satisfaction they offer. When a person is already enjoying such a career, for instance as an airline pilot or surgeon – two professions for which there are stringent health requirements – infection by a disease such as tuberculosis could be critical. In such instances courts would be compelled to take into account the damage caused by total loss of career.[499]

As for loss of earning capacity which the plaintiff avers he/she would have had if not for the injury (and which the plaintiff did not have at the time of injury) the observation *obiter* of Diplock LJ in *Browning* v. *War Office*[500] is relevant: 'A plaintiff is not entitled to damages for loss of capacity to earn money unless it is established that he would, but for his injuries, have exercised that capacity in order to earn money.'[501] In every claim for specific compensation concerning earning capacity, the plaintiff has the burden of showing clearly and convincingly that there was actual loss of future income owing to the injury or illness caused.

Liability under international convention

When there is incontrovertible evidence of a person contracting a disease as a result of being contaminated in an aircraft while on board, liability issues pertaining to the airline arising from the incident may involve principles of private air carrier liability. The Montreal Convention of 1999[502] which emerged consequent to the Diplomatic Conference on Private Air Law of the International Civil Aviation Organization held from 10 to 28 May 1999, provides that the carrier is liable for damage sustained in the event of death or bodily injury of a passenger upon condition only that the accident which caused the damage so sustained took place on board the aircraft or in the course of any of the operations of embarking or disembarking. Later in this section, liability issues under the Montreal/Warsaw regime will be addressed with a view to determining whether, in general terms, the infection of a passenger with tuberculosis could be considered an 'accident' if the negligence of the carrier can be shown.

Accident generally defined The Warsaw Convention stipulates that an 'accident' should cause injury or death to a passenger[503] if it were to be considered for liability. Halsbury states:

> the word accident (or its adjective accidental) is no doubt used with the intention of excluding the operation of natural causes such as old age, congenital or insidious disease, or the natural progression of some constitutional, physical or mental defect, but the ambit of what is included by the word is not entirely clear ... What is postulated is the intervention of some cause ... so as to be fairly describable as fortuitous ... it covers any un-looked for mishap or an untoward event which is not expected or designed ...[504]

Perhaps the first known attempt at definition was in a case reported in England in 1900[505] where a man, in the course of lifting heavy machinery, vomited blood owing to an abnormality of his internal organs. Smith LJ, interpreting section 1(1) of the Workmen's Compensation Act of 1897 under which the action was brought for compensation under a personal accident insurance policy, held that the death of the man was due to disease and therefore did not accord with the true sense of the word accident.[506] Collins LJ, agreeing with the view expressed by Smith LJ, decided that an accident should be fortuitous and unexpected and in this case the event which led to the death of the worker was not fortuitous.[507] In a case which followed,[508] where a workman had to balance a beam in such a way as to avoid falling and in the course of which precarious exercise he strained the muscles of his back, Collins MR held that an accident, to be compensated, should be fortuitous and unexpected,[509] to which Matthew LJ added that the criterion should be to determine what would happen within the course of employment and what would not.

Both the cases cited seem to accord with Halsbury's inclination to treat accident as a fortuitous event. Analogically, the approach of the judges to an accident caused to an airline passenger would seemingly have included the dual criteria of there being an unexpected or fortuitous event not contributed to by the inherent ill-health of the passenger and which should have occurred within the course of his carriage by air. The later case of *Fenton* v. *Thorley and Co. Limited*[510] qualified the somewhat restrictive definition of the word 'accident' adopted in the earlier cases. Lord Macnaughten, while recognizing that an accident should be an unlooked for mishap or an untoward event which is not expected or designed,[511] observed that the earlier definition could even make a stupid act performed by a person compensable, if such was fortuitous. In this case an appeal of an apparently healthy man who ruptured himself by an act of over-exertion during employment was deemed by the House of Lords to have qualified to be allowed compensation under the rubric of 'accident'. Perhaps the most significant statement on the applicant's position was by Lord Robertson, who said: 'No one out of a law court would ever hesitate to say that this man met with an accident ... the word "accident" is not made inappropriate by the fact that the man hurt himself.'[512]

Lord Lindley, dealing with the term 'accident' in the same case, held that 'The word "accident" is not a technical legal term with a clearly defined meaning. Speaking generally, but with reference to legal liabilities, an accident means any unintended occurrence which produces hurt or loss.'[513] His lordship went on to say:

> every injury must have a cause. The proximate cause may be an internal strain; but if, as in this case, the strain is occasioned by an effect to overcome an obstacle accidentally presented to a workman in the course of his employment I am not prepared to say that the Act[514] does apply.[515]

Viscount Haldane LC in a later case,[516] while agreeing with Lord Macnaughten's view in *Fenton* v. *Thorley*,[517] qualified the decisions further by stating that Lord Macnaughten did not exclude intentional acts of third parties from the purview of the term 'accident'. In this case, where a schoolmaster was killed by a premeditated assault of two schoolboys, the assault was considered an accident and compensation was allowed.

In *R.*v. *Morris*,[518] a more recent case decided in 1971, the term 'accident' was interpreted to mean in the broadest possible terms 'any unintended occurrence'. This was a case where two cars interlocked in pursuance of the driver of one vehicle pushing the other which had refused to start. Lord Widgery CJ, in examining the word 'accident', has seemingly depended upon the quantum of damage[519] more than on anything else to determine whether an accident had occurred. If this approach were to be followed, the English law would show a decided inconsistency with the more laudable approach taken in *Fenton*'s case.

A valid criticism which may lie against the English common law is that at no point has there been an attempt to define the word 'accident' in concrete terms. The only positive step seems to have been that which was taken by Lord Lindley in *Fenton*'s case,[520] where his lordship stated that, although there is no technical definition of the term itself, an occurrence may be considered accidental in the case of a workman if an obstacle presents itself within the course of the activity which led to the occurrence. In assessing the term 'accident', American law is not as explicit as the English law, although it is noteworthy that American courts have excluded unforeseen and unexpected incidents from the purview of the word 'accident'. In *Kinavey* v. *Prudential Insurance Co. of America*,[521] where the deceased fell from a bridge after intoxicating himself and placing himself in a position of grave risk on a railway bridge, the court held that nothing unusual or unforeseen occurred as the risk was extremely likely to have been realized under the circumstances. Accordingly, compensation was not required to be paid to the deceased's dependants by the insurance company that had covered the life of the deceased.

In a later case,[522] decided in 1957, the principles applied by the court were substantially the same as in *Kinavey*'s case where the operative criterion applied was that any act of the deceased or wounded in which he voluntarily undertook a grave risk would effectively preclude the dependants of the deceased from invoking the word 'accident' in their claim. In this case the deceased had lain down on a busy highway and been killed by a vehicle. He was of sound mind and had been warned by his companions of the grave danger of his act. The court held that death was due to the voluntary assumption of risk by the deceased and that the incident did not occur accidentally.

Voluntary assumption of risk appears to be the prominent factor which excludes compensation in the United States of America for claims relating to death or injury by accident. In a 1951 case,[523] this principle had been expressly laid down where a court refused the award of compensation in an instance where the insured died as a result of participating in 'Russian Roulette'. Similarly, in a case decided earlier,[524] the courts had held that, even if a person's not being aware of a particular susceptibility to risk is assumed, no award of compensation would be available to the injured person by the person who allegedly causes him the injury. It appears to be clear, therefore, that American law seems to run parallel to the English common law to insist on unexpected events to be classified as accidental. The heavy reliance on voluntary assumptions of risk underscores this fact.

The common law of Canada has, in more than one instance, expressly recognized the principle enunciated by Lord Macnaughten in *Fenton* that the word 'accident' can be attributed to an unexpected incident or one which is undesigned. In a 1940 decision,[525] Crocket J spelt out the fact that an accident is an untoward event.[526] In this case a worker incurred internal injury in the course of her duties while operating a new hand embossing machine. The decision is very clear, in that, as in *Fenton*, the claim was found to be compensable notwithstanding the risk, since the employee had to take the risk involved to perform her duties. Courts in Canada have refused compensation in instances where consequential damage is caused by a person's voluntary behaviour which leads to the injury. In *Travellers' Insurance Company* v. *Elder*,[527] where a customer in a restaurant used abusive language and was assaulted as a result, the court held that the injuries were effected directly and independently of causes other than through accidental means.

A noteworthy feature in the *Travellers' Insurance Company* case is that the court had relied upon the fault of the claimant as a basis for rejecting his claim[528] and on the fact that the claimant had placed himself in a position that would objectively be considered to have brought about an assault upon himself. This approach was seen in another case[529] where a deer poacher shot at another while poaching, which invited retaliation resulting in the death of the poacher. The Nova Scotia Supreme Court held that death had not been caused accidentally since the deceased, by his act of firing at the other, had invited the retaliatory shot. The rationale in the case appears to be that, if the injury caused is calculated to be foreseeable by the injured, such injury would not be considered accidental.

The test of foreseeability has been strongly applied in the case of *Candler* v. *London and Lancashire Guarantee and Accident Company of Canada et al.*,[530] where the court had pronounced that an injury which is the reasonable consequence of a voluntary act of the injured cannot be considered as having been caused by accidental means. In this case the deceased met with his death by falling from the twelfth floor of a hotel. The insurance company with whom the deceased had held a life insurance policy denied compensation on the grounds that the deceased had been in an advanced state of intoxication. Grant J stated:

> The purpose of his [the deceased's] action to show his friend that he had sufficient nerve to take the risk of falling, that was obviously associated with his actions, was so evident to Simmonds [the friend] that, to use his words, he was petrified at the display. His efforts to dissuade Candler from engaging in such act consisted partly in telling him that he need not so act. ... His statement that he would show he still had nerve is the conclusive evidence that he appreciated the risk involved.[531] His acts on the night in question in assuming the dangerous position he did on the top of the coping could have no useful purpose whatever except the obvious opportunity to convince Simmonds that he possessed sufficient nerve to accept the challenge that was associated therewith ...

> His conduct was foolhardy and attended with the most obvious danger ... I therefore hold that Candler's death was not caused either by accidental means or by accident.[532]

Grant J seems to have assiduously followed the objective test of foreseeability and attributed the cause of death to consequential injury arising from the initial act of intoxication of the deceased. This interpretation has precluded the death of the deceased from being considered an accident.

There are two assumptions that emerge from the decision in *Candler*'s case. One is that, in determining the occurrence of an 'accident', the courts in Canada would inevitably consider the cause of the accident as a relevant fact. The other is the incontrovertible assumption that, if the incident arises out of the foreseeable consequences of an act of the deceased or injured person, the incident itself would not be considered for compensation.

It is very clear that the three jurisdictions of the United Kingdom, the United States and Canada recognize at common law certain basic facts in determining whether a given incident can be termed an 'accident'. They are that (a) the incident should constitute an unexpected, fortuitous or untoward happening; (b) it should not be a consequence of irrational conduct of the deceased or injured person; and (c) the incident should be one which is not reasonably foreseeable by the deceased or injured.

Perhaps the only exception is *Fenton* v. *Thorley*, where it was recognized that an injury may be compensable even if caused with foreseeability if the risk was foreseen but was inevitable. Be that as it may, the most critical problem in this area where all three jurisdictions are concerned is that the common law has not offered an acceptable definition of the word 'accident'.

Comments

As regards an accident, particularly where it is established that the airline knew or ought to have known of the risk involved, it is highly arguable that, on the strength of the broad interpretation of the *Tseng* case,[533] courts may be inclined to treat the contracting of any disease as an accident. Also relevant to this issue is the 1996 Supreme Court decision in *Zicherman* v. *Korean Air Lines*,[534] which ruled that it was quite evident that the English word 'damage' or 'harm', which was reflected in the official French text of the Convention as 'dommage', has a wide application and was, in fact, used by the Warsaw Convention drafters in its classical French law sense of 'legally cognizable' harm.

It must be emphasized that, in selling an airline ticket for travel by air, an airline offers a composite service, not only to carry a passenger from point A to B, but also to ensure that transportation is accomplished in a safe and sanitary manner. Therefore the services offered by the airline in the area of clean air in the cabin become extremely relevant and critical to the issue.

The aerotoxic syndrome cannot be addressed in isolation, but should be considered as one more health-related occupational hazard for cockpit and cabin crew. Together with sleep loss-induced fatigue, and substance abuse cabins which permit smoking, the aerotoxic syndrome should be addressed within a composite health-related problem. To counter the collective problem, an airline has to adopt a safety culture which addresses issues of contamination in the aircraft with inherent difficulties related to crew resource management as common problems. Individual case studies and brainstorming should be carried out regularly to address potential problems and an efficient internal audit process should monitor progress made. A deficiency rectification system should be in place to remedy lapses without loss of time.

Airlines should strictly enforce the ICAO resolution on smoking[535] in the cabin, which quotes World Health Organization resolutions and those of the International Labour Organization to the effect that occupational health and safety are interrelated, and apply the same principle to air quality in general, supporting further research on the effects of contaminants on passengers and crew, particularly in relation to anoxia and hypoxia. Both cabin crew and technical crew should be encouraged to report instances of contamination and experiences of sick feeling within the cabin and cockpit, without the risk of reprisals from management. If these precautions are taken and measures adopted accordingly, an airline need not be concerned about being found guilty of reprehensible conduct.

8 PRIVACY OF AIRLINE PILOTS

Introduction

From a purely statistical standpoint, the 1990s were not favourable to aviation safety. The number of airline accidents for the decade increased by 28 per cent as compared to the previous decade and fatalities rose by 12.5 per cent. It is reported that a total of 11 950 people perished in 480 accidents in the decade, as against 10 600 fatalities in 370 accidents in the 1980s.[536] Of course, the number of passengers increased by 32 per cent and the number of flights also rose, by 30 per cent,[537] in the 1990s over the previous decade, making it possible to accept the notion that it would not be surprising to expect an increase in the accident rate of aircraft operated by commercial airlines.

Although most of the accidents that have occurred can be traced to identifiable causes, some accidents have yielded no coherent pattern of activity that would enable investigators to arrive at acceptable conclusions. The Silk Air crash was one of them. In December 1997, a Silk Air B737-300 operating a flight from Jakarta to Singapore crashed in Indonesia, killing 104 passengers and crew on board. Two theories regarding the accident are propounded: that some catastrophic malfunction of the aircraft led to the crash, or that the crew committed suicide.[538] The aircraft plunged vertically from its cruising altitude directly into the Musi River in Southern Sumatra without any distress signal being emitted or any indication from the cockpit to air traffic control that the aircraft was experiencing problems. Unfortunately, much of the debris had been washed away by the fast flowing waters of the river when accident investigation commenced, leaving little, if any, information for deduction as to the cause of the accident. A significant factor, however, was that both the cockpit voice recorder and flight data recorder had stopped functioning immediately prior to the commencement of descent. It is reported that the captain had been demoted from his position of flight instructor shortly before the crash and had allegedly been heavily in debt.[539]

The Singapore police investigating the crash had reportedly classified the case as involving suicide-cum-murder by the pilot.[540] The suicide theory had seemingly led to pressure being brought upon the family members of the pilot to release documents pertaining to the state of his affairs to the Air Accident Investigation Commission (AAIC) of Indonesia. Consequently, the documents were released by the deceased captain's family members in Singapore following pressure from authorities to lift secrecy laws governing personal bank accounts, in order that the state of mind of the captain prior to the crash could be determined.

At aviation law, the distinction between an accident which causes death or injury to passengers through a mechanical defect in the aircraft or other extraneous reason such as adverse weather conditions and an accident of an aircraft which is found to have been mechanically defect-free and travelling in turbulence-free weather is significant if, in the latter instance, the aircraft meets with an accident caused by the wilful misconduct of the carrier. In this instance, if the suicide theory were allowed to prevail, the dependants of passengers killed in the crash could argue that Silk Air was guilty of wilful misconduct in allowing a crew member whose mental state did not admit of his ability to fly an aircraft to do so.

Liability issues at air law

Warsaw Convention of 1929

Generally in law an accusation has to be proved by the person who alleges it. Therefore a presumption of innocence applies to an accused person until he is proven guilty. However, in the instance of carriage by air of passengers, the airline is presumed liable if a passenger alleges personal injury or if his dependants allege his death has been caused by the airline.[541] Of course the airline can show in its defence that it had taken all necessary measures to avoid the damage[542] or that there was contributory negligence[543] and obviate or vitiate its liability. This curious anomaly of the law imposing on the airline a presumption of liability is contained in the Warsaw Convention,[544] article 17 of which states:

> The carrier shall be liable for damage sustained in the event of the death or wounding of a passenger, if the accident which caused the damage so sustained took place on board the aircraft or in the course of any of the operations of embarking or disembarking.

To control the floodgates of litigation and discourage spurious claimants, the convention admits of certain defences the airline may invoke and above all limits the liability of the airline to passengers and dependants of deceased passengers in monetary terms. The Warsaw system therefore presents to the lawyer an interesting and different area of the law which is worthy of discussion.

Article 17 of the Warsaw Convention needs analysis in some detail in order that the circumstances in which a claim may be sustained against an airline for passenger injury or death be clearly identified. Further, the defences available to the airline and the monetary limits of liability need to be discussed.

The Warsaw Convention stipulates that an 'accident' should cause injury or death to a passenger[545] if it was to be considered for liability. Under the convention, two key factors govern the civil liability of airlines: the presumption of liability that is imposed upon the airline and the liability limits that apply to protect the airline from unlimited liability and spurious claimants. There are two other factors which operate as adjuncts to the initial concepts. They are that the airline may show certain facts in its defence to rebut the presumption and that, if the airline is found to be guilty of wilful misconduct, it is precluded from invoking the liability limits under the Warsaw Convention. Viewed at a glance, the said four concepts seem to be grouped into two sets of balancing measures. The end result is that, while on the one hand the airline is subject to stringent standards of liability, on the other it is protected by two provisions which limit its liability in monetary terms and allow a complete or partial defence in rebuttal of the presumption.

Article 20(1) of the Warsaw Convention provides that the airline shall not be liable if it proves that the airline and its agents had taken all necessary measures to avoid the damage or that it was impossible for the airline and its agent to take such measures. Shawcross and Beaumont are of the view that the phrase 'all necessary measures' is an unhappy one, in that the mere happening of the passenger injury or death presupposes the fact that the airline or its agents had not in fact taken all necessary measures to prevent the occurrence.[546] The airline usually takes such precautions as making regular announcements to passengers on the status of a flight, starting with instructions on security and safety measures that are available in the aircraft. These measures are taken by the airline to conform to the requirements of the Warsaw Convention that the airline has to take all necessary measures to prevent an accident in order that the presumption of liability be rebutted. Thus, in a case decided in 1963,[547] it was held that a passenger who leaves her seat when the aircraft goes through turbulent atmosphere is barred from claiming under the Warsaw Convention for personal injury. Here it was held that an admonition by the airline that the passengers were to remain seated with their seat belts fastened during the time in question was proof of the airline having taken the necessary measures as envisaged in the Warsaw Convention.[548] This case also established the fact that 'all necessary measures' was too wide in scope and that a proper interpretation of the intention of the Warsaw Convention would be to consider the airline being required to take all 'reasonably necessary measures'.

In a more recent case, Chapman J imputed objectivity to the phrase 'reasonably necessary measures' by declaring that such measures should be considered necessary by 'the reasonable man'.[549] A similar approach was taken in a subsequent case where the court held that the airline should show more than the fact that it was not negligent in order to invoke article 20(1) of the Warsaw Convention.[550] The United States also follows this approach of objectivity. In *Manufacturers Hanover Trust Co.* v. *Alitalia Airlines*,[551] it was emphasized that the airline must show that all reasonable measures had been taken from an objective standpoint in order that the benefit of the defence be accrued to the airline. Some French decisions have also approached this defence on similar lines and required a stringent test of generality in order that the criteria for allowing the defence be approved.[552]

The airline which has the burden of proof cannot seek refuge in showing that normal precautions were taken. For example, normal precautions in attending to the safety of the passengers prior to a flight is not sufficient. If, therefore, the airline cannot adduce a reasonable explanation as to why the accident occurred despite the reasonably necessary precautions being taken, it is unlikely to succeed in its defence.[553] In so far as the requirement of impossibility to take precautions is concerned, the courts have required clear evidence of the difficulties faced by the airline in avoiding the disaster. In one case of a crash landing the court required that it was insufficient for the airline to show that the aircraft was in perfect condition and that the pilot took all steps to effect a good landing. The airline had to show that the weather conditions were so bad that the aircraft could not land in another airport.[554] In *Haddad* v. *Cie Air France*,[555] where an airline had to accept suspicious passengers who later perpetrated a hijacking, the court held that the airline could not deny boarding to the passengers who later proved to be hijackers. In that instance the airline had found it impossible to take all necessary precautions and was considered sound in defence under article 20(1). A similar approach was taken in the case of *Barboni* v. *Cie Air* France,[556] where the court held that, when an airline receives a bomb threat whilst in flight and performs an emergency evacuation, a passenger who is injured by evacuation through the escape shute cannot claim liability of the airline since it would have been impossible for the airline to take any other measure.

If the airline proves that the damage was caused by or contributed to by the negligence of the injured person, the court may, in accordance with the provisions of its own law, exonerate the carrier wholly or partly from his liability.[557] Contributory negligence under the Warsaw Convention has been treated subjectively as and when cases are adjudicated. The courts have not set an objective standard as in the earlier defence. For instance, in *Goldman* v. *Thai Airways International Ltd.*[558] it was held that a passenger is not guilty of contributory negligence if he keeps his seat belt unfastened through the flight and suffers injury when there is no sign given by the aircraft control panel to keep the seat belt on. However, if a passenger removes a bandage or brace that he is required to keep on for an existing injury and he suffers injury in flight owing to the removal of the support, he will be found to have contributed to the negligence resulting in his injuries.[559]

Article 25(1) of the Warsaw Convention states that the airline shall not be entitled to avail itself of the provisions of the Warsaw Convention which exclude or limit its liability if the damage is caused by the wilful misconduct or by such default on the part of the airline as, in accordance with the law of the court to which the case is submitted, is considered to be equivalent to wilful misconduct. Article 25(1) extends this liability to acts of the agent of the airline acting within the scope of his employment and attributes such wilful misconduct to the airline. Such action as the failure of the technical crew of the aircraft to monitor weather conditions and the failure to execute a proper approach in adverse weather conditions are examples of wilful misconduct of the airline.[560] Similarly, the failure of a crew which is going off duty to inform the incoming crew of a defect in the aircraft or any such relevant issue which would affect the safety of the aircraft could be construed as an act of wilful misconduct on the part of the airline.[561]

The effect of article 25 is that the plaintiff becomes entitled to lift the limit of liability of the airline as prescribed in article 22 of the Warsaw Convention if he proves that the airline was guilty of wilful misconduct. Thus the burden of proof falls on the plaintiff and if he succeeds he may claim an amount over and above the prescribed limits of airline liability. The limitation of liability of the carrier that the Warsaw Convention imposes could be circumvented by the plaintiff proving that the carrier was guilty of wilful misconduct in causing the injury. Wilful misconduct as an exception to the limitation of liability rule appears in all three air law conventions that admit of liability limitations.[562] The original French text of the Warsaw Convention states that, if the carrier causes the damage intentionally or wrongfully or by such fault as, in accordance with the court seized of the case, is equivalent thereto, he shall not be entitled to claim the limitation of liability.[563] Drion[564] maintains that the English translation inaccurately states that the liability limitations of a carrier will be obviated if the damage is caused by his *wilful misconduct* or by such *default*.[565] The contentious issue in this question is, what kind of misconduct is required? Drion is of the opinion that, by approaching the issue in terms of conflicting concepts, the question whether *faute lourde* as proposed originally in the French text and for which there was an English equivalent of 'gross negligence' was in fact more appropriate than the word *dol* which now occupies the document and for which no accurate English translation exists, has emerged.[566] Miller[567] takes a similar view when she states that the evils of conceptualistic thinking that had pervaded the drafting of article 25, which rendered it destitute of coherence, has now been rectified by the Hague Protocol which has introduced the words 'done with intent to cause damage or recklessly and with knowledge that the damage would probably result'.[568]

This confusion was really the precursor to diverse interpretations and approaches to the concept of wilful misconduct under article 25 of the Warsaw Convention. The French government took steps by its Air Carrier Act of 1957 to rectify ambiguities in this area by interpreting *dol* in the convention as *faute inexcusable*, or deliberate fault, which implies knowledge of the probability of damage and its reckless acceptance without valid reason,[569] making a strong analogy with the Hague Protocol's contents. This interpretation, needless to say, brought out the question whether such reckless acceptance would be viewed subjectively or objectively.

The Belgian decision of *Tondriau* v. *Air India*[570] considered the issue of article 25 of the convention and the Hague interpretation. The facts of the case were usual, involving the death of a passenger and a consequent claim under the convention by his dependants. The significance of the case lay, however, in the fact that the Belgian court followed the decision of *Emery and others* v. *SABENA*[571] and held that, in consideration of the pilot's negligence under article 25, an objective test would apply, and the normal behaviour of a good pilot would be the applicable criterion. The court held:

> Whereas the plaintiffs need not prove, apart from the wrongful act, that the pilot of the aircraft personally had knowledge that damage would probably result from it, it is sufficient that they prove that a reasonably prudent pilot ought to have had this knowledge.[572]

The court rationalized that a good pilot ought in the circumstances to have known the existence of a risk and no pilot of an aircraft engaged in air transport ought to take any risk needlessly. The Brussels Court of Appeal, however, reversed this judgment and applied a subjective test, asserting that the Hague protocol called for 'effective knowledge'. Professor Bin Cheng seems to prefer the objective test in the interpretation of 'wilful misconduct' in article 25, on the grounds that a subjective test would defeat the spirit of the convention and that judges would be 'flying in the face of justice in search of absolute equity in individual cases'.[573]

Peter Martin, analysing the Court of Appeal decision in *Goldman* v. *Thai Airways International Ltd*,[574] agrees with Bin Cheng and criticizes the lower court decision which awarded Goldman substantial damages for injuring his hip as a result of being thrown around in his seat in turbulence, in an instance where the captain had not switched on the 'fasten seat belt' sign.[575] Martin maintains that Goldman failed to prove that the pilot knew that damage would probably result from his act, as envisaged in the Hague Protocol principle. Being an aviation insurance lawyer, Martin is concerned that, while the English courts have a proclivity towards deciding article 25 issues subjectively, insurance underwriters could view the breach of the limits stringently. Both on the count of the need for objectivity and on the count of the adverse effects on insurance, it is difficult to disagree with Cheng and Martin.

The question of air carrier liability and the approach taken in its context by the Warsaw Convention has seen the emergence of the scholarly analysis of two issues: should liability of the carrier be based on fault and consequently on the principles of negligence and limited liability, or should liability be based on strict liability? Drion, in his 1954 treatise on liability,[576] enquires into the various rationales and scenarios that may come up in an intellectual extrapolation of the subject. He examines the fact that an insurance system for liability, which would be inextricably linked to a strict liability concept, would be desirable, as a plaintiff would be able to claim compensation from an impecunious defendant through the latter's insurer, on the deep pocket theory,[577] and that insurance underwriters might, in their own interest, be impelled to formulate aviation accident preventive schemes, strengthening the effects of accident prevention.[578] Drion also puts forward eight rationales for the rebuttable limitation of liability presumption that appears in article 17, quantified by article 22 of the Convention: maritime principles carry a limitation policy; the protection of the financially weak aviation industry; the risks should be borne by aviation alone; the existence of back-up insurance; the possibility of the claimants obtaining insurance; limitation of liability being imposed on a *quid pro quo* basis on both the carrier and operator; the possibility of quick settlement under a liability limitation regime; and the ability to unify the law regarding damages.[579]

These rationales, and whatever else may form considerations of policy in the assessment of whether a liability system should be based on negligence or strict liability should be addressed with the conscious awareness that, while the convention imposes a rebuttable presumption of limited liability on the carrier, the contributory negligence of the plaintiff can exculpate the carrier and obviate or apportion compensation. More importantly, wilful misconduct of the carrier transcends liability limits and makes the liability of the carrier unlimited. Strict liability, on the other hand, as proposed in the Montreal Protocols 3 and 4,[580] does not admit of breaking liability limits, sets a maximum limit of compensation that the carrier has to pay, and makes this limit unbreakable by such extraneous factors as the carrier's wilful misconduct.

The ultimate question therefore is, does one keep the Warsaw–Hague concept of fault and limited liability, or does one embrace a system of strict liability which assures the aggrieved party of pecuniary recompense, while obviating the need for lengthy determinations of who was at fault after the fact? In other words, does one point a finger at the carrier in the first instance, then limit his liability and again break the limit if he is at fault, or make the carrier pay a sum of money, the maximum limits of which have been set, with the assurance that such limits would not shoot up unconscionably if the carrier was negligent?

The convention unified legal principles relating to air carrier liability, thus precluding the application of scores of differing domestic laws.[581] However, it did not succeed in presenting to the world unequivocally objective and quantified rules of liability. This precludes a plaintiff from knowing that, as a rule, he will be compensated if he is injured in an air accident, since the convention admits of challenge on the grounds of the plaintiff's conduct before, during or after the accident. The strict liability principle introduced by the Guatemala City Protocol[582] and carried through by the Montreal Protocols, on the other hand, has been applauded on the grounds that

> First, it gets money into the hands of the passengers much more quickly. Second, it saves transaction expenses which include legal fees and other substantial litigation costs. Third, it provides compensation to passengers in those factual situations where no responsible party is at fault, such as in an act of terrorism.[583]

Alexander Tobolewski points out very validly that actual aviation practice in terms of aviation insurance by the airlines has nothing to do with limitation of liability and claims, since airlines insure their fleets and liabilities for colossal amounts in the insurance market.[584] He suggests, therefore, the harmonization of the law and actual practice (presumably by infusing a more specific quantum in damages) and simplification of the system of recovery, *inter alia*, both of which strongly suggest a regime such as the one envisaged in the Montreal Protocols.[585] Werner Guldimann concludes:

> The most important and urgent matter in the present decade is the continuation of the efforts undertaken by ICAO to re-establish the former universality and uniformity of the Warsaw system by having the Montreal Protocols No 3 and 4 rapidly ratified by the greatest possible number of contracting States.[586]

The Montreal Convention of 1999

In May 1999, the Convention for the Unification of Certain Rules for International Carriage by Air was concluded in Montreal at an International Air Law Conference called by the International Civil Aviation Organization (ICAO) to modernize the Warsaw Convention which has been amended and supplemented over the years. The new convention modernized and consolidated a 70-year-old system of international instruments of private international air law into one legal instrument that will provide an adequate level of compensation for those involved in international air accidents. Article 17.1, which is similar to the corresponding provision in the Warsaw Convention, provides:

> The carrier is liable for damage sustained in case of death or bodily injury of a passenger upon condition only that the accident which caused the death or injury took place on board the aircraft or in the course of any of the operations of embarking or disembarking.

However, unlike the Warsaw Convention, which has no strict liability provisions, the new convention makes the carrier strictly liable for the first 100 000 special drawing rights (SDR) of damage and it cannot, by virtue of article 21.1, exclude its liability. The carrier's liability, however, can be wholly or partially exonerated, to the extent that the carrier proves that the damage was caused or contributed to by the negligence or other wrongful act or omission of the passenger. Unlike the Warsaw Convention, which breaks the limits of liability and makes the carrier's liability unlimited in the case of the carrier's wilful misconduct, the Montreal Convention obviates unlimited liability of the carrier by stipulating in article 21.2 that the carrier is not liable for damages in excess of 100 000 SDR if the carrier proves that the damage was not caused by the negligence or other wrongful act or omission of the carrier or that the damage was solely due to the negligence or other wrongful act or omission of a third party.

The distinction between the two conventions is quite subtle in that, whereas the Warsaw Convention *prima facie* imposes liability on the carrier and limits its liability, only to break the limits if the plaintiff proves misconduct, the Montreal Convention imposes strict liability up to a certain amount and places the onus of proof of negligence of the passenger or non-negligence of the carrier upon the carrier itself in order to retain the limit of liability. However, until such time as the Montreal Convention comes into effect, with 30 ratifications, the Warsaw Convention will still be considered applicable law in this area.

Mental health of pilots in command

With respect to medical fitness, Annex 1 to the Chicago Convention of 1944,[587] which is the seminal legal instrument regulating international civil aviation, contains, in 1.2.6.1, a standard according to which 'license holders shall not exercise the privileges of their licenses and related ratings at any time when they are aware of any decrease in their medical fitness which might render them unable to safely exercise these privileges'.

In 1.2.6.1.1 of the annex, a recommendation is addressed to all contracting states which 'should, as far as practicable, ensure that license holders do not exercise the privileges of their licenses and related ratings during any period in which their medical fitness has, from any cause, decreased to an extent that would have prevented the issue or renewal of their Medical Assessment'.

Paragraph 6.2.2 of the same annex provides a standard on the physical and mental requirement for any class of Medical Assessment and makes it mandatory for an applicant for a licence or its renewal to be free of, *inter alia,* 'any active, latent, acute or chronic disability ... such as would entail a degree of functional incapacity which is likely to interfere with the safe operation of an aircraft or with the safe performance of duties'. In accordance with 6.3.2.2 (Class 1 Medical Assessment for applicants for or holders of commercial pilot licences, airline transport pilot licences, flight navigator and flight engineer licences), 6.4.2.2 (Class 2 Medical Assessment for private pilot licences and glider and free balloon pilot licences) and 6.5.2.2 (Class 3 Medical Assessment for air traffic controller licences), the applicant shall not have an 'established medical history or clinical diagnosis of ... alcoholism, drug dependence ... such as might render the applicant unable to safely exercise the privileges of the license applied for or held'.

Annex 6 to the Chicago Convention, Part II, 4.12 deals with the fitness of flight crew members and states that 'pilot-in-command shall be responsible for ensuring that a flight: a) will not be commenced if any flight crew member is incapacitated from performing his duties by any cause such as injury, sickness, fatigue, the effects of alcohol or drugs; b) will not be continued beyond the nearest suitable aerodrome when flight crew members' capacity to perform functions is significantly reduced by impairment of faculties from causes such as fatigue, sickness, lack of oxygen'.

The question which would inevitably emerge from the suicide allegation in respect of the Silk Air crash is whether technical crew members should be assessed for mental stability in the course of the physical checks they undergo periodically. The International Federation of Airline Pilots' Associations (IFALPA) has reportedly insisted: 'The very rarity of the event [suicide] means the system is working, and we would not support any suggestions to institute random or periodic psychological testing.'[588]

In the above context, it becomes critical that, if financial records of a pilot in command are required to be divulged in order to ascertain his wilful misconduct, the plaintiff proves there is a causal nexus between the accident and the mental condition of the pilot in command. Also, if the carrier were to be found directly liable, the plaintiff would have to prove that the carrier concerned wilfully neglected to test the person concerned for mental instability, in spite of a requirement for such testing being in force. The operative criterion here would be the existence of such a requirement, which is vehemently denied by IFALPA. Captain Ted Murphy, President of IFALPA, has stated that suicide by a pilot has not been proved to be the cause of any airline accident. He claims that attempts to draw such conclusions about the Silk Air accident is purely speculative and premature.[589] Although, as discussed above, ICAO regulations require that it is mandatory for a pilot to be free of any latent mental disease or instability, nowhere is it explicitly or implicitly stated that, if such a condition exists in a pilot that would deprive him of the mental stability needed to pilot an aircraft safely, the carrier concerned would be held liable. Of course, if the carrier knew of such a condition or ought to have known the existence of danger, it would be viewed differently by the courts.

Privacy issues

The question of whether existing common law affords any principles which admit of the protection of the privacy of an individual was raised as far back as 1890,[590] and the conclusion was that the law did indeed recognize a right to privacy and that an invasion of this right would constitute a tort.[591] However, the right to free expression, as enshrined or otherwise embodied in many democratic states' constitutions, may seriously inhibit the scope of the tort, and as the United States Supreme Court eloquently described, 'the right could obliterate one of the most noteworthy legal inventions of the 20th Century; the tort of publication of private facts'.[592]

However, it has consistently been recognized that courts may, for purposes of establishing or addressing defamation issues, require private information to be divulged to a court as privileged communication. Warren and Brandeis have stated: 'The right to privacy does not prohibit the communication of any matter, though in its nature private, when the publication is made under circumstances which would render it a privileged communication according to the law of slander and libel.'[593] The libel and slander paradigm could be applied analogically to the instance of a claim for personal information, which may assist the court in the award of damages in respect of death or injury, where the public benefit is at stake.

In addition to the general principles discussed above, the Silk Air adjudication, which transcended territorial boundaries, may involve the need to discuss information stored by a bank as a modern multinational enterprise operating in several jurisdictions. In the Silk Air case, at least two jurisdictions – Indonesia and Singapore – were involved, and the issue that data stored by a bank's computer may flow on a trans-boundary basis to other branches of the bank before such data are released through a court order to the public is a matter of consideration. A noteworthy fact about trans-border data flow is that laws of privacy and disclosure, in the same manner as laws related to the collection, storage and dissemination of personal information, may differ from country to country. The advent of modern information systems poses a threat to the earlier principles governing the collection and storage of data and their release, which, in their pristine purity could be established clearly and in the context of the jurisdiction concerned. Now, owing to the complexities of computer data storage and the existence of diverse multinational privacy laws, courts may need to have recourse to a unified system of laws that have been set on a global or regional level.

A sound analogy in data flow harmonization is the document containing the OECD[594] Recommendations Concerning and Guidelines Governing the Protection of Privacy and Trans-border Flows of Personal Data,[595] made in 1980. The OECD Guidelines seek to strike a balance between discouraging restrictions on trans-border data flows and assuring privacy protection. This is done by expressly encouraging OECD member states not to restrict trans-border data flows to other member states while at the same time encouraging member states to adopt municipal laws protecting individual privacy within their territories. These two approaches are balanced in turn by the principle that an OECD member, which is the source of the data concerned, could restrict the flow of data from its territory to another member state only if that recipient state has not enacted privacy laws affording a subject the protection at least equivalent to that granted by the source state.

On the issue of the use of the data, disclosure to third parties can only take place if such disclosure falls within the scope of the originally specified purpose or if the disclosure is authorized by law.

The Council of Europe (COE)[596] Convention for the Protection of the Individual With regard to Automatic Processing of Personal Data,[597] adopted in 1981, applies to automated personal files such as those maintained at a bank and requires that, unless appropriate safeguards are established, certain sensitive data may not be automatically processed. Subsequent proposals made by the OECD in 1992 go a step further by requiring that each EC member state enacts legislation providing an identified minimum level of privacy protection, while effectively precluding member states from stopping trans-border data flows between EC member states on grounds of privacy protection. There is no indication in the proposal as to whether there could be a trans-border data flow between an EC member state and a non-EC member state. However, according to the 1992 European Draft Directive to United States Law,[598] if the United States law does not provide adequate protection within the meaning of the EC Directive, there could be no trans-border data flow from a member state of the EC to the United States.

There being no regional consensus in the form of a treaty in Asia on privacy aspects of trans-border flows of sensitive and personal information, courts would apply domestic laws as applicable, but the existing guidelines in Europe may prove to be analogically interesting to any region which contemplates harmonizing laws in this area.

In determining the justification for disclosing the deceased pilot's financial statements in order to determine his mental state, two key issues have to be addressed: first, if such records were disclosed, would the plaintiff have been able to establish a causal link between the fact that the pilot was heavily in debt and the mental state which may have impelled him to commit suicide; and second, does the pilot or his estate have a right to privacy which is inviolable or is such a right conditional upon the ability of the plaintiff to satisfy the above requirement?

Financial information of a person is personal to him. Personal information has been defined as that which consists of those facts, communications or opinions which relate to the individual and which it would be reasonable to expect him to regard as intimate or sensitive and therefore to want to withhold or at least to restrict their collection, use or circulation.[599] American common law identifies the public disclosure of embarrassing private facts about a person as a tort.[600] In order to be identified as a tort, public disclosure of embarrassing private facts should be made publicly, in that it should be disclosed to a large number of people as against a small group; the facts disclosed must be private; and the facts disclosed must be offensive to a reasonable person of ordinary sensibilities.

In general, for a breach of confidence action to succeed, three general requirements must be satisfied: the information must be confidential, in that it must be shared strictly between the parties intended, such as bank and client; the information should have been imparted under circumstances which imposed confidentiality on the keeper of such information; and there must be an unauthorized use of such information without the consent of the party or parties concerned.[601] Linked to the last requirement is the inexorable fact that confidential information may be disclosed for the public benefit. The seminal case of *Gartside* v. Outram,[602] decided in 1857, which held that disclosure of information that would prevent or shed light upon acts which are civil or criminal wrongs is justified, was embellished in a 1973 decision[603] which held that public disclosure of personal information, if such resulted in obviating or clarifying the mysteries of acts 'destructive of the country or its people' is within the law. Thus the need for disclosure of personal information and its use may outweigh considerations of confidentiality if the public interest is at issue.[604] In the 1981 case of *British Steel Corporation* v. *Granada Television Ltd*,[605] the House of Lords distinguished the release of information related to an act of mere incompetence from the release of information related to an act of wilful misconduct and concluded that one would be justified in releasing to the public personal information in the latter circumstances. In this case, the documents concerned reflected the issue of mismanagement in an institution, which, in the eyes of the House of Lords, was not sufficient to breach confidentiality. The defence of public interest in privacy litigation reached its highest recognition in 1984, when the Court of Appeal held that personal information could even be published in the press, irrespective of the method in which such information was obtained and the motive of the publisher, if disclosure of such information was of benefit to the public.[606]

The issue of privacy, as applicable to banking law, was initially recognized only as a partially investigated branch of the law.[607] However, in 1969, Diplock LJ put the issue of ambivalence regarding secrecy between banker and client to rest by observing:

> Such a duty exists not only between solicitor and client, but for example between banker and customer, doctor and patient and accountant and client. Such a duty of confidence is subject to, and overridden by, the duty of any party to that contract to comply with the law of the land … For example, in the case of banker and customer, the duty of confidence is subject to the overriding duty of the banker at common law to disclose and answer questions as to his customer's affairs when he is asked to give evidence on them in the witness box in a court of law.[608]

It is therefore clear from the above discussion that, in the perspective of a banker or, as in the case of the Silk Air accident, the relatives of the deceased captain, overriding power is wielded by the 'public interest' criterion, and a court order for disclosure of confidential financial details would render ineffective the general principles pertaining to privacy and the secrecy of information.

Comment

Although the public interest criterion is overriding and absolute, the disclosure of financial details of a deceased pilot in order to establish his state of mind, which in turn may impute wilful misconduct to the carrier, involves two key factors: first, the plaintiff must show, even if the financial details of the pilot were such that one could draw an inference that he would be desperate enough to commit suicide, that the state of mind of the pilot was at the time suicidal; second, the plaintiff must also show that the pilot in fact committed suicide. The probative potential of both these links is too tenuous and remote, in the absence of other circumstantial evidence such as statements by the pilot prior to or during the flight which give the inference of despair on his part.

Although in the Silk Air case the disclosure of financial information was calculated to obtain higher awards of compensation for the victims' dependants at values beyond the limitation of liability of the carrier as prescribed in the Warsaw Convention, it is difficult to envision how this could be done by the invocation of article 25 of the convention without a coherent linkage between the accident, the establishment of a suicidal mental state of the pilot and the fact of suicide.

NOTES

1 International Conference on the Reduction of Noise and Disturbance Caused by Civil Aircraft. See Michael J.T. Smith, *Aircraft Noise*, New York: Cambridge University Press, 1989, p.22.
2 Convention on International Civil Aviation, signed at Chicago on 7 December 1944, Doc 7300/8, 8th edn, 2000 (hereafter referred to as the Chicago Convention). See Annex 16, Aircraft Noise, 2nd edn, 1988 (first published simply as 'Aircraft Noise' in 1971).
3 See Lord Rayleigh, *The Theory of Sound*, 2nd edn, London: Dover, 1945, p.21. For more recent discussions on aircraft noise, see A.R. Frey and L.E. Kinsler, *Fundamentals of Acoustics*, 3rd edn, Chichester: Wiley, 1982, p.82 and P.M. Nelson (ed.), *Transportation in Noise Reference Book*, London: Butterworth, 1987, p.321.
4 K.D. Kryfer, *The Effects of Noise on Man*, Toronto: Academic Press, 1985, p.1.
5 D.V. Harper, 'Regulation of Aircraft Noise at Major Airports: Past, Present and Future', *Transportation Law Journal*, 17, 1988, 121.
6 Ibid., at 120.
7 J. Grey, *Noise, Noise, Noise*, Philadelphia: The Westminster Press, 1975, p.72.
8 Ibid.
9 Abey-wickrama *et al.*, 'Mental Hospital Admissions and Aircraft Noise', *Lancet*, 2, 7633, 1969, 1275–7.
10 Alexander Cohen, 'Noise and Psychological State', National Centre for Urban and Industrial Health, United States Public Health Service, Cincinnati, Ohio, 1968, 25pp.
11 (1936) 13 L.G.R. 73.
12 Ibid., 75.
13 *Williams* v. *Storey* (1957) 2 L.G.R.A. 226.
14 Ibid., 233; also 236.
15 Ibid.
16 [1962] N.S.W.R. 641.
17 Ibid., 644.

18 [1952] V.L.R. 222.
19 Ibid., 231.
20 Ibid., 241.
21 *Schofield* v. *City of Moorabbin* [1967] V.R. 22.
22 Ibid., 24.
23 [1976] 1 W.L.R. 1101.
24 Ibid., 1103.
25 *OECD and the Environment*, Paris, 1979, 108. This definition has also been adopted by the Law of the Sea Conference. See article 1(4), A/CONF.62/WP 10/Rev.3.
26 Charter of the United Nations and Statute of the International Court of Justice, United Nations, New York, article 1.3.
27 Ibid., article 13.1.b.
28 Article 55(*a*).
29 Article 55(*b*).
30 Article 62(1).
31 P. B. Stein, 'The Price of Success: Mitigation and Litigation in Airport Growth', *Journal of Air Law and Commerce*, 57, Winter 1991, 555.
32 Ibid.
33 See *Thornburg* v. *Port of Portland* (1962) 233 Or. 178, 376 P.2d. 100 at 101, note 1.
34 328 U.S. (1946) at p. 256.
35 The Fifth Amendment provides that private property shall not be taken for public use without payment of compensation. See also the cases of *Griggs* v. *Allegheny County* 326 U.S. at 84 (1962) and *Batten* v. *United States* 306 F.2d. 580 (10th Cir. 1962) which awarded damages for diminishing of value of property under the United States' Constitution.
36 *Supra,* note 33.
37 391 P.2d. 540 (1964).
38 Ibid., at p.545. See also *Aaron* v. *City of Los Angeles*, 40 Cal.App. 3d. 471, 115 Cal. Rptr. 162 (1974) which held that compensation should be awarded to persons for property values affected by aircraft noise even though the property was not located within a direct flight path of the Los Angeles airport.
39 The *Island of Palmas* case (1928) 11 U.N.R. I.A.A. at 829.
40 Ibid.
41 J.G. Starke, *Introduction to International Law*, 10th edn, London: Butterworths, 1989, p.3.
42 (1949) *I.C.J.R.* 1, 22.
43 J. Barros and D. Johnston, *The International Law of Pollution*, New York: The Free Press, 1974, p.69.
44 Charter of the United Nations and Statute of the International Court of Justice, *supra*, note 26, article 38(1).
45 Sharon Williams, 'Public International Law Governing Transborder Pollution', *University of Queensland Law Journal*, 13, 1984, 136–7.
46 W.V.H. Rogers, *Winfield and Jolowicz on Tort*, 2nd edn, Oxford: Clarendon, 1979, p.339.
47 *Nova Mink Ltd.* v. *Trans-Canada Airlines* [1951] 2 D.L.R. 241.
48 Ibid., 254.
49 *Per* Lord Atkin in *Sedleigh-Denfield* v. *O'Callaghan* [1940] A.C. 880, 886.

50 *Per* Dixon J in *Torette House Pty, Ltd.* v. *Berkman* (1940) 62 C.L.R. 637, 652.
51 *Salmond on Torts*, ed. R.F.V. Heuston, 17th edn, London: Butterworths, 1977, p.49.
52 *Per* Cleary J in *Morgan* v. *Kyatt* [1962] N.Z.L.R. 791, 794 (C.A.).
53 4 De G & Sm 315; [1851] 64 E.R. 849.
54 Ibid., 322. See also [1851] 64 E.R. 849, 852.
55 Ibid., 12.
56 *Per* Harris J in *Oldham* v. *Lawson* [1976] V.R. 654, 655.
57 *Haddon* v. *Lynch* [1911] V.L.R. 230.
58 *McKenzie* v. *Powley* [1916] S.A.L.R. 1.
59 *Daily Telegraph Co. Ltd.* v. *Stuart* (1928) 28 S.R. (N.S.W.) 291.
60 Ibid., 295, where his lordship cited *Harrison* v. *Southwark and Vauxhall Water Company* [1891] 2 Ch. 409.
61 [1930] S.A.S.R. 295.
62 *Field and Others* v. *South Australian Soccer Association (Incorporated) And Shields* [1953] S.A.S.R. 224, hereafter referred to as *Field*'s case.
63 (1872) L.R. 8 Ch. App. At 8. See also *Field*'s case.
64 [1906] 1 Ch. 234. See *Field*'s case, 231.
65 *McMahon* v. *Catanzaro* [1961] Qd.R. at 22 Q.W.N. 28.
66 *Aldridge* v. *Clough*, unreported S.C. Decisions of Western Australia No. 1246 of 1979.
67 [1930] S.A.S.R. 295 at 297.
68 [1930] St. R. Qd. 325.
69 *Victoria Park Racing and Recreation Grounds Company Ltd.* v. *Taylor and Others* (1937) 58 C.L.R. 479.
70 [1942] S.A.S.R. 213 [S. Ct.].
71 Ibid., 219.
72 Ibid., 220.
73 [1948] V.L.R. 269.
74 *Fraser* v. *Booth* (1950) 50 S.R. (N.S.W.) 113.
75 Ibid., 116.
76 (1953) 90 C.L.R. 170.
77 Ibid., 176.
78 [1955] V.L.R. 332.
79 Ibid., 335.
80 257 N.E. 2d. 870.
81 The defendant's investment in the plant was in excess of $45 000 000.
82 *Boomer*, *supra*, note 80, at 872–3.
83 [1961] 1 W.L.R. 683.
84 (1979) W.A.L.R. 771.
85 [1963] N.S.W.R. 1624. The facts of this case are similar to the facts of *Aldridge* v. *Clough*.
86 *Aldridge* v. *Clough*, *supra*, note 66, 11.
87 Ibid., 5.
88 *Supra*, note 61.
89 [1948] V.L.R. 269.
90 Ibid., 272.
91 [1955] V.L.R. 332.

92 Ibid., 337.
93 *Kidman* v. *Page* [1959] Qd. R. 53.
94 *Tipping* v. *St. Helen's Smelting Co.* [1865] 1 Ch. App. 66.
95 [1893] 2 Ch. 447.
96 Ibid., 449.
97 [1977] Q.B. 966 (C.A.).
98 Ibid., 986.
99 (1879) 11 Ch. D. 852. In this case the plaintiff, who was a physician, was hindered in his work by the noise and vibrations from the neighbouring confectionery shop.
100 [1977] Q.B. 966 at 986-7.
101 [1955] V.L.R. 332.
102 [1895] 1 Ch. 287. Lindley LJ stated at 316: 'Neither has the circumstance that the wrongdoer is in some sense a public benefactor (e.g., a gas or water company or a sewer authority) ever been considered a sufficient reason, for refusing to protect by injunction an individual whose rights are being persistently infringed' (cited at 337 in *Munro* v. *Southern Dairies Ltd*).
103 [1980] 3 All E.R. 329.
104 Ibid., 333.
105 Ibid.
106 [1977] Q.B. 966 (C.A.).
107 [1895] 1 Ch. 287.
108 The other remedies are abatement without recourse to legal proceedings, summary proceedings for penalties or abatement of statutory nuisances and criminal proceedings.
109 [1976] V.R. 654.
110 [1975] 1 All E.R. 787.
111 Ibid., 794., cited at 658 in *Oldham* v. *Lawson*, *supra*, note 109.
112 [1964] A.C. 326, cited at 658 in *Oldham* v. *Lawson*, *supra*, note 109.
113 *Bone* v. *Seale*, *supra,* note 110, at 795, and cited at 658 in *Oldham* v. *Lawson*, *supra*, note 109.
114 [1942] S.A.S.R. 213 [S. Ct.].
115 These instances were first discussed by Smith LJ in *Shelfer* v. *City of London Electric Lighting Company* [1895] 1 Ch. 287.
116 *Spencer* v. *Silva* [1942] S.A.S.R. 213 [S. Ct.] at 222.
117 257 N.E. 2d. 870.
118 [1973] 1 N.S.W.L.R. 466.
119 [1953] Ch. 149, *supra*, note 118.
120 Ibid., 188, cited at 467–8 in *Vincent* v. *Peacock.*
121 *Vincent* v. *Peacock*, at 468, *supra*, note 118.
122 [1980] V.R. 163.
123 *Per* Farwell J in *Royal Insurance Co. Ltd.* v. *Midland Insurance Co. Ltd.* (1908) 2 R.P.C. 95 at 100. This case is also cited in *Grasso* v. *Love*, *supra*, note 122, at 167.
124 [1980] V.R. 163 at 167.
125 I.C.F. Spry, *Equitable Remedies* (1971) 342–3.
126 Ibid. See also *Grasso* v. *Love* [1980] V.R. 163 at 167.
127 *Supra*, note 2.
128 Article 9.
129 Article 44(*a*).

130 Article 44(*d*).
131 Article 44(*n*).
132 Article 44(*i*).
133 Article 37(*b*).
134 For more details on CAEP, see L.F. Mortimer, 'Ambitious Programme of Future Work to be Undertaken by CAEP', *ICAO Journal*, August 1992, 6. See, also, John Crayston and Jane Hupe, 'ICAO facing complex and evolving challenges in the environmental field', *ICAO Journal*, September 1999, 5.
135 Only two aircraft that will meet standards beyond those prescribed in Chapter 3 of Annex 16 to the Chicago Convention will be in production after the year 2000, namely the Boeing 747-400 and the Airbus A321. It is expected that, by the year 2007, more than 70 per cent of the world airline fleet would meet the most stringent of the proposals under consideration by CAEP. See Chapter 3½ *The Avmark Aviation Economist*, January/February 1995, p.10.
136 See John Crayston and Jane Hupe, *supra*, note 134, 6.
137 See *Annex 16 to the Convention on International Civil Aviation*, 2nd edn, 1988, Vol. 1, Foreword.
138 Sonic boom was identified in 1970 as 'a phenomenon peculiar to supersonic flight. It is caused by the mach waves that an aircraft inevitably generates aerodynamically when it flies at a speed greater than that of sound. Roughly speaking these waves take the form of compression waves from the bow and the stern separated by expansion waves … these waves extend from the aircraft as an audible pattern of roughly conical shape, much as the water waves from a boat extend from it as a visible pattern of roughly v-shape, and just as the water waves from a boat cause a disturbance that often extends to and travels along a neighbouring shore as the boat passes by, so do these shock waves from an aircraft cause a disturbance that normally extends to and travels along the ground as the aircraft flies over. The passage of these shock waves is perceived as a sonic boom. See ICAO Doc 8894, SPB/11, at 1–5.
139 See ICAO Doc 9064, SBC/2, at 4–1.
140 See Assembly Resolutions in Force (as of 6 October 1989), ICAO Doc 9558 at II-18.
141 Assembly Resolutions in Force (as of 2 October 1998), ICAO Doc 9730, ICAO: Montreal, at I-36.
142 Perry Flint, 'Breaking the Sound Barrier', *Air Transport World*, 3, March 1999, 29.
143 It was reported that American Airlines is installing the Raisbeck System on 52 B 727 aircraft and hush-kitting 20 more. United is installing hush-kits on 75 B 727 aircraft and 24 B 737–200s. Delta is hush-kitting 104 727s and 54 737–200s. Southwest, TWA, Alaska Airlines and US Airways are other carriers who plan to hush-kit their Chapter 2 aircraft. See Perry Flint, ibid., 34.
144 David Esler, 'The Latest Noise about Noise', *Business and Commercial Aviation*, December 1999, 53.
145 'Europe Considers Delaying Hushkit Ban', *Aviation Daily*, Thursday 7 October 1999, p.1.
146 Article III of WTO requires each party to publish promptly all relevant laws, regulations, administrative guidelines and all other decisions, rulings or measures of general application, by the time of their entry into force.
147 WTO's national treatment philosophy provides foreign services and services suppliers

with treatment no less favourable than that accorded to a country's own services and service suppliers.

148 For a detailed discussion of the ITO, see Robert R. Wilson, 'Proposed ITO Charter', *American Journal of International Law*, 41(4), October 1947, 881 and 882.

149 U.N. Economic and Social Council, Official Records, 134th Session, 546th meeting (5/SR.546, 11 September 1951). See also Report of the *ad hoc* Committee on Restrictive Business Practices (E/2380, 30 March 1953).

150 *Focus Newsletter*, WTO, Geneva, January/February 1995, p.2.

151 See speech of Peter D. Sutherland, Director General of WTO, *World Trade Organization Press Release*, PRESS/1, 27 January 1995 (95–0156) at 1.

152 Ibid., p.5.

153 General Agreements on Tariffs and Trade, Multilateral Trade Negotiations Final Act Embodying the Results of the Uruguay Round of Trade Negotiations (done at Marrakesh, 15 April 1994), 33 *I.L.M.* 1125 (1994), Annex 1B, Part II Article II.

154 Ibid., article III.

155 Ibid.

156 See Matsushita, 'The Structural Impediments Initiative: an Example of Bilateral Trade Negotiation', *Michigan Journal of International Law*, 12(2), Winter 1991, 436–49.

157 *United States* v. *Aluminium Company of America*, 148 F. 2d 416 (2d Cir. 1945).

158 See BNA, *Antitrust and Trade Regulation Report*, vol. 67, no. 1685 (20 October 1994) at pp.488 *et seq*.

159 *Ahalstrom Osakeyhtio* v. *Commission* (1988) ECR 5193.

160 *United States* v. *The Watchmakers of Switzerland Information Center Inc. et al.*, 133 F. Supp. 40.

161 Ibid., 41.

162 731 F.2d 909 (1984).

163 Ibid., 910.

164 148 F. 2d 416 (2d Cir. 1945), *supra*, note 157.

165 731 F.2d 909 (1984) at 945–6.

166 *In re Uranium Antitrust Litigation, Westinghouse Electric Corporation* v. *Rio Algom Limited et al.* 473 F.Supp. 393 (1979).

167 A tying arrangement is the sale of one item (the tying product) only on condition that the buyer would take the second item (the tied product) from the same source. Such arrangements are *per se* unreasonable and violative of antitrust laws if the tie-in involves two distinct products, and the party has sufficient economic power in the tying market to impose significant restraints in the tied product market.

168 See, generally, Eleanor Fox, 'Antitrust, Trade and the 21st Century – Rounding the Circle', Record of the Association of the Bar of the City of New York, pp.535–88.

169 Petersmann, 'Proposals for Negotiating International Competition Rules in the GATT–WTO World Trade and Legal System', *Aussenwirtschaft*, 49, Jahrgang (1994), Heft II/III: Ruegger S. 231–77.

170 'Report of the GATT Secretariat to the Second Meeting on Sustainable Development', 16–31 May 1994, Let/1873, 94-0438.

171 'Note by the GATT Secretariat prepared for the Second Meeting of the Commission on Sustainable Development', included in the Report cited *supra*, note 170.

172 The World of Civil Aviation 1999–2002 – ICAO Circular 275–AT/115 at para. 5.2.

173 Ibid., para. 5.11.
174 Ibid.
175 Ibid., para. 5.30.
176 Chicago Convention. See ICAO Doc 7300/7, 7th edn, 1997.
177 Article 28 of the Chicago Convention calls on each contracting state, so far as it may find practicable, to provide airport and air navigation facilities, in accordance with the standards and practices recommended or established in pursuance of the convention.
178 Vienna Convention on the Law of Treaties, U.N. Doc A/CONF.39/27 (23 May 1969).
179 The *pacta sunt servanda* which is enshrined in Article 26 of the Vienna Convention provides that every treaty in force is binding upon the parties and must be performed by them in good faith. The validity of a treaty or of the consent of a state to be bound by a treaty may be impeached only through the application of the Vienna Convention, which by article 42.1 requires that one of the following circumstances exist: (a) that a treaty be derogated only in circumstances the treaty in question so specifies; (b) that a later treaty abrogate the treaty in question; and (c) that a *novus actus interveniens* or supervening act occur, making the performance of the treaty impossible. See R.I.R. Abeyratne, *Legal and Regulatory Issues in International Aviation*, New York: Transnational Publishers Inc, 1996, pp.11–20.
180 Doc 9082.
181 See R.I.R. Abeyratne, 'Taxation in the Field of International Air Transport – Legal Aspects', *Air and Space Law*, XVI(3), 1991, 106–18. Also by the same author, 'Recent Developments in Taxation of Air Transport – The ICAO–IATA Symbiosis', *Air and Space Law*, XX(2), April 1995, 48–59.
182 ANSConf-WP/4 at para. 5.1.
183 Ibid., para. 5.3.
184 *Supra*.
185 See ICAO Circular 3-AT/1, Airport Economics, May 1948 at p.9 for an early definition of 'airport'.
186 Rigas Doganis, *The Airport Business*, London & New York: Routledge, 1992, p.7.
187 The World of Civil Aviation, 1999–2002, *supra*, note 172, at p.52.
188 Ibid.
189 Ibid., p.53.
190 'Statements by the Council to Contracting States on Charges for Airports and Air Navigation Services', Doc 9082/5, 5th edn, 1997, para. 14.2.
191 Doc 9082/5, *supra*, note 190, para. 24.
192 Ibid., para. 14(vii).
193 *Airport Economics Manual*, 1st edn, 1991, Doc 9562, Chapter 6, para 6.3, p.50.
194 Ibid., para. 4.60, p.40. It should also be noted that certain concession-type facilities are established at an airport to provide services considered necessary for passengers, visitors and/or persons working at the airport. Such facilities may include cafeterias, post offices and tourist information counters. See *Airport Economics Manual*, *supra*, note 193, para. 6.11.
195 Conference on Airport and Route Facility Management (CARFM) 1991.
196 Doc 9161/3.

197 Marcel Boiteux, 'Peak-Load Pricing', in James R. Nelson (ed.), *Marginal Cost Pricing in Practice*, Englewood Cliffs: Prentice-Hall, 1964, p.59.
198 ANSConf-WP/14 at p.2.
199 ANSConf-WP/80 at p.2.
200 See Appendix, ANSConf-WP/14.
201 Report of the Conference on Economics of Airports and Air Navigation Services – Air Transport Infrastructure for the 21st Century, Montreal, 19–28 June 2000, Doc. 9764, ANSConf 2000, Recommendation 19.
202 Ibid., recommendation 20.
203 ANSConf-WP/14.
204 ANSConf-WP/54.
205 Chicago Convention, ICAO Doc 7300/7, 7th edn. 1997.
206 Ibid., article 10.
207 Ibid., article 68.
208 The World of Civil Aviation 1998–2002, *supra*, note 172, Table 5.6.
209 Outlook for Air Transport to the Year 2005, ICAO Circular 270-AT/111, p.37. See also A32-WP/105, p.4.
210 James Ott, 'Alliances Spawn a Web of Global Networks', *Aviation Week and Space Technology*, 23 August 1999, p.53.
211 Adam M. Pilarski, 'Columnist Bureaucrats and the Transition to the Market Economy', Neil Garston (ed.), *Bureaucracy: Three Paradigms*, Boston: Kluwer Academic Publishing, 1993, p.207.
212 Adam M. Pilarski, 'Airline Privatization: As a Response to Globalization', in Darryl Jenkins (ed.), *The Handbook of Airline Economics*, 1st edn, 1999, Washington, DC: Aviation Weekly Group, p.204. See also Maxim Boycko, A. Shleifer and R. Vishney, *A Theory of Privatization*, Boston: Howard University Press, 1993, p.1.
213 Harry P. Hatry, *Privatization: The Provision of Public Services by the Private Sector*, Jefferson, NC: McFarland & Company, 1999, p.263.
214 Ibid.
215 'Update', *Airport Privatization*, Airports Council International, no. 6 September 1998, p.4.
216 Ibid., p.3.
217 See 'Report of the Ad hoc Working Group on Comparative Experiences with Privatization on its Second Session', United Nations Conference on Trade and Development, Geneva, 1993, p.12.
218 *ICJ Reports* 1970, at 32.
219 Vienna Convention on the Law of Treaties, United Nations General Assembly Document A/CONF.39/27, 23 May 1969.
220 *Barcelona Traction, Light and Power Company Limited, ICJ Reports*, 1974, 253 at 269–70.
221 *Yearbook of International Law Commission*, New York: United Nations, 1976, vol. II, pt one, p.29.
222 *ICJ Reports*, 1970 at 32.
223 1925 RIAA ii 615 at 641.
224 *In Re. Chorzow Factory (Jurisdiction) Case (1927) PCIJ*, Ser. A, no. 9 at 21.
225 *ICJ Reports* (1949), 4 at 23.

226 Carl Q. Christol, *Space Law Past, Present and Future*, Deventer: Kluwer Law and Taxation Publishers, 1991, p.231.
227 Report of the International Law Commission to the General Assembly on the Work of the 1st Session, A/CN.4/13, 9 June 1949, at 21.
228 *Entick* v. *Carrington* (1765) 19 St. Tr 1030.
229 [1946] AC 543.
230 [1966] AC 552, [1966] 1 All ER 582, HL.
231 In *Fisher* v. *CHT Ltd. (No 2)* [1966] 1 All ER 88, CA, the owners of a club and the defendants who ran a restaurant in the club under licence from the club were both held to be occupiers. In *AMF International Ltd.* v. *Magnet Bowling Ltd.* [1968] 2 All ER 789, a contractor (as well as the owner) was an occupier of the whole building although part of the building was separated by a screen beyond which he went only to attend to heating and lighting. It is doubtful whether someone who has granted a right of way occupies that right of way: see *Holden* v. *White* [1982] QB 679, [1982] 2 All ER 328, CA. A highway authority which owns the land but has not adopted the highway is not an occupier of the highway: see *Holmes* v. *Norfolk County Council* (1981) 131 NLJ 401. A highway authority does not occupy a footpath on land owned by another although it has a statutory obligation to maintain it: see *Whiting* v. *Hillingdon London Borough Council* (1970) 68 LGR 437.
232 *Humphreys* v. *Dreamland (Margate) Ltd.* [1930] All ER Rep 327, HL.
233 *Hartwell* v. *Grayson Rollo and Clover Docks Ltd.* [1947] KB 901, CA. However, a contractor merely painting a house is not an occupier. See *Page* v. *Read* (1984) 134 NLJ 723.
234 *Hawkins* v. *Coulsdon and Purley UDC* [1954] 1 QB 319, [1954] 1 All ER 97, CA.
235 *Greene* v. *Chelsea Borough Council* [1954] 2 QB 127, [1954] 2 All ER 318, CA. See also *Harris* v. *Birkenhead Corporation* [1976] 1 All ER 341, CA where a local authority, having acquired a house by compulsory purchase, occupies it even before its staff enter it.
236 Cmd 9305.
237 Section 1.
238 Section 2(2) of the Occupiers' Liability Act, *supra*, note 237.
239 *Greenhalgh* v. *British Railways Board* [1969] 2 QB 286, [1969] 2 All ER 114, CA, *per* Lord Denning MR at 292–3.
240 Section 2(3).
241 *Cooke* v. *Midland Great Western Rly of Ireland* [1909] AC 229 at 238 (*per* Lord Atkinson), HL; also *Gough* v. *National Coal Board* [1954] 1 QB 191, [1953] 2 All ER 1283, CA. The cases are legion, but they all turn on their particular facts, as with, for example, *Williams* v. *Cardiff Corporation* [1950] 1 KB 514, [1950] 1 All ER 250, CA (a grassy slope with broken glass at the foot is a trap for a four-year-old child). The principle stated in the text also applied at common law in the case of adults suffering from mental or physical handicap and, it is submitted, will continue to apply to them under the Act.
242 See *Glasgow Corporation* v. *Taylor* [1922] 1 AC 44, HL which concerned liability for brightly coloured poisoned berries in a park and within easy reach of the child. Their decision can be contrasted with *D (a minor)* v. *Department of Environment (NI)* [1992] 4 BNIL 117, where there was no liability when a six-year-old climbed a tree and fell out.

243 See *Phipps* v. *Rochester Corporation* [1955] 1 QB 450, [1955] 1 All ER 129, containing an excellent review by Devlin J of the rights of child visitors which was applied in *Simkiss* v. *Rhondda Borough Council* (1982) 81 LGR 460, CA.
244 *Roles* v. *Nathan* [1963] 2 All ER 908, CA.
245 Here it is valid to consider whether 'danger' means the peril or the thing which creates the peril.
246 *White* v. *Blackmore* [1972] 2 QB 651, [1972] 3 All ER 158, CA.
247 Section 2(5).
248 *London Graving Dock Co. Ltd.* v. *Horton* [1951] AC 737, [1951] 2 All ER 1, HL.
249 *Bunker* v. *Charles Brand & Son Ltd.* [1969] 2 QB 480, [1969] 2 All ER 59. See also *McMillan* v. *Lord Advocate* 1991 SLT 150n.
250 *Longhurst* v. *Metropolitan Water Board* [1948] 2 All ER 834, HL; *Caminer* v. *Northern and London Investment Trust Ltd.* [1951] AC 88, [1950] 2 All ER 486; *Bolton* v. *Stone* [1951] AC 850, [1951] All ER 1078, HL. Sometimes it is not clear on which tort a judgment is based. See Denning LJ in *Mint* v. *Good* [1951] 1 KB 517 at 526, [1950] 2 All ER 1159 at 1168, CA.
251 [1948] 2 All ER 662; cf. *Wheeler* v. *Morris* (1915) 84 LJKB 1435, CA.
252 For example, *Hilder* v. *Associated Portland Cement Manufacturers Ltd.* [1961] 3 All ER 709, [1961] 1 WLR 1434. In this case the defendant occupiers of a field allowed children to play football in the field and were held liable to a motor-cyclist who, when driving along the adjoining highway, was knocked off his machine by a ball kicked by the children from the field.
253 *Hughes* v. *Percival* (1883) 8 App Cas 443, HL: the premises for the benefit of which the present rule applies are those in respect of which someone other than the defendant has a vested interest in possession. See also *Murphy* v. *Brentwood District Council* [1990] 2 All ER 908 and 926 (*per* Lord Bridge).
254 *Goldman* v. *Hargrave* [1907] 1 AC 645, [1966] 2 All ER 989, PC. Water normally percolates from the defendant's land to the plaintiff's, and the defendant pumps out the water from his land, and by so stopping the subterranean flow causes settlement damage to the plaintiff's land; the plaintiff has no remedy, because the defendant has no duty to adjoining occupiers in respect of percolating water; *Langbrook Properties Ltd.* v. *Surrey County Council* [1969] 3 All ER 1424, [1970] 1 WLR 161.
255 *Bradburn* v. *Lindsay* [1983] 2 All ER 408.
256 [1933] 1 KB 551; the principle on which this case was based was approved *obiter* by Parcq J in *Bishop* v. *Consolidated London Properties Ltd.* (1933) 102 LJKB 257 at 262.
257 [1918] 1 KB 247, CA (not cited in *Cunard* v. *Antifyre Ltd.*).
258 [1938] 2 KB 577 at 594–5 (*per* Greer LJ), [1938] 2 All ER 1, CA.
259 [1939] 3 All ER 329.
260 Convention on International Civil Aviation, signed at Chicago on 7 December 1944. See ICAO Doc. 7300/7, 7th edn, 1997.
261 Ibid., preamble at p.1.
262 Ibid., Article 44(*a*).
263 ITA Press 284, 1–5 April 1997, p.10.
264 Argentina, Brazil, Colombia, Costa Rica, Cuba, Dominican Republic, El Salvador and Panama.
265 ICAO Assembly Working Paper A31-WP/73, EX/26 at p.2.

266 Chicago Convention. ICAO Doc 7300/6.

267 See ICAO Assembly Working Paper A29-WP/39, EX/8, Appendix at p.8.

268 See R.I.R. Abeyratne, 'Aircraft Engine Emissions and Noise', *Environmental Policy and Law*, 24(5), September 1994, 238–50. See also, by the same author, 'General Principles of Liability of States as Providers of Space Technology in the Field of Air Navigation', *European Transport Law*, XXIV(5), 1994, 553–69; 'The Evolution from FANS to CNS/ATM and Products Liability of Technology Producers of the United States', *Zeitschrift für Luft-und Weltraumrecht* (German Journal of Air and Space Law), 43(2) June 1994, 156–86; 'The Liberalization of Air Transport Services with GATT: Some Legal Issues', *Trading Law and Trading Law Reports*, January–February 1994, 165–81; 'The Challenge of Airports and Planning Laws', *Environmental Policy and Law*, 23(2), April 1993, 262–74; 'Legal Aspects of the Unlawful Interference with International Civil Aviation', *Air and Space Law*, XVIII(6), 1993, 262–74; 'The Effects of Unlawful Interference with Civil Aviation on World Peace and the Social Order', *Transportation Law Journal*, 22(3), Spring 1995, 449–94; 'The Air Traffic Rights Debate – A Legal Study', *Annals of Air and Space Law*, XVIII(I) 1993, 3–44; 'The Economic Relevance of the Chicago Convention: A Retrospective Study', *Annals of Air and Space Law*, XIX(II) 1994, 3–80; 'The Worldwide Air Transport Conference and Air Traffic Rights – A Commentary', *European Transport Law*, XXX(2), 1995, 131–47; and 'Tobacco Smoking in Aircraft – A Fog of Legal Rhetoric?', *Air and Space Law*, XVIII(2)1993, 50–60.

269 See A31-WP/206, EX/87, 30/9/95, Corrigendum 2/10/95.

270 Annual Report of the Council 1996 (ICAO Doc. 9685) at p.2.

271 See 'ICAO Projects Long-Term Moderate Traffic Growth of 5 Per Cent per Year', a paper published by the ICAO Secretariat in *ICAO Journal*, December 1994, 20.

272 Saeed A. Al-Ghamdi, 'Alternative Approach to Implementation of CNS/ATM Systems Would Impose User Charge', *ICAO Journal*, April 1993, 20.

273 Ibid.

274 Provisional International Civil Aviation Organization: the predecessor of ICAO.

275 Report on the Conference on Air Navigation Services in Iceland, Geneva, 8–26 June 1948, ICAO Doc. 7000-JS/550, at 7.

276 Ibid., at 8.

277 Ibid., article 44.

278 Ibid., article 44(*c*).

279 Ibid., article 69.

280 Ibid., article 72.

281 Ibid., article 74.

282 Ibid., article 23.

283 Ibid., article 76.

284 Agreement on the Joint Financing of Certain Air Navigation Services in Iceland (1956), ICAO Doc. 9586-JS/682.

285 Ibid.

286 Ibid., article III(1).

287 Ibid., article VII(1).

288 Assembly Resolution A16-20.

289 Gerald F. Fitzgerald, 'ICAO and the Joint Financing of Certain Air Navigation Services', *Annals of Air and Space Law*, XII, 1987, 57, 59, 60.
290 See *Airline Business*, March 1998, p.35.
291 Report on the Conference on Airport and Route Facility Management, ICAO Doc 9579 – CARFM (1991), Recommendation 2/24 at p.38.
292 Statements by the Council to Contracting States on Charges for Airports and Air Navigation Services, 5th edn, 1997, Doc 9082/5 paras 32–3 at p.10.
293 Binal Ghosh, *Huddled Masses and Uncertain Shores*, Deventer: Martinus Nijhoff, 1998, p.4.
294 'The New Trade in Humans', *Economist*, 5 August 1995, p.45.
295 Paul J. Smith (ed.), *Human Smuggling*, Washington, DC: The Centre for Strategic and International Studies, 1997, p.9.
296 *Trafficking and Prostitution: The Growing Exploitation of Migrant Women from Central and Eastern Europe*, Geneva: International Organization for Migration (IOM), 1995, p.12.
297 Jonas Widgren, *Multilateral Co-operation to Combat Trafficking in Migrants and the Role of International Organizations*, Vienna: ICMPD, 1994, pp.5–6.
298 A/RES/51/60.
299 Revised Draft, United Nations Convention Against Transnational Crime, A/AC.254/4/Rev. 8, 7 April 2000.
300 Ibid., article 3.1(*b*).
301 Revised draft Protocol against the Smuggling of Migrants by Land, Air and Sea, supplementing the United Nations Convention against Transnational Organized Crime, A/AC.254/4/Add.1/Rev. 5, 20 March 2000.
302 Ibid., article 2.
303 Ibid., article 3.
304 Ibid., article 3 *bis*.
305 Facilitation Division, Report of the 7th Session, 14–30 May 1968, ICAO Doc 8750-FAL/564, Agenda Item 2.3, at 2.3–4. See also AT-WP 1079, 1/12/70, Attachment A, which sets out the Terms of Reference of the Panel.
306 Agenda Item at 2.3–5.
307 See ICAO, AT-WP/1183, 13/9/73, at 7 and 22. The passport card has been identified as a passport in card format as well as an improved conventional passport, both possessing machine-readable characteristics.
308 Ibid., at 8.
309 Pamela Shaw, 'Cutting Red Tape', *ICAO Journal*, January 1991, 8–9.
310 Ibid., 7.
311 Ibid.
312 The Technical Advisory Group comprised experts nominated by eight of the ten states that had originally participated in the ICAO Panel on Passport Cards. At present, the group has 12 members from ICAO contracting states, 12 observers from ICAO contracting states and three observers from international organizations.
313 Chicago Convention. For full text see ICAO Doc 7300/6, 7th edn, 1997.
314 See 'Machine-Readable Passports', ICAO Doc 9303/2, 2nd edn 1990, at 6.
315 'Machine-Readable Travel Documents', Doc. 9303, Part 2, Machine-Readable Visas, 1st edn, 1992. The second edition of this document was released in 1994.

316 See 'Machine-Readable Travel Documents', Doc. 9303, Part 3, Size 1 and Size 2 Machine-Readable Official Travel Documents, 1st edn, 1996.
317 'Machine-Readable Travel Documents', Doc. 9303, Part 4, Machine-Readable Crew Member Certificate, 1st edn, 1996.
318 See Report of the Technical Advisory Group on Machine-Readable Travel Documents, 11th Meeting, TAG-MRTD/11 Report, Montreal, 1–3 September 1999.
319 Ibid., para 2.1.3.
320 See FAL/10-WP/17, Recommendation A.
321 Facilitation Division, Report of the Tenth Session (7–23 September 1988), ICAO Doc. 9527, FAL/10 (1988), Recommendation No. A-44.
322 Annex 9 to the Chicago Convention, Recommended Practice 3.5.1.
323 See FAL/10-WP/18, 29/1/88.
324 Annex 9, Chicago Convention, 10th edn, Recommended Practice 3.8.1.
325 Annex 9, Chicago Convention, 10th edn, April 1997, at 3.5.2.
326 The full text of the resolution is as follows:

International co-operation in protecting the security and integrity of passports

Whereas the passport is the basic official document which denotes a person's identity and citizenship and provides an assurance for the State of transit or destination that the bearer can return to the State which issued the passport;
Whereas international confidence in the security and integrity of the passport is of prime importance in the functioning of the international travel system;
Taking into account the resolution adopted by the United Nations General Assembly which requests that ICAO consider ways and means to enhance international co-operation to combat the smuggling of aliens, while emphasizing that such efforts should not undercut the protection provided by international law to refugees;
Taking into account the resolutions adopted by the United Nations General Assembly and the Economic and Social Council which request that Member States establish or improve procedures to permit the ready discovery of false travel documents, that States co-operate bilaterally and on a multilateral basis to prevent the use of fraudulent documents, and that States take measures to provide penalties for the production and distribution of false travel documents and the misuse of international commercial aviation; and
Whereas high level co-operation among States is required in order to strengthen resistance to passport fraud, including the forgery or counterfeiting of passports, the use of forged or counterfeit passports, the use of valid passports by imposters, the misuse of authentic passports by rightful holders in furtherance of the commission of an offence, the use of expired or revoked passports, and the use of fraudulently-obtained passports.

The Assembly:
1. *endorses* the actions taken by the Council through the Air Transport Committee to strengthen and approve specifications for machine readable passports as they relate to security of such documents;
2. *requests* the Council to study specific actions and measures for enhancing the effectiveness of controls on passport fraud, including the possible preparation of

necessary SARPs and guidance material, to be implemented by Contracting States in the interests of maintaining the integrity and security of passports and other travel documents; and

3. *calls upon* all Contracting States to intensify their efforts to safeguard the security and integrity of their passports, to protect their passports against passport fraud, and to assist one another in these matters.

327 Chicago Convention, *supra*, note 313.
328 Annex 9, *supra,* note 322, Chapter 3, section E, 3.38.1.
329 Ibid., 3.38.
330 Ibid., 3.38.2.
331 Ibid., 3.39.
332 Ibid.
333 Ibid., 3.39.1.
334 Ibid., 3.40.3.
335 Ibid., Recommended Practice 3.40.2.
336 It is noteworthy that the ICAO Facilitation Panel which met in Montreal, from 17 to 21 November 1997, has suggested two new Recommended Practices to Annex 9 which provide:

1 the appropriate public authorities of Contracting States either singly or jointly should enter into co-operative arrangements such as memoranda of understanding with the airlines providing international services to and from that State, setting out guidelines for their mutual support and co-operation in countering the abuses associated with travel document fraud. Such arrangements should assign mutual responsibilities to the public authorities and to the airlines, in the ascertainment of the validity and authenticity of the travel documents of embarking passengers, and in the necessary steps to prevent the loss or destruction of documents by passengers en route to their destinations; and

2 Contracting States are encouraged to make arrangements such as memoranda of understanding (MOUs) with other Contracting States with the intention of permitting the positioning of 'liaison officers' at airports or to establish other forms of international co-operation in order to assist airlines to establish the validity and authenticity of the passports and visas of embarking passengers. (See Facilitation Panel Report, First Meeting, Montreal, 17–21 November 1997, at 1–4).

337 For a more detailed discussion of the legal nature of the passport, see R.I.R. Abeyratne, 'The Development of the Machine Readable Passport and Visa and the Legal Rights of the Data Subject', *Annals of Air & Space Law*, XVII (II), 1992, 12–14.
338 In conformity with article 22 of the Chicago Convention, which confirms the agreement of all contracting states to adopt all practicable measures to prevent unnecessary delays to aircraft, passengers and crews, especially in the administration of laws relating to immigration, quarantine customs and clearance, ICAO is actively seized of the development of a machine-readable travel document which uses various devices to secure the passport, visa and other travel documents against fraud.
339 *R.* v. *Halmo* (1941) 76 C.C.C. 116 (Ont. C.A); also *R.* v. *Kulbacki* (1966) 1 C.C.C. 167 (Man. C.A.).

340 *R.* v. *Nixon* (1990) 80 C.C.C. (3d) 16 at 21 (Ont. C.A.).
341 849 F Supp. 276 (SDNY 1994).
342 Ibid., 281.
343 'SPT – Covering the Legalities for Vision and Reality', *Airlines International*, IATA, March–April 2000, p.62.
344 *The New Encyclopedia Britannica*, vol. 11, Micropaedia, 15th edn, p.739.
345 Ibid.
346 See Brian Dexter, 'Cramped Airline Seats can Kill, Studies Find', *The Toronto Star*, 30 January 2000, p.2.
347 R. Virchow, *Gessamelte Abhandlungen zur Wissenschaftlischen*, Frankfurt: Meidinger, 1856, p.324.
348 K. Simpson, 'Shelter Deaths from Pulmonary Embolism', *Lancet*, vol. 2, 1940, 744.
349 J. Homans, 'Thrombosis of the Deep Leg Veins due to Prolonged Sitting', *N. Engl. J. Med.*, 250, 1954, 148–9.
350 See P.H. Beighton and P.R. Richards, 'Cardiovascular Disease in Air Travel', *British Heart Journal*, 30, 1968, 367–72; R.E.C. Collins and S. Field, 'Thrombosis of Leg Arteries after Prolonged Travel', *British Medical Journal*, 1979, 1478; J.M. Cruickshank, R. Gorlin and B.B. Jennett, 'Air Travel and Thrombic Episodes: The Economy Class Syndrome', *Lancet*, 1988, 497–8; J. Holliday, 'Atypical Presentation of Multiple Pulmonary Embolism in a Young Air Traveller', *J. R. Coll. Gen. Prac.*, 1985, 497; J. Homans, 'Thrombosis of the Deep Leg Veins due to Prolonged Sitting', *N. Engl. J. Med*, 250, 1954, 148–9; J.A. Lederman and A. Keshavarzian, 'Acute Pulmonary Embolism following Air Travel', *Postgrad. Med. J*, 59, 1983, 104–5; M. Naide, 'Spontaneous Venous Thrombosis in Legs of Tall Men', *JAMA*, 148, 1952, 1202;, I.S. Symington and B.H.R. Stack, 'Pulmonary Thromboembolism after Travel', *Br. J. Chest*, 71, 1977, 138–40.
351 Farhad Sahiar and Stanley R. Mohler, 'Economy Class Syndrome', *Aviation, Space and Environmental Science*, October 1994, 957.
352 Ibid., p.3.
353 Mercer A. Brown, 'Venous Thromboembolism Associated with Air Travel: A Report of 33 Patients', *Aviation, Space and Environmental Medicine*, 69(2), 1998, 154–7.
354 Ibid., at 155.
355 See R. Sarvesvaran, 'Sudden Natural Deaths Associated with Commercial Air Travel', *Med Sci Law*, 1, 1986, 38.
356 R. Milne, 'Venous Thromboembolism and Travel; Is there an Association?', *J.R. Coll Physicians*, vol.1, 1992, 49.
357 The term 'economy class syndrome' was ironically coined by a business class traveller. See J.M. Cruickshank, R. Gorlin and B. Jennett, 'Air Travel and Thrombic Episodes: the Economy Class Syndrome', *Lancet*, 2, 1988, 498.
358 *Tseng* v. *El Al Israel Airlines*, 1195 ct. 662 (1999).
359 *Air France* v. *Saks*, 470 U.S. 390 at 404 (1985).
360 *Laor* v. *Air France*, 1998 WL 886979 (SDNY 18 December 1998).
361 Convention for the Unification of Certain Rules for International Carriage by Air, done at Montreal on 28 May 1999.
362 Ibid., article 21.2(*a*) and (*b*).
363 Convention for the Unification of Certain Rules Relating to International Carriage by Air, 12 October 1929.

364 1999 Westlaw 7724 (12 January 1999).
365 John G. Fleming, *The Law of Torts,* 6th edn, Sydney: The Law Book Company, 1983, p.1.
366 Warsaw, 4–12 October 1929.
367 *Supra*, note 363.
368 *Second International Conference on Private International Law, 4–12 October 1929, Warsaw, Minutes* (translated by Robert C. Horner and Didier Legrez), Littleton CO: Fred B. Rothman & Co, 1975, p.21.
369 Ibid., p.58.
370 Ibid., pp.59–66.
371 Ibid., pp.251–2.
372 Fleming, *supra*, note 365, p.2.
373 Robert H. Horner and Didier Legrez, *supra*, note 368, p.47.
374 Lee S. Kreindler, 'The IATA Solution', *Lloyd's Aviation Law*, 14(21), 1 November 1996, 5.
375 Ibid., 6.
376 Sean Gates, 'IATA Inter Carrier Agreement – The Trojan Horse for a Fifth Jurisdiction?', *Lloyd's Aviation Law*, 14(23), 1 December 1995, 2.
377 *Shawcross and Beaumont Air Law*, 4th edn, reissue 1988, VII(152).
378 Ibid., VII(116).
379 Ibid., VII(117).
380 Chicago Convention, Annex 13.
381 *Shawcross and Beaumont Air Law*, 4th edn, reissue, 1988, VII(153).
382 *Air France* v. *Saks* 105 S. Ct. 1338 (1985).
383 Ibid.
384 *Husserl* v. *Swiss Air Transport Co. Ltd.* 485 F.2d. 1240 (2nd Circ. 1975); *Day* v. *Trans World Airlines Inc.* 528 F2d 31 (2nd Circ. 1975); *Evangelinos* v. *Trans World Airlines Inc.* 550 F2d. 152 (3rd Circ. 1976). See also *Salerno* v. *Pan American World Airways* 19 Avi Cas 17,705 (SDNY 1985).
385 *Arkin* v. *Trans International Airlines Inc.* 19 Avi Cas 18,311 (EDNY 1985).
386 *Abdulrahman Al-Zamil* v. *British Airways Inc.* 770 F2d. 3 (2nd Circ. 1985).
387 *Seguritan* v. *Northwest Airlines Inc.* 86 A.D. 2d. 658 (2d Dept. 1982). See also *Lloyd's Aviation Law*, 1(4) August 1982, 1.
388 *Vincenty* v. *Eastern Airlines* 528 F. Supp. 171 (D.P.R. 1982). Also *Lloyd's Aviation Law*, 1(3) July 1982, 2.
389 *Sprayregen* v. *American Airlines Inc.* 570 F. Supp. 16 (SDNY 1983). See also *Warshaw* v. *Trans World Airlines Inc.* 443 F. Supp. 400 (ED Pa. 1977); *Pironneau* v. *Cie Air-Inter* (Pan CA 3 July 1986). Cf. *De Marines* v. *KLM Royal Dutch Airlines* 586 F 2d 1193 (3rd Circ. 1978).
390 See *Warshaw* v. *Trans World Airlines Inc*, *supra*, note 389.
391 *O'Leary* v. *American Airlines* 475 NYS 2d. 285 (A.D. 2d Dept. 1984).
392 105 S. Ct. 1338 (1985).
393 Ibid., 1345.
394 *Abramson* v. *Japan Airlines Company Ltd.* 739 F. 2d. 130 (3rd Circ. 1984).
395 *Scherer* v. *Pan American World Airways Inc.* 387 NYS 2d. 581 (1976).
396 Supra, note 387.
397 *Rosman* v. *Trans World Airlines Inc.* 34 NY 2d. 385 (1974).

398 *Husserl* v. *Swiss Air Transport Co. Ltd.* 388 F. Supp 1238 (SDNY 1975).
399 *Krystal* v. *BOAC* 403 F. Supp. 1332 (DC Cal. 1975); *Karfunkel* v. *Cie Nationale Air France* 427 F. Supp. 971 (SDNY 977); *Borham* v. *Pan American World Airways Inc.* Avi Cas. 18,236 (SDNY 1977).
400 See R.I.R. Abeyratne, 'The Human Stress Factor and Mental Injury in American Tort Law – A Patchwork Quilt?', *The Anglo American Law Review*, 15(4), 1986, 338–60.
401 398 S.W.2d. 170.
402 Ibid., at 273–4.
403 19 Avi Cas (CCH) 17,377 (SDNY 1985).
404 606 F. Supp. 656 (SDNY 1985).
405 Ibid.
406 *Supra*, note 387.
407 Bin Cheng, 'What is Wrong with the Montreal Additional Protocol No. 3?', *Air Law*, XIV (6), 1989, 232.
408 The Warsaw Convention of 1929 was amended by The Hague Protocol, 1955; the Guadalajara Convention, 1961; the Guatemala City Protocol, 1971; and the Montreal Protocols, 1, 2, 3, 4, of varying dates. It should also be noted that the Montreal Agreement of 1966, a private arrangement between air carriers, also purported to amend the Warsaw Convention. Hereafter, joint references to all these instruments will be referred to as the 'Warsaw system'.
409 Peter Martin, '50 Years of the Warsaw Convention, A Practical Man's Guide', *Annals of Air and Space Law*, IV, 1979, 234.
410 Ibid.
411 Bin Cheng, 'Wilful Misconduct, From Warsaw to the Hague …', II, *Annals of Air and Space Law*, 1977, 99. 55. René Mankiewicz also uses the word 'shambles' when he describes the Warsaw Convention. See René H. Mankiewicz, 'From Warsaw to Montreal With Certain Intermediate Stops', *Air Law*, XIV (4), 1989, 26.
412 Peter Martin, *supra*, note 409, 239.
413 *Warren* v. *Flying Tiger Line Inc.* 352 F. 2d. 494 (CA9 1965); *Mertens* v. *Flying Tiger Line Inc.*, 341 F. 2d. 841 (CA2 1965).
414 21 Avi 18,228 (1989).
415 [1983] 3 All ER 693.
416 D.A. Kilbride, 'Six Decades of Insuring Liability Under Warsaw', *Air Law*, XIV (4/5), 1989, 187.
417 18 Avi 17,778, 1984.
418 *SS Pharmaceutical Co. Ltd.* v. *Qantas Airways Limited* [1988] 1 *Lloyd's Law Reports* 319.
419 *Tasman Pulp and Paper Co. Ltd.* v. *Pan American World Airways Inc.* and others; see *Annals of Air and Space Law*, XI, 1987, 323 for a detailed account.
420 Ref. LE 3/27, 3/28–91/3, at 5.
421 Mankiewicz, *supra*, note 411, 59.
422 Michael Milde, 'ICAO Work on the Modernization of the Warsaw System', *Air Law*, XIV (4/5), 1989, 206.
423 *Supra*, note 387.
424 *Supra*, note 391.
425 See Convention for the Unification of Certain Rules Relating to International Carriage

by Air, signed at Warsaw on 12 October 1929, reproduced in *Annals of Air and Space Law,* XVIII (II), 1993, 339.

426 Ibid., article 25.2.

427 H. Drion, *Limitation of Liabilities in International Air Law,* The Hague: Martinus Nijhoff, 1954, para. 181, p.212.

428 Ibid., para. 181.2, p.213.

429 Ibid., paras 181.4 and 5, p.213.

430 *Second International Conference on Private International Law, 4–12 October 1929, Warsaw, Minutes*, translated by Robert C. Horner and Didier Legrez, Littleton CO: Fred B. Rothman, 1975, p.42.

431 [1952] 2 All ER 1016 at 1022.

432 *Goepp* v. *American Overseas Airlines*, New York Supreme Court, Appellate Division (1st Dep) 16 December 1952; [1952] US Av R 486; IATA ACLR, No. 12.

433 *Grey* v. *American Airline Inc.* 4 Avi. 17,811 (2d Cir. 1955).

434 *Wing Hang Bank Ltd* v. *Japan Air Lines Co.* 12 Avi. 17,884 (SDNY 1973).

435 932 F.2d 1475, 1479 (D.C. Cis), cert denied, 1125.ct.616 (1991).

436 No. 93 C 1510, 1994 Westlaw 17 1522 (N.D. Ill. 2 May 1994).

437 Ibid.

438 *Supra*, note 435.

439 866 F. Supp. 588 (DDC 1994).

440 Ibid.

441 1995 Westlaw 151 793 (EDNY 27 March 1995).

442 No. 94–2392 (6 Cir. 15 March 1996).

443 Ibid.

444 25 Avi. Cas (CCH) 17, 259 (Sup. Ct. App. Tm. N.Y. 1st Dep't. 1996).

445 920 F. Supp. 408 SPNY (1996).

446 See *Koirola* v. *Thai Airways International*, 1996, Westlaw 402403 (N.D. Calif. 26 January 1996).

447 See 'Thai Airways found Guilty of Wilful Misconduct in 1992 Kathmandu Crash Litigation', *Lloyd's Aviation Law*, 15(6), 15 March 1996, 1.

448 Ibid., 2–3.

449 86 F. 3d 498 (6th Cir. 1996).

450 1999 Westlaw 7724 (12 January 1999).

451 'Contaminated Cabins Can Spread Disease, Special Report: Cabin Safety', Highlights of the Southern California Safety Institute's 17th Annual International Cabin Safety Symposium, Part II, Disease in the Cabin, *Air Safety Week*, 14(11), 20 March 2000, Washington, DC, p.1.

452 See Ruwantissa I. R., Abeyratne, 'The Spread of Tuberculosis in the Aircraft Cabin – Issues of Carrier Liability', *Transportation Law Journal*, 27(1), Winter 2000, 42–3.

453 *Supra*, note 451, p.2.

454 See R.B. Rayman and C.B. McNaughten, 'Smoke/fumes in the Cockpit', *Aviation Space and Environ. Med.*, 54, 1983, 738–40; L.B. Smith, B. Bhattacharya, G. Lemasters, P. Succop, E. Puhula, M. Medvelovic and J. Joyce, 'Effect of Chronic Low Level Exposure to Jet Fuel on Postural Balance of US Air Force Personnel', *Journal of Occupational and Environmental Medicine*, 39, 1997, 625–32.

455 ESA, 'Atmosphere Quality Standard in Manned Space Vehicles', European Space

Agency P55-03-401, Paris, June 1992, 7. Also R.B. Raymond and C.B. McNaughten, *supra*, note 454, 739.

456 Douglas McArthur, 'Frequent Flying may be hazardous to your Health', *The Globe and Mail*, Wednesday 17 May 2000, p. R12.

457 Ibid.

458 Alex Kirby, 'Air Crews Fear Toxic Leak Effects', *BBC News*, SCI/TECH (*http://news.bbc.co.uk/hi/english/sci/tech/newsid_946000/946943.stn*).

459 Ibid. According to the same report, an Australian pilot has reportedly claimed that he frequently smelt a strange odour on the aircraft he was piloting – a vomit-type smell, like dirty socks or an acrid, oily smell.

460 J.J. Cottrell, B.L. Leibovitz, R.G. Fennell and G.M. Kohn, 'Inflight Arterial Saturation: Continuous Monitoring by Pulse Oximetry', *Aviation Space Environ. Med.*, 66, 1995, 30–126.

461 H.N. Huttgren, 'High Altitude Medical Problems, Current Topics in Medicine', *Sci. Am. Med.*, IX, 1992, 16.

462 C. Thibeault, 'Cabin Air Quality, Special Committee Report: Cabin Air Quality', *Aviation Space Environ. Med.*, 68, 1997, 2.

463 'Carbon Monoxide Levels in Cabins Need to be Measured for Potential Hazard, Expert Urges', *Air Safety Week*, Washington, DC, 13(42), 18 October 1992, p.1.

464 Pierre Sparaco, 'Combating Fatigue to Enhance Safety', *Aviation Week and Space Technology*, 4, 1996, p.49.

465 Ibid., p.54.

466 See Morris L. Hawk, 'The Kingdom Ends, In re Cincinnati Radiation Litigation and the Right to Bodily Integrity', *Case Western Reserve Law Review*, 45, 1995, 977–97.

467 483 U.S. 699 (1987).

468 494 U.S. 210 (1990).

469 15 Av. Cas. (CCH), 18, 235 (Iowa Sup. Ct. 1980).

470 Ibid., 18, 238.

471 Michael Grossman and Philip Price, *Tobacco Smoking and the Law in Canada*, Toronto: Maxwell, 1992, section 16.

472 W. Winfield and B. Jolowicz, *Winfield and Jolowicz on Tort*, 12th edn, London: Butterworths, 1984, p.54.

473 Ibid.

474 See A.S.R. Peffers, J. Bailey, G.L. Barrow *et al.*, 'Vibrio parahemolyticus gastroenteritis and international air travel', *Lancet*, 1, 1973, 143–5. See also R.G.A. Sutton, 'An Outbreak of Cholera in Australia due to Food Served in Flight on an International Aircraft', *Journal of Hygiene*, 72, 1974, 441–51; M.S. Eisenberg, K. Gaarslev, W. Brown *et al.*, 'Staphylococcal Food Poisoning During Air Travel', *Lancet*, 2, 1975, 595–9; and F.R. Ratzinger, 'Disease Transmission by Aircraft', *Aeromedical Review*, 4, 1965, 1–10.

475 'Tuberculosis and Air Travel', Guidelines for Prevention and Control, WHO/TB/98–25 World Health Organization, Geneva, 1998, at p.7. The humidity level of a home or office building is usually 40–60 per cent.

476 See Farrol Kahn, 'Sick Aircraft', *The Aviation Quarterly*, 3, July 1998, 166.

477 Chicago Convention, 7th edn, 1997, Doc. 7300/7.

478 World Health Organization, *International Health Regulations*, 3rd annotated edn, Geneva: WHO, 1983.

479 *R.* v. *Sansregret* (1985) 18 CCC (3d) 223 (S.C.D.).
480 The other types of wrongs are wrongs exclusively criminal; civil wrongs which create no right of action for unliquidated damages, but give rise to some other form of civil remedy exclusively; and civil wrongs which are exclusively breaches of contract.
481 This definition of a tort was cited with approval in the case of *Anglo-Saxon Petroleum Co. Ltd.* v. *Damant* [1947] K.B. 794 at 796 and in *Philip Morris Ltd.* v. *Airley* [1975] V.R. 345 at 347.
482 See A. Seavey, 'Harm is the Tort Signature Principles of Torts', *Harv. L.R.*, 56, 1942, at 73.
483 [1964] AC 326, [1963] 2 All ER 625.
484 Ibid., 348, 633.
485 (1966) 39 ALJ 480.
486 Ibid., 486. This view was endorsed at English common law in 1980 in the case of *Lin Poh.choo* v. *Camden and Islington Area Health Authority* [1980] AC 174, [1979] 2 All ER 910.
487 [1969] 3 All ER 1528.
488 Ibid., 1532.
489 See *Fletcher* v. *Autocar and Transporters Ltd.* [1968] 1 All ER 726 at 750 *per* Salmond LJ.
490 *Ward* v. *James* [1966] 1 QB 273, [1965] 1 All ER 563.
491 *Gage* v. *King* [1961] 1 QB 188.
492 *Shearman* v. *Folland* [1950] 2 KB 43.
493 See *The Esso Malaysia Case* [1975] QB 198. In the case of loss of future income, courts may take into account the sums that may have been payable in the future by the plaintiff as income taxes, which would naturally be deducted from the compensation payment. See *British Transport Commission* v. *Gourley* [1956] AC 1985.
494 [1975] 2 All ER 1107, [1975] 1 WLR 1054.
495 *Conolly* v. *Camden and Islington Area Health Authority* [1981] 3 All ER 250.
496 [1981] 3 All ER 852, [1982] 1 WLR 71.
497 [1977] 1 All ER 9, [1977] 1 WLR 132.
498 *Cook* v. *Consolidated Fisheries Ltd.* [1977] 1 All ER 36.
499 See *Morris* v. *Johnson Matthey & Co. Ltd.* (1967) 112 Sol.Jo 32, CA and *Hearnshaw* v. *English Steel Corporation Ltd.* (1971) 11 K1R 306.
500 [1963] 1 QB 750, [1962] 3 All ER 1089.
501 Ibid., at 754, 1093.
502 Convention for the Unification of Certain Rules for International Carriage by Air, Montreal, 1999. The Montreal Convention, which was signed by 52 contracting states of ICAO on 28 May 1999, would need 30 ratifications before coming into effect. Until then, the Warsaw Convention provisions and those of its instruments shall remain applicable for the most part in instances of adjudication relating to private air carrier liability.
503 Ibid., article 17.
504 See Halsbury, *Laws of England*, 3rd edn, vol. 22, London: Sweet and Maxwell, 1990, para. 585, p.293.
505 *Hensey* v. *White* [1900] 1 KB 481.
506 Ibid., 484.
507 Ibid., 485.

508 *Boardman* v. *Scott and Witworth* [1902] 1 KB 43.
509 Ibid., 46.
510 [1903] AC 433.
511 Ibid., 446–7.
512 Ibid., 452.
513 Ibid., 453.
514 Workmen's Compensation Act of 1897.
515 [1903] AC 433 at 455. See also *Trim Joint District School Board of Management* v. *Kelly* [1914] AC 667 at 669, and generally *Anderson* v. *Balfour* [1910] 2 IR 497 and *Nisbett* v. *Rayne* [1910] 2 KB 689.
516 *Board of Management of Trim Joint School* v. *Kelly* [1914] AC 667.
517 [1903] AC 433.
518 [1971] 1 All ER 384.
519 Ibid., 392.
520 [1903] AC 433.
521 (1942) 27 A. 2d. 286.
522 *Alred* v. *Prudential Insurance Co. of America*, 100 S.E. 2d. 226.
523 *Thompson* v. *Prudential Insurance Co.*, 66 S.E. 2d. 119.
524 *Evans* v. *Metropolitan Life Insurance Co.*, 174 p. 2d. 961.
525 *Workmen's Compensation Board* v. *Theed* (1940) 3 DLR 561.
526 Ibid., 557.
527 (1940) 2 DLR 444.
528 Ibid., 448, 449.
529 *Turner* v. *Northern Life Ass'ce Co.* (1953) 1 DLR 427.
530 (1963) 40 DLR 408.
531 Ibid., 422.
532 Ibid., 423.
533 1999 Westlaw 7724 (12 January 1999).
534 116 S. Ct. 629 (1996).
535 Resolution A29-15, Assembly Resolutions in Force Doc. 9730, ICAO, Montreal (as of 20 October 1998), 1–42.
536 David Learmont, 'Preparing for Safety', *Flight International*, 25–31 January 2000, p.56.
537 Ibid.
538 See 'Family of *Silk Air* Pilot Releases Financial Documents', ITA Press 337, 16–30 June 1999.
539 Ibid.
540 'Singapore Police Probe Silk Air Crash as Suicide', *Air Letter*, Monday 6 September 1999, No. 14 319, p.2.
541 *Shawcross and Beaumont, Air Law*, 4th edn, reissue, 1988, VII (152).
542 Ibid., VII (116).
543 Ibid., VII (117).
544 Convention for the Unification of Certain Rules Relating to International Carriage by Air, signed at Warsaw on 12 October 1929; see *Annals of Air and Space Law*, XVIII (II), 1993, 323.
545 Ibid., article 17.
546 *Shawcross and Beaumont Air Law*, *supra*, note 541, VII (116).

547 *Chisholm* v. *British European Airways* [1963] 1 Lloyd's Rep. 626; also *Grein* v. *Imperial Airways Ltd.* [1937] 1 KB 50 CA at 69–71, *per* Greer LJ.
548 See *Chisholm* v. *British European Airways*, *supra*, note 547, at 629.
549 *Goldman* v. *Thai Airways International Ltd.* (1981) 125 Sol Jo 413 (High Ct); also in [1983] 1 All ER 693.
550 [1986] 2 All ER 188.
551 429 F Supp. 964 (SDNY 1977).
552 *Preyvel* v. *Cie Air France* (1973) 27 RFDA 198; also *Rivière-Girret* v. *Ste-Aer-Inter* (1979) Uniform L.R. 173.
553 *Panalpina International Transport Ltd.* v. *Densil Underwear Ltd.* [1981] 1 Lloyd's Rep. 187.
554 *Mandreoli* v. *Cie Belge d'Assurance Aviation*, Milan 1972 (1974) Dir Mar 157.
555 (1982) 36 RFDA 342.
556 (1982) 36 RFDA 355.
557 Warsaw Convention, *supra*, note 544, article 21.
558 [1983] 3 All ER 693.
559 *Bradfield* v. *Trans World Airlines Inc.* 152 Cal. Rptr 172 (Ca. CA 1972).
560 *Butler* v. *Aeromexico* 774 F. 2d. 499. (11th Cir. 1985).
561 *Piano Remittance Corp.* v. *Varig Brazilian Airlines Inc.* 18 Av. Cas (CCH). 18, 381 (SDNY 1984).
562 The Convention for the Unification of Certain Rules Relating to the Assistance and Salvage of Aircraft at Sea, Brussels, 1938; the Rome Convention, 1933; and the Warsaw Convention, 1929.
563 Article 25.
564 H. Drion, *Limitation of Liabilities in International Air Law*, Deventer: Martinus Nijhoff, 1954, p.195.
565 Ibid.
566 Drion, *supra*, *Limitation*, p.200.
567 Georgette Miller, *Air Carrier's Liability Under the Warsaw System*, Sydney: Butterworths, 1979, p.200.
568 Protocol to Amend Convention for the Unification of Certain Rules Relating to International Carriage by Air, signed at Warsaw on 12 October 1929, Article XIII. See *Annals of Air and Space* Law, XVIII (II), 1993, 351.
569 Miller, *supra*, *Air Carrier's Liability*, p.202.
570 *Revue Française de droit aérien* (RFDA) 1977 at 193.
571 5 December 1967; RFDA 184.
572 Transcript of judgment, p.4.
573 Bin Cheng, 'Wilful Misconduct, From Warsaw to the Hague and From Brussels to Paris', *Annals of Air and Space Law*, 11, 1977, 99.
574 (1983) *Law Society's Gazette*, 8 June 1983, p.1485.
575 Peter Martin, 'Intentional or Reckless Misconduct, From London To Bangkok and Back Again', *Annals of Air and Space Law*, VIII, 1983, 145–9.
576 H. Drion, *supra*, *Limitation*, p.7.
577 Ibid., p.8.
578 Ibid.
579 Ibid., pp.12–13.
580 Additional Protocols Nos 3 and 4 to Amend Convention for the Unification of Certain

Rules Relating to International Carriage by Air, signed at Warsaw on 12 October 1929, as amended by the Protocol Done at the Hague on 28 September 1955; and at Guatemala City on 8 March 1971. See *Annals of Air and Space Law*, XVIII (II), 1993, 467–515.

581 *Reed* v. *Wiser* 555 F. 2d. 1079 (2nd Cir) at 1090.

582 Protocol to Amend Convention for the Unification of Certain Rules Relating to International Carriage by Air, signed at Warsaw on 12 October 1929, as amended by the Protocol Done at the Hague on 28 September 1955. See *Annals of Air and Space Law*, XVIII (II), 1993, 409.

583 Nicholas Mateesco Matte, 'The Warsaw System and the Hesitation of the United States Senate', *Annals of Air and Space Law*, VIII, 1983, 164.

584 Alexander Tobolewski, 'Against Limitation of Liability, A Radical Proposal', *Annals of Air and Space Law*, III, 1978, 263.

585 Ibid., 266.

586 Werner Guldimann, 'A Future System of Liability in Air Carriage', *Annals of Air and Space Law*, XVI, 1991, 104.

587 Convention on International Civil Aviation, signed at Chicago on 7 December 1944, at Doc. 7300/7, 7th edn, 1997.

588 James T. McKenna, 'U.S., Egyptians Split on Suicide Theory', *Aviation Week and Space Technology*, 22 November 1999, p.43.

589 Ibid.

590 Samuel D. Warren and Louis D. Brandeis, 'The Right to Privacy', *Harv. L. Rev*, 4, 1890, 197.

591 Ibid., 198.

592 *Florida Star* v. *B.J.F.*, 491 U.S. 524 at 550 (1989).

593 Warren and Brandeis, *supra*, note 590, 216–17.

594 The Organization for Economic Cooperation and Development (OECD) was created in 1960 by 20 founder states. Subsequently, other states have gained OECD membership. The OECD's philosophy is to maintain an open economy system.

595 See 20 I.L.M. 422 (1981).

596 The Council of Europe is an intergovernmental organization composed primarily of European nations. It has no legislative jurisdiction over its members. Its aim is to achieve greater unity between its members for the purpose of safeguarding and realizing ideas and principles which are their common heritage and facilitating their economic and social progress.

597 20 I.L.M. 317 (1981).

598 See generally Jonathan P. Graham, 'Privacy, Computers and the Commercial Dissemination of Personal Information', *Tex. L. Rev.*, 65, 1987, 1395.

599 Raymond Wacks, *Personal Information – Privacy and the Law*, Oxford: Clarendon Press, 1989, p.26.

600 Prosser, *Privacy*, New York: Law Book Co., 1968, p.383, adopted by the *Restatement of the Law of Torts*, para. 867.

601 *Saltman Engineering Co. Ltd* v. *Campbell Engineering Co. Ltd* (1948) 65 RPC 203, [1963] All ER 413 at 415 *per* Lord Greene MR.

602 (1857) 26 LJ Ch (NS) 113 at 114.

603 *Beloff* v. *Presssdram Ltd* [1973] 1 All ER 241.

604 See *Weld-Blundell* v. *Stephens* [1920] AC 956 at 965, where the court held that

'danger to the state or public duty may supersede the duty of the agent to the principal'.

605 [1981] 1 All ER 417.

606 See *The Lion Laboratories Case* [1984] 2 All ER 417.

607 *Tournier* v. *National Provincial and Union Bank of England* [1924] 1 KB 461.

608 *Parry-Jones* v. *Law Society* [1969] 1 Ch at 9, [1968] All ER 177 at 180.

Chapter 6
Conclusion

Although we may not be able to expect spectacular advances during the first few decades of the new millennium, new large aircraft, such as the Airbus A 3XXX and the larger version of the Boeing 747 will, by themselves, have revolutionized air travel during the first decade. The drastic increase in demand for capacity will overrun supply, and the skies will be so crowded that at least in certain regions, such as North America and Europe, the air traffic management system will be 'gridlocked' unless the new satellite navigation of the CNS/ATM system is introduced quickly.

As regards market demand for air transport services, the prognosis is ominous. In the coming decades there will be increased global income and consumption (and greater inequality in their distribution); a growing population (but, with smaller families, levelling out by the middle of the 21st century); an ageing population (more than doubling the number of over-60s by 2030); and a higher proportion of dependent to productive people. It is also worthy of note that the wealthier segments will have increased disposable income and leisure time. These economic factors will bring to bear a demand for the following:

- increased urbanization,
- increased migration,
- further globalization of markets and liberalization of trade rules,
- further shifting of taxation from progressive to regressive and from direct to indirect,
- increased strains on the environment,
- a continuing information revolution (which will, *inter alia*, redefine the nature of white-collar work through teleworking and outsourcing – towards the 'virtual office').

The above trends personify a fundamental global issue as we enter the 21st century, the dichotomy between economic growth and social justice. Fortunately, the first three of these trends are predominantly positive for air transport, although more consumption in terms of air transport capacity will epitomize and define global issues in air transport. There are two types of mega-trends affecting the airline industry today: country mergers and airline mergers. Both these trends affect the airline industry profoundly. Of these, the unification of Europe has been the largest single influence on international airlines. Within these two mega-trends are smaller trends that individual airlines have to follow just to remain competitive. They are privatization, the use of information technology, removing infrastructure constraints and governmental restraints and, most importantly, changing travel patterns. These trends have given rise to the new phenomenon in the global aviation scene that survival (if not success) of airlines is now dependent, not on pricing, but on service. This new phenomenon calls for the airline product to be similar to one from the entertainment industry, bearing in mind that a passenger spends 70 per cent of his total travel time in the aircraft on long-distance flights. To counter strong alliances between countries and airlines, the smaller carriers (as well as the big ones) are now going in more for glamour and in-flight luxury to score on the 70 per cent in-flight time. Personal video screens for every seat, satellite-assisted telephone facilities and teleconference services are some of the luxuries offered. Indeed, as David Shoenfeld, International Marketing Vice President of Federal Express said, 'If you view your services as flying between terminals, you miss the point.'

The view that 'marketing is determined from the view of the customer' is becoming more valuable now more than ever before. To survive, airlines have to build 'brand recognition'. An INTRAMAR study, conducted on 44 of the world's most profitable and financially successful airlines, reveals that Singapore Airlines received an extremely high PAX/SAT index rating, coming second among all airlines of the world. The first was Swissair.

There are twelve important factors influencing passenger choice: flight punctuality; excellence of in-flight service; superiority of aircraft; comfortable seats; clean cabins, seats and washrooms; good food and beverages; superior first class; superior business class; efficient reservations systems; pricing; good check-in service and attractive frequent flyer programmes. At least seven of these factors are entirely dependent on the quality of the aircraft. The foremost important factor – punctuality – cannot, indeed, be achieved with ageing aircraft. The matter becomes more crucial to a relatively small airline, running a small fleet of aircraft, where, if one aircraft is grounded for reasons of repair or maintenance, the entire flight schedule of the airline would be in disarray, leading to delays down the line. Connecting services would be disrupted and passengers stranded. It is needless to envisage the effect this catastrophe would have on the airline's good name. No amount of superior in-flight service would atone for a six-hour delay where a connecting passenger has to sit inside an unknown airport terminal. It is therefore necessary for any airline to seriously consider removing one of its most burdensome infrastructural constraints – its ageing aircraft.

Another compelling reason for airlines to modernize their fleets is that ageing aircraft do not conform to noise restrictions imposed by many countries and thus face being barred from certain airports. The noise issue has become a crucial environment issue in the world aviation community. At the 27th Session of the Assembly of the ICAO held in Montreal in 1989, when the matter of possible noise restrictions on subsonic jet aircraft was taken up, the main concern of the assembly was to achieve a balance between the desire to protect the environment around airports against unnecessary noise and the desire to avoid excessive costs associated with accelerated replacement of noisier aircraft, particularly where these aircraft were registered in countries which did not themselves intend to introduce noise-related operating instructions. In the sessional discussions, the Airport Associations Co-ordinating Council (AACC, now Airports Council International, ACI) noted that aircraft noise represented a major constraint upon the future viability and capacity of the aviation system. Unless concerted international action was taken, there would be a proliferation of various local legislation banning noisy aircraft from their airports – a measure that would have a devastating effect on air commerce. The airline industry has recognized the need in many states to address political and other concerns relating to the environment and the fact that the noise climate in areas adjacent to airports is linked to the ability of airports to provide expanded travel facilities to meet the growing demand for air travel.

The standards of the international community on ageing aircraft are now clear. States have been given the right by the international civil aviation community to start phasing out aircraft from 1 April 1995 until the year 2002. What this means is that airlines that have in their fleets ageing aircraft would have to commence modernizing their fleets soon. If they fail to modernize their fleet their ageing aircraft will not be admitted to countries which have phased them out by legislation. The need for modernizing ageing aircraft fleets has become more compelling than ever, and is amply reflected by the recommendations made by the Fourth Meeting of ICAO's Committee on Aviation Environmental Protection (CAEP) which was held from 6 to 8 April 1998. CAEP has recommended the reduction by an average of about 16 per cent of levels of nitrogen oxides (NO_x) that aircraft engines are currently allowed to emit under Annex 16 to the Chicago Convention. CAEP has also recommended that states implement ICAO's new Communications, Navigation, Surveillance and Air Traffic Management systems (CNS/ATM), thereby implicitly requiring aircraft to be equipped with the modern facilities onboard to comply with the satellite navigation systems introduced by the CNS/ATM systems.

Another measure taken by CAEP at its Fourth Meeting which would have a serious impact on airlines with ageing fleets, needing them to consider the modernization of their fleets, was CAEP's commitment to carry out more work in the future to establish new noise standards for jet aeroplanes that would be more stringent than the present Chapter 3 Standards in Annex 16. The Fifth CAEP meeting, held in January 2001, addressed these issues in greater depth.

Apart from the compelling marketing reasons and environmental factors discussed above, a modernized fleet would succeed in sweeping an airline to success if the acquisition of aircraft was managed prudently. For example, the new aircraft would have to be placed in the fleet just before the airline reached peak utilization of its aircraft. New air traffic rights of the airlines would have to be negotiated beforehand and existing ones reviewed for maximum utilization. The fixed costs of the new aircraft would have to be analysed well beforehand to maximize profits. The resale value of the old aircraft, when they are ultimately phased out in order for newer aircraft to be brought in, should also be given serious consideration. Engineering and maintenance facilities and costs thereof for new aircraft have also to be carefully thought out.

To capitalize on changes in their competitive environment, competent airline managers now need to know that, in the foreseeable future, there will be a few mega-carriers operating in America, Europe, Asia and the Pacific Rim and that these carriers will probably be composites of strong strategic alliances between powerful airlines and powerful regional states. They will be well equipped to offer the quality of service and punctuality that modern glamour requires of air travel. To compete with these carriers for a fair share of the market, a smaller airline would have to offer a comparable product.

Modernized fleets would effectively preclude recurring aeromedical problems such as the economy class syndrome and the aerotoxic syndrome. They would also provide a better working environment for both technical and cabin crew.

At the 33rd Session of the Assembly of the International Civil Aviation Organization, held in Montreal from 25 September to 5 October 2001, a resolution was adopted containing a consolidated statement of continuing policies and practices related to environmental protection.[1] This resolution was a response to the need to incorporate new ICAO policies and guidance material regarding aircraft noise and other developments in that field since the 32nd Session, held in 1998, in particular, to achieve a balanced approach to noise management. The resolution also addressed, *inter alia*, the issue of aircraft engine emissions, including an increased and improved understanding of emissions, notably a possible means of limiting or reducing greenhouse gases from aviation.

Over the past decade, there has been continuing awareness that aviation may contribute to adverse environmental impacts on the world and that it behoves the world aviation community to achieve maximum compatibility between the safe and orderly development of civil aviation and the quality of the environment. This is particularly significant in the context of ICAO's role in developing international air transport so as to meet the needs of the people to ensure safe, regular, efficient and economical air transport.[2] The philosophy of Resolution A33-7 is based on the fact that adverse environmental effects of civil aviation activity can be reduced by integrated measures embracing technological developments, proper operating procedures, appropriate organization of air traffic and strategic use of airport planning, land use planning and market-based measures. ICAO's role, in this delicately balanced operation, is to strive to achieve harmony between the benefit occurring to the world community through civil aviation and the harm caused to the environment in certain key areas through the progressive advancement of civil aviation.

With regard to aircraft noise, the resolution, in Appendix B, makes reference to Annex 16 to the Convention on International Civil Aviation (Chicago Convention)[3] which contains noise certification standards for subsonic aircraft and ICAO's 'Policies on Charges for Airports and Air Navigation Services' (Doc. 9082) which has policy guidance on noise-related charges. In the context of these documents, and particularly with regard to more stringent aircraft noise standards adopted by the Council in June 2001 for inclusion in Annex 16, the Assembly requested the Council to continue with vigour the work related to the development of standards, recommended practices and procedures and ensure that work conducted by the Council's Committee on Aviation Environmental Protection (CAEP) continues expeditiously in order that appropriate solutions can be developed as soon as possible.

In following up revisions made by the Council in June 2001, the Assembly, through the resolution, urged contracting states to adopt a balanced approach to noise management, taking full account of ICAO guidance, applicable legal obligations, existing agreements, current laws and established policies, all to be given due consideration when addressing noise problems at international airports. Contracting states are urged to adopt appropriate mechanisms in implementing this balanced approach, notably in establishing a transparent process based on objective, measurable criteria for the assessment of the noise problem; in evaluating likely costs and benefits of various measures with a view to achieving maximum environmental benefit; and in providing for dissemination of the evaluation results that may be used in consultation with stakeholders and in dispute resolutions.

As part of the balanced approach, Resolution A33-7 encourages states, *inter alia*, to conduct studies, support research and technology programmes aimed at reducing noise at source and to work closely with each other to ensure that their noise management programmes are harmonized taking into consideration the particular economic exigencies of developing countries and also taking particular care so as not to derogate the non-discrimination principle enshrined in Article 15 of the Chicago Convention.[4]

Resolution A33-7, in Appendix D, urges contracting states not to introduce any phase-outs of subsonic jet aircraft which exceed noise levels contained in Volume 1 of Annex 16 to the Chicago Conventio[5] before giving consideration to a clear determination as to whether normal attrition of existing fleets of such aircraft will provide the necessary protection of noise climates around airports and whether necessary protection can be achieved by regulators preventing their operations from adding such aircraft to their fleets through either purchase or lease/charter/interchange, or alternatively by incentives to accelerate fleet modernization. Before phasing out subsonic aircraft that may exceed the above-mentioned noise levels, the resolution also calls upon contracting states to give careful thought to whether, alternatively, effective noise management can be achieved by applying regulations preventing operations of such aircraft through restrictions limited to airports and runways, the use of which has been identified and declared by these states as generating noise problems and limited to time periods when greater noise disturbance is caused. Finally, contracting states are called upon to consider implications of any restrictions for other states concerned, through consultation and reasonable notification of the application of restrictions.

One of the most significant achievements of Resolution A33-7 lies in the skilful balance achieved in offering a compromise to contracting states which, despite the above-mentioned criteria, decide to phase out aircraft which comply with noise certificates standards in Volume 1, Chapter 2 of Annex 16 but which exceed the noise levels in Volume 1, Chapter 3 of Annex 16. This compromise recommends that such states frame any restrictions so that Chapter 2-compliant aircraft of an individual operator which are operating at present to their territories may be withdrawn from such operations gradually, over a period of not less than seven years. The resolution also requests contracting states not to restrict before the end of the above period the operations of any aircraft less than 25 years after the date of issue of its first individual certificates of airworthiness, and not to restrict before the end of the period the operations of any currently existing wide-body aircraft or of any fitted with engines that have a bypass ratio higher than 2 to 1. Contracting states are required to inform ICAO, as well as the other states concerned, of all restrictions imposed.

Finally, the resolution urges states not to introduce measures to phase out aircraft which comply, through original certification or recertification, with the noise certification standards in Volume 1, Chapter 3 or 4 of Annex 16 and, in particular, not to impose any operating restrictions on Chapter 3-compliant aircraft, except as part of the balanced approach to noise management developed by ICAO and in accordance with Appendices C and E to the resolution which address issues pertaining to phase-out of subsonic aircraft and local noise-related operations at airports.

Resolution A33-7 also addresses growing concerns about environmental problems in the atmosphere such as global warming and depletion of the ozone layer, noting that the Agenda 21 action plan adopted by the 1992 United Nations Conference on Environment and Development calls on governments to address these problems with the cooperation of relevant United Nations bodies. Particular reference is made to the Kyoto Protocol, adopted by the Conference of the Parties to the United Nations Framework Convention on Climate Change (UNFCCC) in December 1997 (referred to in some detail later on) which recognizes ICAO as the primary body responsible for the regulation of aviation-related environmental issues on aircraft engine emission, and which calls upon developed countries to pursue limitation or reduction of greenhouse gases from 'aviation bunker fuels' working through ICAO.

The Assembly recognized that market-based measures, which will be described in some detail below, are policy tools that are designed to achieve environmental goals at a lower cost and in a more flexible manner than traditional regulatory measures. Particularly in the context of controlling greenhouse gas emissions, the Assembly recognized that there has been increasing recognition by governments of the need for each economic sector to pay the full cost of the environmental damage it causes and market-based measures for protecting the environment were particularly relevant in this regard. It was the Assembly's view that any charges imposed, based on the costs of the mitigating or environmental impact of aircraft engine emissions to the extent that such costs can be properly identified and directly attributable to air transport, should be applicable only in so far as they are consistent with Article 15 of the Chicago Convention and ICAO's policies on taxes and charges.[6] The Assembly noted with approval analyses, conducted by CAEP, concluding that an open emissions trading system, whereby the total amount of emissions would be capped and allowances in the form of permits to emit carbon dioxide could be bought and sold to meet emission reduction objectives, was a cost-effective measure to limit or reduce carbon dioxide emitted by civil aviation, particularly in the long term. Short-term voluntary measures, where industry and governments agree to a target and/or to a set of actions to reduce emissions, would serve as a first step towards such long-term measures.

The Assembly required the Council of ICAO to develop guidance for states on the application of market-based measures aimed at reducing or limiting the environmental impact of aircraft engine emissions, particularly with respect to mitigating the impact of aviation on climate changes. Above all, contracting states and the Council are encouraged through Resolution A33-7 to take into account the interests of all parties concerned, to evaluate the costs and benefits of various measures with the goal of addressing aircraft engine emissions in the most cost-effective manner and to adopt actions consistent with ICAO policies. The Assembly endorsed the development of an open emissions trading system for international aviation and requested the Council to develop guidelines for open emissions trading for international aviation, as a matter of priority.

In making its recommendations and requests, the Assembly took into consideration the work of the CAEP which, at its Fifth Meeting (CAEP/5), held from 8 to 17 January 2001, CAEP identified market-based measures as being policy tools that are designed to achieve environmental goals at a lower cost and in a more flexible manner than traditional regulatory measures. CAEP considered three types of measure: emissions-related levies – generically, referring to charges and taxes; emissions trading – a system whereby the total amount of emissions would be capped and allowances in the form of permits could be bought and sold to meet emission reduction objectives; and voluntary measures – mechanisms under which industry and governments agree to a target and/or a set of actions to reduce emissions.

Under emission-related levies, three options were considered by CAEP: a fuel (or en route emissions) tax with revenue going to the national treasury; a revenue-neutral aircraft efficiency charge; and an en route emissions charge with revenue returned to the aviation sector.

The main findings of the analysis conducted by CAEP on these three options are that, in the context of a fuel tax, it raises legal issues concerning air services agreements and ICAO policies and, if not applied worldwide, could cause tankering practices (by which aircraft would carry extra fuel for later segments rather than purchasing the fuel locally). With regard to a revenue-neutral charge, CAEP felt that it would be consistent with ICAO policies but would require an acceptable method to be developed for defining aircraft efficiency, and could not be implemented in those areas which do not have en route charges. An en route emissions charge would be consistent with ICAO policies, assuming that revenues were recycled to the aviation sector, but, if not applied worldwide, could raise equity and competitiveness issues and would necessitate further guidance for the use and distribution of the revenue collected.

In designing an emission trading regime, It was the view of CAEP that the key issues are the scope of trading (that is open trading across sectors, or closed trading within the aviation sector alone) and the distribution of emission permits or allowances (that is, grand-fathering, based on past or current use, or auctioning through a bidding process). Since such a system is untested for aviation, there would need to be rules for participation and the establishment of administrative mechanisms for recording trades and monitoring and ensuring compliance.

As for voluntary measures, CAEP advised the ICAO Council that an industry initiative, where a set of actions and/or a target to be met should be proposed, based on a negotiated agreement between industry and government to take a set of actions, and/or to achieve a specific emission target; and a hybrid option, under which one of the two above-mentioned options is used in conjunction with another market-based measure.

The main findings were that voluntary measures alone cannot achieve an ambitious emission reduction target. They would have to be used in conjunction with other measures. In addition, these voluntary measures allow industry to enhance its ability to undertake activities related to 'capability building'. They are primarily looked at as transitional measures. A key issue is the need to ensure that any such action would be to the advantage of the participants if market-based or other regulatory measures were imposed at a later date.

CAEP/5 concluded that a closed emissions trading system does not show cost–benefit results to justify further consideration, and felt that an open emissions trading system would be a cost-effective solution for CO_2 emission reductions in the long term, but cannot be implemented until the Kyoto Protocol has entered into force and an emissions cap has been agreed. Further work is necessary to develop an emission trading system and to study the consequences for developing countries, and ICAO should continue to play a leadership role, particularly in the development of proposals for caps, consistent with the responsibility given to ICAO in Article 2.2 of the Kyoto Protocol.

The essential philosophy of emissions trading in environmental protection is based on a certain flexibility allowed to market forces to reach the lowest cost involved in an operation while at the same time achieving an environmental target which has already been set. The word 'trading' correctly denotes an exchange, and when applied to the aviation context means a certain trade-off between airlines whose fleets pollute more than others and low polluting airlines. The trade-off could take the form of a 'purchase' by the high polluting airline of the reduction level of a low polluting airline. Emissions trading would encourage airlines to seek innovation in technology and to reduce their emission levels.

Emissions trading of levels of pollution between airlines differs fundamentally from the existing expectation of each airline maintaining a standard level of emission by its aircraft. When airlines traded emission levels, the rates at which their aircraft pollute the atmosphere would be taken as a whole and be applicable to a whole fleet, so that an airline which is over and above its permitted pollution level could join another airline which is below the standard level of pollution required of it, thus making the average pollution between the two more acceptable than if taken individually. This mechanism encourages a low polluting airline to achieve even lower standards, in order to trade its levels with high polluting airlines.

The Third Conference of the Parties to the United Nations Framework Convention on Climate Change (Climate Change Convention)[7] was held from 1 to 11 December 1997 at Kyoto, Japan. Significantly, the states parties to the Convention adopted a protocol (Kyoto Protocol)[8] on 11 December 1997 under which industrialized countries have agreed to reduce their collective emissions of six greenhouse gases[9] by at least 5 per cent by 2008–12. Ambassador Raul Estrada-Oyuela, who had chaired the Committee of the Whole established by the Conference to facilitate the negotiation of a Protocol text, expressed the view that the agreement 'will have a real impact on the problem of greenhouse gas emissions and that 11 December 1997 should be remembered as the Day of the Atmosphere'.[10]

The Kyoto Protocol, in Article 1(*a*)(v) calls on each state party to achieve progressive reduction or phasing out of market imperfections, fiscal incentives, tax and duty exemptions and subsidies in all greenhouse gas-emitting sectors that run counter to the objective of the Convention and application of market instruments. The subject of emissions leading to trading is addressed initially in Article 3 of the Protocol which requires states parties to ensure that their aggregate anthropogenic carbon dioxide equivalent emissions of the greenhouse gases listed in Annex A do not exceed their assigned amounts, calculated pursuant to their quantified emission limitation and reduction commitments inscribed in Annex B. The provision also requires states parties to the Protocol to reduce their overall emissions of greenhouse gases by at least 5 per cent below 1990 levels in the commitment period 2008 to 2012. Article 3(6) goes further, in providing that states parties shall be allowed a certain degree of flexibility in implementation of Article 3 and the reduction of their emission standards.

The subject of emissions trading is explicitly addressed in Article 6, which states that, for the purpose of meeting its commitments under Article 3, any party included in Annex I may transfer to or acquire from any other such party emission reduction units resulting from projects aimed at reducing anthropogenic emissions by sources or enhancing anthropogenic removals by sinks of greenhouse gases in any sector of the economy provided the parties concerned approve of such trading, and, *inter alia*, such trading actually results in a reduction in emission by sources.

Article 17 sets out that the Conference of the Parties shall define the relevant principles, modalities, rules and guidelines, in particular for verification, reporting and accountability for emissions trading. It also provides that the parties included in Annex B to the Protocol may participate in emissions trading for the purposes of fulfilling their commitments under Article 3. Such trading shall be supplemental to domestic actions for the purpose of meeting qualified emissions limitation and reduction commitments under Article 3.[11]

Once the Protocol has entered into force,[12] Annex I parties must submit an annual inventory of emissions to the Convention Secretariat,[13] enabling expert review teams to provide a full assessment of such parties' compliance with the Protocol.[14] These expert assessments will be reviewed by the Conference of the Parties serving as the meeting of the parties to the Protocol,[15] which will adopt decisions on implementation.[16]

Article 12 of the Protocol is also noteworthy in that it defines a clean development mechanism (CDM) which introduces the concept of joint implementation by a developed country and a developing country.[17] The mechanism admits of the advantage afforded to the parties concerned, in developed countries gaining the benefit of the partnerships in emissions trading with developing countries which are more cost-effective in financing such projects. The CDM achieves the dual goal of enabling developing countries to operate projects which result in emission reductions which contribute to the objectives of the UNFCCC[18] – and also enabling countries specified in Annex I of the Kyoto Protocol which finance such projects through the CDM to use emissions reductions to reduce their own emissions *in toto*.[19]

The mechanism is supervised by an executive board and the responsibility of establishing procedures to make certain that proper verification of projects is achieved in a transparent manner devolve upon the Conference of the Parties to the Protocol.[20] By virtue of Articles 12(10) and 3(12), Annex I countries could contribute to their own emission reduction targets under the Protocol by using emission reductions from jointly implemented projects under the CDM during the period 2000–2008.

A watershed provision of the Kyoto Protocol lies in Article 2.2, which stipulates that parties included in Annex II shall pursue limitation or reduction of emissions of greenhouse gases not controlled by the Montreal Protocol[21] from aviation and marine bunker fuels, working through the International Civil Aviation Organization and the International Maritime Organization, respectively. This lays the regulatory responsibility for emissions trading with regard to aircraft engine emissions squarely on ICAO.

Resolution A32-8 of ICAO, referred to earlier, and containing a consolidated statement of continuing ICAO policies and practices related to environmental protection, urges states to refrain from unilateral environmental measures that would be harmful to the development of international civil aviation. On the subject of aircraft engine emissions, the resolution, in its Appendix F, makes mention of the fact that the Kyoto Protocol calls for developed countries to pursue limitation or reduction of greenhouse gases from aviation bunker fuels, working through ICAO, and invokes Appendix A, which calls upon the ICAO Council to maintain the initiative in developing policy guidance on all aviation matters related to the environment and not leave such initiatives to other organizations.

Appendix H of A32-8 refers to ICAO's policies on charges and taxes[22] and the policy statement issued by the ICAO Council on 9 December 1996 in the form of a Council Resolution of an interim nature, and urges states to follow the current guidance of the Council on emission-related levies. The Council is similarly exhorted by the Assembly, through A32-8, to continue to pursue the question of emission-related levies with a view to reaching a conclusion prior to the next ordinary session of the Assembly in 2001.

The policy statement of the Council dated 9 December 1996 takes into consideration the fact that a number of states consider it desirable to use a levy to reflect environmental costs associated with air transport, while other states do not consider it appropriate to impose such a levy under the present circumstances. The Council goes on to state that it considers the development of an internationally agreed environmental charge or tax on air transport that all states would be expected to impose would appear not to be practicable at the time, given the differing views of states and the significant organization and practical implementation problems that would be likely to arise.

According to the Council Statement, ICAO is seeking to identify a rational common basis on which states wishing to introduce environmental levies on air transport could do so. The Council strongly recommends in its statement that any environmental reviews on air transport which states may introduce should be in the form of charges rather than taxes and that the funds collected should be applied in the first instance to mitigating the environmental impact of aircraft engine emissions, for example by (a) addressing the specific damage caused by these emissions, if that can be identified, (b) funding scientific research into their environmental impact, or (c) funding research aimed at reducing their environmental impact, through developments in technology and new approaches to aircraft operations.

Finally, the Council urges states that are considering the introduction of emission-related charges to take into account the non-discrimination principle in Article 15 of the Convention on International Civil Aviation and the work in progress within ICAO and, in the meantime, to be guided by the general principles in the 'Statements by the Council to contracting States on Charges for Airports and Air Navigation Services' (Doc. 9082/4) and the following principles adapted from those agreed by the 31st Session of the ICAO Assembly: that there should be no fiscal aims behind the charges, the charges should be related to costs, and the charges should not discriminate against air transport compared with other modes of transport.

As part of its efforts to monitor the issue of emissions and economic instruments in that regard, and also to reach a conclusion prior to the 33rd Assembly Session of ICAO in the year 2001, the Council of ICAO actively pursued the issue also through its Committee on Aviation Environmental Protection (CAEP). CAEP, at its 4th meeting (CAEP/4) held in April 1998, identified as an integral part of its work programme the need to address emissions inventories for future scientific assessments; long-term emissions burden estimates used for quantifying benefits of regulatory charges; and the effectiveness of operational measures to reduce aircraft emissions or their effect on the atmosphere.[23] The meeting also noted that further work on market-based options for reducing emissions was necessary.

The CAEP/4 Report, which was considered by the 32nd Session of the ICAO Assembly, presented a report on emissions-related levies which was quite extensive. CAEP/4 basically envisioned four options for levies: a fuel levy, a ticket levy, a route levy and an airport levy. With regard to the application of a levy, the Report considered a revenue-neutral application, a general taxation application, a levy application based on a preventive-cost approach and an application involving paying damages or compensation for third party injury. The Report also considered the efficacy of each levy option and application as well as implementation aspects of environmental levies in the context both of their relation to levy collection and as to the application of levies. As a pivotal point to the whole exercise, CAEP/4 examined the role of ICAO with regard to such levies.

The 33rd Session of the Assembly, in considering the work of both CAEP/4 and CAEP/5, endorsed the development of an open emissions trading system for international civil aviation and requested the Council to develop, as a matter of priority, guidelines for open emissions trading for international aviation, focusing on establishing the structural and legal basis for aviation's participation in an open trading system, and including key elements such as reporting, monitoring and compliance, while improving flexibility to the maximum extent possible consistent with the UNFCC process.

There is no room for doubt that development in aviation and the environment over the years has now led the international community in general, and the aviation community in particular, to a crossroads, where a delicately balanced formula between market demand and sustainability has to be reached. This is indeed true in the context of both aircraft noise and engine emissions.

As for market demand, it is incontrovertible that, notwithstanding the short-term effects that may be felt as a result of recent setbacks, economic analysts are of the view that air transport is still the most expensive of all modes of transport (road, rail, air and sea) to operate in terms of per kilogramme of mass carried.[24] This essentially means that commercial air transport is predominantly offered to the high-value/high-yield end of the market, that is, to the business community, the tourism industry and the time-critical freight industry dealing with overnight documents and high-value/high-perishable items.

The total scheduled traffic (domestic and international) carried by the airlines of contracting states of ICAO in 1999 is estimated to have been at about 369 billion tonne-kilometres performed, an increase of about 6 per cent over 1998.[25] The airlines of these states carried a total of 1558 million passengers and some 28 million tonnes of freight in 1999. The freight figure compares with 26 million tonnes carried in 1998.[26] Compared with previous years, the carriage of international freight showed an increase of 9 per cent in 1999.

ICAO records that, between 1989 and 1998, the reported number of commercial aircraft in service increased by about 60 per cent, from 11 253 to 18 139 aircraft. In

1998, 1463 jet aircraft were ordered, compared with 1309 in 1997, and 929 were delivered, compared with 674 aircraft in 1997. In 1998, the total scheduled traffic carried by airlines of the 185 contracting states of ICAO amounted to a total of about 1462 million passengers and about 26 million tonnes of freight. In the years 1988–99 the total tonne-kilometres performed, or, in other words, total scheduled airline traffic, grew at an annual rate of 5.2 per cent.[27] Passenger kilometres growth during this decade was 4.6 per cent and freight tonne-kilometres growth was 6.6 per cent for the same period.[28] These figures[29] are reflective of the rapidly increasing frequency of aircraft movements at airports, calling for drastic management of aircraft movements in terms of noise and airport capacity.

In 2000, world gross domestic product (GDP) grew by approximately 4.4 per cent in real terms. The industrialized countries showed a 4 per cent increase, with North America showing a robust 5.3 per cent growth and Europe achieving 3–5 per cent. Africa's economy achieved a 3.6 per cent growth within an overall growth for developing countries which was at 5.6 per cent. Asia and Pacific countries reflected a significant 6.7 per cent and South America and the Caribbean recovered to post a healthy 4.3 per cent GDP growth.[30] General views offered by both the Organization for Economic Cooperation and Development (OECD) and the World Tourism Organization in the context of the future of aviation after the September 2001 crisis are encouraging, in that the GDP of countries, which is essentially tagged to consumerism, is expected to stabilize by mid-2002 and increase in 2003.

In the air transport sector, the total scheduled traffic carried by airlines amounted to a total of 1647 million passengers and some 30.2 million tonnes of freight. This was an 8 per cent increase over 1999.[31] Countries continued to expand the international air transport network, by concluding with each other 73 bilateral air services agreements in 2000, compared to 67 in 1999. Over 70 per cent of these agreements showed a marked trend towards liberalization, with 17 'open skies' agreements concluded, within an overall figure of 83 such agreements concluded at the time of writing. With these figures and prognoses one can be reasonably confident that market demand for air transport will regather its momentum and the demand for aircraft and services will increase in the near future.

With regard to sustaining ability, the regulators of the environmental impact of aviation will necessarily have to bear in mind the vibrant significance of the balanced approach suggested by Resolution A33–7. Essentially, the term 'sustainable development' in the context of environmental protection means 'development which the environment can sustain without being polluted'. The notion that environment is an inextricable and integral part of sustainable development and that environmental issues were not *sui generis* or stand-alone issues but were incontrovertibly linked to their economic, political and social contexts is critical in the context of aviation and environmental protection. Environmental issues are the necessary corollaries to social processes and should be addressed on the basis of equity, care for nature and natural resources and development of society.

Environmental management is therefore the key to effective sustainable development. This should involve a necessary diversion from the mere cleaning up or repairing of damage to being a sustained social activity which brings to bear the need to force development to keep pace with the environmental equilibrium and stability of the world.

Another integral part of sustainable development is economics, and it is in this broad context that a link can be drawn between sustaining ability and market demand in the field of commercial aviation. Economics not only plays a key role in societal decision making, but it also integrates environmental issues with distribution, ownership and control, identifying economic development and social issues as major elements in the management of a society. Another aspect of the role of economics in sustainable development is reflected in the very nature of sustainable development itself, in that it requires a delicate balance between the needs of the present generation and the long-term environmental well-being of a society. If, for instance, the alienation of environmental assets were to enrich the present generation, but would adversely affect future generations, the management of this dichotomy could be addressed by considering, primarily, the economic implications of unsustainable development.

Another factor which influences sustainable development is globalization, which calls for intervention at the international level to ensure that development could be sustained environmentally. In this context, in addition to the implementation of international environmental agreements, it becomes necessary to analyse critically the impact of the global economy and the liberalization of trade on environmental issues. In any aspect of trade, including trade related to the aviation industry, any bifurcation of environment and sustainable development becomes arbitrary and cosmetic. With this in view, sustainable development in aviation should be internationally managed in three component elements:

1 environmental assessment, through evaluation and review, research and monitoring and the exchange of views on the environment;
2 environmental management, through comprehensive planning that takes into account the effects of the acts of humans on the environment; and
3 supporting measures, through education, training and public information and also through financial assistance and organizational arrangements.

Any balanced approach towards environmental management should essentially be based on these guidelines.

NOTES

1 See ICAO Resolution A33-7, 'Consolidated Statement of Continuing ICAO Policies and Practices related to Environmental Protection, A33-7', *Resolutions Adopted by the Assembly*, Provisional Edition, October 2001, p.15.
2 See Convention on International Civil Aviation, Doc 7300/8, 8th edn 2000, Article 44(d).
3 *Supra*, note 2.
4 Article 15, *inter alia*, generally requires that any charges that may be imposed or permitted to be imposed by a contracting state for the use of airports and air navigation facilities by aircraft shall not be higher than those that are payable by national aircraft of the state imposing such charges.
5 These noise levels will be discussed in some detail later.
6 ICAO's policies on taxes and charges are contained in Doc. 8632. These policies recommend, *inter alia*, the reciprocal exemption from all taxes levied on fuel taken on board by aircraft in connection with international air services, and reduction, to the fullest possible extent, or elimination, of taxes related to the sale or use of international air transport.
7 (1992) 31 I.L.M. 849. On the negotiations and text of the Climate Change Convention, see D. Bodansky, 'The United Nations Framework Convention on Climate Change: A Commentary' (1993) 18 *Yale J. Int. L.*, 451–558. See also J. Barrett, 'The Negotiation and Drafting of the Climate Change Convention', in R. Churchill and D. Freestone (eds), *International Law and Global Climate Change* (1991), pp.183–200.
8 Kyoto Protocol to the United Nations Framework Convention on Climate Change, UN Doc. FCCC/CP/1997/L.7/Add.1.
9 Carbon dioxide, methane, nitrous oxide, hydrofluorocarbons, perfluorocarbons and sulphur hexafluoride.
10 UN Environment Programme (UNEP) Press Release, 11 December 1997.
11 The subject of emissions trading falls within the purview of the Intergovernmental Panel on Climate Change (IPCC), which was established in 1988 by the World Meteorological Organization and the United Nations Environment Programme (UNEP) to assess the scientific basis and impact of climate change. The IPCC's first scientific report was published in 1990 and recommended the negotiation of a framework convention to combat global warming. The United Nations Framework Convention on Climate Change (UNFCCC) was adopted on 9 May 1992 and the treaty entered into force on 21 March 1994. This chapter, being a legal one, will not address details of these bodies. For an extensive treatment of the IPCC's work and the UNFCC, see Colin Warbrick and Dominic McGoldric (eds), 'Global Warming and the Kyoto Protocol', 47 *ICLQ*, April 1998, 446–62.
12 The Protocol will enter into force 90 days after 'not less than 55 Parties to the [Climate Change] Convention, incorporating Parties included in Annex 1 which accounted in total for at least 55% of the total carbon dioxide emissions for 1990 of the Parties included in Annex 1' have ratified Art. 24 of the Protocol.
13 Ibid., Art. 7 (1). The Secretariat is located in Bonn, Germany. Its postal address is P.O. Box 260 124, D-53153, Bonn, Germany.
14 Ibid., Art. 8(1).
15 Ibid., Art. 8(5). When the Conference of the Parties meets as the meeting of parties to

the Protocol, those states that are party to the Convention but not to the Protocol may participate, but only as non-voting observers (ibid., Art. 13(1) and (2)). Parties to the Protocol will meet annually (Art. 13(6)) to review the implementation of the Protocol (Art. 13(4)).

16 Ibid., Art. 8(6).

17 See J.K. Parikh, 'Joint Implementation and North South Cooperation for Climate Change', 1995, 7 (1) *International Environmental Affairs*, 22–41.

18 *Supra*, see note 10.

19 See Article 12(3) of the Kyoto Protocol.

20 Article 8 of the Protocol.

21 'Montreal Protocol on Substances that Deplete the Ozone Layer' (1987) 26 *I.L.M.* 1550. The Montreal Protocol controls gases such as chlorofluorocarbons, which not only have ozone-depleting characteristics but also contribute to the greenhouse effect. The Kyoto Protocol has, by explicitly excluding the Montreal Protocol's role in ICAO's mandate, included carbon dioxide, nitrogen oxides and compounds of sulphur emissions within ICAO's purview.

22 As contained in Doc. 9082 ('Statements by the Council to Contracting States on Charges for Airports and Air Navigation Services') and Doc. 8632 ('ICAO's Policies on Taxation in the Field of International Air Transport').

23 CAEP/4, Committee on Aviation Environmental Protection, Fourth Meeting, Montreal, 6–8 April 1998, ICAO: Montreal, p. i-8.

24 'The Supply of Air Freight Capacity to Asian Markets', Working Paper 42, Bureau of Transport Economics, Commonwealth of Australia, 2000, p.1.

25 'The World of Civil Aviation 1999–2002', ICAO Circular 279-AT/116, ICAO, Montreal, p.27.

26 Ibid.

27 Ibid., para. 5.11.

28 Ibid.

29 The above figures were extracted from 'The Annual Report of the Council – 1998', Doc. 9732, ICAO: Montreal, p. 6.

30 'Annual Report of the Council 2000', ICAO, Doc. 9770, p.1. Also 'Airline Financial Results Remain Positive in 2000 Despite Soaring Fuel Prices', ICAO News Release, P10 05/01.

31 ' Annual Report', p.2.

Index